LEAVING HOME
TOWARDS A
NEW MILLENNIUM

A Collection of English Prose by
Pakistani Writers

LEAVING HOME

TOWARDS A
NEW MILLENNIUM

A Collection of English Prose by
Pakistani Writers

Selected and Edited by
Muneeza Shamsie

OXFORD
UNIVERSITY PRESS

OXFORD
UNIVERSITY PRESS

Great Clarendon Street, Oxford OX2 6DP

Oxford University Press is a department of the University of Oxford.
It furthers the University's objective of excellence in research, scholarship,
and education by publishing worldwide in

Oxford New York

Athens Auckland Bangkok Bogotá Buenos Aires Cape Town
Chennai Dar es Salaam Delhi Florence Hong Kong Istanbul Karachi
Kolkata Kuala Lumpur Madrid Melbourne Mexico City Mumbai Nairobi
Paris São Paulo Shanghai Singapore Taipei Tokyo Toronto Warsaw

with associated companies in Berlin Ibadan

Oxford is a registered trade mark of Oxford University Press
in the UK and in certain other countries

© Oxford University Press 2001

The moral rights of the author have been asserted

First published 2001

ISBN 0 19 579529 6

Typeset in Times
Printed in Pakistan by
Mas Printers, Karachi.
Published by
Ameena Saiyid, Oxford University Press
5-Bangalore Town, Sharae Faisal
PO Box 13033, Karachi-75350, Pakistan.

For
Saleem, Saman, and Kamila
with love

THANKS

I would like to thank Ameena Saiyid, the Managing Director of OUP, for being such a source of strength as always, to Yasmin Qureshi for her help, and Daleara Jamasji Hirjikaka and Faisal Nazir for their co-operation. I owe a particular debt to Richard Hardwick and the British Council in Pakistan for the opportunity to attend the 25th Cambridge Seminar on The Contemporary British Writer, where discussions on multi-culturalism and migration, provided me with much food for thought. I also thank my husband, Saleem and my daughters, Saman and Kamila, for their constant interest and support, but Kamila deserves a special word for solving my computer problems and for acting as a liaison between me and some of my contributors, during her months in England.

CONTENTS

III: VOTING WITH THEIR FEET

INTRODUCTION

The history of mankind is the story of migration, adaptation, mutation and change; of dominant cultures absorbing the influence of others; of nomadic horsemen sweeping down to agricultural valleys as conquerors and becoming farmers; or itinerant monks and traders and preachers carrying tales and secrets of one land to another. Then there has been the traffic of human beings as slaves, bonded labour or booty across oceans, or great religious, political and racial persecutions which have led to heroic treks to far-flung lands, in search of liberty and survival.

The twentieth century saw an unprecedented movement of people across the globe, due to advances in technology. There was a vast fanning out of people from South Asia, to the developed world, for a variety of reasons, ranging from employment and education to a quest for political and intellectual freedom. There are also few parallels in history to the mass migration, the exchange of population at Partition in 1947. This traumatic event, which marked the retreat of the British Empire and the birth of two independent countries, India and Pakistan, left some ten million refugees and almost one million dead. The reverberations haunt the very fabric of South Asia still. Other pressures have come to bear on urban and rural life in Pakistan, due to the breakdown of traditional village life and the influx of rural migrants to the cities or oil-rich states. Today, even an arranged marriage within the community, does not mean that a bride will continue to follow the same living patterns as her mother and grandmother did, or remain in the same village or city.

This has led to many stresses in contemporary life. At the same time, there has been a subtle process of adjustment and integration, which Intizar Hussain, described as 'acculturation' in his essay 'My Fifty Years in Lahore'.[1] He expressed a universal truth about migrant and host communities when he said:

> The process of acculturation is never smooth or easy. It brings in its wake many tensions, conflicts and rifts. In fact we in Pakistan, are locked in the situation of Sartre's *No Exit*. Migration has landed us in a position where we have no choice but to live together: and no matter whether we love and respect or hate each other, we are influenced and being influenced by each other, without noticing it.

The aim of this book is to explore the Pakistani experience of 'Leaving Home' in a wider perspective and to generate a dialogue on different types of migrations and draw upon parallels, contrasts and variances. This includes perceptions of history, identity, memory, multiple belonging, text—and perhaps the very definition of the term 'home', in a mobile eclectic world, at the dawn of a new millennium.

Today, the English language occupies a global domination unprecedented in history. What the long-term impact will be on other world languages, remains to be seen, but the recognition of this *lingua franca*, the concept of a global village and the presence of diverse migrant communities in the West is largely responsible for the increasing interest in the new literatures in English.

The idea for a book about migration began to grow while I was putting together my previous book, *A Dragonfly in the Sun: An Anthology of Pakistani Writing in English*.[2] This was a retrospective volume, consisting of English fiction, poetry and drama by writers of Pakistani origin, living in Pakistan and in the diaspora. Among the issues which, emerged from this, was that a large number of Pakistani writers of English fiction were living in far-flung countries such as England or America. Their

---

1. Originally written as a speech for 'Promised Lands', a seminar at the Goethe Institute, Karachi, October 1997.
2. Muneeza Shamsie, ed., *A Dragonfly in the Sun: An Anthology of Pakistani Writing in English*, OUP, Karachi, 1997.

work charted a course across the societies in which they lived and the homeland that they or their parents had left behind. To them, the act of writing itself was a process of reclamation or of re-defining themselves and their history and thus creating a new narrative and a new space for themselves in the cannons of Anglo-American literature and world literature in English.

On the other hand, in Pakistan, many questioned the 'Pakistani' identity of Pakistani English writers who had migrated, or had Pakistani parents and lived elsewhere. The problem of identity has been further complicated by the fact that Pakistan is an ideological state. The concept behind it, that of a separate homeland for Muslims, was essentially a trans-geographical one as a response to the Muslim demand for political rights in an undivided India. Nevertheless geography has continued to assert itself in the body politic of Pakistan, creating conflicts of language and ethnicity. Conversely, South Asian migrants to the West find themselves on the same side of political and cultural spectrum i.e. as a minimized and often, stereotyped minority.

All these disparate influences have produced a nascent, but enormously rich and stimulating literature in English by writers of Pakistani origin. As the Karachi-born expatriat Aamer Hussein, says:

> I haven't discarded notions of commitment and belonging. But a modest lack of ideological dogma is crucial to the engaged writer. I claim, with fiction as my only instrument, the native's right to argue and discuss my history with my compatriots. I guess that makes me a Pakistani writer.

The ability of so many Pakistani English writers to perceive themselves in universal terms, yet identify with Pakistan has also had a powerful impact on Pakistani English writing. In her incisive review of *A Dragonfly in the Sun*, Anita Desai commented on the extent to which the imagination of the Muslim writer in Pakistan has been captured by the history and culture of the wider Islamic world.[3] Of course Pakistani English writing and Indian English writing have strong echoes, having shared a common history. Inevitably they also bear a close kinship to trends in Anglo-American literature as well as that of Commonwealth countries where English was acquired as the direct result of the colonial encounter. The development of Pakistani English writing has been discussed already in *A Dragonfly in the Sun* and in Tariq Rahman's academic study, *A History of Pakistani Literature in English*.[4] Suffice it to say here that in the nineteenth century, South Asian English poetry, fiction and drama was very derivative; original, creative work only began to evolve in the twentieth century. However, English was used very effectively for non-fiction writing ranging from treatises, memoirs, travelogues and newspaper articles long before that.

According to Zamir Niazi,[5] India's first newspaper, *Hicky's Bengal Gazette or Calcutta General Advisor,* was established in 1780 by a British trader, James Augustus Hicky, to expose corruption and irregularities among the 'Nabobs' of the East India Company. From the very beginning, the press in India assumed the role of dissent from authority. An increasing number of Indians began to write in English, as British rule was established in India and English became the official language. English newspapers published by Indians sprang up alongside those in the vernacular languages. They played a pivotal role in explaining the Indian point of view to the British, forging reformist movements within India, as well as a national identity and ultimately the Independence Movement and The Pakistan Movement. Furthermore, because English was the language of the colonial power, the acquisition of English during the Raj became a form of migration in itself: it meant establishing a dialogue with the British on British terms and thus being

---

3. Anita Desai, 'Englished Diaspora', *The Times Higher Education Supplement*, London, 8 May 1998.
4. Tariq Rahman, *A History of Pakistani Literature in English*, Vanguard, Lahore, 1991.
5. Zamir Niazi, *The Press in Chains,* Royal Book Company, Karachi, 1986.

sensitive to a different world of ideas, living, and conduct.

For this reason, it was decided to begin this book symbolically with a Prologue named 'Leaving Home'. This consists of an extract from the seminal work, *The Travels of Dean Mahomet, A Native of Patna in Bengal Through Several Parts of India While in the Service of the Honourable East India Company, Written by Himself in a Series of Letters to a Friend.* Published in 1794, *Travels* is believed to be the first book in English by a writer of South Asian origin.

In *Travels* Sake Dean Mahomet's narrative pre-dates and foreshadows the Raj. He provides an eyewitness account of events, which led to British hegemony over India. As the poet and scholar Alamgir Hashmi[6] has said, *Travels* establishes the sub-continent as one of the first regions beyond Britain and America to use English for literary purposes. This also dates South Asian English literature to the same era when many indigenous and provincial literatures of South Asia began to assert themselves, as centralized Mughal authority and thus the influence of the court language—Persian—waned.

Sake Dean Mahomet left his Patna home to serve with the East India Company, and later sailed to Ireland with his young Anglo-Irish patron, Godfrey Evan Baker. He married an Irishwoman and ultimately settled in England.[7] His book was published in Cork to explain India—and himself—to his new European friends. Michael H Fisher, author of the excellent *The First Indian Author in English*, believes that *Travels* may have been encouraged by the writings of the Black African writer, Olaudah Equiano, who wrote in English and had toured Ireland. Fisher also points out that although Dean Mahomet emulated the style of European travel writers and often identified with the European officers that he served in India, he retained a consciousness of himself as an Indian. His narrative provided

6. Alamgir Hashmi, 'Prolegomena to the Study of Pakistani English and Pakistani Literature in English', the International Conference on English in South Asia, University Grants Commission, Islamabad, January 4-9, 1989.
7. Michael H Fisher, *The First Indian Author in English: Dean Mahomed (1759-1851) in India, Ireland and England*, OUP, Delhi, 1996.

insights into India and its society, very different to that of any European. He was also reaching out to an Anglophone audience in a very specific way and, in the process, he was at pains to rectify the existing European notions of 'heathens', 'Mahometans' and the exotic east. Opposite the title page of *Travels*, there is a sketch of Dean Mahomet with long, curly, collar-length hair, in the European style, and a coat and cravat. Underneath is the inscription 'Dean Mahomet, an East Indian'. He embodies the duality of all South Asian writing in English.

Today, most Pakistani English fiction is being written in the diaspora, but there is also some good, non-fiction writing with a literary quality by writers living in Pakistan. Many of them are contributors to Pakistan's English press. Therefore it was decided to include fiction, essays and memoirs in this volume to extend the scope of the book and to organize material according to linkages or contrasts, rather than by genre. Hopefully this will not only highlight the manner in which fiction and non-fiction reflect each other but also reveal the close affinity between work written or published in the diaspora and in Pakistan. In the process of selection, it was decided to cover as broad a spectrum of opinions as possible; a short story was given a preference over an extract from a novel, unless the latter was complete and could stand on its own. There, the title of the chapter has been used or a new title has been given with the author's help, or consent, for the purposes of this book.

Some of the work included here has been published elsewhere, but there was a conscious decision not to repeat any that had appeared previously in *A Dragonfly in the Sun*. Except for the Prologue, all the work in this volume was written after Partition.

Leaving Home: Towards a New Millennium is basically divided into three sections, which follow a loose chronology, beginning with 1947. They touch upon three distinct waves of migration and their aftermath, although there is much that overlaps. 'Part I: When Borders Shift', opens with Partition and deals with contemporary issues related to that. 'Part II: Go West!', focuses largely on the migration to the West and issues of conflict or integration and intermarriage. 'Part III: Voting with their Feet', looks at those left behind, the movement of people within Pakistan and to the oil-rich Gulf, and at the importance that words, language and story telling assume, during a prolonged exile.

Part I begins with 'When Borders Shift', a harrowing and powerful extract from Bapsi Sidhwa's novel, *The Bride*. She describes the mass movement of humanity across the Indo-Pakistan borders in trains that were set upon, when the boundaries between the two countries were so arbitrarily drawn across the Punjab in August 1947. At the heart of the story, there is Qasim, a man from the northern hills, who has come to the cities to find work, but his tribal culture sets him apart from people of the plains.

Several works in this volume revolve around more than one form of migration. 'The Native Alien's Story', an extract from Zulfikar's Ghose's novel, *The Triple Mirror of the Self,* provides a view of Partition and its aftermath, through the eyes of Roshan, a Muslim boy in Bombay, as his cosmopolitan world becomes increasingly fragmented. In the background stands the ship, which will eventually carry him and his family to England.

The departure of the British and the remnants of a 'Little England' in the Punjab is the subject of Athar Tahir's essay, 'Momento Mori', and is complemented by his short story, 'Rajling', about colonial attitudes. In 'The Colour of the Lahore Sky', Sorayya Y Khan gives a different context to the presence of a European woman in post-independence Pakistan. A naturalized American of Dutch origin, Irene, comes to live with Javed, her Pakistani husband, in Lahore. The narrative not only brings out the differences and similarities between East and West, but also links up many migrations and the cataclysmic events of Partition and World War II in Europe.

Hamida Khuhro's essay, 'Another Kind of Migration', describes the changing face of Karachi. She provides vivid glimpses of pre-Partition Karachi life, of World War II, the Pakistan Movement and her family's involvement in the Muslim League. She goes on to describe the influx of Muslim refugees from India, the exodus of Hindus from Pakistan and the search for a 'national' culture, all of which irrevocably altered the face of Karachi as she had once known it.

Karachi also forms the backdrop to my story, 'A True Princess', about an aristocratic family divided by Partition between India, Pakistan and Britain. The tenuous hold of the past, its customs, class and traditions, blight the lives of a displaced, erstwhile princess and her adopted daughter. Intizar Husain's essay, 'My Fifty Years in Lahore', has already been quoted above. He describes the process of adaptation and adjustment that he has witnessed, and which he perceives as a dynamic, creative process, since his migration to Pakistan from India in 1947.

Partition was a watershed in the history of South Asia but twenty five years later, Pakistan too was divided when East Pakistan formed an independent Bangladesh. In her essay, 'Leaving Bangladesh', Aquila Ismail relives the terror faced by her family and a people largely forgotten by history, the 'Urdu speaking' minority. They were stranded in a hostile Bangladesh and were instinctively associated with the brutal military action, although she says:

> We had no part in the decisions on either side, but were merely cannon fodder that necessarily accompanies such acts by men in power.

The poet and journalist Kaleem Omar, takes a nostalgic look at the carefree East Pakistan he once knew, in his essay, 'A Land that was Lost to Me.' Moazzam Sheikh's story, 'The Idol Worshipper', develops the theme of loss and reclamation and the ambiguities of war.

The Urdu poet, Fahmida Riaz is unique because she lived in India as a political exile. There she switched languages to write *People*, her unpublished, first and only English novel because she felt so cut off from her roots in Pakistan. The extract reprinted here, 'Amina in High Waters', provides a fascinating insight into a political exile's sense of alienation and limbo; it also portrays the conflicts of a strong public figure, a woman activist, struggling against an untenable marriage, which has reduced her to emotional bondage and a personal paralysis.

Part II begins with 'Go West Young Man!' by Javed Qazi, which gives an entertaining account of a Pakistani student's unrealistic expectations of America and his confusing encounter with American culture. Afzal Haider's brief story, 'Tribes', packs in much about history, migration, and racial exclusion in the United States and revolves around the chance conversation between a naturalized American, born in India, and a native American Indian.

As a writer and political activist, Tariq Ali has never been deterred or hampered by national or other boundaries. His interest in Marxism and Islamic history has led to a clear commitment to universalism. Exiled from Pakistan for his politics, he found a larger canvas for his ideas. From being a student leader in Pakistan, he became one in Europe during the 1960's. One of the great icons of that era was Che Guevara. Tariq Ali describes his quest for him in South America, in a spellbinding account from his memoir, *Streetfighting Years*. He says:

> The secret of Che's appeal is not difficult to fathom. He was a successful revolutionary leader in Cuba, where he held high office. Yet he had left the relative safety of Havana to resume the struggle in other lands. In his person, theory and practice were in complete harmony. Such a display of internationalism had not been seen since the twenties and thirties...

In 'Leela Lean', actor Zia Mohyeddin's records his memories of director David Lean's legendary Indian wife. His account is at once sumptuous, dazzling and poignant, as it moves between fantasy and reality, from the stage and film sets of Britain and America to a harsher world of solitude and exile.

The burden of colonial history, the timelessness of good literature, the commemoration of love, create a rich tapestry, a merging of cultures in Sara Suleri's chapter, 'What Mama

Knew', from her memoir, *Meatless Days*. Through her writing she reclaims, enshrines and celebrates the lives of her sister Iffat and their Welsh-born mother, who were both killed in hit-and-run accidents in Lahore.

To Anwer Mooraj, the son of a German mother, Berlin was the city he once considered as his home. In his essay, 'Kameradschaft in Berlin', he weaves in the memories of pre-War innocence, with post-War glimpses of that divided city, which he visited at different intervals.

In the first half of this century it became customary for the ruling and professional classes of South Asia, to send their sons abroad to England or Europe to acquire foreign degrees. By the 1960s, South Asian women had also started filtering into western academia. Among them was Anita Dass Schwaighofer who then met and married a European and settled in Paris. Her remarkably honest 'A Parisian Odyssey', is the story of that difficult adjustment. Hers is not simply the tale of a Pakistani woman coming to terms with French culture, but also of a woman belonging to a Christian minority in Pakistan, who finds countrywide celebrations in France at Easter and Christmas providing a new awareness for her.

The British-born Hanif Kureishi has carved a niche for himself with his intelligent and ruthless writing about multi-cultural, contemporary British life and the exclusion, overt and covert, that Asian Britons battle against. His story, 'We're not Jews', provides a chilling and finely observed portrait of British racism. Here the home that an Englishwoman, Evie and her son, Azhar, have left, is no more than a bus ride away. But Azhar's father is a Pakistani. Because of that, amidst unconcerned passengers on that bus, the school bully and his father—a childhood friend of Evie's—subject Evie and Azhar to taunts and jeers.

Rukhsana Ahmad's story, 'The Treatment', highlights a particularly disturbing aspect of migration: rich childless couples in the West kidnapping poor children from the Third World. Talat Abbasi's 'A Bear and its Trainer', is strongly permeated with feminism, as it describes the revenge of a long-suffering

Pakistani women who, mocked and demoralized by her husband since their Karachi wedding, is to be finally abandoned in America for another woman. Adam Zameenzad says much about oppression and gender roles in his story, 'Just like Home', which turns an ordinary London day into a nightmare.

In the title essay of 'Part III: Voting with their Feet', the columnist Irfan Husain contemplates on the state of Pakistani society today and why the brightest and the best want to leave. Humair Yusuf uses a quiet and subtle humour in his short story, 'MM Hashmi, Superintendent of the Passport Office', to parody officialdom and the exodus of young men from the country. Mahir Ali sums up the unfortunate political history of Pakistan in 'A Letter from a Father to his Daughter' to explain why he chose a voluntary exile in distant Australia.

Humera Afridi's witty '(Trans)Migrations of the Heart' elaborates on her instinctive reaction, 'Ha! A post-modern rendition of the arranged marriage!', when she accepted a proposal by her American cousin. This was followed by three weddings to the same man: a civil ceremony in the United States, a traditional Pathan wedding in the family village, and a sophisticated reception in urban Karachi.

Humera Afridi's cosmopolitan account provides a stark contrast with that of another Pathan girl, Saima Sarwar, who dared to demand a divorce from her husband. She was shot dead in her lawyer's office in Lahore for dishonouring her family. 'In the Name of Honour' by IA Rahman looks at the implications of this *cause celebre* which outraged Pakistani liberals but was applauded by many politicians and the orthodox.

Religion, migration and psychological aberration form the backdrop to Akbar S Ahmed's analysis, 'Migration, Death and Martyrdom in Rural Pakistan'. This looks at the 1983 Hawkes Bay Incident, when Saiyyid Willayat Hussain Shah, a one-time labourer in Saudi Arabia, gained unprecedented importance in his Punjab village, due to his daughter's religious hallucinations. In accordance with the divine instructions that she had received, he led her and almost forty Shi'as from the Punjab to the Arabian

Sea at Hawkes Bay, in the belief that a path would open in the sea, which would lead them to Karbala in Iraq, their holy city.

Nadeem Aslam's poetic 'Rainbow Dust', an extract from his novel, *Season of the Rainbirds*, filters economic hardship and the absence of a father in Saudi Arabia, through the eyes of a young child. 'The Zoo' by Tariq Rahman describes skewed bureaucratic priorities and the plight of rural migrants in overcrowded Pakistani cities. In 'Hiatus', Tahira Naqvi delves into the conflicts of a Pakistani woman, who comes from America to visit her much-loved Lahore family but prevaricates at the idea of returning for good. Kamila Shamsie's essay, 'Mulberry Absences', looks at the importance that language, words and their meanings assume after long absences from home. This theme is developed further in Aamer Hussein's ambitious story, 'Summer, Lake and Sad Garden', which moves in and out of countries, cities and time and provides a wonderful portrait of political and personal exile, as well as a clever interplay of history, interpretation and text.

Ultimately this book closes with 'Elephants and Jaguars' by Roshni Rustomji, an essay about story telling, revisions and adaptations, about how tales are carried from one culture to another. Through these oral and literary traditions, they cross the oceans and are transposed and transmuted into newer, wondrous forms and bring entire continents closer together.

Muneeza Shamsie
Karachi, 2000

PROLOGUE
LEAVING HOME

SAKE DEAN MAHOMET

Sake Dean Mahomet (1759-1851) was the first South Asian to have written a book in English. He left home to become a camp follower in the East India Company Bengal Army and later became a subaltern officer. In 1784, he sailed to Ireland with his Anglo-Irish patron, Godrey Evan Baker. His book, *The Travels of Dean Mahomet, A Native of Patna in Bengal Through Several Parts of India While in the Service of the Honourable East India Company, Written by Himself in a Series of Letters to a Friend in two volumes*, was published in Cork, in 1794. Written as a series of letters to a fictitious friend, the autobiographical *Travels* is dedicated to William Baillie Esq, Colonel in the Service of the East India Company. According to Michael H Fisher,[1] it remains the only Indian account of life in the East India Company in the eighteenth century. Fisher reveals that in 1786, Sake Dean Mahomet married Jane Daly, an Irishwoman, and in 1807, he moved to England with her. He settled in London's fashionable Portman Square and helped popularize vapour baths as a health cure and later, the Indian arts of massage (*malish*) and shampooing (*champi*), as therapy. He also set up an Indian restaurant, the 'Hindoostanee Coffee House', but became bankrupt and together with his wife, he moved to the fashionable seaside resort of Brighton. There he became a 'Shampooing Surgeon' and set up an enormously successful Indian Medicated Vapour Bath where he employed Indian herbs and other such items and treated the elite of society, including George IV. He began to lose prominence by the Victorian era, however, and was largely forgotten by history until recently. He also wrote *Cases Cured by Sake Deen Mahomed, Shampooing Surgeon, Inventor of the India Medicated Vapour and Sea Water Baths*, (1820) and *Shampooing, or Benefits Resulting from the use of the Indian Medicated Vapour Bath* (1822).

---

1. Michael H Fisher, *The First Indian Author in English: Dean Mahomed (1759-1851) in India, Ireland and England*, OUP, Delhi 1996.

THE TRAVELS OF DEAN MAHOMET[2]

Volume I
Letter I

DEAR SIR,
SINCE my arrival in this country, I find you have been very
anxious to be made acquainted with the early part of my Life
and the History of my Travels: I shall be happy to gratify you;
and must ingenuously confess, when I first came to Ireland, I
found the face of everything about me so contrasted to those
striking scenes in India, which we are wont to survey with a
kind of sublime delight, that I felt some timid inclination, even
in the consciousness of incapacity, to describe the manners of
my countrymen, who, I am proud to think, have still more of
the innocence of our ancestors, than some of the boasting
philosophers of Europe.

Though I acknowledge myself incapable of doing justice to
the merits of men, whose happy manners are worthy the
imitation of civilized nations, yet, you will do me the justice to
believe, that the gratification of your wishes, is the *principal*
incitement that engages me to undertake a work of this nature:
the earnest entreaties of some friends, and the liberal
encouragement of others, to whom I express my
acknowledgements, I allow are *secondary* motives.

The people of India, in general, are peculiarly favoured by
Providence in the possession of all that can cheer the mind and
allure the eye, and tho' the situation of Eden is only traced in
the Poet's creative fancy, the traveller beholds with admiration
the face of this delightful country, on which he discovers tracts
that resemble those so finely drawn by the animated pencil of
Milton. You will here behold the generous soil crowned with

---

2. From *The Travels of Dean Mahomet, A Native of Patna in Bengal Through
Several Parts of India While in the Service of the Honourable East India
Company, Written by Himself in a Series of Letters to a Friend.* The text
used here is from the original source in the British Library and retains its
spellings and grammar.

various plenty; the garden beautifully diversified with the gayest flowers diffusing their fragrance on the bosom of the air; and the very bowels of the earth enriched with the inestimable mines of gold and diamonds.

Possessed of all that is enviable in life, we are still more happy in the exercise of benevolence and goodwill to each other, devoid of every species of fraud or low cunning. In our convivial enjoyments, we are never without our neighbours; as it is usual for an individual, when he gives an entertainment, to invite all those of his own profession to partake of it. That profligacy of manners too conspicuous in other parts of the world, meets here with public indignation; and our women, though not so accomplished as those of Europe, are still very engaging for many virtues that exalt the sex.

As I have now given you a sketch of the manners of my country, I shall proceed to give you some account of myself.

I was born in the year 1759, in Patna, a famous city on the north side of the Ganges, about 400 miles from Calcutta, the capital of Bengal and seat of the English Government in that country. I was too young when my father died, to learn any great account of his family: all I have been able to know respecting him, is, that he was descended from the same race as the Nabobs of Moorshadabad. He was appointed Subadar, in a battalion of Seapoys commanded by Captain Adams, a company of which under his command was quartered at a small district not many miles from Patna, called Tarchpoor, an inconsiderable fort, built on the side of a little river that takes its rise a few miles up the country. Here he was stationed in order to keep this fort.

In the year 1769, a great dearth overspread the country about Tarchpoor, where the Rajas Boudmal, and his brother Corexin resided, which they took an advantage of by pretending it was impossible for them to remit the stipulated supplies to the Raja Sataproy, who finding himself disappointed in his expectations, sent some of his people to compel them to pay: but the others retired within their forts, determined on making an obstinate defence. My father having received orders to lead out his men to the scene of dispute, which lay about twelve miles from the fort he was quartered in, marched accordingly, and soon after his arrival at Taharah, took the Raja Boudmal prisoner, and sent him under a strong guard to Patna, where he was obliged to account for his conduct. My father remained in the field, giving the enemy some striking proofs of the courage of their adversary; which drove them to such measures, that they strengthened their posts and redoubled their attacks with such ardour, that many of our men fell, and my lamented father among the rest; but not till he had entirely exhausted the forces of the Raja, who, at length submitted. The soldiers, animated by his example, made Corexin a prisoner, and took possession of the fort.

Thus have I been deprived of a gallant father, whose firmness and resolution was manifested in his military conduct on several occasions.

My brother, then about sixteen years old, and the only child my mother had besides me, was present at the engagement, and having returned home, made an application to Capt Adams who, in gratitude to the memory of my father, whose services he failed not to represent to the Governor, speedily promoted him to his post. My mother and I suffered exceedingly by his sudden yet honourable fate in the field: for my brother was then too young and thoughtless, to pay any great attention to our situation.

I was about eleven years old when deprived of my father, and though children are seldom possessed of much sensibility or reflection at such immature years, yet I recollect well no incident of my life ever made so deep an impression on my mind. Nothing could wear from my memory the remembrance of his tender regard. As he was a Mahometan, he was interred with all the pomp and ceremony usual on the occasion. I remained with my mother sometime after, and acquired a little education at a school in Patna.

Letter II

DEAR SIR,

IN a few months after my father's fate, my mother and I went to
Patna to reside: she lived pretty comfortably on some of the
property she was entitled to in right of her husband: the rest of
his substance with his commission, came into the hands of my
brother: our support was made better by the liberality of the
Begum and Nabob, to whom my father was related: the Begum
was remarkably affectionate and attentive to us.

The Raja Sataproy had a very magnificent palace in the centre
of the city of Patna, where he was accustomed to entertain
many of the most distinguished European Gentlemen, with
brilliant balls and costly suppers. My mother's house was not
far from the Raja's palace, and the number of Officers passing
by our door in their way thither, attracted my notice, and excited
the ambition I had already had of entering on a military life.
With this notion, I was always on the watch, and impatiently
waited for the moment of their passing by our door; when, one
evening in particular, as they went along, I seized the happy
opportunity, and followed them directly to the palace, at the
outward gates of which there are sentinels placed, to keep off
the people and clear the passage for the Gentlemen; I however
got admittance, on account of the respect the guards paid my
father's family. The Gentlemen go to the palace between seven
and eight o'clock in the evening, take tea and coffee, and
frequently amuse themselves by forming a party to dance; when
they find themselves warm, they retire to the palace yard, where
there are marquees pitched for their reception; here they seat
themselves in a circular form, under a *semiana*, a fort of canopy
made of various coloured double muslin, supported by eight
poles, and on the ground is spread a beautiful carpet; the Raja
sits in the centre; the European Gentlemen on each side; and the
Music in the front. The Raja, on this occasion, is attended by
his Aid-du-Camps and Servants of rank. Dancing girls are now
introduced, affording, at one time, extreme delight, by singing
in concert with the Music, the softest and most lively airs; at

another time, displaying such loose and fascinating attitudes in their various dances, as would warm the bosom of an Anchoret; while the servants of the Raja are employed in letting off the fire-works, displaying, in the most astonishing variety, the forms of birds, beasts, and other animals, and far surpassing anything of the kind I ever beheld in Europe: and to give additional brilliancy to the splendor of the scene, lighted branches blaze around, and exhibit one general illumination. Extremely pleased with such various entertainment, the Gentlemen sit down to an elegant supper, prepared by the utmost skill, by an Officer of the Raja, whose sole employ is to provide the most delicious viands on such an occasion: ice-cream, fowl of all kinds, and the finest fruit in the world, compose but a part of the repast to which the guests are invited. The Raja was very happy with his convivial friends; and though his religion forbids him to touch many things handled by persons of a different profession, yet he accepted a little fruit from them; supper was over about twelve o'clock, and the company retired, the Raja to his palace, and the Officers to their quarters.

I was highly pleased with the appearance of the military Gentlemen, among whom I first beheld Mr Baker, who particularly drew my attention: I followed him without any restraint through every part of the palace and tents, and remained a spectator of the entire scene of pleasure, till the company broke up; and then returned home to my mother, who felt some anxiety in my absence. When I described the gaiety and splendor I beheld at the entertainment, she seemed very much dissatisfied, and expressed from maternal tenderness, her apprehensions of losing me.

Nothing could exceed my ambition of leading a soldier's life: the notion of carrying arms, and living in a camp could not be easily removed: my fond mother's entreaties were of no avail: I grew anxious for the moment that would bring the military Officers by our door. Whenever I perceived their route, I instantly followed them; sometimes to the Raja's palace, where I had free access; and sometimes to a fine tennis court, generally frequented by them in the evenings, which was built by Col Champion, at the back of his house, in a large open square, called Merfevillkeebaug: here, among other Gentlemen, I one day, discovered Mr Baker, and often passed by him, in order to attract his attention: he at last, took particular notice of me, observing that I surveyed him with a kind of secret satisfaction; and in a very friendly manner, asked me how I would like living with the Europeans: this unexpected encouragement, as it flattered my hopes beyond expression, occasioned a very sudden reply: I therefore told him with eager joy, how happy he could make me, by taking me with him. He seemed very much pleased with me, and assuring me of his future kindness, hoped I would merit it. Major Herd was in company with him at the same time: and both these Gentlemen appeared with distinguished eclat in the first assemblies in India. I was decently clad in the dress worn by children of my age: and though my mother was materially affected in her circumstances by the precipitate death of my father, she had still the means left of living in a comfortable manner and providing both for her own wants and mine.

Volume II
Letter XXXI

DEAR SIR

IN the year of 1781, Captain Baker, after his appointment to the command of the Seapoy's battalion, in the second brigade, with Lieutenants Simpson and Williamson, two companies of Europeans, and two companies of Seapoys, marched from Barahampore, in order to join the second brigade in Caunpore: on his promotion, he appointed me market-master to supply the bazar. We halted at Denapore to refresh the party, and draw their pay; and as they proceeded on their march, I was dispatched, with an escort of two Seapoys to Gooldengunge, which was considered the cheapest market, to purchase corn for the army, and had in my possession for that purpose, four hundred *goolmores*, with bills on the Commissary there, amounting in all to fifteen hundred pounds sterling. As we journeyed onwards, one of the Seapoys happened to trample some melons in passing through a plantation near the river side, and on being observed by the proprietor, who desired him to be more cautious in his career, he returned him some impertinent answer, which roused the peasant's resentment, and discord expanding her gloomy wings, a battle ensued; the neighbouring cottagers thus alarmed, flocked to their friend's assistance, and cruelly stabbed his adversary, who fell a breathless corpse beneath their murderous weapons. The other Seapoy made off through the country, but I was dismounted from my horse, which I was obliged to leave behind, and having plunged into the Ganges, on whose verge I stood trembling for my fate, with the utmost difficulty I gained the opposite shore, fainting under the fatigue of my exertions in crossing the wide river, with my clothes on, and such a weight of gold about me. A few of the peasantry, who beheld me thus struggling for life, ran to my assistance, and after supporting me to the next cottage, kindly ministered what relief was in their power. As the night approached, I sunk to rest, and forgot the dangers of my late journey in the sweet oblivion of sleep. Next morning, finding myself tolerably restored, I made my acknowledgements to these humane people, whose foot-steps, in all ruling Providence must, in that crisis, have directed, to save me from impending dissolution; and having gone forthwith to the Fouzdar of Gooldengunge, and given him up my money and bills, I related the story of my adventures; he seemed much affected at the recital, and detained me till the supplies for the use of the troops were purchased; a part was sent by water to Caunpore: and the rest by land, consisting of several loads of corn drawn by bullocks, with which I travelled and joined the army at Buxar. From the early intelligence of the Seapoy, who escaped before me, the greatest surprize, and even doubt of the reality of my existence at my arrival, was almost graven on every countenance, as the prevailing opinion unanimously agreed on by all parties, was, that I had fallen a sacrifice with the other Seapoy to the rage and resentment of the country people.

From Buxar we marched for Caunpore, where we arrived in the latter end of February. On the first of March, Captain Baker took the command of the battalion of Seapoys in Major Roberts' regiment, to which he had been recently promoted, and by his recommendation, I was appointed Jemidar in the same battalion.

Having received an account of the insurrections of the Morattoes in the vicinage of Caulpee, on the banks of the river Jemina, the entire brigade by order of Colonel Morgan, proceeded to that town, and a part of the main army in different detachments, scoured the neighbouring country, in order to disperse those disturbers of the public tranquility, who, after some slight skirmishes, entirely fled, overawed by the terror of our arms.

We remained a few weeks in Caulpee, and then returned to Caunpore, where our stay was of no long continuance.

About this time, Governor Hastings having required of Cheytsing his stipulated subsidies, towards defraying the expenses of the late war with Hyder Ally; and finding him either unwilling or unable to pay them, sent a guard consisting of two companies of Seapoys to arrest him: the alarming news of his being made a prisoner, soon spread through the country, and roused the indignation of his troops, who were seen in a large body, crossing the river from Ramnagur to the palace, in which he was confined. The two companies of our Seapoys, who formed the guard in an inclosed square outside the palace, were mostly massacred by this powerful force which rushed onward, like an irresistible torrent, that sweeps all away before it.

Ramjaum, one of the Raja's Generals, after killing a serjeant of the Seapoys, who opposed his entrance, broke into the royal mansion, and made way for the soldiery, who escorted their Prince through a garden which led to the river. As the banks were high above the surface, they let him down by turbans tied together, into a boat that conveyed him to the other side, whence he escaped under the friendly shade of night, to Lutteefgur, one of his strongest fortresses, with a chosen band of men to protect him.

Letter XXXII

DEAR SIR,
THE day following, a large party of the Raja's, with Ramjaum at their head, went in pursuit of Governor Hastings, who proceeded to Chunargar; and having fought him in vain, they returned to Ramnagur, where they attacked a strong body of the English under the command of Capt Mayaffre, of the artillery, who was hemmed in on every side by the narrow streets and winding alleys of the town, with which he was unacquainted. Being thus exposed to the fire of the enemy from all quarters, and particularly to that of a covered party that greatly annoyed him, he fell in the scene of battle, with upwards of one hundred and fifty of his men, among them were Captain Doxat, and Lieutenants Stalker, Symes and Scott, besides eighty wounded. After many brave struggles, Captain Blair, at last effected a regular and steady retreat, which gained him much honour. He prevented the eager pursuit of the enemy, who followed him till he came within a few miles of Chunar, from having any bad effect. This success gave fresh ardour to the Raja's friends, and plunged Governor Hastings into new difficulties.

Ramjaum having put Ramnagur into a state of defence, conducted his principal troops to a fort called Pateetah, to which a detachment under the command of Major Popham was directed, composed of what men could be spared from the garrison of Chunar. In the meantime Captain Blair was dispatched with his battalion and two companies of grenadiers to surprise the fort; and Lieutenant Polhill, who just arrived from Allahabad, with six companies of Seapoys from the Nabob Aspah-doulah's life guards, was ordered to encamp on the opposite shore, in order to keep the communication at that side open. In two days after his arrival, this spirited Officer, defeated a considerable body of the enemy at a small fort called Seekur, where he found a vast quantity of grain, which proved an acceptable prize, as it was much wanted.

Major Popham and Captain Blair having arrived within about a mile of Pateetah, nearly at the same time found a party of the enemy in seeming readiness to oppose them. They fought on both sides, with great ardour and intrepidity, till victory perplexed with doubt, waited the arrival of Lieutenants Fallow and Berrille, whose gallant conduct with the united bravery of their countrymen, preponderating in the scale of her unbiassed judgement, induced the Goddess to bestow on them, her unfading laurels, as the reward of their exertions. After a dreadful carnage of killed and wounded on each part, the conquered fled for refuge to their fort, and the victors advanced to Chunar to recruit their losses. At the commencement of these commotions, Governor Hastings dispatched a courier to Colonel Morgan, at Caunpore, with instructions directing him to send an immediate reinforcement to Chunar: three regiments were accordingly sent with the utmost expedition; two of which were under the command of Majors Crabb and Crawford with one company of artillery, and two of European infantry; and the other under Major Roberts, which marched by the route of Lecknow. Early on the tenth of September, Majors Crabb and Crawford, at the head of their respective corps, appeared within view of Chunar on the opposite shore: the following day, the Nabob Aspah-doulah arrived and encamped at the same side of the river; and shortly after Major Roberts came from Lecknow, with his troops. The English crossed the river, and joined Major Popham, who had now the command of four complete regiments, one battalion of Colonel Blair, another of the Nabob's life guards, two companies of Europeans, one of artillery, and one of French rangers. From this main body, Major Crabb, with one detachment, proceeded against Lutteefgur; Major Crawford with another, crossed the mountains to Seckroot and Lora; and two companies under the direction of Captain Baker, and Lieutenant Simpson, advanced towards Pateetah with a twelve pounder, which they played on the north side of the fort, for, at least an hour, with good effect, till an *halcarah*, who just arrived, informed them that there was a large tank on the eastern situation with a great heap of earth thrown up about it, which might answer the purpose of a temporary battery. When the tank was discovered, and found adequate to the description given of it, an

additional supply of cannon and ammunition was directly sent
for. We now began the siege with the most lively ardour, and
continued it for three days without intermission: on the fourth
morning, at three o'clock, Captains Baker and Gardner kept up
a brisk cannonading, and threw the enemy into the utmost
confusion, amidst which, Captain Lane, Lieutenants Simpson
and Williams with whom I adventured and three companies of
determined Seapoy grenadiers, stormed the fort and rushed on
the disordered enemy with manly resolution. After some
opposition, they evacuated their stronghold, with Ramjaum at
their head, and made off towards Lutteefgur, leaving their
military equipage, elephants, camels, bullocks, &c. behind them.

Captain Baker distinguished himself in this action, as in many
others, by the greatest exertions, and displayed the courage of
the active soldier united with the experience of the hoary veteran.

While memory dwells on virtues only thine
Fame o'er thy relics breathes a strain divine.

Major Crabb having met Ramjaum on his way to Lutteefgur,
gave him battle, and obliged him with his vanquished forces to
fly for shelter to Lora, and from thence to Bidgegur, whither
Cheyt-sing had escaped. The Raja, however, not finding himself
safe in Bidgegur, fled for refuge to the mountains among the
Morattoes, taking with him what diamonds and other valuable
effects he could possibly convey on his camels.

PART I
WHEN BORDERS SHIFT

BAPSI SIDHWA

*O*ne of Pakistan's most widely read English language writers, Bapsi Sidhwa divides her time between Pakistan and the United States, but for most of her life she has lived in Lahore, where her books are largely set. Her novel, *Ice-Candy-Man* (Heinemann, 1988) about Partition—published as *Cracking India* (Milkweed, 1991) in the United States—won Germany's 1991 Liberature Prize and has been made into a film, *Earth* (1998). Partition and tribal customs, feature in her earlier work, *The Bride* (Cape, 1982). She is a committed feminist, has a great eye for comedy and has written two other novels, *The Crow Eaters* (Cape, 1978) and *The American Brat (*Milkweed, 1993*).* She has taught in many American universities, was a Bunting Fellow at Radcliffe College and received the 1993 Lila Wallace-Reader's Digest Award. She has been showered with honours in Pakistan, including The Pakistan Academy of Letters Award, the Patras Bokhari Award and the *Sitara-e-Imtiaz.* She was a Visiting Scholar at the Rockefeller Foundation in Bellagio, is also on the board of *Inprint,* Houston, and the Distinguished Writer-in-Residence and Professor of English at Mount Holyoke College, Massachusetts. She is now putting together a collection of short stories.

WHEN BORDERS SHIFT[1]

I

In the chaotic summer of 1947 there was serious political unrest in the North Indian plains. Savage rioting erupted and many minority groups felt insecure. One by one the hill-country tribesmen fled Jullundur. For a time Qasim, loath to return to his life in the mountains where he would be under pressure to re-marry, stayed on. He did not want to expose himself again to the bonds of love.

Hysteria mounted when the fertile, hot lands of the Punjab were suddenly ripped into two territories—Hindu and Muslim,

---

1. From the novel, *The Bride.*

India and Pakistan. Until the last moment no one was sure how the land would be divided. Lahore, which everyone expected to go to India because so many wealthy Hindus lived in it, went instead to Pakistan. Jullundur, a Sikh stronghold, was allocated to India. Now that it was decided they would leave, the British were in a hurry to wind up. Furniture, artifacts and merchandise had to be shipped, antiques, curios and jewellery acquired and transported. Preoccupied with misgiving and the arrangements attendant on relocating themselves in their native land, by the agony of separation from regiments, Imperial trappings and servants, the rulers of the Empire were entirely too busy to bother overmuch with how India was divided. It was only one of the thousand and one chores they faced.

The earth is not easy to carve up. India required a deft and sensitive surgeon, but the British, steeped in domestic pre-occupation, hastily and carelessly butchered it. They were not deliberately mischievous—only cruelly negligent! A million Indians died. The earth sealed its clumsy new boundaries in blood as town by town, farm by farm, the border was defined. Trains carrying refugees sped through the darkness of night— Hindus going one way and Muslims the other. They left at odd hours to try to dodge mobs bent on their destruction. Yet trains were ambushed and looted and their fleeing occupants slaughtered.

Near Lahore, men—mostly Sikhs—squat on either side of the rail-tracks, waiting. Their white singlets reflect the moon palely. These Sikhs are lean and towering, with muscles like flat mango seeds and heads topped by scraggly buns of hair, loose tendrils mingling with their coarse beards. They are silent, listening, glancing at the luminous dials of wrist-watches.

They have raised a barricade of logs across the tracks, and the steel rails swerve slightly where the lines disappear in blackness. On either side, ploughed stretches of earth spread black wings to the horizon.

At first the men, bunched in loose groups, welcome the diversion when a voice rises:

'I saw them myself—huge cauldrons of boiling oil and babies tossed into them!'

Then losing interest in what they have heard so often, their faces turn away. By now these tales arouse only an embarrassed resentment. They are meant to stir their nobler passions, but the thought of loot undermines that resolve.

An old Sikh stands up. He wears a loose white muslin shirt, which makes him look bigger in the moonlight. They know him to be the sole survivor of a large family in the Montgomery district. They whisper, 'It is Moola Singh, cousin of Bishan Singh.'

Seething with hatred, his hurt still raw, Moola Singh resents their apathy. From the depths of his anguish, his voice betraying tears, he shrieks: 'Vengeance, my brothers, vengeance!'

He swallows hard. 'I thought we would stay by our land, by our stock, by our Mussalman neighbours. No one can touch us, I thought. The riots will pass us by. But a mob attacked our village—Oh, the screams of the women, I can hear them still...I had a twenty-year-old brother, tall and strong as a mountain, a match for any five of them. This is what they did: they tied one of his legs to one jeep, the other to another jeep—and then they drove the jeeps apart...'

Moola Singh stands quite still. The men look away despite the dark. Their indignation flares into rage.

'God give our arms strength,' one of them shouts, and in a sudden movement, knives glimmer. Their cry, *Bole so Nihal, Sat siri Akal*, swells into the ferocious chant: 'Vengeance! Vengeance! Vengeance!' The old Sikh sinks to his knees.

II

Sikander cut his way frantically through the ripe wheat as he ran towards the mud walls of his hut. His wife Zohra, standing in the courtyard, watched him. In the heat-hazed dawn neat

squares of rippling wheat stretched towards the horizon and—
riding on sudden swells of the breeze—came the distant chants
of *Hari Hari Mahadev*! *Bole so Nihal. Sat siri Akal*! And an
occasional, piercing, *Ya Alieeee*! An ugly bloated ebb and flow
of noise engulfed everything. The corn, the earth, the air and
the sky seemed full of threat.

The child saw her father's brown legs flash towards them
through the green stalks. Something in his movement checked
Munni's usual delighted greeting. She clung to her mother's
sari.

Sikander, panting, reached the open yard. He shouted, 'A train
is leaving at four o'clock from Ludhiana. We must make it.'

Zohra turned her face away, sick with fright and the
realization of loss. The moment she had vaguely dreaded hit her
like a physical blow.

The angry chants, fragmented by the distance, urged them
into action.

'Hurry, for God's sake,' panted Sikander.

Zohra dragged out their tin trunks and bed-rolls. Listlessly
she wrapped odds and ends into clumsy cloth bundles. The calf
and two goats were tethered, ready for departure.

Sikander ran round to the back and, trotting abreast of the
horse, brought their two-wheeled *rehra* to the spread of luggage.
'We can't take all this!' He cried. 'A trunk apiece, that's all.
Hide the jewellery somewhere on your body. Come on, hurry
up.' He bustled Zohra out of her stunned apathy. Munni was
lifted into the cart. Sikander hauled in the calf and goats while
Zohra fetched the sleeping baby boy from inside. They drove
through the fields on to a dirt road.

The train at Ludhiana station already swarmed with Muslims
who had boarded it at earlier stops. Panic-stricken families were
abandoning their animals and possessions in an attempt to get
on. Zohra glanced back at their mound of luggage now scattered
and indistinguishable among the mounting litter of tin trunks

and bundles. Their goats had already run off. She pressed closer to Sikander, roughly yanking Munni by the hand. The baby, secure on her hip, looked about him with interest.

Carrying the calf, protecting it with his arms, Sikander forced a way for his family. Inches from the train they were suddenly pushed back by a swell in the crowd. Sikander dropped the calf. Lunging desperately, he at last got a grip on an open window. Quickly he clambered on to the roof of a compartment. Zohra held up the baby. Someone took him and passed him to his father. Lifting Munni, arms outstretched, Zohra too was hoisted up by friendly hands.

'Abba, the calf! There it is!' cried Munni, pointing it out. It tottered below them on spindly, unsteady legs, its face raised, mute and trusting.

'Get the calf, Abba. Don't leave it, she's a baby, she'll die!'

'Shush,' her mother scolded. 'We haven't room for ourselves and you want to take that beast!'

'Abba, don't leave the calf…I want my calf,' Munni wailed, and Zohra, overwrought and on the verge of tears herself, raged, 'Shut up, or I'll slap you.'

'Don't be angry with the child,' said Sikander, holding his daughter close.

A few paces from them, jammed between two men, a boy sat cradling a newborn calf. Munni dug her face into her father's shirt. She wept inconsolably.

The train sped through the throng awaiting it at Jullundur and stopped instead at a siding a few furlongs past the station. It was a pre-arranged halt and the small, clandestine group awaiting it squeezed in as best they could. Qasim, a holstered pistol slung across his chest, a rifle swinging down his back, walked rapidly towards the engine, scanning the compartments. He tried one, but was churned out by the pressure of brown bodies. Afraid that the train might leave without him, he began to run. Just as it pulled away, he hauled himself on to the roof of the carriage nearest the engine.

Sitting on the roof, Qasim could see the refugees who had been by-passed at the station closing in like a tide. Men and women carrying children surged forward with their cattle. The train picked up speed. There was an angry roar from the scrambling mass, and some, leaving their families, rushed forward.

But the train, with an indifferent hiss, drew away into the growing darkness.

An old man with a wispy beard sits next to Qasim. Their legs dangle over the roof and from time to time the old man, afraid of losing his balance, grips Qasim's thigh. He chirps like a bird, philosophizing, sermonizing, relating the histories of various members of his family in his impeccable Aligarh Urdu. Qasim, who has picked up only a broken, make-do Urdu in his three years in the plains, is at a loss before the onslaught of such poetic fluency. Yet he nods his head. He gathers that the old man is from Central India and is eager to settle in Pakistan with his wife, four sons and their families, all of whom are scattered about the train.

Smoke from the engine spews into their faces, and except for their irritated red eyes, they are black with soot. Brushing away sparks and tears, patches of Qasim's skin show unexpectedly white. Tall and bristling with weapons, he is unmistakably a mountain tribal. His narrow eyes, intent on the landscape, combine wariness with the determination of a bird of prey.

It is nearly four years since Qasim left his mountain village. From the remote Himalayan reaches of Kohistan, he had travelled straight to Jullundur where his cousin worked as a messenger in a British firm. His cousin found him a job as watchman in the National and Grindlays Bank. The work suited Qasim perfectly. He stood all day, resplendent in a khaki uniform and crisp turban, guarding the bank entrance. The double-barrelled gun that he stood beside him and the bullet-crammed bandolier swathing his chest gladdened his heart and gratified his pride, for a gun is part of a tribal's attire. It shows his readiness to face his enemy and protect his family's honour.

Touchy and bewildered to begin with, Qasim nevertheless had been fascinated by Jullundur, a busy city in the North Indian plains. Each common object he saw was to him a miracle. Torches, safety-pins, electric lights, cinemas and cars whirled magically before his senses. The language posed a problem. Although he spoke Hindko, a distorted mixture of Punjabi and Pushto, Qasim was able to follow only very little of the zestful Punjabi spoken in Jullundur. Urdu and Hindustani were entirely beyond him.

In the evenings, with his Kohistani friends, Qasim perched atop the backrests of park benches, seeking with his mind's eye the heights and valleys of the land he had left. Like prime-hooded hawks, the tribesmen squatted on the thin edges of roofs and walls, and their eyes sank into the women's brisk buttocks and bare midriffs. Qasim developed a taste for spicy curries and vegetables, a far cry from his daily mountain diet of flat maize bread soaked in water.

The difference was greatest in the really basic values. The men of the plains appeared strangely effeminate. Women roamed the streets in brazen proximity. These people were soft, their lives easy. Where he came from, men—as in the Stone Age—walked thirty days over the lonely, almost trackless mountains to secure salt for their tribes.

The old man has not spoken for some time. Nervously he glances at Qasim's pistol when the holster stirs between them. He is certain the jerks will trigger a shot and shatter his thigh. At last he pats Qasim gingerly on the back.

'Do you think you could move this thing to the other shoulder, Khan Sahib?'

Qasim obligingly shifts the holster strap.

The old man gives a thin smile. Holding on to the roof-edge with one hand, he combs his scant beard.

'Say, why do you carry this dangerous weapon?' he asks in fatherly tones.

'To kill my enemies.'

In the dark, Qasim feels the man's shoulder twitch and move away. Enjoying the situation, he boasts: 'I killed a *baboo* just before getting here.'

'Why...what had he done?'

'I settled a score with him before leaving.'

Qasim pats his gun.

'But why?' persists the old man.

'He was a bloody Hindu bastard!' says Qasim with a finality that checks the old man's curiosity back into his throat.

It was a fact. Qasim had killed a man before leaving.

His enmity with Girdharilal, a puckish, supercilious little clerk, had started a few months after he became watchman at the bank. Besides his clerical work, Girdharilal was responsible for cleanliness in the bank building, right down to the toilets.

Qasim performed his ablutions before reporting for work, but sometimes he was compelled to use the public place reserved for lesser employees. It was of sophisticated Indian style: a clock-shaped china basin embedded in the floor to squat over, with a rusty chain dangling from the ceiling to manipulate the flush. A tap was at hand and a mug stood under it ready for use.

On his rare visits, Qasim left the contraption clogged with stones and scarps of smooth-surfaced glass. Colleagues visiting the lavatory later would rush out in consternation. Girdharilal had the mess cleared out a couple of times and everyone wondered who had caused the mischief. Happily oblivious, Qasim understood none of their talk.

But Girdharilal had his suspicions. One day he followed Qasim and discovered him to be the culprit. He accosted him directly, asking, 'Did you throw the stones in there?' Qasim, who did not follow the quick-spoken, alien words, merely smiled. A bunch of peons and clerks gathered around them. They explained the charge to Qasim. Admitting the facts, still smiling, he looked from one astonished face to the next, wondering what really was the matter. But there was no mistaking Girdharilal's truculence. He spluttered and gesticulated insultingly. He poked him in the ribs, and the smile left Qasim's face.

He realized he was being ridiculed. And then Girdharilal used a particularly vile obscenity. 'You filthy son of a Muslim mountain hog!' he cried. Qasim's face darkened. Lifting the slightly-built man he pressed him against a wall, and with his hands around the clerk's neck, he started to choke him. Death was the price for daring such an insult to his tribe, his blood, his religion.

Frantic cries rang out of 'Murder! Murder! The Pathan will kill him!' and the two were wrenched apart.

Girdharilal, faint with shock, trembled while Qasim hurled abuse and threats of vengeance at him in his hill dialect. Girdharilal did not catch a single word, but he could not miss the meaning.

A senior officer appeared. The situation was explained to him, and Qasim was ordered to apologize. He refused, and his clansman was sent for. After a roaring argument, the clansman finally persuaded Qasim to say the necessary words. He uttered them with the grace of a hungry tiger kept from his victim by chains. An uneasy peace ensued. Qasim learnt from his cousin that killing, no matter what the provocation, was not acceptable by the laws of this land. He would be caught and hanged. These were the plains, with no friendly mountains to afford him sanctuary.

Time passed. Tales of communal atrocities fanned skirmishes, unrest and panic. India was to be partitioned, and that summer the anger and fear in people's minds exploded. Towns were automatically divided into communal sections. Muslim, Hindu, Sikh, each rushed headlong for the locality representing his faith, to seek the dubious safety of strength in numbers. Isolated homes were ransacked and burnt. The sky glowed at night from the fires. It was as though the earth had become the sun, spreading its rays upward. Dismembered bodies of men, women, and even children, lay strewn on roads. Leaving everything behind, people ran from their villages into the towns.

Qasim had not been to work for a month. Riots were in full swing in Jullundur.

One night, defying the curfew, Qasim stealthily made his way to Girdharilal's quarters on the first floor of a squalid tenement.

He stood on the landing, letting his eyes get accustomed to the dark. Then, pressing a shoulder against the cheap wood, he quietly tried to force the doors. They were chained to each other from inside.

'Who's there?' a woman's frightened voice called.

Qasim paused. Regaining his composure, he knocked politely.

'I want to speak with Girdharilal. It is urgent,' he said, disguising his accent.

Girdharilal cleared his throat noisily. Any intruder would know there was a man in the house. Qasim heard him shuffle into his slippers. Next, the chain was being slackened enough for him to peep through the crack.

'Who is it?'

Qasim examined the slit of light, bright at the top, but dark where the clerk's face and naked torso blocked it. The crack looked paler where the light filtered through the white loin-cloth between his legs.

'Who is it? Speak up,' asked Girdharilal, peering into the dark, unable to see who it was.

Slipping the muzzle of his pistol between the door panels, Qasim felt it touch soft flesh. He pulled the trigger.

As he raced away, the clerk's wretched moan and a woman's scream rang in his ears. He wondered that Girdharilal had had time to moan. His hand twitched, and the naked gun still seemed to jump as crazily as it had when he fired it. Even as he fled, lights all over the building were coming on.

The next day Qasim heard of the train and rushed to board it.

The train glides through the moon-hazed night, with a solid mass of humanity clinging to it like flies to dung.

From time to time a figure loses its hold, or is forced off and drifts away like discarded rubbish. A cry, then silence.

Compartments and lavatories are jammed with stifled brown bodies; some carry the dead weight of children asleep on swaying shoulders. Women hold on to flush chains, they lean on children cramped into wash basins. The train speeds on.

Zohra sits on the train roof within the protective crook of Sikander's outstretched arm. He holds on to a projecting water-spout to secure his family against the sway and jerk of the train. The girl sleeps cramped between his legs, her head bobbing on his chest. Zohra holds the baby snugly between her thighs and breasts. The baby presses against a sachet of gold and silver ornaments hanging from her neck. The metal bruises her flesh and the young mother makes little squirming shifts.

Sikander feels a dampness along his thighs. Glancing over his shoulder he sees a black wetness snaking its path down the slope of the roof. In desperation, men and women urinate where they sit. He feels the pressure in his own bladder demanding relief.

'God, let me hold out until Lahore,' he prays.

Whistles screaming their strident warning, the train speeds through Amritsar. Past the station it slows, resuming its cautious, jerky passage. They are nearing the border with Pakistan. Already the anticipation of safety lulls the passengers, and tensions lessen. Here and there a head slumps down in sleep.

Zohra has been praying silently. Now that the danger has abated, she dares to think out loud.

'What about the five hundred rupees we lent to Meera Bai for her daughter's wedding?'

An emaciated old woman crouching next to her peers inquisitively into her face.

Sikander looks fixedly into the darkness. He doesn't answer. Zohra senses his tension, and bitterness shoots through to her. They have abandoned their land, their everything, and she thinks to remind him of money lent to a Hindu woman they will never see again. Abashed, she lays her head against his arm, mutely begging forgiveness.

III

Qasim has no conception of the city the train is rolling towards. Swaying with the motion of the train, his life in transition, his future uncertain, he absently scans the shadowy flat landscape.

Another forty-five minutes and they will cross the border. The engine is taking a bend. Momentarily the smoke in front drifts to one side and Qasim has a glimpse of the tracks ahead.

It is enough. His wary mountain instincts warn him. In a flash he turns to the old man shouting, 'Jump!' Terrified by the tribal's erratic behaviour, the old man leans back, but Qasim slides off the roof.

Rolling neatly down the gritty embankment, he scuttles towards the deep shed of a clump of trees. Night engulfs him.

As the centre carriage moves past him he sees the train buck. Only now does the engine-driver realize there is something farther down the track. A roar rises from the mass of jolted refugees. The train's single headlight flashes on. It spotlights the barricade of logs and some unaligned rails. White singlets flicker in and out of the glare. The train brakes heavily and the engine crashes into the logs. People are flung from their scant hold on footboards, roofs and buffers. Women and children pour from the crammed compartments.

Now the mob runs towards the train with lighted flares. Qasim sees the men clearly. They are Sikh. Tall, crazed men wave swords. A cry: *Bole so Nihal*, and the answering roar, *Sat siri Akal*! Torches unevenly light the scene and Qasim watches the massacre as in a cinema. An eerie clamour rises. Sounds of firing explode above agonized shrieks.

A man moves into Qasim's range. He is shouting, 'Run, Zohra! Run into the dark.' Qasim can just hear him above the clamour. He is a young, broad-shouldered man, and the peasant *lungi* wrapped around his legs causes him to stumble.

❖

Sikander pushed Zohra and the children off the train and yelled, 'Run. Hide in the dark.' He watched from on top. Zohra was pushing her way through the swirling bodies. She was almost beyond the range of his vision when he saw an arm clutch at her. The sea of faces swayed beneath him. Pin-pointing her position he leapt, clasping his knife. He half slid, half fell down the embankment and sprang up. A Sikh, hair streaming, lashed a bloody sword. Another slowly waved a child stuck at the end of his spear like a banner. Crazed with fury, Sikander plunged his knife into the Sikh's ribs. He stumbled over soft flesh and the mud slushy and slippery with blood. 'Zohra! Munni!' he screamed, barely conscious of his own futile voice.

Forcing his way forward, he is suddenly without his *lungi* and his long, surprisingly scrawny legs trample the live body of a child. He is moving towards a young woman. The flap of her *burkha* is over her head. A Sikh, sweat gleaming on his naked torso, is holding one breast. She is screaming. Butting a passage with his head, Sikander pushes past the woman and stabs her tormentor. Again and again he plunges his knife into the man's back. Frantically waving her arms, the woman is swept away.

'Run into the dark, Zohra! Run!' he screams. A white singlet flashes before him. Sikander crumples to the ground, astonished by the blood gushing from his stomach. A woman tramples over him. He tries to ward off the suffocating forest of legs with

his arms. More and more legs trample him, until mercifully he
feels no pain.

◈

Qasim sees figures flee the glare like disintegrating wisps of
smoke. He sits still, in the undergrowth, biding his time.
Although he is horrified by the slaughter he feels no compulsion
to sacrifice his own life. These are people from the plains—not
his people.

The carnage is subsiding. Already they are herding and
dragging the young women away. The dying and the dead are
being looted of their bloodied ornaments and weapons. An eerie
silence settles on the stench of blood.

◈

Qasim, as far as he knew, was alone. He moved swiftly, in
shadows, aware that he had to cross the border before daylight.

He had barely started when suddenly a short form hurtled out
of the dark at him. He stopped, his heart pounding. That same
instant he realized it was a child, a little girl.

Clinging to his legs, she sobbed, 'Abba, Abba, my Abba.'
For a moment Qasim lost his wits. The child was the size of his
own little Zaitoon lost so long ago. Her sobs sounded an eerie,
forlorn 'echo from his past. Then, brutally untangling her
stubborn grasp, he plunged ahead.

The child stumbled after him, screaming with terror.

Fearing the danger from that noise, Qasim waited for the
child to catch up. He slid his hand beneath his vest and triggered
a switch. A long thin blade jumped open in his hand. His fingers
were groping for the nape of her neck when the girl pressed
herself to him for protection.

Qasim gasped. Was it a trick of the light? Quietly, with one
hand, he closed the knife. She looked up and in the mould of
her tear-stained features, he caught an uncanny flash of

resemblance to his daughter thrashing in the agony of her last frenzy.

Kneeling before her, he sheltered the small face in his hands.

The girl stared at him. 'You aren't my Abba,' she said in accusing surprise.

Qasim drew her to him. 'What is your name?'

'Munni.'

'Just Munni? Aren't all little girls called Munni?'

'Just Munni.'

'You must have another name...Do you know your father's name?'

'My father's name was Sikander.'

Her use of the past tense startled him. It showed a courage and a forbearance that met the exacting standard of his own proud tribe.

'I had a little girl once. Her name was Zaitoon. You are so like her...'

She leaned against him, trembling, and he, close to his heart, felt her wondrously warm and fragile. A great tenderness swept over him, and recognizing how that fateful night had thrown them together, he said, 'Munni, you are like the smooth, dark olive, the zaitoon, that grows near our hills...The name suits you...I shall call you Zaitoon.'

A simple man from a primitive, warring tribe, his impulses were as direct and concentrated as pinpoints of heat. No subtle concessions to reason or consequence tempered his fierce capacity to love or hate, to lavish loyalty or pity. Each emotion arose spontaneously and without complication, and was reinforced by racial tradition, tribal honour and superstition. Generations had carried it that way in his volatile Kohistani blood.

Cradling the girl in his arms, he hurried towards Lahore.

ZULFIKAR GHOSE

*B*orn in Sialkot, Zulfikar Ghose moved to Bombay in 1942, migrated to England in 1952, and has taught at the University of Texas at Austin since 1969. He has published an autobiography, *The Confessions of a Native-Alien* (Routledge, 1965), several collections of poetry, *The Loss of India* (Routledge, 1964), *Jets from Orange* (Macmillan, 1967), *The Violent West* (Macmillan, 1972), *A Memory of Asia* (Curbstone, 1984), *Selected Poems* (OUP 1991), and five books of literary criticism, including *Hamlet, Prufrock and Language* (Macmillan, 1978), *The Fiction of Reality* (Macmillan, 1983), *Shakespeare's Mortal Knowledge* (Macmillan, 1993). He dislikes the idea of writers being pigeonholed into cultural or geographical categories however and believes only good literature matters. He has written over ten novels, including *The Murder of Aziz Khan* (Macmillan, 1967, OUP, 1998), about the tussle between a small Punjab farmer and a group of industrialists. The leitmotif in all his novels is alienation, but most are set in South America which, he says, has definite resonance with South Asia. His acclaimed historical trilogy, *The Incredible Brazilian* (Macmillan, 1972/75/78), was translated into many languages. He has also written a stream of consciousness novel, *Crump's Terms* (Macmillan, 1975) and a complex tale of multiple migrations and exile, *The Triple Mirror of the Self* (Bloomsbury, 1992). More recently, he published a collection of short stories, *Veronica and the Gongora Passion* (TSAR, 1998). He is married to the Brazilian artist, Helena de la Fontaine.

THE NATIVE ALIEN'S STORY[1]

Author's Note: 'Time's Outcast' and 'The Station of the Dead' are chapters from the last part of my novel, The Triple Mirror of the Self. *The setting is Bombay, the time just before and after the Partition. In the previous chapter there has been a huge explosion in the city—ammunition-loaded British ships have blown up in the harbour; thousands of people, misinterpreting the explosion as some catastrophe associated with the demand for independence from the British, begin to flee from Bombay;*

---

1. From the novel, *The Triple Mirror of the Self.*

there is communal violence; Roshan, a Muslim boy, is severely beaten by a Hindu gang. 'Time's Outcast' finds him in a clinic. When Roshan resumes his life, he finds that the familiar scenes of his Bombay have changed: independence is at hand, there is talk of partition, communal riots have begun, a Hindu militancy fills the air of Bombay. 'The Station of the Dead' is set soon after the Partition and includes a foreshadowing of Gandhi's assassination and Roshan's emigration to England. Readers who know my autobiography, Confessions of a Native-Alien, *and some of my early poems, such as 'The Body's Independence', will see certain themes and images from those early works, written almost thirty years before the novel, recurring in* The Triple Mirror of the Self, *so enduring has been the spiritual pain generated by the events before and after the Partition.*

Time's Outcast

'Look at the sea, how still! Like a sheet of glass,' Nurse Nabuco said, glancing back from the window at Roshan's mother who sat in a rattan chair next to his bed. 'Just like our sweet, quiet patient. So silent and so beautiful!'

His mother's eyes were closed while she obsessively flicked the beads of a rosary and quietly repeated some prayer, moving her lips urgently as if she feared the time for its completion was insufficient. Hearing the nurse's amiable chatter, she shook her head, like one awakening suddenly, opened her eyes, and leaning forward, blew her breath, which was charged with prayer, at the face of her son and kept blowing while she turned her head so that the length of his body would be touched by her pious plea.

Nurse Nabuco came to the side of the bed and leaned over his face. 'When you're stronger, we'll place a chair next to the window so you can look at the sea. Would you like that?'

Roshan's still eyes saw her face a foot away from his. Dark brown and almost triangular, the chin was so pointed, with curly black hair, and dark brown eyes that gleamed so generously bright he almost felt a warmth from them on his cheeks. 'So calm he is!' she said, turning her face to the mother.

The mother's fingers worked at the rosary. The whisper that escaped her lips was a fragment of Arabic.

Nurse Nabuco touched Roshan's cheekbone with her finger tips and softly drew them down his face. She traced the outline of his lips with her index finger and then tapped his nose gently. 'Hello, handsome,' she said, smiling. 'Ain't I your favourite girlfriend?' She stroked his cheek, her face very close to his. 'Won't you speak, my beautiful darling?'

The mother spoke aloud the conclusion of the Arabic prayer and blew her breath again at her son. Nurse Nabuco withdrew from the bed, and said to the mother, 'The doctor must be right. He hears everything. You can tell it from the rhythm of his breath. He knows everything.'

'How can we be sure? He won't say anything.' There was despair in the mother's voice.

Nurse Nabuco walked to the window and drew the curtain halfway across to cut the glare. 'Like a mirror, the sea,' she said, as she did so. 'The doctor's quite certain though he's waiting for the tests to be completed,' she said to the mother. 'He will be all right, you'll see. Before you know it, there'll be delegations of mothers coming to ask you for his hand, he's so, so handsome. Such a catch! Do you know what, if you didn't sit there watching him I think I'd steal him myself!'

The mother would have been scandalized by such an assertion from a Christian girl did she not believe Nurse Nabuco was only trying to cheer her up.

'But I'm an old woman,' Nurse Nabuco said, mockingly self-deprecating. The mother could not help laughing, knowing the nurse had only the previous week turned twenty-one. She had brought a piece of her birthday cake to share with her favourite patient.

'Hai-ay,' the nurse clicked her tongue and sighed dramatically. 'Here is my prince charming, but what can I do, his mother watches him like a dragon!'

The mother laughed aloud now. Nurse Nabuco was too comical. 'Go on with you,' she said.

Nurse Nabuco glanced at the patient to see if her talk had had any effect on him. He remained as before. Eyes open, breathing quietly, silent.

She looked out at the wide curve of Marine Drive. The usual crowd thronged Chowpatty beach. Beyond Malabar Point the ocean had begun to swell and white points of gleaming light seemed to pierce the vast blue. She drew the curtain across the entire window. How sad it was, the handsome boy just lying there as if the world about him were water and no sound reached him.

Roshan heard each of her words. The warm, amiable quality of her voice sounded clearly in his ears. Her Goanese-Bandra accent was just like Miss Miranda's though Nurse Nabuco's speech had a ring to it which Miss Miranda's did not. There was a distinct music in her voice. He wanted to tell her that her voice was lovely. Her Christian name was Carolina, she had said, and he wanted to tell her it was a charming name. Each time she leaned over him and talked to him with her face so close to his he wanted to tell her she was beautiful. It was not the presence in the room of his mother that prevented him. There were times when his mother went to the bathroom and Nurse Nabuco was alone with him. He was unable to talk. His voice would not come. He could speak no words.

His senses were sharper than before, and his capacity for knowing the world he inhabited had intensified. His memory was so vivid, he sometimes felt himself present again in some past event and was astonished, when he realized he had only been remembering, at the re-appearance of forgotten tastes and smells. Sometimes it seemed the remembered event was not one from the past but from the future, but that, he was convinced, was merely a confusion in his brain. But he could not work out how long he had lain in this room. He knew it was a room in a clinic on Marine Drive in the city of Bombay. He did not need to be placed by the window to see the ocean. He could see it with his eyes closed. He knew, too, that it was an expensive clinic, and that his father had gone into debt to save his son. But he could not tell how long he had been there. Weeks, months. He had no system of reckoning time. It was almost as if he had been cast outside the dimension of time and could only float among random appearances of images of events that claimed to be his reality.

The British soldiers had taken him to the nearest hospital after Bhatia had pleaded with them. The blows he had received made him look mortally wounded and the British officer, not wanting a communal riot in the streets when his government had enough problems with the war and had just suffered a setback with ammunition-loaded ships blowing up in the docks in Bombay, had seen the immediate necessity of trying to save the boy. But the hospital had found nothing to be alarmed about. Bruised ribs, a slight cut inside the upper lip. No more. He was kept overnight for observation and discharged the next morning. The parents' relief at his recovery was brief, however. Roshan would not leave his bed. He would not explain what, if anything, pained him: he uttered no sound. Specialist doctors were consulted. He was moved to the clinic on Marine Drive.

A doctor would come, carry on a silent manipulation of his body. Tapping the chest, holding the tongue down with a wooden stick and peering into his throat, looking through a glass into his ears. Some days a second doctor came with him, and probed and fingered like Roshan had often seen his mother do at the market when buying chicken. The two men stood aside and looked gravely at the floor as they whispered to each other. Nurse Nabuco fluttered about the room. His mother sat there, fixed like an idol in a Hindu temple, her breath coming from her as if it were incense that floated continuously about her head. His father and Zakia visited every evening. Zakia had become quiet and watched him with round, worried eyes, staying by the window and sometimes pulling the curtain in front of her. His father talked with a bold cheerfulness that masked his anxiety. Without turning his head to look, Roshan could see his father have a whispered talk with his mother while Zakia observed them though she pretended to be looking out at the crowd on Chowpatty beach. Roshan did not need to direct his eyes at an object in order to see it. And though the parental whispering was distant and muffled, the words reached him as clearly as if they had been spoken in his ear. Money problems, the father was talking about. 'Ninety per cent of my head is thinking of the boy all the time, how can I do any business? What if...?' The mother stopped him quickly with, 'Don't say that!' *Allah...Allah*, came from her lips.

He never needed to look or to listen. Yet all experience reached him with great clarity. When he attempted to focus on the present it dissolved instantly into the past and he fell into the habit of re-enacting events in his memory with such an obsession for minutiae that the particular event seemed to be happening for the first time and it was a surprise to discover at its conclusion that he had been lying in a bed and only dreaming about the past. Sometimes the discovery of his condition seemed merely an imagined event, as if his healthy body was running about chasing a soccer ball on Juhu beach and only imagined an unpleasant fate, thereby superstitiously preventing its happening. One day when his father and Zakia came, he saw them leave and return again the next day, and then he saw them returning a month later, having done so on each of the intervening days, and all their successive comings and goings happened in that one instant of their latest arrival. He thought that years had passed while he lay there. His eyes always open, he was certain that he never dreamed any more. He would see a mountain, its series of jagged, snow-covered peaks sharply defined against a deep blue sky, and he was certain he stood there in the cold atmosphere. Their Pathan servant Nabibullah Khan was there, in a valley at springtime with the snowy mountain in the distance. Whether it was a past or a future moment, or merely the eternally self-deleting present, seemed vastly irrelevant. He was in a train, which was like the Frontier Mail, and perhaps it was so because it was so far north and mountains could be seen from the window, but beyond its terminus he travelled on horseback and then on a canoe. Even the canoe had to be abandoned and he was obliged to proceed on foot. 'We shall arrive at the icy waters yet,' a voice behind him said, but when he looked back there was no one there, only roots hanging from trees with vast trunks, forming a curtain so thick he was surprised it had not prevented his passage.

'Drink it all up,' said Nurse Nabuco, holding his hand that held a glass and gently tipping the cold water into his mouth. 'You need a lot of water in this heat. O the glare!' When he had drunk the water, she went and drew the curtain across the window. His mother's breath blew over his body.

A vast crowd had gathered on Chowpatty beach. People had come from the suburbs on lorries that flew the orange, white and green flag with the blue wheel at the white centre. They were shouting slogans in Hindi. The city was in a turmoil of independence. Thousands of people were massed upon the cricket pitches on the Maidan. The flag flew from buildings. Loudspeakers rang aloud with patriotic songs and with speeches. The voice of the people pierced the sky. The sky flowered with fireworks and burst with echoes of cheering humanity.

A group of orange-capped youths roamed the narrow streets behind Mohammed Ali Road. Very little light fell upon the deserted streets from the buildings, which had most of their doors and windows closed. Inside the closed flats, people sat grimly silent. The festivities of independence seemed a distant rumour, as if the celebrating country were just past the horizon across a border which excluded them.

Then someone saw the youths in the streets and could tell in the darkness that their caps were coloured orange. It was a provocation. They had got their India and were flaunting it. Coming to their doors and yelling in Hindi and Marathi. Abusing the name of God. Telling them to eat pig. Two men, armed with knives, ran out of an alley, shouting the name of God. There were screams in the night. Puddles of blood. Vengeful crowds flowed into the narrow streets. Roshan was running before them. A line of policemen, bamboo sticks in hand, charged from a side street and held the crowd. Shots were fired in the air. Roshan slipped into a doorway. A man stood there holding a dagger in the air, looking with horribly gloating eyes at the blood dripping from the blade. Roshan ran past him and came to a courtyard. A crowd sat there on the ground, wailing and crying in the direction of the open door of a room. There was a bed in the room. Mahatma Gandhi lay on it. He had just died.

The radio was on in the room. Nehru was talking. Bells were ringing. The night air boomed with fireworks. The hour of destiny. Soft as a lover's, Nehru's voice. A train had stopped in a vast plain green with sugarcane and wheat. It carried the dead lying in their blood that still flowed from their flesh. No sound, no motion, just the slow oozing out of the blood from the carriages of the stopped train in the middle of that vast green land. Gandhi's head was propped against pillows, he stared sadly at the people gathered round his bed beseeching him to take a sip of water. But several fires had started in the village and women were running down the dusty streets calling to their men to come back from the dead. Lorries, decorated with garlands of marigold flowers and flying the tricolour, rushed through the streets, the men in them shouting in jubilation. Roshan was in one of the lorries, squeezed among the men. He, too, was wearing an orange cap on his head and shouting with the men. Hindustan, Hindustan.

Squeezing the warm water out of the sponge, Nurse Nabuco scrubbed it across Roshan's chest. 'Here is the heart that beats only for me,' she said in her ringing, cheerful voice, rubbing the chest with a white towel when she had sponged it. 'You're going to be nice and clean, as for a wedding party.' She inhaled deeply, bowing her head quickly so that her nose nearly touched his left nipple and her lips seemed to graze his skin, and said, 'And you smell so fresh you could be getting ready for your own wedding! Ain't I your lucky bride!' And she smacked her lips just above his left nipple while at the same time putting the sponge into its enamel bowl and slapping away the towel so that Roshan's mother, sitting nearby with her rosary, heard nothing untoward and kept her eyes closed, concentrating on her prayer. The sudden kiss sent a shivering sensation through Roshan but his body seemed to remain immobile and his eyes did not blink.

Nurse Nabuco combed his hair and re-arranged the pillows behind his head. She caressed his cheek. 'There,' she said, 'his imperial majesty is ready to receive the ambassadors.' She leaned back and asked the mother, 'Doesn't he look just royal? Hai-ay, I shall go to an early grave, I know, with a broken heart.'

The mother completed her prayer and opened her eyes. She stood up, saying, 'Help me with this chair. They'll be here soon.'

The two women carried the rattan chair with its faded pale green cushions and placed it near the window. Nurse Nabuco came back to the area that had been cleared and did a quick pirouette. Her skirt fanned out and swirled around her knees. Footsteps could be heard in the corridor and she stopped, smoothing her skirt down her thighs.

'There you are, Carolina!' a bright voice said from the door. Roshan recognized the voice a second before he saw Miss Miranda come into the room. A thrill passed through his body though its surface remained still.

'Alicia!' Nurse Nabuco greeted Miss Miranda. She stepped back, stood erect, threw an arm in the direction of Roshan, and said, 'His imperial majesty the emperor of Bombay and his dominions of Elephanta, Ajanta and Ellora welcomes you to his court!'

The two girls laughed as if what had been spoken was some private joke that they had long shared between them. But Roshan's mother, a little alarmed by the outburst of gaiety, whispered loudly, 'Nurse!'

Without turning his head, Roshan saw that more people were entering the room behind Miss Miranda. There was little Miss Mimi Engineer, the art teacher from the lower school, who was always seen in a stooping posture, with her face shaking continuously as if her life were dedicated exclusively to making the gesture of refusal. Even when she expressed agreement or accepted a gift the movement of her face suggested disapproval and rejection. But she had beautiful grey eyes and a sensuous mouth, making her a puzzling contradiction to men attracted to her, for when they gazed at those features the eyes would never stay still for any prolonged contemplation and the mouth would appear to quiver nervously, so that the men inevitably turned away from her in frustration. Behind her walked Father Marconi, his hands clasped across his protruding stomach. He had undone the top two buttons of his white cassock and sweat could be seen to have collected at the base of his neck. He kept his head lowered as though he wished to regard only the ground below his feet, so that as he looked up his eyebrows remained raised and gave him the appearance of someone for whom experience is a succession of surprises. He was followed by Bhatia and Adi, both looking like model senior students, with their hair perfectly in place and their mouths shut.

Not seeing Roshan at the school for several weeks, Miss Miranda had set her little boys questioning the senior ones and had been able to piece together a loose and somewhat wrinkled fabrication of what had transpired. Then a chance meeting with Nurse Nabuco, a family acquaintance, had given her precise information that she wore about her like mourning, desperately wanting to go and see Roshan but not knowing how to do so in the face of the obstructive social conventions. She set her little spying boys at work again and had confirmed what she already vaguely knew that Roshan's closest friends were Bhatia and Adi. The plan she hit upon was to take a delegation from the school to visit the sick boy. She chose Miss Mimi Engineer from among her colleagues because the art teacher never talked in the staff common room, and then persuaded Father Marconi that it was the duty of the spiritual leader of the school to visit one of his brightest pupils who had been hospitalized. Father Marconi's going with them would serve two purposes: he would make the visit look official and since he would go in the school car, an old black Morris with curtains at the windows, it would save her the expense and the discomfort of travelling by bus.

She allowed Father Marconi to step forward and stand beside the bed, his head bent low. Roshan's mother saw him from the window and felt alarmed. Father Marconi seemed to be saying a prayer. She quickly turned her head away and looked out of the window. She was terrified that the Christian priest might make the sign of the cross over her son and thus nullify every prayer that she had uttered. His hands still clasped upon his stomach, Father Marconi made a quick little gesture with his right index finger which could be seen as the sign of the cross and which need not be generally noticed. Having done his duty, he stepped back and turned his lowered head to glance round the room. He decided that his next duty was to say a few words of consolation to the mother. She heard his steps approaching and began vigorously to flick the beads on her rosary.

Miss Miranda took his place by the bed and stared sadly down at Roshan's unblinking eyes. Nurse Nabuco came and stood next to her and said with her customary extravagance, 'Look at him, Sindbad the Sailor, Mr Number One Pirate of the blue oceans, plunderer of treasures and stealer of girls' hearts, Oh I could die!'

While Nurse Nabuco's voice rang in the room, Miss Miranda leaned closer to Roshan, and said in a whisper, 'Oh, Roshan my darling!' She withdrew quickly, closing her mouth tight and swallowing hard to suppress a choking sensation. Miss Mimi Engineer had come up to her other side and glanced down at Roshan, her head saying no, no, no. Bhatia and Adi remained behind by the door and saw glimpses of their recumbent friend much of whose body was blocked by the women standing near the bed.

The mother flicked the beads of the rosary furiously and opened her eyes. Father Marconi stood right in front of her and her eyes fell upon the cross on his chest. 'Allah, Allah,' she whispered to herself, terrified that the communication she had established with heaven was being sabotaged. It was bad enough, the Hindus on Chowpatty beach making their idolatrous offerings to the ocean, obliging her to close the window to prevent their prayers entering the room and polluting her pure devotion, but this priest had to come right in with his cross. She had stealthily observed his feet since he had entered, even when pretending to keep her eyes closed. He had walked into the room in a straight line, turned sharp left to the bed, then retreated and completed the intersecting line before following along the straight line to where she sat by the window, thus making a sign of the cross on the floor. She knew the tricks of these Christians. 'Allah, Allah,' she whispered. Father Marconi looked down upon her and said, 'So sorry.'

Bhatia and Adi were able to stand by the bed when the women stepped back and went to talk to the mother. 'Watch it, Roshan,' Bhatia whispered into his friend's ear, 'I wouldn't have a single thought in my mind, if I were you. The Short Wave's right here in this room. I didn't even say what I just said!' He added in a very low voice, 'You should have seen us in his old hearse. The Short Wave was squeezed against Miss Mimi and her head seemed charged with electricity, shaking faster than ever.'

Adi, who heard Bhatia's attempt to be funny, was not amused and looked sadly down at his friend. He had not known till the last minute that Miss Mimi Engineer was to be one of the party. She depressed him. As soon as he saw her come to the car with her eternally shaking head he went quiet and had scarcely spoken a word since. Miss Mimi Engineer paraded the curse of the Parsees, to be fair and beautiful and pathetically deformed at the same time, to appear from one perspective gifted by nature and from another to be conspicuously mocked. He lamented his fate, seeing in Miss Mimi Engineer a model for the wife that would be chosen for him, with whom he would have children who would perpetuate the curse. It was another of the dilemmas that made him want to remain celibate, but he knew that would be impossible, for already, at 16, he felt that if he could not find soon some way of experiencing real sex he would have to take up a shocking suggestion made to him by a male cousin.

Roshan saw himself arrive at the school, late as usual in order to miss the first period of compulsory moral instruction that he loathed. Being a senior boy and having been appointed to the team of monitoring prefects, he had worked out with the other prefects a mutually beneficial system of ignoring among themselves the very precepts they obliged others to observe. It was Holy Week again, and passing the long room where Brother Batista used to play the organ while the Christian boys lustily sang the hymns, he heard the little bells ringing. Always

Ram-Ram in there, Shiva, Krishna, tinkle, tinkle, and great puffs
of incense. He hurried past and pretended he was patrolling the
corridors, looking for miscreants and shirkers. From the open
windows of the classrooms he could hear the moral instruction
going on in top gear. In front of each class stood a fat little man
with an orange cap on his head shouting away in Hindi so pure
it sounded like Sanskrit. He walked into the lower school to
escape from the harshness of the alien language. Miss Miranda
had gone and Miss Bhosle was back. Luckily she did not see
him pass her door. But the next classroom had a teacher who
too looked exactly like Miss Bhosle. The lady teacher in each
of the succeeding classes wore a sari and had a large round dot
on the middle of her forehead. Going back to the senior school,
Roshan had to pass the principal's room. Father Marconi had
gone. A new principal sat there, a man named Mr Bhagwan. He
was talking loudly in Hindi to Mr Ramdas and Mr Krishan.
Roshan remembered that his first lesson, after the moral
instruction period, was with Mr Krishan who taught Hindi
grammar and that later in the day Mr Ramdas expected the class
to recite by heart sixty lines from a Sanskrit epic. As he walked
through the corridor, the bells from the temple became louder
and louder. The boys in all the classrooms had stood up and had
donned orange caps on their heads. They were all chanting
loudly in Sanskrit. Then they were shouting at the top of their
voices. Hindustan, Hindustan.

Allah, Allah, he heard vaguely and felt his mother's warm
breath blow across his face. Then he thought the air that touched
him came off the side of a white mountain peak, imbuing him
with the cool grace of heaven. He opened his eyes. His mother
was just then retreating from his bed and going out of the room.
Nurse Nabuco had come in with her little white enamel basin
and a towel folded over her arm. 'Time for a bathy-bath,' she
said cheerfully, 'the hour for a scrubby-scrub, *and...*' she
paused, putting down the basin and the towel and lifting
Roshan's head away from the pillow to begin removing his
pyjama top, before adding triumphantly, 'the minute to take off
his clothy-clothes!'

She sponged his forehead and cheeks, his neck, shoulders and chest. She rubbed the fluffy white towel over his face and then the chest, moving her hand vigorously and letting the towel slip and continuing to stroke him with her moist little hand. 'Here we go round Roshan's heart, Roshan's heart, giving him a warning,' she sang as she stroked, 'and here we go kissy-kiss early in the morning!' And she quickly threw her face at his chest and kissed him smack-smack on each nipple. He gasped at the sudden pleasure that ran through his body. A low, distant sound had escaped his lips. Nurse Nabuco looked up at his face. His lips were slightly open in their attempted expression of delight. Nurse Nabuco glanced around and listened. The mother had not returned yet and nor could her footsteps be heard outside. Nurse Nabuco regarded Roshan with eyes that beamed with a new brightness. 'Ah-hah!' she exclaimed, and then dropped her face against his and kissed him long and hard on the mouth, driving her tongue into it.

'Ooooh!' came from Roshan's mouth when she withdrew from it, hearing the mother's footsteps down the corridor. She looked amazedly at him. First, her surprise was with herself, at the sudden snatching of pleasure from the captive boy, but then the greater surprise that she had in the process released his voice that had remained silent for so many months. She gave him a quick little smack on the mouth again, saying, 'And what do you say to that'—giving him another kiss—'and that'—one more—'and that?' one more. 'Oh Carolina!' he responded. 'That's my wonderful Roshan,' she said, kissing him once more, and then beginning to busy herself with the towel and the basin for the mother had just reached the door.

The Station of the Dead

Bells were ringing in the new temple near the suburban railway station. Roshan and Mona walked past it hurriedly towards the old iron bridge. The priest's voice in the temple seemed to pursue them down the street. Ram, Ram. Mona was swinging

his Walter Hammond bat and talking about a recent visit to
Amritsar. The Frontier Mail up, the Punjab Mail down. Mona
was comparing the two trains. Chandru and some of the other
boys were trailing behind them. They had stopped to go into the
temple and were now coming out with a line of ash smeared
across their foreheads. Each train had its unique points. Mona
wished he could travel on both simultaneously. There was one
station in the Punjab that both the trains used to go shooting
through at top speed, Mona said. But now they slowed down
and crawled through the empty station. Everyone held his breath
when the train crawled through making no noise. The blood on
the platforms still looked fresh. Five months after independence
there was still fear. Anything could happen. There were still
murderers about. A drop of cold moisture fell in Roshan's
stomach. It is the station of the dead, Mona was saying. No
train stops there but no one dare speed through there either. A
train going to the new country of Pakistan had been forced to
stop there. Everyone on it had been killed. I wanted to put my
head out of the window, Mona was saying. But all the windows
had been pulled up. To keep out the smell of death. Mona
swung his Walter Hammond bat in his right hand as he walked.
He had flung his left hand over Roshan's shoulder. Roshan
remembered the time three or four years earlier when he had
been alone with Mona in Chandru's flat and they had desecrated
the Hindu kitchen. They had kissed each other on the lips. No
trains go through the station of the dead at night, Mona was
saying. No one wants to run over ghosts.

Chandru and the others had caught up with them. They came
to the bridge and scampered up the steps to get away from the
potent smell of human excrement. A dozen families now made
their home under the bridge, having put up some kind of a
lean-to on the side away from the station and used the station
side as their lavatory. Coming to the bridge, the thing to do was
to hold your breath and run. But when the boys reached the top
of the bridge and were hastily crossing it a man standing
half-way across it stopped them. His eyes were swollen and red.

He looked distraught. He raised his arms with the palms of his hands to the boys and said, 'Where are you all going?'

Mona held up his Walter Hammond bat and answered, 'To play cricket.'

'Ah, to play cricket,' the man nodded his head, and repeated with an exaggerated suggestion of irony in his voice, 'to play, of course, to play.' He paused, looked down at his feet, which were bare, and suddenly stared up at the boys with tears flowing down his cheeks, 'And it is nothing to you that Gandhiji is dead. Oh no, it is nothing to you that the Mahatma has been assassinated! Hay Ram, Gandhiji gives his life for your freedom and all you can do is to play!' He fell to weeping uncontrollably for a few moments. The boys stood petrified, not knowing what to say. They had heard the news the previous day. It had not occurred to anyone that it was somehow wrong to carry on living. Several had talked about the assassination late into the night and listened to the speeches and reports on the radio. But by the morning the shock had passed. Gandhi wasn't going to come back if they didn't play cricket.

A train had arrived at the station and many people who had disembarked were coming up the bridge. The weeping man turned aside. The boys stood back to let the crowd pass. Roshan held on to an iron post as he looked down the tracks. Another train was approaching from the opposite direction. Immediately below him a swarm of naked children were playing between the tracks. His hand on the iron post slid down and encountered some embossed letters. He looked closely, for the letters had become the same colour as the weathered old iron, and read:

HOSKEN & BULLER
LIVERPOOL

and then clasped his hand over the words as though he needed to conceal them from the eyes of others.

'Let's go home,' Chandru said, turning around. All the boys, released from the tension by Chandru's decision, quickly

followed him and the group became swallowed by the crowd
flowing over the bridge.

Roshan and Mona walked past the temple where some of the
Hindu boys again disappeared. Bells were ringing. The priest's
voice echoed from within the temple. Ram, Ram. '*Hé Ram*,'
had been Gandhi's last words. And Nehru's voice had come on
over the radio. *The light has gone out of our lives and there is
darkness everywhere.* Nehru's voice like a betrayed lover's. The
light has gone out, Roshan repeated walking past the temple.

Chandru caught up with Roshan and Mona some distance
from the temple. The three walked silently towards the block of
buildings down the road, where they lived. From a side street
there suddenly burst upon their hearing the sound of drums
being beaten. It was an erratic pounding sound. Soon some
bugles joined in. The combination was not musical so much as
noise intended to catch people's attention. A band of some forty
or fifty youths marched down the street led by the bugles and
the drums. They wore orange-coloured cloth caps and chanted
slogans in Hindi. They were marching in the direction of the
temple and grew louder as they approached it.

A bus was coming down the street. The procession came out
of the side street and obliged the bus to halt. 'How much money
you got?' Mona asked. Neither Roshan nor Chandru needed to
count the coins in their pockets. 'And I have two rupees,' Mona
added when they had said they possessed eight annas each.
'Let's go to town!' They ran to the bus stop and waited for the
procession of the orange-capped men to pass. The drummers
were beating furiously as they approached the temple. The
bugles had become shrill. Roshan remembered the new Hindu
students at the school. They were not like his friend Bhatia.
They carried orange-coloured caps in their pockets and wore
them during the lunch break when they paraded by themselves
on the edge of the cricket ground. The new Hindi teacher Mr
Shevlankar led them on their martial exercises. Mr Shevlankar
was short and fat, with a round, bald head that seemed to rest on
his shoulders without the need of a neck. He did not wear a suit
and a tie like some of the other male teachers who were not

priests, but dressed like a Maharashtran in a white shirt of coarse cotton over a *dhoti*. When he came to a class he spoke only in Hindi. He spoke loudly and his voice boomed out of the window and the door into the corridor and down the length of the school. You could hear him when he was in another class. He spoke a Hindi which even Bhatia could not understand. Suddenly he would roll his eyes and chant in his booming voice from some Sanskrit epic. 'The man's crazy,' Bhatia said. 'Complete number one lunatic.' But everyone had to say 'Yes, sir,' to him in Hindi. 'I wish the Short Wave would tell him to pipe down,' Bhatia said, 'his yelling gets on my nerves.' Adi laughed cynically and said, 'That's just what he'd like, just what he's trying to provoke. If the Short Wave says anything that can remotely be interpreted as criticism of Hindus, that's the end of the Catholic mission. Goodbye Father Brooks, Father Mendoza, go to sleep forever, here come the orange caps!' Roshan found it impossible to learn the Hindi alphabet and had come to an arrangement with Bhatia. He wrote Bhatia's English essays and Bhatia wrote his Hindi exercises. The strategy in class was to remain dumb except to say 'Yes, sir,' in Hindi. They had yet to work out a plan to cope with the coming exams.

The procession finally cleared out of the street and disappeared into the temple where the bells began to ring louder than before. The three friends boarded the double-decker bus, climbed up the steps and found seats at the front, above the driver. The bus crossed the middle of the island, from Sion in the north to Fort in the business district. The conductor came up. 'Where are we going?' Roshan asked. 'Let's make it to VT,' Chandru said. 'No, no, let's make it the end of the line,' Mona said, who sat by himself with the Walter Hammond bat held between his knees.

The bus went off the main road before approaching Dadar to serve an area inhabited principally by Parsees. Roshan looked down on a park where seven old Parsee men sat in a line, their heads tilted up. One of them was talking but the others also had their mouths open. Their eyes seemed made of glass. There was one who could not control the nervous movement of his face.

Just like Miss Mimi Engineer with her beautiful grey eyes. Always saying no-no-no-no with her face. Mona saw the Parsee men on the bench and said, 'Hey, Roshan, what's worse, to kiss a pork eater or to kiss a crow eater?' Roshan answered: 'It depends on how carefully the moustache's been trimmed.' Chandru laughed and said, 'You Punjabis!'

The bus filled up at Dadar. A man boarded it a few stops later. He carried a basket in his left hand and in the other he held up three or four black arm bands of which the basket was full. 'In remembrance of Gandhiji, four annas, in mourning for the father of the nation, four annas,' he chanted in Hindustani though his voice betrayed the intonation of an Urdu speaker. No one paid him any attention. The conductor ignored him at first but when the man became louder to see if he could get a customer and at the same time cut his price by 50 percent, the conductor shouted at him, 'Go stick them on your grandmother's nose, this isn't the bazaar.' The man left, saying 'What a way to talk, hai-Ram.' Roshan felt sorry for the man whose features and accent clearly marked him as a Muslim but who was pretending to be a Hindu.

Some of the shops were closed. Black sheets were draped over their padlocked doors. Groups of men stood talking on the pavement by the textile mills. The conductor kept ringing the bell all the way to Byculla to inform the driver not to stop, the bus being full. There, several people left the bus and as many got on it. The crowds on the pavement now became immense and spilled on to the road, slowing the already congested traffic. A general noise of vociferous humanity filled the air but no words, or slogans, could be distinguished in the waves of a muffled sort of roar that swept across the road. The slow progress came to a halt when the bus reached a junction on Mohammed Ali Road. There vast crowds thronged the streets in every direction. The noise was louder, shriller. The traffic crawled forward a few yards at a time. The crowd in one street was running towards some distant destination. Then a bell was heard. A fire engine trying to get through. When the bus had

moved a little farther and another side street came into view
smoke could be seen rising from a building.

Roshan observed, without seeing, the recurrence of history
that he had already witnessed during the months he had been
sunk into silence. Someone behind him in the bus was saying,
'But it was a Hindu who killed Gandhiji.' Someone else
answered him, saying, 'No, no, the Muslims had to be behind it,
why should a Hindu want to kill the Mahatma?' Roshan did not
need to raise his hands to his ears to stop the words from
entering. His body had evolved silent procedures with which to
block out unpleasant sensations. His Hindu and Sikh friends
were silent. Chandru looked out sadly at the crowd which
seemed to be driven by some agitators in its midst, for now
Hindi slogans could be heard. Mona stroked his Walter
Hammond bat and wondered whether he should not let his hair
grow, like other Sikhs.

More bells could be heard. They seemed to be ringing with a
desperate urgency as if someone wanted to clear away some
vast obstruction with one loud gesture. Car horns added to the
din. Some siren had also gone off. Then the bus began to move
uninterruptedly, though slowly. An unfamiliar smell came
through the windows. A smarting, searing sensation hit the eyes.
Someone shouted, 'It's tear gas!' People without handkerchiefs
pulled up their shirt ends to protect their eyes. Roshan bent his
head towards his lap and held a handkerchief against his eyes.
Tears had sprung from them.

The bus accelerating, the air in it, which had possessed only
a momentary hint of tear gas, cleared. Roshan wiped his face
and put away his handkerchief. His eyes were red. Most of the
passengers left the bus at Victoria Terminus. 'Hey, Roshan,'
Mona asked when the nearly empty bus moved on, 'if VT is
Victoria Terminus, what's VD?' Roshan answered: 'Victoria
Dermatitis.' Mona asked: 'What's dermatitis?' Roshan
answered: 'Inflammation of the skin.' Mona said, 'I thought
yours was cut off!' Roshan answered: 'That's correct, which is
why I can't get VD.'

They left the bus at Flora Fountain and stood laughing in front of the bare-breasted maiden in one corner of the monument erected some decades before by the British who could not have guessed that Indian boys would re-name it Lowra Fountain, the substitute word being a common native word for the organ just referred to by Mona. Exchanging coarse jokes, they walked away towards Colaba, Mona with his Walter Hammond bat on his shoulder as if he carried a rifle.

The emptier streets, with their cleaner buildings, and the sense of camaraderie that sprang from the sharing of vulgar jokes restored the easy gaiety that characterized their friendship. They were released from the tension that had closed them from one another in a strange mood of resentment and regret when the bus had stopped on Mohammed Ali Road.

But here too, near the shipping warehouses, a crowd had gathered, though a thin one. Some office clerks stood in a group and shouted at the sparse traffic going to the docks to stop work as a sign of mourning. The people in the few taxis and cars and a number of luggage-laden lorries that went past looked curiously at the demonstrators as if their shouts were aimed at someone else and proceeded with their business. The clerks seemed content merely to be gazed at, for theirs was the sort of demonstration calculated not to achieve any real end but only to make the demonstrators feel good. Mona, walking with a military air with the Walter Hammond bat on his shoulder, led the boys away from the futile spectacle of the clerks and headed towards the Gateway of India.

They stopped at a cafe for a cup of tea. The radio was on and played a selection of sad songs from Indian films. Men sat at the tables, drinking tea and smoking cigarettes, and talked animatedly. One behind Roshan was saying, 'Believe me, Pandit Nehru can cry all he wants to impress the public but secretly he must be glad. Now he won't have Gandhiji to stop him sending troops into Kashmir.' His companion clicked his tongue in disapproval of an expression that was nearly sacrilegious. 'Believe me,' the other said, 'time will prove it, Pandit Nehru will be glad not to have Gandhiji to nag at his conscience any more.' 'Hay-ay,' his companion seemed saddened by the prognosis.

Mona ordered a boiled egg and toast. Chandru went to the counter and bought cigarettes for himself and Roshan to smoke with their tea. Roshan moved to another chair so that he could be closer to the radio and not have to listen to the man analyzing Gandhi's death as the Prime Minister's opportunity. But the whole room seemed to be talking about the same subject and though Roshan listened to the playback singer Mohammed Rafi's Urdu words that flowed lugubriously from the radio the words he heard again and again were Nehru-Gandhi, Gandhi-Nehru being uttered by the men around him.

A cool breeze blew through the arch of the Gateway of India. The usual crowd strolled about the precincts of the monument. Evening was falling. Mona leaned upon his Walter Hammond cricket bat as if he stood at the crease. Roshan bowled an invisible ball at him. Mona drove the invisible ball into the crowd. Chandru leaped up and caught the invisible ball and threw it jubilantly into the sky. The three friends walked through the arch of the Gateway of India. A small vessel was sailing back from Elephanta Caves. But from their left came the urgent noises of an ocean liner. A bell rang out several times. A steam whistle blew startlingly loudly. Just at that moment the crowd strolling about the precincts of the Gateway of India began to run in the direction of the cafe. 'It's Gandhiji, it's Gandhiji!' someone shouted.

The three friends ran after the crowd. People had packed into the cafe and stood in a mass between the tables. Most of the crowd was obliged to stand outside on the pavement. Everyone was dead silent. The Hindi words on the radio could be heard in the street. Everyone's head was bowed. It was evening on the banks of the Jumna river in the nation's capital. Gandhiji's pyre had just been lit.

It is a beautiful fire, the flames evenly distributed. In the middle of the pyre there is a round orange glow brightening each moment like a glorious sun. And now the Mahatma's body is framed in a dance of flames.

A small heap of ash, Roshan saw ... and already observed the ceremony twelve days hence on the banks of the Ganges, at the confluence of the sacred rivers, the Ganga and the Yamuna, over a million people crowding the banks, of the immersion of the ashes, and Nehru speaking in the language of India. *The last journey has ended. The final pilgrimage has been made* and a tide of garlands rises around the ashes in the voyage of the self without being towards ... but now Roshan again heard the commentary on the present and shrank from it, withdrawing from the crowd and began to hasten towards the Gateway of India, hearing a ship's bell strike.

The white P & O ocean liner had just begun its journey to England. Roshan stood under the arch of the Gateway of India and watched the brilliant white ship slowly sailing past, its decks crowded with people who still waved in the direction of the dock. *SS Stratheden*, he read. He had climbed to the topmost deck and stood away from the crowd and watched the Gateway of India receding as the steaming ship left the murky waters of the harbour and entered the blue ocean. The monument looked like a small box of matches on the edge of a table. Tiny people moved around it like ants. Roshan went to the opposite side of the deck. The ship was sailing past some small islands, each with a hilltop temple. He walked to the bow and finding the crow's nest unmanned settled in it, making himself a position from where he could not see the land. The stiff breeze that had been blowing exhilaratingly over the deck was nearly a gale here. The ship was racing through an immensity of blue. A cold, benumbing spray blew at his face, hitting his eyes like sharp needles.

M ATHAR TAHIR

*P*oet, critic, translator and short story writer, M Athar Tahir was the 1974 Rhodes Scholar for Pakistan at Oriel College, Oxford, the 1979 Rotary International Scholar at the University of Pennsylvania and the 1984 Hubert H Humphrey Fellow to the University of Southern California. Now a senior civil servant, he has published five volumes of Pakistani English poetry; a collection of short stories, *Other Seasons*, (Sang-e-Meel, 1990); of essays, *Punjab Portraits* (Sang-e-Meel, 1992); of poems, *Just Beyond the Physical* (Sang-e-Meel, 1991) and *A Certain Season* (OUP, 2000). He won the Shah Abdul Bhitai Award and the 1991 Book Council Award for his pioneering work on the Punjabi poet, *Qadir Yar: A Critical Introduction* (Punjab Adabi Board, 1990). He has collaborated with Christopher Shackle on *Hashim's Sassi* (Vanguard, 1986) and published books on Pakistani art, including *Lahore Colours* (OUP, 1997) which won the Allama Iqbal Award and he is now putting together *Pakistan Colours*. He is a Fellow of the Royal Asiatic Society and was decorated with the *Tamgha-e-Imtiaz* in 1998.

MOMENTO MORI

The high spire is visible for miles; silent and remote like a forgotten sentinel. Nearby a green meadow slopes down towards the river. A country church perhaps in the Cotswolds, Sussex, or the lush counties of Southern England. A village church idyllically skirted by a river, straight from the pages of Thomas Hardy or the paintings of John Constable. Only the river gives it away. It is too tricky, too muddy, too broad, to be English.

Travelling from Lahore to 'Pindi one comes across the church as one nears Jhelum. From a distance it seems large, imposing. From the tree-lined road that leads to a rickety gate, small. The spire, perhaps inspired by that of the Salisbury Cathedral, gives it the Gothic grace that holds and lifts the eye.

The path leading to the unpainted door is overgrown. The low boundary wall is falling. A workman is repairing what he can. The railing is rusty. The churchyard is ploughed and planted with vegetables. A few gaily dressed children dart about. Under a shabby canopy some people sit talking. One of them stirs the ladle leisurely in a cauldron of tea. Another shouts advice. They are making ready for a wedding.

The building is uncared for. Bricks show under the flaking whitewash. Broken panes stick in the windows. The area under the arches is unswept. The main door is locked. The entry is from the transept. The door like all the doors and windows is unpainted, the wood has cracked. Inside there is a jumble of old boxes and clothes. There is paper, litter and thick dust everywhere.

Some broken furniture is piled in a corner. The chancel is dark, unlit. The altar window is broken at places. The fake stained glass has peeled off. The pews are unpolished, and coarse to touch. Not in neat rows. They seem discarded, in store. The fine church organ is broken and some pipes are missing. But it is not beyond repair. The inside walls were whitewashed years ago. High up the wooden arches still hold the dark ceiling.

Sitting there in the afternoon silence, disturbed only by the passing chirp or caw of a bird, one realizes that here is a monument to the dead.

Dead are those that came down its path to a lit and polished interior. Dead are those who were beckoned hence by the ringing of Sunday bells. Dead, who came to honour the dead in the wake of tolling bells. Dead, who came to joyous peeling of bells to join in holy matrimony.

All that remains of the dead are six plaques and ecclesiastical things. A white marble lectern was erected 'To the Glory of God and in Memory of 35 soldiers of HM XXIV Regt of Foot who were killed in action at Jhelum on 7 July 1857 or died of wounds subsequently, and who were buried in the cemetery of this Church by their Comrades and Descendants of the South Wales Borders (24th Regt) December 1937'. What prompted this show of patriotism some 80 years later, one wonders. Perhaps the knowledge that this land was slipping from their grasp.

The wall towards the river shows two tablets. One in brass commemorates 'Lt-Colonel KS For-Strangway, Deputy

Commissioner of Jhelum. Died 8 July 1912'. The other in marble is in the memory of 'Major Arthur Henry Montague of the 21st Punjabis who died at Jhelum on 18 December 1907'.

The four plaques on the other wall are all in brass too. One simply states 'Major Harvey Francis Holland. 22nd Punjab Infantry. Died 10 June 1903'. The oldest plaque in the church is in the memory of 'Lt-Colonel Halford Fellowes, Commander of 32 Pioneers. Born 16 October 1833. Entered into rest 9 April 1879 in the return march from Kandahar'. Presumably of noble birth, his coat of arms is engraved on the left of the inscription in Gothic script.

The plaque below it, commemorates four officers of the 37th Dogras who died during the stay of the Regiment in Jhelum from 1910 to 1914. Since no bravery or heroism is implied, perhaps they succumbed to malaria and dysentery that were forever plaguing the colonists. The inscription is a mix of Gothic and simple lettering. Some letters are still visible, highlighted in red. The last plaque is also inscribed in Gothic and straight letters some of which are in red. This is to the memory of 'Clarence Edward Lees. Lt 34th Pioneers who died at Landi Kotal, Khyber Pass, of Enteric Fever, on 13 June 1898. Aged 29 years and 4 months, by his widow'.

Both these plaques were made by P Orr and Sons, Artmetal Workers of Madras and Rangoon. Surprising. Well into the twentieth century plaques had to be imported from Madras. The visitor wonders what happened to the metal-work training that the Mayo School of Arts at Lahore imparted.

The pulpit with cement sides is raised on a cement base. The front is made of marble with crosses and a Gaelic interlacing pattern. 'To the Glory of God and in memory of Major AHB Joyce, MC 1st Bn, 1st Punjab Regiment who died at Multan, while attached to the 2nd Bn, on 11 September 1937', the inscription reads. It was erected by his 'Brother Officers and other Friends'.

Diagonally across the floor from the pulpit, near the main entry is a stone and marble baptistery. Eight small pillars in red marble probably from Nowshera are mounted on a white marble base, and hold up the baptism bowl which a wooden lid with an iron handle covers. This fine piece is solid and basic in form, with a Norman feeling to it. It was gifted to the church in memory of 'Gunners Northover and Campbell, killed in action at Jhelum, July, 1857'.

Each plaque, each object tells a tale. A tale of imperialism, of individual valour and loss. A tale which to the inheritors of the church is dead. Recalling Rupert Brooke's sonnet, 'The Soldier':

> *If I should die think only this of me:*
> *That there is some corner of a foreign field...*

The visitor leaves for the world of the living.

But as he walks away he wonders at the indifference of the Christian organizations in Pakistan. If the church cannot be looked after, then the Cantonment Board of Jhelum should purchase, renovate and convert it into a military museum. Left to itself, one more historic monument worth preserving will be lost. And soon the picturesque spire will no longer mark the journey to, and through, Jhelum.

RAJLING

> *A darkness in the weather of the eye*
> *Is half its light.*
>
> – Dylan Thomas

We sat down at a table in the restaurant picked at random. There were two ladies at the table next to ours. The one facing me was middle-aged, stout, discreetly dressed in black with stubby little fingers, manicured and all, wearing large rings. Round her neck hung a little pendant, which glinted dully as she leaned forward to spoon her dish of rice, splattered with curry. While my companion and I talked, I heard her talking about some disease. My companion later told me she was telling her companion:

'If you have to have a disease, dear,' (as if she were making up her mind about the colour of cloth), 'diabetes is quite the best disease to have.'

We talked on, but I could not help noticing that she was eavesdropping. They had finished their meal. While the other lady—those scare-crow type of skeletal women, of which Britain has such an abundance—got up and in a school-marmish way trotted off to the toilet, the fat lady opened her fat black handbag. Her rings glittered. Extracting a five-pound note, she placed it in the saucer. The slight silence which our mastication created, she seized upon and intervened.

'I am sorry I could not help overhearing your conversation, but I have such,' her voice made an arc of the last word and her fat body stretched and sank dramatically, 'a passion for India.' As an afterthought she added defensively, 'and of course, Pakistan.'

'Hum,' I said neutrally. My companion turned to look at her.

'I was there for years.' Her years stretched and faded away. 'At Bombay, Madras, Karachi, Delhi and Rawalpindi.'

'Lahore?' I asked.

'And yes, Lahore,' she said, in a tone suggesting, how could I forget that? 'My grandfather was there,' she added quickly. 'He got a VC in the Indian Mutiny.' She had established her position.

'You mean the War of Independence,' I said. She was not listening. A faraway look came, and went, in her eyes.

'We had an orderly who still writes to us,' she started again. 'He can't really write you know, he goes to the letter-writer,' she confided. 'We still,' and this 'still' was more emphatic than the first, 'send him a little money every year. Oh! I have a passion for India. And Pakistan. I don't agree about India being divided on a religious basis you know. It's so boring. But I do like the way Jinnah went about it. Without even once going to prison. I imagine if I were a Muslim, I could agree to partition.'

Her words flowed nicely and easily as her tone oozed with condescension. All the while, she held the saucer in her right hand like a Greek goddess, resting it above her shoulder on the back of the chair. The five-pound note visible, prominent. The waitress came and took it away.

'And oh! those bazaars,' she dragged with relish. 'You can find everything there. How I miss them. And those sweets you were talking about.'

Her stubby fingers leapt to her quivering mouth. She held them there to cover her mouth as she gulped the saliva down.

'Have you gone back, since?' My companion asked.

'Oh, one never goes back,' she said poetically. 'One always goes again. But never back.'

I nodded.

Encouraged she carried on.

'The *samosas*, they make them so deliciously.' Her fingers shot to her mouth. The waitress came back with the change. It was a pound note and some coins. The lady barely looked at the saucer and waved her away. The waitress, flustered, thanked her profusely.

The lady obliquely eyed us to see the effect.

'I do miss the bazaars,' she resumed.

Her twiggy companion had trotted back. The lady pushed the chair back and struggled her bulk out of it.

'I have such a passion for India. And of course Pakistan.'

She got up and leaned fatly on my companion. 'You will forgive me for interrupting dear, but I have such...'

I guessed the rest.

Just before she rolled off after her friend she leaned towards me and said:

'O the great departed Raj.'

She could not resist it.

SORAYYA Y KHAN

*O*he daughter of a Pakistani father and Dutch mother, Sorayya Y Khan, was educated in Europe and the International School, Islamabad and received her degrees in the United States, from Allegheny College and the Graduate School of International Studies, Colorado. She now lives in Ithaca, New York. Her fiction has appeared in various literary journals and anthologies. In Canada, her story, 'In the Shadow of the Margalla Hills', won the Malahat Review's 1995 First Novella Prize. She is a Fulbright Research Scholar for 1999-2000 in a Creative Writing Programme in Pakistan and Bangladesh to research her novel-in-progress.

THE COLOUR OF THE LAHORE SKY[1]
(1956-1959)

I

Peace arrived at Five Queen's Road slowly and reluctantly, the way a grey sky becomes less heavy before the sun. It was not the kind of reprieve that might have been chosen, but nonetheless a quiet surrender that made it possible for lives to be lived. The stranglehold that gripped the house was much like a wrestler's, only kinder because the flourishing car shops and the bursting sweepers' colony allowed those within it the freedom to breathe, the luxury of movement. But the many years of pushing and pulling, partitions erected and removed, boards hammered together and pried apart, layers of paint falling in packets to the ground, was more than anyone could have imagined when the house was nothing but a fancy and the slope upon which it sat, overlooked vast empty grounds. For years now, it had been impossible to see the facade of the house from the road. Those whose livelihoods carried them by the corner of Lawrence and

---

1. From an unpublished novel, *Five Queen's Road.*

Queen's Road where the house once stood so boldly, no longer even saw it. When the postman traded his bicycle for a motor scooter and sped up the dwindling rise from the bottom of the driveway to the top, he believed that the house and the slope on which it stood had sunk, the same way old people curve and shrink when the burdens of their lives become too heavy to shoulder.

When Five Queen's Road began to shed itself, it did so finally and completely, without the promise of a new coat of paint or the hope of a more abundant one. Time between owners had grown until it filled the distance in between them and it became almost impossible to recall the blooming lavender bushes or the majestic perennials whose annual deliverance had once lent the carefully sculpted grounds of Five Queen's Road extraordinary colour and fragrance. It was then that another foreigner travelled through the constricted vein of what was left of the driveway and arrived on the porch of Amir Shah's library underneath the scattered shade of the early spring blossoms of his bougainvillea.

The first time she came to Five Queen's Road, she came as a guest and, much was done to mend the crumbling house. But the next time, and all the times after that, she came as family and little allowance was ever made that this woman, Irene, had once had a life beyond the tired and worn dwelling in which she and Javaid began their life in Pakistan.

The preparation of the house for Irene's arrival was so deliberate, it was as if her approval rested on the perfection of each detail. The effort was set in motion one night with Amir Shah's interruption at the dinner table. He had never done so much as brush the crumbs underneath his plate from the edges of the table at the end of his dinner. But when news reached him that Javaid was bringing home his wife, he began noticing the crumbs underneath his plate and everyone else's. That night, when the idle chatter of his family was flowing in one ear and out the other, and their tiring practice of raising their voices to address him had turned from being curious to absurd, he pounded his glass on the table so hard the water emptied in every direction.

'Do the house,' he exclaimed, as though he had said it before and been ignored. After the water had been sponged from the table cloth and he had taken his evening tea outside, Hamid translated Amir Shah's command.

'The house needs order,' he said.

Yunis worked the hardest. He shook the carpets, swept away the dust, filled the holes in the roof, and hurt his back doing whatever could be done to save the garden of Five Queen's Road. He dug borders around the trees and outlined a few flower beds, not because there was anything in them, but to suggest what had been. He shook brown and withered leaves from bushes and trees so they would appear only empty rather than dead. The night before Irene's arrival, he lifted the garden hose to the bougainvillea and aimed the trickle of water on all the blossoms in reach so the colour and smells would be fresh in the morning. He was joined in his work by the frenzy of a family determined to make something of what was left of the house. Bushra removed the curtains and began the tedious process of washing out the stains of many years of use. Hamid consulted several contractors about the possibility of renovating a bathroom and making warm water flow from one of the taps. Rubina stopped reading newspapers to her husband in the morning and in the evening, and she overlooked the fact that her husband's walking cane needed to be polished. Instead, every moment of her spare time was spent working in a house in which she no longer lived for a brother who had been gone so long the days of his absence stretched into years.

A few years after Javaid boarded the plane in Pakistan, surrounded by a ring of family he did not know he had, Javaid met Irene in America. Until they met, Irene thought of 1955 as the tenth anniversary of the end of the Second World War; Javaid considered it only as the eight year marker since Partition

and the birth of Pakistan. She was not as far away from home as
he was, but the stretch of ocean she had sailed on from her
country, Holland, to America often seemed that far to her.
Surviving World War II had left her with a life to live, but also
furnished her with an imagination that could conjure up the
most tangible visions at the least bit of notice. Although she had
lived in Holland all her life, she grew up with the tales of her
grandfather, a Dutchman, who had taken it upon himself to see
as much of the world as he could, collecting pieces of it in his
trunks and carrying it home. She was so entranced with the
fantastic accounts of his travels, that she could concentrate on a
tiny detail from which one of her grandfather's stories would
unfold from memory. She had learned this skill lying in bomb
shelters, trying to think over the sound of planes and gunfire
and the cries of fear in between. It was in those moments when
she first began to dream of being somewhere else, of leaving
the old country for the new one. What she most looked forward
to was leaving behind all the reminders of war, the bare
skeletons of buildings, and moving to a new city where
everything was whitewashed and peaceful, where office
buildings stood tall, and sported large panes of clean and
unbroken glass, and the people who worked in them took all of
it for granted, because they understood that was the way life
was supposed to be. It was ten years before she brought herself
to the shores of the new country, the time it took for her to grow
from a child to an adult, witness her father abandon his family,
and care for her mother confined to a hospital bed for two years
as if too sick to die. Although the new country was as she had
supposed, by then her need to imagine had become a habit that
could not be unlearned. She often thought of home. When she
took her lunch break at work and walked between the tall
buildings in Chicago, she imagined the nurse washing what was
left of her mother's hair, turning her over, and drawing the
curtains, all before the late morning sun rose over Amsterdam.

   But she occupied herself with different worlds as well. The
faraway worlds had inspired the miniature paintings hanging in
her grandmother's room and the semblance of music her

grandfather tried to pick out on the instruments he had
accumulated in his travels to the East. Without the daily
sustenance of her grandfather, Irene decided to do some
exploring of her own. She studied the city university bulletin
that her office mates used as a doorstop at work, and found an
array of subjects so diverse she picked straws to determine her
selection. In the first year she learned to decipher the Arabic
script in some of the books her grandfather had collected. In the
second year, her curiosity in Arabic led to an interest in Islam,
and she mastered the daily prayers almost as easily as the simple
songs so much a part of her childhood. Her teacher invited her
to help organize an Asian cultural function that spring, a series
of dances, films, and exhibits, as cluttered as the university
bulletin she had first studied.

It was there, one evening, in a room filled with smoke and
urgent sitar strains, that she met Javaid. He was the only man
amidst tables of many who toasted the speaker with ice water
rather than the champagne Irene had selected. Javaid, a few
inches shorter than she, rose politely when his friend introduced
her, but then stumbled on his words, confusing his 'v's with his
'w's in an Urdu-speaking idiosyncrasy he thought he had
overcome. Nonetheless, he impressed Irene with his knowledge
of Holland, all gleaned from an uncle's travels in Europe years
earlier. Over the next few months, in a slow and gentle courtship,
she found in him a companion to share in fact and in dreams,
places she had never been. Later, Irene said it was as if Javaid
gave life to a part of her she did not know she had and in this
way he made her whole. But Javaid told a fair share of stories
that she could scarcely grasp. Javaid described the English to
her, what it had been like to sing 'God Save the King' every
morning before school began and in the mandatory daily school
prayer, give thanks to the Empire for the schools, the railroads,
the hospitals, the roads it had brought to his land. They laughed
together at the absurdities, but in her heart, Irene could not
reconcile the England she had seen, the dark stricken country
that had suffered at least as much as her own, with what she
heard. It was similar to the way she had felt when her

grandfather spoke to her in the shelter above the noise of bombing raids, and he described the lushness of the Indonesia he had visited, the markets of fresh produce, the brilliant sand on beaches he thought should glow in the night. Irene told Javaid she would take him to England one day and show him what she meant. He promised he would take her to Pakistan, and then, slowly and without saying that this is what they were doing, they began to plan what would become a lifetime together.

Had it not been for Hamid, Amir Shah's brother, their lives might not have been woven into one. Javaid would not have seen the cold winter sun rise over Amsterdam in mid-morning and Irene would not have come to Five Queen's Road. Even before Javaid left Pakistan to study in America, there had been talk of marriage to the daughter of a family friend, but Javaid, who was not interested in beginning his life abroad tied to a woman he did not know and did not want, avoided the formality of an engagement or even a promise. Hamid was never inclined to take such talk seriously, at first, because he had always been reluctant to recruit one person to enter another's life, and later, because his own experience with his heart had made it impossible.

Many years earlier, before Partition, Hamid had travelled abroad to study philosophy. Upon his return to Pakistan, Hamid had fallen in love with the sixteen year old sister of a friend of his. Their marriage was opposed by her family. Although he did everything he could think of to appease her family, especially the father, whose determination not to allow his daughter to leave the house wavered ever so slightly when Hamid brought him gifts of imported chocolates and sweets, still her parents refused his hand in marriage to their daughter. They said he was too old for her, and even though he was fifteen years older than she, Hamid was as unprepared for their decision as he was inconsolable. In response, he swore he would never marry, but two years later when his beloved married a man ten years her senior and he was invited to her wedding, Amir Shah urged him to reconsider.

'There are only two things that give meaning to our lives,' Amir Shah said to him. 'Children and God.'

Possibly because the idea of children moved him or he had immersed himself in loneliness long enough or he wished merely to put a stop to this sort of conversation, Hamid agreed that the search for his wife should begin. There was only one condition he insisted on, that he would decide whom he would marry. And, with that, he carried Amir Shah's Holy Quran into the back garden and placed it on a bench. Without looking, he opened the holy book to a random page and ran his index finger down the faded calligraphic text. When his finger settled, he opened his eyes, and the word on which his finger lay was the name he pronounced would one day belong to his wife.

For months, Amir Shah's family searched for a Sakina, but every day, his friends and their friends related to him that they could not find a woman by that name. Hamid, meanwhile, discovered his heart healing from the disappointment his beloved had brought him. But then came the day he was told that an eligible woman by the name of Sakina existed, and he was invited to meet her. He was startled by the news, but he knew he could not go back on his word, so he dressed in his nicest suit and went to her house.

Hamid did not see much of Sakina. He was taken to her room where she lay in her bed, covered with a sheet from her toes to her chin. He was told that she was ill with the flu and was under doctor's orders not to rise from her bed. Sakina kept her eyes averted, focused on the two sharp points that poked through the sheet and appeared as though they might be the bulges of bent knee caps. Hamid, standing near the side of her bed, contemplated that whoever lay underneath the sheet would be his wife one day. He studied her face, searching for some sign of the flu or hint of person, but instead found perfectly drawn lipstick, eyes carefully shaped with kohl, and the creamy wrapping of foundation that in the dim light of her bedroom lent Sakina the appearance of a tarnished porcelain doll. Just before he turned to leave, Sakina's hair caught his attention and he remained put for a few months longer. Her jet black hair was pulled away from her face and after one set wave, was piled underneath her head with pins or netting that he could not see. He wondered how she had managed to do her hair, whether her mother had set it for her or the family hairdresser had come to do the job at her bedside. Then he began to cough and his eyes turned teary red. Sakina's mother rushed him from the room, apologizing for the germs that infected her daughter and her house. Hamid had not caught the flu, however, he had only been suddenly overcome by the clash of scents near Sakina's bed, her sweet perfume mixed with the powerful smell of hair spray, the body splash her mother had rubbed on her forearms just before they arrived, and the cologne he knew was on his neck, but all of a sudden, did not resemble the fragrance he had handled in his bathroom.

At their engagement, where Hamid and Sakina stood next to each other and sat side by side, the truth could no longer be concealed. The moment he saw Sakina upright for the first time, Hamid realized that she had not had the flu the morning of his visit, and this, among other reasons, was why she had appeared as though someone had spent hours readying her for the occasion, fixing her hair, applying her make up, and cloaking her in a variety of scents, the combination of which incited his allergic reaction. The fact was that Sakina was short, so short that she could not find anyone to marry her and so desperate to change this, that her mother fabricated the scheme of confining her to her bed to conceal her size. But Sakina's mother had not been sure of success until she received a marriage proposal. She had watched Hamid as his eyes rested on the two points that poked from the sheet and although he had assumed the bulges were bent knees, Sakina's mother feared he knew they were the rounded tips of her daughter's patent leather shoes.

Amir Shah called Hamid to the side and conferred with him. He presented the option of cancelling the entire affair before the ceremony began, and even though Hamid hesitated before he said no, he did not consider breaking his word. His studies in philosophy provided him with the many arguments he might have used to do so, but the time spent abroad had also confirmed his sense of principle, the importance of his word. He returned to his seat next to Sakina, and as they were joined together in an unlikely and lopsided union, he was determined to bear whatever was his due.

Hamid was married to Sakina for only two years before she left him, childless, a widower, and closer to God than he had ever been. Despite Amir Shah's pronouncement, marriage did not bring children, and even though Amir Shah had not said anything about happiness, Sakina's explained death after a bout with the flu, robbed Hamid of whatever happiness he had learned to feel. So when Javaid sent Amir Shah and Hamid like-minded letters that explained meeting Irene and his desire to spend the rest of his life with her, the two of them had a discussion. There was no question of where Hamid's sympathies lay. Hamid had more respect for destiny than ever before, and berated himself for choosing a wife as frivolously as he had, for playing with his life and hers so lightly, and for taking leave of the reasoning his studies demanded. He had not allowed destiny to come to him, he had played with it in mid-course, as though it were a child accustomed to having conditions placed on it. Hamid believed that Javaid would not have met Irene if he were destined to marry the daughter of a family friend and, therefore, could not help but suppose that their unexpected marriage was imminent.

'Let him marry whomever he wants,' he said, thinking of Javaid's right to happiness. 'If he marries who you want him to and she dies two years later, you will not be able to forgive yourself.'

Amir Shah did not acknowledge that he heard Hamid. Later, when a sketch of this conversation was recounted for Javaid, he filled in Amir Shah's silence. *She is not like us*, Javaid imagined Amir Shah thinking, *how will she take to this country? Because of her differences, people will not always be kind to her.* Had Javaid shared his intention to marry Irene in person rather than in a letter, Amir Shah would have reached for Javaid's shoulder then. *Consider this*, he would have said, not because he did not want Javaid to make his own decision, but because he wanted Javaid to understand.

There had not been a discussion like this, or even a semblance of one, when Irene's mother received the letter that contained her daughter's intentions to commit her life to a husband whose country was not inscribed on the fading map that hung in the parlour. There had been no one for her to confide in when she got Irene's letter, partly because the people she would have wanted to tell were dead, but also because she didn't have a need to discuss the news with anyone. The letter surprised her only because she wasn't expecting it, not because the decision was beyond her daughter's character. Although Irene's mother had little patience for her own father's stories of the East, it would have been difficult to ignore Irene's reaction, the transfixed look that appeared on her face the moment he spoke of Indonesia, even when it was a mention of something as simple as the clarity of the ocean and a horizon that could not be separated from it. Although Irene's mother did not participate in the world they built for themselves while the bombs dropped nearby and she flinched with each noise, she envied how in moments such as those they were deaf to the sounds of war. So it was her own father that she thought of when she read Irene's letter, refolded it according to the original creases, and returned it to its envelope. Irene was not going to Indonesia, but she was going east, to a continent far away from the reminders of the war. If he had still been living, she would have pulled herself from her bed, walked the few steps down the corridor to where his room had been, and laid it on his desk next to his collection of pipes and tobacco. 'She always dreamed of seeing that ocean,' she would have said to him, 'and now she will.'

Unlike the difficulties Javaid had informing his family of their decision, Irene had not spent months rewriting letters, agonizing over every word and phrase, and with great difficulty, selecting the gentlest version she had composed. She had sat down in front of her typewriter during lunch break at work one afternoon in one of the tallest office buildings in Chicago, and although her fingers moved more slowly than they had been trained to, she wrote what came to her mind. *He is kind*, she wrote her mother, using a word so simple it might have described her grandfather, and then added, *only he is more than that. He soothes me. He has given me something new, a life without war, a new country if I want it, and brothers and sisters, uncles and aunts, whose names I am still learning. You see what I mean*, she had said, not as a question, but as a fact. And, her mother did see, even in the darkness of her bedroom in Amsterdam where she considered the letter from her daughter. Her hand trembled, but only with weakness, as she wrote her response. She said that the most important thing was for Irene to live the life she wanted. *You did not want the war*, she said and implicit in this was neither did you want your father's leaving, your grandparents' dying, my illness. *You have my blessing*, she felt compelled to write, although her daughter had not been so formal to request it.

When the engagement was official, her mother did not tell many people the news, not because she lacked the strength or enthusiasm, but because she knew what many of them would say. They found out anyway, though, and although they didn't do so within earshot, she knew with the certainty of someone who had been privy to such remarks on other occasions exactly what they were saying. One of them? Can she really want dark children? Across the ocean, amidst the tall buildings of the new country, and sometimes even in Javaid's presence, Irene heard their echoes. She appreciated the ocean more, the depth and distance between where she sat and where they talked. *Thank you for everything*, she wrote her mother after receiving her response, and enduring those comments was part of what she had in mind.

Summer had scarcely begun by the time Irene arrived at the airport in Pakistan for a visit of undetermined length while her husband searched for a job at home and abroad. The asphalt was hot under her shoes, and the waves of heat that rose from it dried her eyes before she realized that the waving crowd on the roof of the arrival lounge was gathered to meet her. Within minutes of her arrival, she felt something sink inside of her so palpably she almost reached down to lift it up. She heard the name spoken once, 'Yasmin,' and then again and again, by everyone except Amir Shah. She had agreed to the name when she became a Muslim because it was meant to erase the distance between the heritage she owned and the one she was embracing. But she had not counted on the difference between signing it on the marriage license and answering to it when it was spoken. So when she heard the name and knew immediately she could not make it hers, she did as she felt, and said as politely as she could, 'Excuse me?'

What sank so deeply inside of her, and could not be retrieved, was her expectation of what she thought awaited her in her new country. But even as the feeling overcame her, and she slowly forgot what her expectations had been, she heard her grandfather caution her. It was not the first time that she recalled his words, but it was the one time since his death she felt his whisper in her ear and heard the tired, broken rhythm his voice had acquired in old age. 'Living in the past,' he said, 'is for the dead, and living in the future, that is not living.' As she made her way across the asphalt of the makeshift Lahore airport, she saw in the sea of unfamiliar faces what her grandfather had meant. The present was in front of her, and as she embraced her new family for the first time, she began the slow and arduous task of accepting her place in it.

Irene was expecting a child then, and was so ill during her pregnancy that afterwards the people who had watched her struggle during the months of her stay in Pakistan had trouble believing she had delivered a healthy baby. Irene lay in the back garden of Five Queen's Road on a *charpai*, separated from the woven jute by a thin cotton sheet. Every morning, Amir

Shah returned from his prayers in a *tonga* with a block of ice
speckled with saw dust. He placed the ice on a table at the foot
of her *charpai* and sometimes, if he had a moment to spare, he
sat behind it and beat a cool breeze for her with his newspaper.
During the day, she slid her feet on the melting ice block, and
wished that the numbness would spread through her aching body
until the child was born. In the garden of Five Queen's Road
where looking at the sky was the closest she could get to being
in an open space, she thought of how her mother had described
Pakistan, even though she had never left the continent. Put your
face above a boiling kettle, she had said, and then you'll know
how hot it is there. *You were right*, she wrote to her mother,
there are days when the heat makes it difficult to breathe. But
no one, not even Javaid, had warned her of the sky, the solid
sheet of colour that during the entire three months of her stay
was never once interrupted by the slightest scattering of clouds.
On the days when she thought she could not bear the heat
anymore, and the sound of the ice at her feet melting into a
steady trickle of water mesmerized her, she imagined that a vast
pool of crystal clear water hung in the sky and that she lay in
the cool shadow of its lapping waves. And, as she bathed herself
in the blue from the sky every day, she tried to imagine how she
would describe it to her mother when she returned home. She
begged Javaid to take photographs, and after he relented, lay on
his back on the patio and pointed the camera lens into the sky,
she was disappointed to discover that the sky of the photographs
was nothing like the open space above Five Queen's Road that
she had studied so intimately and that had given her so much
solace in those difficult months.

The child she was carrying slowly consumed Irene's body,
drowning her in a fatigue so encompassing she sometimes spent
her waking hours dreaming of sleep. She struggled to coax
nourishment into her body, from the smallest teaspoon of
yoghurt to the ripest pulp of a mango, but it was useless to fight
a body more aligned to her child than to itself. The only food
that provided relief was a special tea, a blend of herbs Amir
Shah's relative had brewed for her child when he refused her

milk a week after he was born. The tea gave Irene some relief, but did not replenish her energy, and she wondered if what kept her on the *charpai* was more than the child.

If Irene had been able to draw herself from the colour of the sky above her or the ripples of movement inside of her, she might have taken notice of much that passed her by. Later, she would discover that her sojourn on a *charpai* in the garden of Five Queen's Road was witness to an important time. Shortly after the summer sun sank into autumn and Yunis' plaster remnant withstood yet another column of notches, uniformed men overtook the country. Easily she remembered the humdrum, traces of which floated towards her in the evenings when those around her reflected aloud on the crises. At the time, she found it hard to digest their words, still unused to the business of a country being conducted at the level of talk rather than with the guns she remembered from the war.

It was not only the distant landscape in which she lived that seemed unnecessary to note. There was much in her more immediate surroundings that she did not absorb. She regarded the world around her with much the same resignation as she regarded the moving contours of her own body, only with less interest. She was unprepared for much of it, from a language she could not understand to a body she barely recognized as her own. Perhaps because of this, her attraction to the sky, her need to describe it over and over again, whether in letters abroad or in conversations with people who lived under it, seemed incomprehensible to everyone but herself.

Irene did not realize that the stretches of day she spent lying on her *charpai* alone were closely monitored by a man she had never met, a man she had not even heard mentioned, and later, a man whose name she never mastered. She was unaware until the day she heard Amir Shah bellow at the screen door of Ram Charan's indoor kitchen and she propped herself up on her elbow to see what the fuss was about.

Ram Charan placed an easy chair and a low stool behind his kitchen door. He spent hours at a time settled in the chair with his feet resting on the stool, observing the comings and goings of the back garden of Five Queen's Road that he always felt had been wrongfully taken from him. Irene's *charpai* stood in a straight line from the door because that is where the shade in the garden fell, in the shape of the elongated image of the low wall that marked off Amir Shah's outdoor kitchen. One afternoon, when Amir Shah returned to the house earlier than expected, removed his shoes and paced the length of the patio in worn socks, he caught sight of Ram Charan reclining in his chair. Although he was not prone to peering in windows, especially those on the side of the house that he had been banned from, Amir Shah looked into the window the same moment Ram Charan raised binoculars to his eyes and pointed them at Irene. Before Ram Charan had steadied the binoculars enough to provide the sharp, focused view he was used to, Amir Shah let out the bellow that brought Irene to her elbows and the vultures in the grown and dusty tree to the tips of the longest branches.

'*Olloo ka patha*,' Amir Shah shouted, planting himself in front of the wobbly screen door, accusing Ram Charan of idiocy.

Ram Charan dropped the binoculars, jumped up from his chair and closed the door with such force that the hinge at the top of the screen door popped open. Then he stood behind the kitchen window in which only a stained cloth hung, called Amir Shah an invader, and ordered him off his property. As before, Amir Shah did not hear him, but responded nonetheless by saying that if he ever caught Ram Charan spying on his daughter-in-law, disgracing her with his filthy eyes, he would feed him to the animals that roamed the car shop settlement and scavenged for food.

Amir Shah did not make a meal of Ram Charan the next time he caught him with binoculars aimed at Irene; he simply did what he had planned to do all along. He returned with the same contractor who had sealed his side of the house from DL Ahmed. And on the first of the month, when Ram Charan was collecting

the rent from the car shop settlements in the front garden, the
contractor went to work nailing boards across the kitchen door
and window, permanently depriving either of a view, and
preventing Ram Charan from ever observing anything, much
less the sight of Irene, in the back garden of Five Queen's
Road.

The boarding of the kitchen, although it did not formally
alter the division of Five Queen's Road, marked the last attempt
to freeze the lines of the house partitioned into two. Ram
Charan's reaction, whatever it might have been, was hidden
behind the fortified boundaries. Yunis swept the kitchen the
following morning, and removed the screen from its hinges so
that the door would close more easily against the pressure of the
boards the contractor had piled, layer upon layer, against the
frame. Over time, as the wooden planks loosened from the
monsoon moisture and rotted with hungry insects, Ram Charan
did not push his weight against the planks and craft an opening
for himself. It was as if whatever it was that had interested him
in the back garden of Five Queen's Road had vanished from his
thoughts.

On the days when she could, Irene spent the early evening
walking up and down the driveway of Five Queen's Road. She
only did this when the pressure of the child she was carrying
did not reduce her legs to wobbly stubs that would not hold her
weight. Javaid joined her when he was home. The two of them
walked beyond the driveway, winding their way along the tight
alleys of the car shop settlement where they kept a tally on the
models of cars they saw in various states of disrepair and, on
different nights, changed their minds about the one they most
wanted to own. The first few times Javaid and Irene strolled in
the car shop settlement, a crowd of children followed them,
rolling their discarded tires with sticks and balancing their
younger siblings on their hips. The scene made Irene
uncomfortable, and she told Javaid so, trying to persuade him

not to take her into the heart of the settlement. But after a few such occurrences, the novelty of Irene wore off, and instead of gathering behind her, the children paused from their playing long enough to wave and giggle when Irene said *asalaam alaikum* to them. If word hadn't already spread that she was unwell, the children would have assumed it on their own, not from the slight bulge in her tummy hidden inside the *shalwar kameez* she wore, but from the sickened complexion of her pallid skin, in stark contrast against the darker browns of her eyebrows, her long hair, and the man who walked at her side.

She felt safe with Javaid. She believed that his only requirement of her was the unspoken oath they had taken in love that each of them would be themselves. But what had come to her so easily and without forethought became cumbersome with their arrival at Five Queen's Road. The languages that surrounded her were different, so much so that she could not know where one word ended and another began. She bought books, memorized words, asked for sentences to be translated, but her efforts both then and in the future were futile. Prior to her future trips to Five Queen's Road, she would immerse herself in lessons, surround herself with vocabulary lists pasted on the walls, determined that this time she would, at minimum, keep the present tense apart from the past tense. However, it seemed she always knew more of the language upon arrival than upon departure, as if in speaking the words she was discarding them, as if in using them she was forgetting them. But those around her immediately learned to discern her one tense from the other, and in this way interpreted her 'I went,' to mean 'I am going,' or her 'you were bringing the tea,' to mean 'please bring the tea.'

During her first visit to Pakistan, Amir Shah hired her a tutor. He was a college professor who sat with her on the porch of Five Queen's Road and said '*tota*' when a parrot flew by and '*darakht*' when it settled on a tree. Her instruction lasted only two or three lessons before she learned that his preoccupation was with palm reading and she offered him her hand. But when he told her she would die from internal haemorrhaging before the child she was carrying would learn to read, she asked Amir Shah to discontinue his visits. Some months later, when she was visiting Amsterdam, she fell on a sheet of ice and gravel and suffered bruises that turned yellow from green and scratches that mended underneath narrow scabs. Then she behaved as though she had put the prophecy to rest, as though the palm reader had mistakenly used internal haemorrhaging to describe the winter beating her body had taken. In a burst of energy, she spread story books on the floor in a fan and let them absorb her while she read to her baby. 'And in the castle sat a prince,' she said and paused before she pointed to the picture of a little boy in a meadow with grass to high it reached his chin.

II

Every so often, before retiring to his library to work into the night, Amir Shah carried his evening tea onto the patio and kept Irene company. Their encounters began slowly, with a mention of the heat or the dust, but over time became much more than that. At first he was unprepared for the swiftness with which she spoke her mind, and her words drew sharp breaths from him more than once. It was not so much that what she said was stark, but that she dared say whatever it was that came to her mind, that when he asked her what she thought of Lahore, she did not hesitate to tell him that she was not sure she had the constitution for it. Her directness seemed vaguely familiar to him, something he recalled from years ago, before his professional training and age made caution and deliberation a way of life. Finally, they grew comfortable with each other and they would speak to each other, then, in the strange pattern of a man who could not hear everything that was said to him and a woman who would not repeat what had been missed. More often than not, their conversations turned into short questions from Amir Shah and detailed responses from Irene. In this way she revealed to Amir Shah stories of her family, where her grandparents had travelled and, one year, how they had wanted to stop in India on their return from Indonesia, but had been advised not to because the late monsoons had ravaged the harbours.

She suspected, later, that it was because of his disfigured index finger that she assumed he had fought in the war. The top half of Amir Shah's index finger on his right hand appeared to be missing. He picked up his tea cup with his thumb and middle finger instead, and the deftness with which he had mastered this skill and others made his deformity less obvious than it would have been otherwise. Irene discovered the top of his finger permanently bent at his knuckle touching a callous in his palm, the day he said to her, waving his hand so close to her face that he almost touched it, 'What was it like for you, this war?'

She told him more than she thought she remembered, about her childhood impressions of the war, fifteen years behind her and several thousand miles away from where she lay. She began with the bomb shelters, because it was the details of the basement in her apartment building to which she sometimes still awoke. There were other memories as well. Opening the door of her home to Germans and being thrust to the side as they ripped their knives through whatever graced the walls, stabbing at the couch and pulling out the stuffing, as though they expected to find a hidden person. Leaving the house early in the morning to search the empty markets for food and passing soldiers carrying their rifles in one hand and thick slabs of freshly baked bread in the other.

'It wasn't only our country that they occupied,' she said. 'They occupied our minds.'

She explained the exhaustion at the end of the day, how it was not uncommon for her to fall into a deep, undisturbed sleep and, sometimes, not even stir with the air raid sirens. She remembered how much energy it took to fight them in her mind, to find it in her to think of something else during the day, that by the time night came, it was a relief to let her eyelids fall and surrender to the comfort of darkness. And on days that passed more quietly than others and it seemed as though she should have had some energy to spare, she had none.

'It look energy to hate them,' she said, turning on her side and staring at Amir Shah's hand, but for the first time seeing the curve of his index finger tucked inside it. 'Can you imagine?' she asked.

The details of Irene's descriptions faded in and out of Amir Shah's strained hearing. 'Pardon,' he had said once or twice, but she spoke over his queries and did not repeat what he had missed. He heard her question, though, and without needing to consider it in the careful and even manner espoused by the courts, he answered it almost immediately. 'Perhaps,' he murmured.

It wasn't so much his answer that led Irene to assume he had fought in the war as it was the image of his finger. She had seen so many people return from the war with bodies different from the ones they had left in, arms and legs so frequently missing that in her dreams she had once seen fields of limbs scattered with fingers and toes. Those who were lucky enough to return with their bodies intact brought back parts that were twisted. A broken shoulder, healed incorrectly and transformed into one arch too many. A leg crudely operated upon, left shorter and with a limp. Amir Shah's finger was familiar to her, a minor war injury never tended to until the curve of his finger eventually caved in and he found the tip of his finger fused into an unnatural position.

'Where were you during the war?' she asked him softly. But he drained his teacup, rose from his seat, and faced the direction of his library, rather than acknowledge her.

She did not ask him again, believing that his lack of response was not about deafness, but rather that it revealed an unwillingness to speak of the war. She had confronted such reluctance before, and in fact, it was impossible to escape after the war ended. Those who had used guns to fight for their country against the Germans came back with parts of themselves too tightly sealed for conversation.

A few weeks later, when the sounds of the birds picking at the bougainvillea near their bedroom window awoke her, Irene shook Javaid awake and asked him where Amir Shah had spent his time during the war.

'Burma?' she asked.

'What war?' is what Javaid first said, the grogginess of sleep making her question virtually incomprehensible.

She did not repeat herself. She lay patiently next to him, knowing his response would eventually come, and when it did, she held Javaid's hand, tapping on the nail of his index finger.

'He hasn't fought in any wars,' Javaid said, and then added, 'He's never been in an army.'

He explained Amir Shah's injury to Irene. His finger had been like that since before they had moved to Lahore, before he had finished his matriculation exams, perhaps even much before that, when he was a child and Rubina was not yet born. He repeated what he had heard Hamid say, that Amir Shah came home with a broken finger one day, and rather than taking himself to a doctor, he discovered that when he bent his finger down as far as it would go, until the tip of it touched the matching callous in his palm, the pain disappeared. He forgot about his index finger then, and before long, when his other fingers grew adept at making up for its loss, he did not need to have it repaired.

'He should put oil on it, though,' Irene said, thinking of how sharp the knuckle had looked to her, as though the bone might pierce through the dry, brittle skin pulled taut around a finger whose purpose had vanished.

She believed Javaid, but she wanted to hear it from Amir Shah, so one evening, when they were sharing a cup of tea, she asked him again.

'Where were you during the war?' she asked. She spoke during an unusual lull from the car shop settlement and he heard her.

He told her where he was in 1939 and how he had listened to the radio address which informed India that England's war was her war and she would also fight to her death. Those weren't the exact words of the radio address, and Amir Shah laughed when he recounted them. The mould of his dentures moved

slightly, and he pushed it back into place with the pointed·
knuckle of his index finger. He did not share the reason for his
laughter with Irene, though. It continued to amuse him, so many
years later, to think India could have fought to her death if she
hadn't even a life, chained and shackled by Kings and Queens
and that the English, for all the roads and hospitals they brought
with them, could not bring themselves to see this. He did say,
though, that with the announcement of the war, the fight for
independence intensified and when that fight was finally won,
Pakistan was born.

'You didn't see the war, then?' she said, and it took a moment
before Amir Shah realized that Irene was no longer talking of
World War II, but a different war, the one that saw the migration
of ten million people across freshly drawn borders, the one
Amir Shah thought of simply as Partition. She had known about
it before she met Javaid, but afterwards, she went to the library
to see what she could find. She came across photographs in
magazines that hinted at the carnage of the summer of 1947,
bullock carts strapped with children, goats, and cooking utensils,
bloated corpses scattered along the riversides in the background.

When she pressed on and asked Amir Shah if he had fought
in it, he needed a moment to consider her question. He first said
he hadn't been a refugee, that six months before Partition, he
was transferred to Lahore from Delhi. It was a fact, he said, that
people had been violently killed with cruelty reserved for
prejudice and a vigilance borne of fear. Knives had been used
to slice body parts he had no intention of describing in front of
Irene. He hadn't been in any fights or set fires to any cars or
houses, although he had slept with a knife under his pillow for
the protection of his family. And then he almost said he hadn't
even seen anyone hurt very badly, but before he could say this,
he thought of DL Ahmed, stabbed in his own garden when the
sun was as its highest point in the sky that blistering afternoon
during the summer of Partition.

He began to tell her, then, in the unhurried and deliberate
manner of a man who might have been putting his thoughts into

words for the first time, the story of how he came to live in Five Queen's Road.

Amir Shah began his account with the long journey, the one from the village near Amritsar to the city of Lahore. It was not only a journey in distance, but in the time it had taken to make. It started with Barra Raouf, his own grandfather, who was the first in his family to learn to read and write. He was employed in a small library as a clerk, and had the responsibility of maintaining correspondence, dusting books, and at the end of the day, returning them to the shelves. But it was a job to wear good clothes to, a job that kept his hands clean, except for the especially busy days when he brought home a splattering of ink on his fingers. His wife rubbed blisters into her hands scrubbing clean his only set of good clothes and then, because she could not wait for the sun to dry them, she pressed them with a slab of iron heated on the fire before she went to bed. She repeated this every night so her husband arrived at work each day in a cotton shirt as white as the material allowed and with only as many creases as her husband collected during his hour and a half walk from where he slept to where he worked. He died on that walk one day, twelve years after it had become part of his life, before any of his sons finished school, but not before he furnished them with the intractable example of how reading and writing moved him. It moved him, not only from the abyss of the undifferentiated lines and curves and dots of letters to the peaks of knowing, with even the most cursory of glances, how all the pieces of the strange drawing came together in a word to mean something. But how this knowledge moved him, literally, bodily, from a sleepy village where he might have lived and died by the kernels of soil to a town or city where armed with an alphabet held firm and constant through the coming and going of the rains, he could, God willing, live and die unburdened by the changing colours of the soil.

Everyone outside of their home assumed it was Barra Raouf who thought this because people were not comfortable accepting that a woman, even one as strong as his wife, could arrange a family around the pursuit of this idea. Besides, it was Barra Raouf who appeared so thoroughly committed that he lived the idea. Little else could explain why he persisted in walking the hour and a half to work and back again even after he began to shed pound after pound along the way until he had nothing but bones left to lose, but before he was called on to give up those, his body gave out. He had not heeded the warnings of the village doctor who warned him to rest, if only for a day or two, long enough to cool whatever it was that was burning up his body and parcelling it away. But inside Barra Raouf's home, among his family, it was understood that it was his wife who gave him the strength to forsake his life in exchange for the prospect of moving. It was she who clung to the idea of moving with a deliberation that frightened her husband, and after she died, her sons, into pursuing this possibility with unparalleled vengeance.

Her name was Amir Bibi, a name that had been part of her youth in the same way that Bibi was the suffix of all young girls' names. But the Bibi had stuck to her name, not in the manner of a young girl who never outgrows the way adults think of her, but because no one ever proposed a stronger, louder name that did her justice. So they stayed with Bibi, and when that suffix blended into her name it took on the meaning of the name that had not been found for her, and whereas all her girlfriends grew out of their names, Amir Bibi continued to grow into hers until it was spoken as a title of respect. When she died, many years later, her name alone graced her gravestone because she did not need her husband's name to help others find her. The caretaker would say her grave was frequented more than any other, and sometimes, it was the first to be sprinkled with flower petals, even if the occasion that brought people to the graveyard was someone else's burial.

When Barra Raouf died, Amir Bibi waited out the forty days of mourning and then packed up her family of four sons, and although she couldn't read or write, she moved them to Lahore with all that she had saved from her husband's weekly wages. As she sat with her sons on the train from Amritsar and observed them following the route on train time tables they could already read, she spoke what was on her mind. She told them she would live as long as it took to see every one of them educated and grown, secure and happy with respectable jobs and family. 'God put me here to give you a better life,' she said, and her sons understood her to mean that she would not give up her life until she had fulfilled her duty to Him. Even though she had never said her allegiance was first to God and then to her family, her sons knew this. As it had been with the perseverance that was moving them from the outskirts of Amritsar to Lahore, they accepted their mother's commitments as if they were their own.

Despite her allegiance to God, Amir Bibi could not know what He had in store for her, and that although the statement she made to her sons would be true, time would prove it less so. Her two youngest sons died shortly after they arrived in the city when the mosque in which they did their homework collapsed and pinned them to the ground with such a force their bodies had to be held together when they were prepared for burial. A few years later, her remaining two sons accomplished what she had meant for them to do, but it wasn't until her sons' children had their own children and she found herself in her nineties that she relinquished her life to God.

Nasim, Amir Shah's father, was the favourite of her two sons, and he took Amir Bibi's mission in life most seriously. For years, Nasim would proudly repeat verbatim the words his mother had spoken on the train to anyone who inquired about his journey from the village to the city. Once Nasim asked Amir Bibi in a tender moment and only partly in jest what kept her going since she had seemingly satisfied Him so completely.

She rubbed her palm, where long after her husband's death she could still trace the outlines of the hard calluses from scrubbing clean her husband's clothes. 'God is not through with me,' she whispered.

The answer took Nasim by surprise, not because it was untrue, but because she could not offer anything more, that God's plan had become too obscure, too intangible, even for her. Soon after, Amir Bibi died, her Holy Quran on her chest, her prayer beads clenched in her fingers, photographs of her children and grandchildren wrapped in an envelope of cloth underneath her pillow.

Nasim named his first son, Amir Shah, after his mother. His friends considered it providence that Amir was a name appropriate for either a boy or a girl, although Nasim believed it incidental because the honour in which he held his mother would have required that he find a way to pass on her name, regardless of what it might have been. Amir Bibi never directly commented on the choice of name, although she indicated that in the future it might be wise to consult his wife, Mariam, before finalizing a name. That would be the last time that Nasim heard his mother express support for his wife.

Later, when Mariam grew from the placid child who signed their marriage contract to a temperamental, uncompromising woman of middle age, she resurrected that comment from her memory as evidence of the only time her mother-in-law offered her any respect. Nasim regretted ever sharing it with her. Even though Mariam felt suffocated by Amir Bibi's intensity which was unlike anything she had detected in the company of women, Mariam worked hard at trying to please her. She continued to provide Amir Bibi with reason after reason for happiness with the births of each of her six sons. Unintentionally, their combined joy in the children blossomed and grew until it filled the void of Nasim's absence, who by the time the last sons arrived was so exhausted from his work, he had barely enough energy to keep separate one son from the other, much less to express his love for them or come to know them.

Nasim was fortunate to find a promising job in the court when he arrived in Lahore. Over time, he worked this way up from a clerical job that was not unlike Barra Raouf's in the village outside Amritsar (except his journey to work lasted only fifteen minutes) to become a court reader, a *munsif*, one of the highest positions in the courts that a Muslim could hope to attain in those days. After both Amir Bibi and Nasim had died, and caring for so many children on her own had worn her nerves, Mariam belittled the work of her husband to her sons. 'He made his money reading out the judgments of others, just as he lived out his life according to the plans of his mother,' she said. Before too long, she learned to cast a shadow of fear over her family in the same way Amir Bibi had done to hers, only without the edge that had endeared Amir Bibi to the children she created and the people whose lives converged with hers.

It took a generation of distance and the insight of her namesake to determine what purpose Amir Bibi's life had come to hold, so long after she had fulfilled her duty to God and provided her own children with a more prosperous life than the one she or her husband had endured. Her need to see her children have a better life did not begin and end with her own children, but instead multiplied onward to her children's children, and if God had not taken her life by then, their children. All of them owed their lives to her and that is why after her death Amir Shah thought he had found the name which honoured her. *Hamari Amma*, he declared her, because it was so: she was the mother of the family. And as Amir Shah spoke her name, he stared at his daughter-in-law, swollen with the child she would bear. It occurred to him how fragments of Amir Bibi's lessons had journeyed with Javaid, only instead of leaving behind the village for the city, he had left his country for another, and in this faraway land Amir Shah had yet to see, Javaid had made a life for himself.

Amir Bibi never saw Five Queen's Road, although if she could have seen the vastness of the house and the beauty of the garden the day her grandson moved into it, even she would have been unprepared for the generosity of it all, from the scope of colours and space to the accident, the twist in God's plan that had put her namesake into it. But Amir Bibi's spirit inhabited the place; so much so that when Amir Shah gave Irene her first tour of Five Queen's Road, he pulled her under the staircase that wound up to the roof and opened the door of a hidden room. This would have been hers, he said. But rather than allow anyone else to reside in it, it was left vacant, filled only once a

year by the *charpais* and prayer benches Yunis brought in during
the monsoons.

Talking with Amir Shah eased Irene's discomfort. The itching
of her belly was soothed by his voice, and although she did not
come to think of him as such, he seemed a kind of ointment to
her, cooling her in a more immediate way than the ice block he
placed at her feet every morning. She felt comfortable with
him, more so when they were alone, but often his mere presence
in a room of unfamiliar faces and languages seemed to still the
panic swelling inside her. It was as though his immense stature,
his proximity to the blue sky, comforted her in the world that
she was ushered into through marriage to Javaid.

But Amir Shah's exuberance in speech, if only toward Irene,
was not unnoticed by anyone. He was regarded as a man of few
words, a man who hoarded his words with the same vigilance
that induced deafness when the words he heard were ones he
could do without. To see him engaged in conversations with
Irene, asking her to repeat what passed him by, was beyond
expectation. Almost everyone felt it was unnatural, although
Rubina was the only one who said so. She told Javaid this, late
one evening, when she was wiping down the dinner table, and
he was reading the day's newspaper headlines to her husband.
Javaid laughed, and drew the newspaper in and out, taking
comfort in the crinkling noise because it made him feel less
alone. Although almost everyone else disapproved of this turn
of events, Javaid secretly welcomed it. Amir Shah had never
had many words to spare for his children, so it was with pleasure
and anticipation that he received them. He received them through
Irene, who recounted to him their conversations as best as she
could remember and who sometimes, in her excitement,
embellished them in ways Javaid immediately identified and
discarded. Javaid knew that a man of restrained speech would
never have taken the liberty to describe the shoes he had worn
at his own wedding or the ceremony at which he had received

his law degree. Although Javaid never found reason to share this with anyone, he was proud that Irene could draw words and stories and lives out of Amir Shah. Even though he'd met most of his father's expectations, he had not received such confidence in return, and he was enchanted that he had brought home a woman who had.

It was more than the late evening conversations with Amir Shah that upset Rubina. She had been curious about Irene, like everyone else in the beginning. She touched her skin, fingered her fine hair, and looked for calluses on her hands. The day family and friends came to congratulate Javaid on his marriage, Rubina helped Irene dress. She fastened and refastened her blouse, pulled it in one direction and then in another before she took it off and altered it, intent on lifting up the scoop neck and lengthening the bottom border so less of Irene's body was exposed. She was slow to wrap Irene's sari, unashamed to stare and unconcerned with the shifting weight of Irene's discomfort.

'A boy,' Rubina said, although she did not have any children and did not know what made these words tumble from her mouth without any forethought or warning. Rubina's proclamation meant nothing to Irene, who could barely comprehend that there was life inside her, much less whether it was male or female.

Rubina continued to survey Irene's unclothed body, as though nothing had been said, but she was not prepared for her impression, that the colour in front of her was less than beautiful. She could not remember a time when she did not consider fair skin more desirable than any other. But she had not counted on the veins, and in between the spaces of blue, Irene's skin seemed hard and lacking, as though the absence of colour was that of feeling. Rubina could not dismiss this shade of thought, and from then on suspected that Irene was a cold woman.

It was not just a matter of colour, and later, when she considered the rift between them from the comfortable distance of time, she knew what else it might have been. She found it impossible to forgive Irene for arriving at Five Queen's Road. The event brought back what she had tried to put behind her,

and it did so with a force so powerful that when she was not
engulfed in sadness she was wrought with wonder that a twist
of fate from so many years past could still do to her what it did.
It was because of Irene that she was reminded, again and again,
of the possibilities that had lit up her life once, in those first
days with her husband when the excitement of going abroad
had thinned the thickness of his glasses. On that warm summer
evening, riding on the back of her husband's new scooter, she
could never have imagined that the promises of marriage could
be so confused, that hers would not take her anywhere, while
Javaid's marriage would bring to Five Queen's Road a woman
with skin so thin the map of her veins shone through.

When Rubina was younger, she had only wanted to paint, so
alive was she with a need to fill monstrous canvasses with
colour. But when that possibility was taken away from her by
Amir Shah because he did not think art an occupation worthy of
his daughter, she painted on smaller surfaces and resigned
herself to marriage. The man chosen to be her husband was a
chartered accountant four months away from being posted to
England. A friend secretly showed her his photograph and that
was the first time she connected a face to his name. She was
unprepared for her disappointment. The photograph caught the
glare bouncing off his glasses and made him appear as though
he only had one eye. Her friend held her in her arms, gently
reminding her of his posting abroad, and Rubina knew she
should be more grateful.

Rubina was small, but no one thought of her as frail until she
sat next to her fiance, Uncle Zafar, at her engagement party in
the back garden of Five Queen's Road. The guests commented
on how tiny she looked, and said marriage would be good for
her because it would put curves where she had none. Rubina
spent her engagement day looking at her feet, fighting the rock
in her throat. The man she was to marry looked worse in real
life than in the photograph, although behind the sturdy black

framed glasses that he wore she did find two eyes. She was slightly comforted to discover that although he was big, he had small hands, much bigger than hers, but small in comparison to the rest of his body. None of this was enough to allay her fears, and later, she would confess to her friend that for the four months between her engagement and marriage, the prospect of their wedding night was enough to send her running to the bathroom, she was so afraid that he would hurt her.

As it happened, neither her wedding night, nor the life she would share with her husband, were what she expected. They did not immediately consummate their marriage because her husband was willing to wait until she overcame her discomfort before he suggested she entrust him with her body in addition to her life. Then, a few days after her wedding, when the course of her life was irreparably changed, she mocked herself for having been so afraid. It was her idea to take the scooter to the movies that night, and even though her husband didn't like to drive in the dark, he agreed. It was dark already when they pulled out of a side road onto a main one, and immediately, Rubina relished the way the wind pressed her face, and how the multicoloured city lights danced as they rushed by on the scooter. She was squinting into the oncoming headlights to make the balls of yellow change shape when the truck ahead of them, packed with bamboo poles much longer than the bed of the truck, braked without warning. Her husband pushed on his brakes as quickly as he could, but he could not prevent the scooter from colliding with the truck, thrusting him against the railing, and among other things shattering his spectacles. The truck sped away, and she was left in the middle of Mall Road pleading for help, waving the bright pink *dupatta* from her new bridal clothes into the traffic. Her husband wiggled on the ground, his legs wrapped around the motorcycle, his hands clutching his wet and bloody face.

Rubina cared for Uncle Zafar day and night, wiping the cakes of dried mucous from his eyes in the morning, replenishing them with fresh eye drops, and cooling them with ice packs. But no amount of care would change the fact that he had lost his eyesight, and with this loss, Rubina watched the possibilities in their lives shrink until their future seemed so small and so narrow it fit into the space between them as they lay next to each other at night. She did what she could for him, though. When he returned to work, every night she put his sunglasses on the top of his wallet where he was sure to find them in the morning. She selected his pants and shirts and ties, and had the feeling that she was dressing him more brightly than he would have dressed himself. He never questioned any decision she made for him, and when he asked questions, they were always of the least intrusive kind. He would ask her to point out his left slipper from the right, something she could not know definitively because the slippers were made out of such soft material they could not always be told apart. He would regularly ask her to forgive him for what had happened, each time with as much feeling as the last, as though he were asking forgiveness for a sin he had committed rather than apologizing for a twist of fate. Once, he asked her if he could call her 'meri ankhein,' because she was his eyes, but then he sometimes called her 'meri jan,' my life instead, which was less original, but endeared him to her very much. It wasn't long after that when her self-consciousness disappeared and she offered to help him bathe his big body with the several buckets of hot water the servant lined up for her. She washed away the softened scabs with a wash cloth and spread soap suds over his bruises that, in the month she bathed him, changed from deep blue to pale yellow in a private colour show that, however briefly, touched on all the hues in between.

After the shock of what had happened lessened, and it was confirmed that they would not be leaving Lahore for England, she came across the canvasses of flowers she had painted and entered in her school competition a few years earlier. It made her unhappy to think that she had moved out of a house where her father would not allow her to hang anything on the walls, and moved into another house where her husband would never be able to see what she hung on his walls. But much later on, when it came time for her daughters to marry, she would not consider marriage proposals from men who wore glasses. When Uncle Zafar told her she was being superstitious, she ignored him, and added another demand, that he only consider men who were not colour blind. She said he had no idea how difficult it was to describe the difference between light purple and violet to someone who was blind, and that there was nothing wrong with wanting her daughter to have a husband who could appreciate every shade of colour on his own.

One evening, a few days before her departure, Irene accompanied Amir Shah to the bazaar and they shared their late evening tea with the owner of a carpet shop. She asked questions about designs and textures, but when Amir Shah asked her to point out her favourite carpet, she did not hesitate. She selected a blue and gold and orange one, and although he did not ask her to explain her preference, she said that she loved the illusions of colours that shifted depending upon the angle of the carpet. Amir Shah made the carpet her wedding gift and when he gave it to her he said that it had been his favourite one as well. The carpet was designed in the pattern of a prayer rug, and if it were used to offer prayers, the top of it would face the direction of the Ka'aba.

'It is beauty, discipline, the path to God,' he said, as much to himself as to her, and when he said this he saw the lives that had gone into the weaving, the hands that worked in unison, the purpose they had served. Irene saw how each colour woven into it was more than one shade, how every line blended into another until the pattern he described was subsumed by a body of infinite possibilities. It reminded her of Rubina's paintings and she said so.

'The painting in her foyer,' she said, assuming Amir Shah would know that she meant the huge purple canvas that captured the expanse of his bougainvillea.

He did not answer her, because for the first time in all their evenings of conversations, they had stumbled on a subject which put them at odds with one another. It was not her intention to frame their differences in Rubina's attempts to study art, but she found herself doing just that. She argued Rubina's case, that she should have been allowed to study art, that even now it was not too late. Amir Shah said little, because he did not need to. He said that God had not put his daughter on this earth to run a wet brush over paper.

'God would not have given her this talent,' Irene said, 'unless He wanted her to use it.'

Perhaps it was her boldest claim of all, that she purported to know what God was thinking, that struck Amir Shah the hardest. He lifted his empty cup and saucer off the ground, pushed the chair behind him as he got up, and walked away without a word.

That was the last conversation the two of them would share before Irene and Javaid boarded the plane for Europe a few days later. Javaid had accepted a job with an international organization, and as a consequence, their lives took them outside the borders of Pakistan.

III

By the time her son arrived, the monsoons had come and gone on Five Queen's Road, the army had not retreated, and Irene was spending colourless mornings in Amsterdam waiting for the sun to push its way into the winter sky and begin its hurried day. She walked around her mother's home in a thin cotton nightgown without regard for the snow and wind outside. Almost before she could comprehend the truth of the baby in her arms the first time she held him, she was consumed by a heat so powerful she thought her toenails would melt. She believed it was her body's way of expelling the vestiges of the Lahore summer it had unwillingly absorbed.

Pregnancy had brought a wanting so complete, she had not believed she could contain it. A child with a mind unafflicted by disease, a body with two eyes and ears, ten fingers and toes, a closed palate, legs with knees in the middle of them and feet at the end. For all this and more she had prayed every day of her pregnancy, always with the nagging suspicion that what she was asking for was greater than her due. When the kicks had started, and she could see the heel of a foot push out her belly, she wondered whose foot her baby would have, whether the toes would be of uneven length like hers or evenly graduated like Javaid's. Not once had she thought of her baby as a boy or a girl, and that may have accounted for her utter surprise when the doctor placed a boy in Javaid's hands and he rested him on her stomach. She explained this to Javaid, that it was almost impossible to think of the being inside of her as a baby, much less a boy or a girl. Even her dreams, those psychedelic tapestries of yellows and reds, greens and purples, that kept her mind reeling in the early months, did not reveal it to her. But after the wanting was over, and her son slept in her arms, it was a simple fact that she found most difficult to digest, that her body should give life not to what it was but what it was not. That miracle would change her life, and never again would she allow a sari blouse to be refitted to conceal the curves in which her own son had lain.

Her surprise was hers alone, and when the news reached Five Queen's Road, it came as though it was expected. Rubina had known that it was a boy since the words tumbled from her mouth the day she helped Irene wrap her sari. The rest had suspected, from the way she carried her swollen belly up tight and high rather than around her hips. Amir Shah read the telegram aloud, pausing only when he reached his grandson's name and found that it was Amir. Had he not already felt a special affection for the child whom he had yet to meet, he would have then.

Soon after his grandson was born, Amir Shah visited Javaid and Irene abroad. They drove to Germany and England, to Holland and France. 'They were here,' Irene would say, and it was understood that she was talking about the Germans who had terrorized her when she was a child and war was ravaging around her. Amir Shah had an idea of how the war had conditioned her from the way she behaved in Germany. When hotel clerks suggested places to visit or food to order, she reacted as though their suggestions were orders and followed them. He asked to see where she had lived as a little girl dependent upon her imagination to survive the war. On what had once been an empty road a mile from where she had lived in Amsterdam, she said that one day she intentionally gave false directions to a group of German soldiers, and when she returned to her home she did not leave the apartment for several days for fear that they would return and punish her, treat her like the sofa in the parlour that bled cotton and springs the whole war because there was never any point in fixing it. The next time the Germans opened the door to the apartment she screamed, 'I didn't mean it,' until her grandfather covered her mouth and stopped her trembling with the strength of his hands. An irritable soldier butted him with a rifle and told him he ought to do something about a child driven to hysterics by something so small as an unannounced visit.

He was reminded, then, of what he liked about Irene so much, that she had not written her war away, that she claimed it as her own again and again with each fear she disclosed.

It was on this trip that Amir Shah and Irene developed their own language, a set of private vocabulary words collected on their travels. They continued to invoke these words in the company of others on her continent and his. But it gave Irene the most pleasure when their secret words were used in Five Queen's Road, and for a moment, there were others who felt uncomfortable in the presence of unknown words.

'*Aqua*,' Amir Shah would say when she asked him what he wanted to drink, and no one besides she would know he meant water. '*Schnell*,' he would say when he wanted her to hurry. '*Ici*,' he would say when he knew she was asking for him. Eventually everyone learned these peculiar words, but Amir Shah did not surrender them. The one time Rubina asked for *aqua* when Irene was refilling Amir Shah's glass, he asked her

what she meant. No one else made her mistake again, even after
his vocal chords grew so weak the only words he spoke came
and went in whispers.

Hamid believed Amir Shah had courted deafness when he
stopped hearing DL Ahmed. The day the roof of Amir Shah's
library caved in behind him and plaster and brick fell to the
floor in a waterfall of noise so thunderous the car shop owners
came running into the house, he knew deafness had triumphed.
It was Baba who saved Amir Shah, pushed him out of the way
just before the beam directly above him broke loose and plunged
to the floor. Amir Shah did not hear anything, and he privately
admitted this to himself when he splashed water on his face and
cleaned his ears before sitting on his prayer carpet for the last
time that night, but he had felt the floor tremble and shake as
though the cracking earth would tear it open. The reason he
continued to hold the heavy law book and did not lift his eyes
from the worn text on the open page was because the earth had
been shifting inexplicably underneath his feet for some time
now and he had discovered that the surest way to make it stop
was to pretend it was not there.

   After his deafness was confirmed by the shattered roof, Amir
Shah was left to improvise. Having spent a life prying into the
minds of his clients, he turned the skill he had perfected in
reading their minds to reading the sounds on moving lips. From
the way he held his head and eyes and cocked his head when he
immersed himself in what was being said, a stranger might not
have known that the conversations were sifted into Amir Shah's
mind by the shape of moving lips and not sounds. But when he
spoke, the pretense crumbled with the first syllable uttered. He
could not hear himself and could not see himself and therefore
had no way of knowing that the veins in his throat were raised
and pulsing and the sounds that came from him were
unexpectedly and unnaturally loud. The stranger would cover
his ears, his family would stare at him and pat their hands in the

air as if his sounds could be quieted and something so slight as
the movement of their hands could convey the problem of vocal
chords drawn too tightly and ears emptied of sound. Ram Charan
was no stranger, though, and although his response was less
swift, what it lacked in immediacy it possessed in severity. He
brought in his own contractor, and had his side of the partitioned
house insulated with foam and covered with a thick cotton
weave. He told Yunis then that it was bad enough that Amir
Shah had stolen half of his house from him, but now that Amir
Shah had finally gone stone deaf, he would be a fool to forfeit
his hearing as well.

Ram Charan wasted his money, and when Amir Shah
discovered how much he had spent upholstering his walls, he
shook with what might have been laughter and only stopped
when his throat went raw trying to make a sound and the stitch
in one of his sides spilled into the other. By then Amir Shah
hardly spoke, not because of how his friends and family had
reacted to the strength of his voice after he became deaf, but
because his vocal chords could not bear the sounds they emitted
and, in the final indication of this, were severed. The doctor
who determined the damage never offered Amir Shah a seat
during the consultation, so when the earth started to move
underneath Amir Shah in shudders that came and went, the
doctor was there as a witness. After several vials of blood were
extracted and analyzed, the doctor wrote a prescription to control
Amir Shah's trembling legs, and it would not be until he felt the
ground give out below him and his heart wind down into death
that Amir Shah sensed the stillness of the earth disrupted in that
way again.

Fifteen months after Irene left Five Queen's Road, all but one
wall of Amir Shah's library came crashing down. In the heap of
rubble there was nothing to distinguish what had been the roof
from what had been a wall, and even the sturdy beam that
barely missed Amir Shah was nowhere to be found in the

collection of brick and plaster that covered the ground. But the remaining wall survived so completely that when the brick and plaster were carried away by the car shop owners and Yunis swept the floor only to discover that it too had disintegrated, it appeared as though this plane of thick cement had been designed to stand solitary in a line that connected to no other. The bougainvillea no longer clung to the wall as it had twenty years before. The deep shade of purple supported the wall, and the soaring branches that wrapped the brilliant sky appeared to hold it all.

Irene had been so entranced with the sky above Five Queen's Road that when she read of these events in Rubina's letter, she found herself unable to call up a memory of Five Queen's Road that was true to the way she had seen it. She knew, of course, the basic facts: that it was yellow and large, but she was confused by the size and she wondered whether she thought of it as large because it was or because the endless ceilings suggested only that it might be. Although she was not concerned with it while she was there, she was surprised that she could not recall the facade of the house, the way it appeared from the road or the driveway. She searched through Javaid's photographs for the answer, but found none. Javaid told her that the reason she could not find any was because there were none, that no one had thought to take a photograph of the house before the sweepers' colony and car shop settlements grew into its edges. But she remembered the lone wall of the library because the first day she arrived at Five Queen's Road the bougainvillea dropped a few blossoms on her hair and as she reached to brush them away she remembered glancing above and wondering how the wall it leaned against could bear the weight of such magnificent colour and clarity.

Javaid was the least surprised by the news. He did not find it unexpected that a man who was not generous with words should lose his capacity to say them as well as to hear them. But Irene digested the news more slowly, and only believed it when she visited Five Queen's Road next and the certainty of it confronted her as clearly as the sky that had once moved her. On the first night of her return, Amir Shah and she carried their cups of tea onto the porch and settled into a waiting so intent it would not have astounded anyone if they had succeeded in coaxing conversation back. Irene's patience was the first to drain.

'Please,' she said to him, disturbing the quiet. She waited for an answer, and when none came, for a simple word. But his grip on words had tightened so severely, not even one slipped out. She leaned forward and touched his hand, the right one with the bent index finger.

'Don't,' Rubina interrupted, and because Irene was as afraid as she was of exhausting his whispers and leaving him with none, she did not ask him again.

Instead, she called for Yunis, and when he arrived, she spoke with him quickly and easily, as though she had never had difficulty with the pronunciation of the aspirated sounds in Urdu or appropriate infinitives or the present tense. *Bring tea*, she told him, *real tea, the way he likes it, with sugar and milk and cardamom pods*. She noticed the stains on his tea cup the same moment her sudden facility with Urdu disappeared, and she struggled to find the vocabulary to ask Yunis to bring the tea in a fresh cup.

Amir Shah shook his head.

'*Aqua*,' he mouthed, and before his lips had even stopped moving, Yunis was standing in front of him with a tall glass of cold water.

It was because she returned with a crawling child, most at home rolling in the ground, and filling his mouth with fistfuls of what he crossed, that her attention was directed to what was around her rather than above her. She held her son's head and forced him to cough up the contents of his mouth in her hands and as she examined the clods of dirt and chips of stones and stalks of dead grass, she considered how untouched they appeared by her son's swallow and realized, then, that she was examining the feeble contents of the garden of Five Queen's Road.

She walked through the house as though she were entering it for the first time. She saw the bathroom Amir Shah had installed for her and wondered how long it had taken him to cover the floor with a paste of cement before dropping to his knees and pressing in the white ceramic tiles. She recollected, now, that he had done it on his own because no contractor would agree to his ambitious renovation plans. There was a tin water container with its own faucet perched above a flame, and all the warm water she had ever used in Five Queen's Road flowed from its tap. A sparrow had once flown through the window when the tank was being filled and it drowned and cooked in the water before the stench revealed its hiding place. In the bedroom she saw an empty nail hanging above the bed that held the garland of one rupee notes that awaited her the first time she set foot in Five Queen's Road. The fragrance of *nargis* that filled her that first night was not one of her grandfather's descriptions, but a bouquet that floated down from the flowers Rubina had strung in between the crisp notes of the garland.

She pulled the nail from its hole and smoothed the bubbles of paint on the wall. She thought, first, there might be a certain synchrony in the wrinkling of the house, because it accompanied the new roundness in Amir Shah's shoulders and the loss of words and sounds from his ears. But her impression was not lasting. It surrendered to the reality of the aging house: Five Queen's Road seemed to move at a pace that outdid the rhythms of those who lived in it, and finally, adhered to an aging process that overtook everyone else's.

She heard Rubina calling her.

'Here,' she answered from her bedroom, although the name, Yasmin, would always be unfamiliar to her. 'I am here.'

It was to the sound of those words that day in December of 1959, two years after she had first laid sight on it, that Irene truly arrived at Five Queen's Road. She was standing next to her bed in Amir Shah's home in Lahore, rubbing a rusted nail between her fingers, leaning against a wall of flaking paint for support. If she could have found the words to explain the sensation that was swallowing her, she might have said that for the first time all of her, the brown in her hair, the stretch of her stomach, and the soles on her feet, was in one place at one time. Her grandfather's warnings against living in the past or in the future echoed in her ears one last time. She took off her shoes and rubbed the soles of her feet onto the chipped and cracked cement of the floor. She was standing in the present now, and where she had come from and where she might go seemed distant in comparison. At last, the habit of being where she was not, of travelling in her imagination to places she had yet to discover, was quieted.

A few minutes later, Rubina found Irene in the bedroom. Irene turned to her and smiled. At that very moment when Irene's eyes met Rubina's, she felt some unnamed part of her in the space between her heart and stomach shrink until it finally sealed itself closed. Then, as if Rubina could not see it for herself, Irene said it again.

'Here,' she said. 'I am here.'

HAMIDA KHUHRO

*D*r Hamida Khuhro was educated at the Universities of Karachi, Cambridge, Oxford, and London. She is a historian and has taught at the University of Karachi and at Oxford and lastly Sindh University where she was Professor of History. She left the University to concentrate on writing and political work. She has published a number of books, including *The Making of Modern Sindh: British Policy and Social Change in the Nineteenth Century Times* (OUP, 1978) and *Mohammad Ayub Khuhro: A Life of Courage in Politics* (Ferozesons, 1999). She has also edited *Sindh Through the Centuries*, and co-edited with Anwer Mooraj, *Karachi: Megacity of Our Times* (OUP,1997).

ANOTHER KIND OF MIGRATION

My experiences of being displaced from my home place, of migrating, although at the time causing a real sense of loss, have been what would be considered routine—from a village childhood to town, from home town to University abroad. Not strictly migrations at all. As a child my most vivid memories are of my village: of the high wall round our family houses—the *kot*—of the lavatories at the end of the garden, well beyond the house; of accompanying my father for walks on the flood *bund* of the river; of sweets from the village *baniya's* shop in return for a handful of grain; of sleeping under a starry sky and listening to terrifying tales of the Day of Judgement; of crossing the *pul-e-sirat* and of witches and ghosts, with distant howls of jackals, which I firmly believed were of the *chirakh* (hyenas)—on whose backs witches rode through the night...I learnt to count on *kories* (shells) and to write on a *pharahi* cleaned with yellow clay (*met*) and using a reed nib.

These are memories so far removed from my present style of life with its computer-driven days that it must count as disturbing a migration as any that we read about. I have left behind those old certainties—of buffaloes being milked at sunset, of waking up to the sound of churning butter in clay pots and the grinding of wheat in stone hand mills (*jand*)—one could push up the *ajrak* to cover one's face as the sun came up early but could not ignore the buzzing of flies, and so, getting up with the sun was unavoidable. My daughter certainly never had these experiences and probably could not imagine them in her thoroughly modern urban Karachi upbringing. So I have migrated from the rural home of my childhood and the term has a meaning for me.

But this has not been my only migration. My most traumatic one is the same as of so many of my generation, the one that occurred at Partition. Unlike millions of Indo-Pakistanis in 1947, I did not move from my second home in Karachi. I continued to live in the house of my parents and the surrounding physical features continued to be the same, more or less, but between the June of 1947 and the following year, my world changed utterly.

I had lived in the small town of Karachi, a comfortable secure town where the tram could take you all the way to the harbour and to Saddar Bazaar. It was a child-friendly city, full of parks and playgrounds. It was bounded by the harbour, Keamari, with its forest of boats—and Clifton beach, and at the other extreme by the Jail. Beyond the Jail were the dry hills with cactus, which burst into life with the rains and became a rewarding hunting ground for wild mushrooms. My memories include an annual circus on Bunder Road at the corner with Garden Road (now the Agha Khan III Road) with its well of death and its roundabouts, its puppet shows and roaring lions—the lion master with his whip and elephants! No daily sight in our camel land. The tram car rides and circus events were under the care of the servants; with parents, there with much smarter treats like car drives to Clifton, ice cream at Cafe Grand, visits to Paradise Cinema or Palace Cinema, (where one could sit in family boxes) and shopping for toys at Mr Paul's toy store on Elphinstone Street.

Even here in remote Karachi there was the presence of The War. Elphinstone Street and Victoria Road would be full of American soldiers with Anglo Indian girlfriends. ABC Chinese

Restaurant had an 'Out of Bounds for Troops' notice on its door. On Bunder Road, outside the Goan Gymkhana grounds, there were large monkey posters warning the public not to speak carelessly. The cinema would be full of soldiers—which would be very strange and somewhat terrifying. The most terrifying experience of our lives was the siren that would sound almost every day and bring the menace of air raids and bombs into our lives. It was no use parents trying to re-assure us that this was only a practice siren and that there was no danger of bombs in Karachi. Then there was the day Prince Aly Khan made a brief stay at our house. He must have been on some secret war mission because he did not put up at any high profile government guest house. We could hear him from upstairs, on the telephone all night, shouting down the line to some far-off place. Then there was Victory in Tunisia Day and sweets distributed at school and a troop parade outside the Sindh Secretariat. I could not understand that if we had celebrated Victory Day, why were we still in a war and it was hardly explained to me at all.

School was the first reality of our lives. First of all the Sindhi school, run by Dadi Jamna, a Congress nationalist, where we were given packets of biscuits and a picture of Gandhi on his birthday. Out of loyalty to the Muslim League, I could not eat the biscuits—it was one of my earlier tests of loyalty. After finishing my three standards of Sindhi, I went to an 'English' school where our class had a colour picture of the two princesses, Elizabeth and Margaret, both blonde and blue eyed. Not strange to us at all—just a fact of life that kings, queens and princesses were the natural order of things. In our Sindhi primer there was a picture of Queen Victoria with a crown, sitting in a chair—or throne I suppose it was—and we felt that here was a suitable Queen for our Indian Empire. It was a matter of some satisfaction that while England was only a kingdom, India was an Empire!

The text books were those that were used in England. We learnt stories of Drake and Raleigh and learnt the geography of England though the geography of India was equally important. We learnt to draw the map of India with all its curves and angles, including the special shape of Sindh and Baluchistan and the cap of Himalayas on the north west corner, and there was such satisfaction from drawing the steep triangle of the Deccan. I still feel bereft of the ownership of that map of India.

There were always more Hindu girls than Muslim and a few Anglo-Indian or English. My closest friends were two Hindu girls, Pushpa Sitlani and Kamala Shivdasani and a Parsee girl— Katie Dubash. We were invited to Kamala's sister's wedding that was held in Guru Mandir on Bunder Road Extension. This was my first visit to a Sindhi Hindu wedding; I was surprised at the simplicity of it. There were no idols or *murtis* a la the Indian movies, just the Holy book, Guru Granth, in the middle of the room on a raised platform, and there were white sheets for every one to sit on.

I was aware of the Hindu religion through the tales of Ramayana and Mahabharata in our story books. Also because of the Holi festival, where we had to be careful not to put on any new clothes, in case we got colour thrown on us. And at Diwali time we were able to buy a lot of clay toys being sold by vendors on the street. Otherwise Hinduism, Christianity, Judaism (there were Jewish girls in our school), the Zoroastrian religion or even Islam did not intrude on our school or social lives. Eid festivals were family oriented; we went off to the village to celebrate Eid. The car journey would be quite long with a break at the Circuit House in Hyderabad and then all the length of Sindh. After Sukkur there were the canal paths, specially strewn with hay for our journey, or else we went by train, with tubs of ice in the compartment to cool the journey, in those days before air-conditioning.

Even politics, fierce and partisan as they were, did not touch our school friendships. I am sure it must have been an instinctive safety valve—not to concern ourselves with politics that we hardly understood, except for green flags and Muslim League Conferences, which the Quaid-e-Azam attended and to which I was taken by my father. Quaid was a figure of awe and reverence; we hung over the staircase for a glimpse whenever he came for lunch—which he always did when he was in

Karachi. A fish menu would be discussed very seriously by the parents—*surmai*, pomfret or ladyfish. The Quaid loved fish—though, alas, Karachi could not produce Bombay Duck!

Then without much warning our world changed in 1947. For more than a year, my father had been making frequent journeys mostly by air, to us an exciting adventure, to Delhi. He would come back with important news about our imminent freedom—but which still seemed so remote—*terra incognita*! True, there was a lot of activity in our house; my father was in charge of building the temporary offices that were to be occupied by the new Government of Pakistan. These buildings were to cover the large empty spaces around the splendid pink Jodhpuri stone building of the Sindh Chief Court and there was a lot of discussion about where all the officers of the government were to be housed. Apart from that there were no dire predictions of disaster or of riots or of any drastic difference to be expected in our lives. But differences there would be, and of so acute a nature, that they would completely transform our lives as if we were transported to a different place, a different country.

First of all, my friends went away almost without warning. Soon the classroom was full of different girls—many more than before and talking of exotic and exalted places like Delhi and Bombay, of Simla and Mussoorie—of the great buildings and of the houses and shops, none of which I had seen and all of which seemed incredibly smart. It gave me a feeling of Alice in Wonderland just to hear of these fascinating, alien places so out of my experience. I felt uncomfortable and apologetic about poor old Karachi with our one Elphinstone Street and no Connaught Place.

It was as if I suddenly found myself in a new school where the geography was the same but the language and the concerns and the people were different. I had to get to know the new people and to make new friends. Eventually I would make some very good friends—friendships which would last for the rest of my life—but it would take a long time to get to know each other, to place each other, and of course there was never going to be a shorthand of a common childhood and growing up till one's teens, of taking for granted that although we spoke English in school, there was Sindhi spoken at home, that we had in common, that we knew each other's place in our familiar social scene and each other's history and did not have to explain ourselves. Suddenly I was the 'new girl' in a school where I had been all my life. So, to begin with, anyhow, there was a formality in my relations with my new and future friends, carefully treading the ground to check the sensitive spots and find common ground, difficulties that I am sure they had as well, even perhaps in greater measure, but I could only feel my own insecurities in the new situation.

My insecurity was not only that there were the new relationships to be built from scratch, but that the shape of the world around me had changed. The physical world of Karachi that I was used to ending at the Jail, became a limitless sea of hutments at Napier Barracks and there were new colonies with strange acronyms for names—PECHS! The town itself once full of green islands and squares now had every inch of space covered in *jhuggies*. The once spacious Saddar became overcrowded with pavement shops, shacks and carts. I kept thinking this could only be temporary—surely tomorrow there will be some proper solution to this choking of the gracious town of Karachi. Housing was so short that my parents gave over some rooms in our house to the incoming families till accommodation could be found for them.

The wonderful world of our imagined independence was turning into a world of squalor and insoluble problems and of a strange new phenomenon. Karachi had wide roads, but only the middle of these roads was raised and covered with tarmac. When the roads were washed or it rained, the water would drain away on the sides into storm drains. I was puzzled to see that though the roads were being covered completely with tarmac, there was no attempt to shape them properly so that the water would drain away—the traitorous thought did come to mind, that the British had gone and perhaps our fellow natives did not quite know how to do things. Then the storm drains were being built over. The one opposite the Taj Mahal Cinema and around the corner of the new Radio Pakistan building became a bazaar. I worried as to how water was going to be disposed off? And when would we get our green islands back? The names changed: Rambagh became Arambagh, Patel Park where I had lived for many years, had become Nishtar Park and a place for public meetings, instead of a children's park with the occasional cricket match in the grounds in the middle. I was pleased that Scandal Point Road where we lived, now in front of the Karachi Gymkhana, was named Khuhro Road, but when that changed to Club Road—my sense of what I suppose was 'alienation', was strengthened.

The alienation was not due just to the loss of a known and friendly atmosphere and its replacement with what felt like a hostile environment. The world had changed drastically. There were new hierarchies to be reckoned with. There were the very grand grandees—the Central Government, master of all it surveyed and was ill disposed to tolerate the powers of the Sindh Government. The tension was almost palpable between the new superpower and our provincial government, or at least those were the vibes we were getting from the stern but stoic attitude of my father, and the mutterings of the officials around. The stories in the papers underlined this tension. The harsh realities of power play were a reminder that now, with freedom had come the ultimate responsibility to solve problems and reach compromises and that no intermediaries were available any more, nor anyone to take the blame for the mess.

But not everyone's thoughts appeared to be on the crisis. There was a strong sense of euphoria at least among the top people. There were the long American cars and lots of garden parties and receptions. Top women floated around in French chiffon saris (Super Nymph was definitely superior to La Parisienne) and silk *ghararas*. There was much discussion about what the appropriate culture for Pakistan could be, since we were now separate and apart from the 'Indian'. The prevalent elite opinion was that 'Mughal' culture embodied what Pakistan was about. Secretly, I was upset that since 'Indian' was a word derived from Indus, which was 'our river', why should we just give it up? No one asked how 'Mughal' could be separated from 'Indian' or even 'Bharati'. From now, although the Taj Mahal and the Red Fort was *theirs*, Mughal was very definitely ours.

So Mughal it was. There were *meena bazaars*—and newspapers full of articles about our rich cultural past of Mughal times. There was a rash of new fashions, *ghararas*—needing a lot of material and very impractical, but that was the fashion. My mother called in help from an obliging neighbour, Saeeda Ahsan whose mother was visiting from UP,[1] to make up some *ghararas* for us.

I was very uncomfortable though I could not explain why. I could see that all was not according to plan. There was a crowded humanity all over the place, obviously not happy, and could not be less concerned with the Mughal past. The problems of governance of the new country, of adjusting the hundreds of thousands of incoming people, of keeping the law and order in a situation which was just barely under control, were real and needed superhuman dedication. This was not to be seen. In January 1948 incredibly, (or perhaps not incredibly given the circumstances) there were riots in Karachi! Luckily my father was in charge. He had the dedication and he would set things right, which he did immediately. But I could not be sure that other things were in such good hands.

Karachi had not only doubled its population in a very short time and was bursting at the seams, it had also changed character and had become a bureaucratic town, full of petty one upmanships—who has a better house—is it the Education Minister or the Interior Minister? The Finance Minister was very angry that his house was not in the enclave with other Ministers' houses, although it was a good enough house in Staff Lines, but at the unfashionable end of the street. The race was on for postings and promotions and every clerk who had come from the Delhi Secretariat thought he was worth an ambassadorship at least.

My world had turned upside down but the reality that had emerged—of grab as grab can, of opportunism and chaos— was certainly not the realization of the Pakistan dream. It was not

1. United Provinces, now Uttar Pradesh in India.

the city of Medina in the days of Caliph Umar that I had been expecting. I was still at the impressionable age, still with illusions, still in the world of history books and heroes, and I found this world alien indeed. Migration had come to me, but not of the Promised Land.

Karachi would never be the same, sleepy, small town again. The town I knew as a child had disappeared as if beneath a wave in the sea. What would emerge from the mass of humanity which was now covering it? As the people slowly dispersed in the new townships and colonies, the city grew in all directions. Manghopir, so distant, almost at the foot of the Baluch mountains, so picturesque a picnic spot, where we went to goggle at the crocodiles, would become just a spot in a crowded shanty town. The drive to Sandspit along the salt flats would turn into a long drive past an endless workshop for trucks along the Lyari village. The shorter drive to Clifton would no longer be on a road with shining sheets of water on both sides, a marvellous sight on a full moon night.

Karachi would emerge as a huge sprawling city with satellite towns, Nazimabad, Liaquatabad et al. Drigh Road and Landhi would become parts of the ever extending city, as would the innumerable ancient villages of fishermen and Baluch tribes. The city bearing the same name as my childhood town, Karachi, which was measured by its rattling tram line, would be a different town—the vast and troubled 'megacity' of Karachi—before the end of my century.

MUNEEZA SHAMSIE

*M*uneeza Shamsie (née Habibullah) was educated in England and has lived in Karachi for most of her life. She is the editor of *A Dragonfly in the Sun: An Anthology of Pakistani Writing in English* (OUP, 1997)—a collection of fiction, poetry and drama. She has written 'The Founding Fathers of Modern Karachi' for *Karachi: Megacity of Our Times*, edited by Hamida Khuhro and Anwer Mooraj (OUP, 1997). She has been a regular contributor of features, interviews and book reviews to *Dawn* since 1982 and also writes frequently for *Newsline*, *She* and *Zameen*. She has spoken at many literary forums and was a delegate to the 1989 Conference on English in South Asia and a Fellow of the 1999 Cambridge Seminar on The Contemporary British Writer. She is now putting together a collection of her short stories.

A TRUE PRINCESS

Soraya had heard so much about Sikander Bagh, although it was in India across the border; she knew its history backwards; she could name every palace functionary who had served Amma Huzoor, her adopted mother. Amma Huzoor had been known as Her Highness The Begum of Sikander Bagh in those days and she still used the title on her letterhead.

Soraya could vividly imagine Amma Huzoor in her crown of diamonds and her regalia, sitting on a cut-glass throne of Bohemian crystal; shimmering court ladies had bowed to her in homage there. Soraya could see herself reclining in the gold and silver palanquins in which Amma Huzoor had been carried; or in her dreams, time would become confused. She would find herself waltzing through the Grand Ballroom with Zein, the dashing Heir Apparent—the Waliahed of Sikander Bagh—while music floated past blazing chandeliers.

Of course Soraya knew that Sikander Bagh was not like that any more; it had merged with India at Independence. Amma

Huzoor's life had crumbled shortly before that. Her husband, His Highness The Nawab of Sikander Bagh had fallen under the spell of another and re-married. Worse, he had expelled Amma Huzoor from the palace and consigned her to oblivion in the Old Fort. That Woman, his new wife, had persuaded him that Amma Huzoor planned to murder him and rule as Regent in the name of her baby son.

Amma Huzoor was not like that.

Amma Huzoor had been a patron of the arts and an enlightened modern Queen. She had established orphanages, schools and hospitals. She had initiated many reforms though the Nawab Sahib had revoked them when she fell from favour. He had denied her access to her children. He had intercepted her correspondence. Amma Huzoor could not even write to Zein, her only son, until he was at school in England. By then, she had run away from Sikander Bagh and was no longer in the Nawab Sahib's power. She always said she considered herself fortunate to have escaped to Pakistan, the new Muslim homeland created by the division of India in 1947.

Soraya often wondered what would have become of her, if Amma Huzoor, her paternal aunt hadn't adopted her. She was three in 1948, when her parents died in a car crash. Soraya's father Major Javaid 'Jacko' Ali Khan had been decorated in World War II and was one of the cleverest cavalry officers in the Pakistan Army. Her Kashmiri mother, with her defiant green eyes had resembled Vivien Leigh.

Soraya's elder sister, Saphia, had looked a lot like their mother, everyone said. Soraya didn't agree. Saphia's eyes had been brown; her short hair wavy, not curly; her features more finely chiselled. Of course Soraya was dark and not in the least beautiful. At thirty three, two grey hairs had already revealed themselves in her long plait. Soraya often wished there were no mirrors in the house at all.

Soraya had lived in Karachi with Amma Huzoor ever since she could remember. There was a time when theirs had been a very exclusive locality, but it was no longer so. All day (and most of the night), the air was thick with the noise and fumes of traffic. The house showed signs of neglect and decay; the gates had rusted; several wooden shutters had jammed; and the paint had started to peel. The garden had been unkept for so long that Soraya felt a thrill of pleasure as she observed a hired gardener mow the lawn. She had almost forgotten how much she loved the smell of freshly cut grass. But she had no time to waste. It was the tenth of November. She had to make preparations to receive Zein, the newly wed Waliahed of Sikander Bagh and his upstart bride, Aliya.

Amma Huzoor was expecting some fifty guests for the ceremonies of welcome. She had taken out the embossed silver bowls, the trays of silver filigree, the antique silk bolsters and covers, encrusted with gold and silver embroidery. She had stored them for years in anticipation of such an occasion. Her daughter, Alex (whose real name was Sikander Sultan Begum) had come down specially all the way from Islamabad to attend. Alex Apa was married to an important Federal Minister. She would be arriving in an official limousine at 9:30 to take Amma Huzoor and Soraya to the airport.

Soraya noticed that the gardener hadn't shut the gate properly. He was so careless, as were all workmen. She told him so. He paid her no attention. She walked resolutely down the front steps and stepped into a puddle. Mud spattered her clean white baggy *shalwar*; her sandals squelched. The driver had flung water all over the drive, to wash Amma Huzoor's tiny car.

Soraya began to haul the gate shut and saw Mr Wajid, their neighbour, hurrying across. He called out to her. His pyjamas were creased; his grey hair wasn't even combed; but then, as Amma Huzoor was so fond of saying, he 'wasn't our class.' Amma Huzoor had stormed into his house once and called him and his family peasants.

Soraya salaamed Mr Wajid politely.

'Bibi,' he said. 'I apologize for intruding at this early hour, but I believe your telephone is not working.'

'The underground cable's snapped,' sighed Soraya.

Amma Huzoor was distraught at such a calamity, just as Zein was coming to stay.

'I have an urgent message for you,' Mr Wajid said. 'I was woken up by a call from the Minister Sahib's office. Your brother's flight has been delayed in London, for six hours, due to a mechanical fault.'

Of course Soraya had no brother of her own, but in Urdu the word for brother and cousin is the same. Besides, Zein treated her as a real brother would, although she hadn't met him until he was grown up: his father hadn't allowed him to visit Amma Huzoor's home before that.

Zein was very democratic in the English way. He had said there was no need for Soraya to address him with an appellation of deference. In England, where he lived, he was simply known as Dr Zein Khan, historian and scholar. But nothing could change the fact that he was every inch a prince, tall and lean, with a handsomely sculpted face and a lock of hair falling on his high forehead. When he laughed, light seemed to dance in his eyes. Soraya longed to see him again, as did Amma Huzoor. She could hardly hide her disappointment at the last minute delay.

'Your guests are being informed by the Minister Sahib,' Mr Wajid continued. 'Here. It's all on this piece of paper.'

Soraya thanked Mr Wajid. She asked him to come in and meet Amma Huzoor. Mr Wajid gave a nervous smile, refused and retreated.

Soraya glanced at her watch. Good heavens! It was 7:55 am: time for her insulin.

'Soraya, have you had your injection?' Amma Huzoor called out to her, a few minutes later, as she always did at 8:05.

'Yes, Amma Huzoor,' Soraya answered from the courtyard. 'Yes. I have.'

Amma Huzoor was dressed for the airport already. A dark chiffon saree edged with silver covered her head and was pinned to the shoulder by an oblong ruby brooch. Her one remaining diamond ring glistened on her finger. She was listening to the BBC as she did every morning. An untidy pile of newspapers lay on her desk; thick books slanted at different angles in her bookcase. The right wall was taken up by a map, dotted with

coloured drawing pins. Amma Huzoor usually adjusted these to
predict world trends, while she listened to the news, but she
wasn't quite herself today. Her grey eyes were a little watery;
her lined face was pinched; and there was a tremor in her strong
hands.

Amma Huzoor adored Zein, yet Zein had married Aliya in
England, last June, against Amma Huzoor's wishes. She had
developed such high blood pressure that she had to be admitted
to Jinnah Hospital; it was only then that a reconciliation took
place between mother and son. He was now stopping in Karachi,
en route to India, where his father was going to welcome the
bridal couple in his dilapidated palace with fireworks and
celebrations.

Amma Huzoor had wanted Zein to marry Soraya. Soraya
had a flawless lineage, Amma Huzoor said. Soraya was a true
princess. Soraya could give him children with impeccable
antecedents, worthy of Sikander Bagh. He had lived in England
for so long, he had forgotten how important things like that
were. Why else would he have married the daughter of the
Nawab Sahib's one-time ADC? Just because her father, Ali
Ahmed, was now a multi-millionaire.

Of course Aliya was very pretty. She had glowing chestnut
hair, thick lashes, a refined well-shaped nose and pale, golden
skin. Soraya could see that in the video of the wedding, which
had been a showy, traditional affair at the Ahmeds' huge
Georgian home in Berkshire. Anyone who was anybody had
been there including Zein's royal father. The camera had zoomed
in on Aliya's trousseau, which had Chanel, Gucci, or YSL
written all over it.

'The plane's been delayed,' Soraya informed Amma Huzoor.

Amma Huzoor didn't believe her.

'How do you know?' she asked.

'Mr Wajid told me.'

'Wajid?' Amma Huzoor cried. 'Wajid? How should he know?
And why were you chatting to him? Haven't I warned you
about those people? We've had enough trouble with them. When
they lured you into their home and tried to palm their son onto

you. All he wanted was to lay his greedy hands on your jewellery.'

'That's not true,' Soraya began to tremble. Her stomach churned. 'That's not true!'

Why did Amma Huzoor have to dredge that up, over and over again? It had been so long ago, although it seemed like yesterday since Soraya had watched the Wajids move in next door; and they paid a neighbourly call with their bespectacled daughter, Nargis. (How Amma Huzoor had laughed afterwards because Nargis was supposed to be doing her BA at Karachi University but was so impressed by the sixteen-year-old Soraya).

Nargis didn't know at the time that Soraya had been expelled from school after school, because she just couldn't learn to read. Nargis wasn't aware that Soraya had been pronounced 'uneducable','retarded' or 'bone lazy'. Nargis never did see Soraya on one of her bad days when Soraya was so overwrought that she couldn't fight back her anger.

Soraya's sister, Saphia was still alive then. Nargis didn't take to her much, though Saphia knew more about literature than Soraya did. Nargis was fascinated by Soraya's ability to rattle off reams and reams of English and Urdu poetry. Soraya loved poetry as much as Nargis did. Nargis started to take Soraya along to poetry recitals. Soon they became firm friends.

Amma Huzoor didn't mind. In fact she was quite glad: Soraya had no other friend and Saphia hated tagging Soraya along. Saphia encouraged her friends to taunt Soraya, giggle behind her back or run away. Nargis never allowed anyone to mock her. Soraya, in turn, never snapped at Nargis's friends or sulked, as she did with Saphia's.

Nargis and her homely buxom mother loved listening to Soraya sing romantic Urdu *ghazals*. Soraya had picked them up from the radio although it was a form of music Amma Huzoor deplored as 'low-brow'. Of course, Amma Huzoor disapproved of rock 'n roll even more. She had no idea that Saphia and her convent-educated crowd danced to it with such abandon.

Soraya didn't know why, but she never told Amma Huzoor or Saphia about Nargis's brother, Tootoo (his real name was Mahmood). Tootoo had been doing his masters in Lahore and he came home for the summer holidays. Soraya didn't pay him much attention at first. He was a weird Marxist, skinny and reedy, with curly hair and a huge Adam's apple. He would often come into Nargis's sparse room, when Soraya was there. He would lean back on the bed on his elbows and chat. He didn't know much about poetry and would grin and say, 'That's because I'm a useless uneducated loafer, you see.' But he knew a lot about other things, particularly history and politics. He didn't agree with Amma Huzoor's views, which Soraya quoted as the gospel.

'The trouble with your Amma Huzoor is that she's never got over being married to a Nawab,' he said. 'She lives in a fantasy world which has nothing to do with reality. Your sister's not too different from all that I hear. I believe she's a terrible snob.'

'Why shouldn't Saphia be snobbish?' Soraya answered, quoting Amma Huzoor once more. 'When she has no equal and is beautiful and clever and is descended from kings?'

'Is that what you really think?' he scrutinized her. Nargis frowned at him. She told him not to upset Soraya. He was standing by the chest of drawers that doubled as Nargis's dressing table. He said, 'Come over here, Soraya.' There was such authority in his voice that Soraya obeyed. 'Now look at yourself in the mirror,' he said. 'And tell me what you see.'

Soraya cowered. She crossed her arms over her face. Why did he want to humiliate her?

'Oh, so that's what they've taught you, is it?' he said. 'Well let me tell you what I see. I see a beautiful girl with thick dark tresses and eyes the colour of emeralds. Your sister can keep that white white skin that our moronic countrymen so admire and her short hairstyle and her Anglo-Indian airs and graces. She's not a patch on you. And I don't care if you can't read, because you are better educated than most girls your age. Though I suppose I have to give your Amma Huzoor some credit for that.'

Tootoo stomped out of the room. Later, Soraya learnt Tootoo went straight to his parents and announced that he wanted to marry her. He asked his parents to formally request Amma Huzoor for her hand. Nargis was so excited that she told Soraya. Soraya turned puce. She was overcome with humility and shyness. (No one had ever proposed for her before, though Saphia had many offers). Before Soraya knew it, Nargis had disappeared and left her alone with Tootoo. Soraya didn't know what to say or do. She pushed him away, when he tried to take her hand, although at his touch, she felt as if she was being consumed by fire. 'Well Soraya,' he smiled. 'What do you think? Will it be so bad? Putting up with a lifetime of me?' Soraya was so overwhelmed that she lurched forward into his arms; it was a moment that she wished she could hold forever.

'If he had really cared for you and respected you,' Amma Huzoor's voice broke into her thoughts, 'he wouldn't have arranged those secret assignations with you and flirted with you as if you were some cheap bazaar girl.'

'He never did!' Soraya screeched. 'He never did! He wanted to marry me! He sent his parents with a proposal.'

'A proposal?' Amma Huzoor pulled herself to her full height. She seemed to fill the room, though she was scarcely five feet. 'A proposal? Who were they to come to Us and propose, as if they were Our equals? What did they think? That just because you have diabetes and no education We'd be willing to dump you on the garbage heap? They have no background. Their son wasn't earning anything. He was absolute scum, the lowest of the low, the way he turned your head and made you his slave.'

'It wasn't like that,' Soraya wept. 'It wasn't.'

'Oh? Wasn't it?' Amma Huzoor taunted her. 'Then pray tell Us, what was it like? What made you so forget yourself and your family honour, that you were ready to elope with him? When We forbade you to see him? He would have made you pregnant and kicked you onto the streets, in no time. Then what would you have done? Saphia saved you,' Amma Huzoor continued. 'Saphia found out your plans. Before anything untoward happened. She stopped you from disaster. What a

wonderful, wonderful girl she was, Saphia. So beautiful and
intelligent and affectionate. She had a maturity far beyond her
years. Everyone loved her.'

Soraya crumpled into the lumpy sofa, her arms wrapped
around her head. It was in this very room, that Soraya had
learnt Amma Huzoor was writing a letter to Tootoo's college
principal, accusing him of obscene behaviour. Tootoo would
most certainly have been expelled. In that era, Amma Huzoor
had been an influential social worker, with direct access to the
President of Pakistan.

Soraya begged Amma Huzoor not to post the letter. She fell
at her feet. She could not bear to live if Tootoo was ruined,
because of her, she wailed. Amma Huzoor started kicking
Soraya, in disgust. Then Saphia rushed in. She picked Soraya
up. She soothed her with pale soft hands. She pacified Amma
Huzoor, wound her arms around her, covered her with kisses
and said, 'Amma Huzoor, throw the letter away. Please. For my
sake. It won't do anyone any good.'

Saphia protected Soraya often, but at other times, she belittled
her: Soraya could never be sure of her.

A signed photograph of Saphia still sat on Amma Huzoor's
desk. Saphia was in a tissue saree spun with gold thread. She
was wearing her mother's emerald necklace and Soraya's
emerald earrings. The photograph was taken in England the day
Saphia was presented to the Queen at Buckingham Palace.
Soraya had never been to England because Amma Huzoor
couldn't afford it. Amma Huzoor had had to sell some of her
own jewellery—and Soraya's—to send Saphia to a finishing
school there.

That was how Zein and Saphia met, exactly as Amma Huzoor
had planned: it was no coincidence that he was at Oxford
University nearby. Amma Huzoor had groomed the exquisite
Saphia for him: he fell in love at first sight. No one accused them
of flirting, although Soraya was sure they did. Saphia flirted with
everyone, when Amma Huzoor wasn't around. Saphia had so
much charm that she even won over Zein's father and That
Woman, his stepmother. The Nawab Sahib personally wrote to

Amma Huzoor on Zein's behalf to ask for Saphia's hand. Until then, the Nawab Sahib didn't want to hear Amma Huzoor's name because she had committed the unpardonable sin of running away.

Shortly afterwards, Saphia developed a malignant tumour. Zein took her from doctor to doctor, but there was no hope. He brought her home to Karachi, with his father's permission, to die among those she loved best. That was the first and the last time that Amma Huzoor, Zein, Saphia and Soraya were together as a family. Alex Apa who lived up north with her landlord husband came down for a fleeting visit too.

Zein was twenty-one years old and very clever. He and Amma Huzoor and Saphia had such a wonderful rapport with each other. Their conversations crackled with wit; their discussions enlivened the hours, even though Saphia was so ill. Saphia was so brave that Soraya wished she could have died in her stead. Saphia still appeared in Soraya's dreams, with her papery face, her bright eyes clinging tenaciously to life. Her last words were for Soraya and Amma Huzoor. 'Look after Soraya and Amma Huzoor for me,' Saphia whispered to Zein. 'Look after them. Promise.' Zein was still holding her hand in his, when the breath left her body.

Amma Huzoor's household had never been the same since.

Over the years, Zein came to Karachi, whenever he could, on the way to Sikander Bagh and back. But it wasn't always easy to get a visa, particularly after the two wars between India and Pakistan. During one of his early trips, Zein found a visiting American doctor in Karachi, who diagnosed that Soraya had dyslexia. Amma Huzoor had never heard of that. The doctor said that there was nothing wrong with Soraya's brain. He explained that she couldn't read, because of the way she perceived certain letters. There were lots of very successful people who were dyslexic, he said. All she needed was special training.

There was no such facility in Karachi. Zein offered to take Soraya to England with him, but Amma Huzoor was shocked. She reminded him that Soraya was not his real sister. People would say she had become his keep. She insisted that he should marry Soraya first. Soraya had the same bloodline as Saphia. Soraya would ensure that his children had Saphia's antecedents. Amma Huzoor spoke to him, again and again of his vow to Soraya's dying sister. If he married Soraya, he could give Soraya the care and security she needed. Otherwise what would become of helpless, innocent Soraya, once Amma Huzoor passed away?

'Oh what is it?' Amma Huzoor's sharp tone forced Soraya to sit up. 'What are you blubbering for? What's that piece of paper in your hand? Wajid's message? Well, why haven't you given it to me?'

Amma Huzoor was terribly upset that her day's plans had gone awry. She fussed and fumed. She summoned Ali Jan and his wife Kallo, her two elderly and faithful servants. She ordered them to shut up the drawing room to keep out the dust and the sun.

Soraya made her way up the dark narrow stairs and blinked at the brilliant sunlight at the top. Two seamstresses salaamed her with due deference. They had once belonged to the palace staff in Sikander Bagh and still worked for Amma Huzoor occasionally. One was adjusting some brocade robes for Soraya to wear at the big dinner Amma Huzoor was giving. The other was altering a grand court outfit for Aliya: it was a glittering, multi-coloured *farshi* pyjama, yards long, which Amma Huzoor had put away, decades ago, for Saphia's trousseau.

Soraya felt quite sick. She tried to calm herself. She settled down crossed legged on the divan, under the covered half of the verandah. Light filtered through the coloured glass panes and cast red, yellow and blue shadows across the tiled floor. Amma Huzoor, who was both a poet and a musician, had composed a bridal song in a festive, classical mode, for Zein's welcome. Soraya was going to sing it for him. Suddenly she grew afraid that she might make a mistake. She needed to practice more. She closed her eyes. She opened her mouth. But no sound came. Crows cawed on the telegraph lines overhead. Soraya took a deep breath. She tried again, but with mounting panic.

A car horn tooted at the gate. Soraya leapt up, ran into her bedroom and looked out. Some relatives had come. They obviously hadn't received the message about the change of plan. Amma Huzoor had taken a tranquillizer and was resting. Soraya knew it was her duty to go down and officiate in Amma Huzoor's stead, but she just couldn't. She curled up on her brass bed. Her body merged into the mattress. Her head grew heavy.

Kallo came. She tried to coax Soraya to her feet. Soraya refused to budge. Kallo's shuffling slippered feet retreated. Soraya's bedroom grew hotter and hotter. The day wore on. Bands of rectangular light filled her room. She couldn't face lunch; or take any medicines or drink any water. At some point Amma Huzoor stormed in, told her to stop wasting time and get up. Soraya continued to lie there in a state of torpor. Then she heard Alex Apa's limousine. She knew it was time to go to the airport, but she couldn't make the effort.

'Soraya, what is this nonsense?' Alex Apa marched in, swathed in French chiffon. A trail of expensive scent wafted in with her. 'Get up.' Alex Apa seized Soraya's hand. Her bejewelled, manicured fingers dug into Soraya. She tried to yank her up. Soraya sank back into the bed. 'Soraya for God's sake!' cried Alex Apa. 'This is no time for a tantrum.'

Soraya didn't answer.

'Poor Soraya Bibi,' one of the seamstresses whispered. 'She loved Saphia Bibi so. When she recognized the outfit I was altering, she became quite strange.'

'Well, honestly, Amma Huzoor, I don't see why you have to give Saphia's bridal clothes to Aliya, even if poor Saphia never wore them,' Alex Apa said.

Alex Apa was the only one of Amma Huzoor's many daughters to migrate to Pakistan, but they didn't get along. Alex Apa couldn't forget that Amma Huzoor had shown such a marked preference for Saphia, although Alex Apa was already married by then.

'I have to make some kind of gesture,' Amma Huzoor cried. 'I have to give Aliya something valuable and rare that Zein will appreciate.'

'I doubt if Zein expects it,' answered Alex Apa. 'And anyway this endless fascination for Saphia, this constant talk, is quite morbid. Saphia died—when? Fourteen or fifteen years ago.'

'Don't you dare talk about her like that,' Amma Huzoor breathed. 'Don't you dare defame her memory. It should have been Saphia that We should have been welcoming today. It should have been Saphia entering this house as Zein's bride. Instead of some ambitious social climber, he's picked up in the streets of London.'

'Oh God!' said Alex Apa.

Soraya was glad they left without her.

'I expect to find you ready, Soraya, by the time I return,' Amma Huzoor called out.

There was plenty of time. Soraya wished that Kallo and the seamstresses wouldn't keep coming into her room and pestering her to change. 'Go away!' Soraya thrashed around in her bed. 'Get out.' Suddenly everyone was back. She heard Zein's voice on the drive below. She wanted to see him so much!

Soraya sat up on her bed. She swivelled herself around. She put her feet down on the floor. With steady steps, she reached the window. Yes, there he was in a grey suit and garlands, towering over everyone, his back towards her. Soraya yearned, with an absolute overpowering desperation to touch his thick dark hair, his long neck and his bony narrow back.

The drive was crowded; some people were still emerging from their respective cars. Zein swung around as the door of Alex's limousine opened. Soraya saw a delicate sandalled foot, the edge of a silk saree. Zein stretched out a firm helping hand to his wife. Aliya kept her head covered and her eyes lowered, as was only befitting a bride, but good heavens! Aliya kept salaaming everyone with deference, even the servants and ex-retainers from Sikander Bagh! What a silly, ignorant creature! What a fool she was making of herself!

'Where's Soraya?' Zein's voice rose. He looked around him.

Soraya leapt away from the window. She cowered against the wall. She had made a dreadful, dreadful mistake. She should have been ready. She should have been downstairs by now. What would he think? Would he ever forgive her?

A group of singers originally from Sikander Bagh started singing.

'Soraya Bibi. Hurry,' Kallo rushed in. She was breathing through her missing teeth, and panting. 'Everyone's enquiring after you.'

Kallo pushed and pulled Soraya's limbs and slipped on her new clothes—a skirt like *gharara*, a co-ordinating shirt and a diaphanous *dupatta*. She shoved on her earrings, snapped on a necklace and escorted her down. Soraya was so hot, hungry, and thirsty that she almost fainted. Kallo's bent husband, steadied her. He told her to sit in the dining room for a minute, take a deep breath and drink a glass of water.

A grey curtain hung in the doorway, between the dining and drawing room. Soraya watched it twist in the breeze. She glimpsed a blur of people beyond. The crowded hexagonal room was spread with white floor cloths. Zein was touching Aliya's toes with strands of grass, soaked in a silver bowl filled with milk and rose petals, to symbolize the washing of her feet, for luck. There was much banter and laughter.

'Soraya Bibi,' Kallo said. 'Come.'

She took her by the elbow.

'No!' screamed Soraya. The voice rose from the core of her being. 'No!'

'Soraya Bibi,' Ali Jan pleaded. 'Your brother has brought home his new bride. It is a day to celebrate.'

'She is not good enough to touch my sister's feet!' screeched Soraya.

'Soraya,' Amma Huzoor stood in the doorway. 'Come here at once.' She took Soraya in a firm grasp and led her into the other room. Soraya bowed low before Zein, her wrist flickering into the courtly triple salaam. He looked through her, as a sign of royal displeasure. He was holding his wife's hand tightly on the divan. His face was furrowed with anger.

'Now salaam his bride,' Amma Huzoor commanded.

Soraya stared at Aliya. She saw a pathetic girl, years her junior, who was so stupid that she was actually frightened of

her and couldn't hide it. Soraya saw no need to treat her with
any deference, even though she was now senior to Soraya in
rank. Soraya made a perfunctory salaam, more as a joke than
anything else.

'Salaam properly,' Amma Huzoor jabbed her in the ribs, hard.

'No,' said Soraya.

She wasn't afraid of Amma Huzoor any more. Zein's
marriage was a farce. She didn't care if the world knew it.

The room was suddenly drowned in a dreadful roar.

'How dare you insult Us?' Zein thundered.

He grabbed his wife and made for the door. Amma Huzoor
seized him by the sleeve. She implored him to stay.

'I know you. You put her up to this,' he said. 'And I will not
stay.'

He freed himself with a jerk.

Amma Huzoor burst into tears.

There was complete confusion. People milled around. Some
tried to console Amma Huzoor; others tried to comfort Aliya,
assuage Zein and dissuade him from leaving. Soon Zein was
sitting there with both his arms around his mother, her head
cradled against his shoulder. He stroked Amma Huzoor's face.
Yes, he said, he knew how hard her life had been. Yes, he realized
how much she had suffered and how valiantly she had coped.

Aliya sat on the sofa, stupefied. Her maternal aunt, who was
a famous gynaecologist, stroked her arm. Her cousin, the
Governor's wife, plied her with tea.

No one bothered with Soraya.

'Ya Allah,' an elderly relative sighed. 'It really is so tragic
that poor Saphia had to die and the Begum Sahib has been left
with this unfortunate, mad girl.'

Soraya had heard that so often that it didn't hurt now.

There were no other ceremonies. No one felt like it any more.
Guests began to trickle away, although one or two did hug her,
as if to say they knew how difficult it all was. Finally, Ali Jan
persuaded Soraya to apologize to Zein and Aliya. He led her to
them in the courtyard. They were chatting to Alex by the
budgerigar cage. Zein barely gave Soraya a perfunctory glance,

but Aliya got up and embraced her. Zein's eyes swept over Aliya in admiration.

A cool breeze began to blow and stars glistened in the clear sky. Aliya said how lovely it was to be home again. Aliya had grown up in Karachi before her family moved to England. She had never adjusted to soggy English winters, she said. She declared it was wonderful to sit out in the open and enjoy the temperate night air. Aliya even relished the sound of noisy rickshaws in the background and the tinny music from the cinema nearby.

After all the guests had gone, Zein and Amma Huzoor fell into a complicated discussion on metaphysics, but Aliya continued chatting to Soraya about this and that. Aliya was an artist. She had illustrated a new edition of Fitzgerald's *Rubaiyat of Omar Khayyam* in England. She presented Soraya a copy after dinner. Soraya loved Fitzgerald/Omar Khayyam. She knew him by heart, as she did Keats and Shelley, Ghalib and Faiz. She was thrilled to possess such a book.

'Will you recite something for us?' Zein asked.

His mood had changed, now that Aliya and Soraya were getting on so well. Quatrain after quatrain fell from Soraya's lips. She forgot everything except the beauty of the words. Zein and Aliya applauded her enthusiastically. Aliya said that she was absolutely spellbound by Soraya's rich voice.

'Oh well. Yes. Our Soraya has many talents,' Zein smiled. 'Don't you Soraya?'

His words made her positively lightheaded. Then he put his arm around his wife. Soraya was filled with such a searing pain, that she didn't know what to do. With a superhuman effort, she fought it down. Aliya, she noted, had a lovely soft face. She had a warmth that Soraya really liked. It was obvious that people were jealous of her, that's why they had told Amma Huzoor so many wrong things about her and dismissed her as some disgusting nouveau riche. After all hadn't she been educated at Saphia's old school?

Soraya confided this to Amma Huzoor later. She had gone into Amma Huzoor's bedroom to say goodnight. Amma Huzoor flicked through Aliya's illustrations and dismissed them with contempt. Amma Huzoor warned Soraya to be very careful of Aliya, though she must pretend to like her for Zein's sake. Aliya was extremely cunning. Aliya had seduced Zein with her body, just as That Woman, his stepmother, had enslaved his father. They were all the same, women like that. They spoke words of honey to you, while all they wanted was to stab you and stab you and stab you in the back.

Soraya hadn't thought of that.

'Just you wait and see,' Amma Huzoor soothed Soraya. 'He'll grow tired of her. He'll marry you one day.'

Soraya wasn't able to sleep well that night. She kept hearing laughter and muffled sounds from Zein and Aliya's bedroom, which adjoined hers. Their bed began to creak with an increasingly fierce rhythm. Soraya became so restless and uncomfortable and breathless that she was sure she was suffocating. She rushed to the window. The sounds wouldn't leave her. She threw open the door leading to a small curved balcony. She took deep breaths. Sweat poured down her.

A light shone from the upper floor of Mr Wajid's house. It came from Tootoo's room. He had become a professor at Karachi University and lived with his parents, in a joint family. She wondered if he knew how frequently she watched him from this vantage point. She could look right into his garden in the winter, when the Indian almond trees shed their leaves. She had seen him stroll there with his petite wife, a colleague of his. She had witnessed his two sons and a daughter grow taller by the year. She had gathered snippets of information about him from the servants. She had seen Nargis on television often, as Urdu poetry's rising star.

Tootoo invariably worked at his desk until late. He was sitting there, running his fingers through his hair in a characteristic gesture and scribbling away. He paused to light a pipe. He leant back in his chair, with a thumb hooked under his arm. For a moment, he turned towards her, but it was unlikely that he could see her.

She was immured by the shadows of the house.

INTIZAR HUSSAIN

*I*ntizar Hussain is one of Urdu's most eminent writers. He was born in Dibai, in north India, did his masters from Meerut and migrated to Pakistan in 1947. He has published seven volumes of short stories, four novels and a novella and his work dwells extensively on Partition and migration. The many English translations of his work include his novel *Basti*, translated by Frances Pritchett (Indus, 1995), and two collections of short stories, *The Seventh Door*, edited by MU Memon (Lynn Reiner, 1998), and *Leaves*, edited by Alok Bhalla (Indus, 1993). He writes a weekly English column in *Dawn*, has translated Attia Hosain's novel, *Sunlight on a Broken Column* into Urdu, *Shikasta Satoon Par Dhoop* (Mashal, 1998), and is the recipient of India's first Yatra Award and the 1999 Pakistan Academy of Letters' Prime Minister's Lifetime Achievement Award.

MY FIFTY YEARS IN LAHORE

I hope I will be forgiven for not discussing the subject at hand—Promised Lands[1]—in an academic way. I will just narrate it, as I have observed and experienced during my fifty years in Pakistan. Let me begin with myself. I am no more the man that I was, at the time I had migrated from India and had put my foot on the soil of Pakistan. One may attribute it to age. But no. The change in me is essentially different to growing old: my cultural being has altered and the process was so slow and subtle, that I was hardly aware of it.

I well remember my early days in Lahore when, clad in my Aligarh pyjama and *sherwani*, with a Rampuri cap on my head, I moved among people who, in their *shalwars* appeared a bit different to those I had been familiar with. Soon, I had to part with the Rampuri cap, as it was not available in the market. But

---

1. This essay was originally written as a speech for the Goethe Institute's 1997 Seminar, 'Promised Lands'.

I stuck with my Aligarh-cut pyjama for almost two decades. In the meantime, I had gradually grown so familiar with the *shalwar* that I liked to wear it sometimes, instead of my favourite pyjama. Perhaps that was an outward expression of the change within me. What I had regarded as a temporary respite from my pyjama, slowly developed into an estrangement from it.

I attributed this to living in Lahore, a city steeped in *shalwar* culture. But on a visit to Karachi, I observed that in that city, which is regarded as the citadel of *muhajirs*, the pyjama culture was in recession, making way for the *shalwar*. As for the dress of women, there too, the *shalwar* appeared to reign supreme. The *arra* pyjama, *gharara* and *lahnga*, so dear to *muhajir* ladies, were no longer in vogue. Now these clothes made their appearance only on formal occasions, such as marriages or Eid; the sari too had retreated into the background.

The infiltration of the *shalwar* in the *muhajir* wardrobe was a great cultural event with far-reaching repercussions. The point is that a certain dress is never a dress alone: it brings with it a certain etiquette, manners and a mental attitude. For *muhajirs*, adopting the *shalwar* meant a migration from their old manners, rooted in a particular culture, to the manners nurtured by the social conditions of this land.

If I am right in my observation, much has changed along with the dress. Social manners peculiar to the people coming from Delhi, Hyderabad and the cities and towns of the UP have altered. The sophistication associated with them is no more. So many customs and expressions, which had evolved under the *Ganga Jamni tahzeeb* have just vanished. For instance, a gentleman from Lucknow living in Karachi will no longer greet his esteemed guest in the polite manner known as *farshi salaam*, followed by an expression such as *banda adab arz karta hai* (your humble servant presents his salutations). My friend Ifthikar Arif, with his *Lakhnavi* background, tried this kind of salaam in Islamabad and suffered for it. He was branded a *khushamdi*— one who has devised a way to flatter Islamabad bureaucrats.

In fact, that whole tradition, of saying salaam in particular, cultivated by the *Ganga Jamni* culture underwent a metamorphosis. Once, a young lady in a *gharara* or *arra* pyjama would bow her *dupatta*-covered head politely, raise four henna coloured fingers to her forehead, with the same politeness, and say *ada'ab* or *taslima'at*. She would never say *as salaam aleikum* or *salamalukum* because in that culture this expression sounded somewhat masculine. *Ada'ab* and *taslima'at* had been conceived as soft expressions suited for ladies. Today, a *muhajir* lady in a *shalwar* is hardly conscious of the fine distinctions between the different ways and expressions of salaam. She will just say *salamalakum*. That is just one instance indicating how century old courtesies that *muhajirs* had brought with them have either disappeared or mutated, because they did not blend in with local manners.

I have a feeling that this is not just a one way traffic. Such situations bring with them, in general, the possibility of a two way exchange, or what may be defined as 'acculturation'. Immigrants, while assimilating influences from the people of their new land, exert their influences imperceptibly, one way or another. The local inhabitants may not like the manners of the incoming people; they might even abhor them and go to the extent of jeering at them and yet, they might be assimilating influences, at an unconscious level. This process brings about a social change in the long run. We can well see that being brought about by immigrants living among the local people. A great part has been played by intermarriages, which are perhaps more common in the Punjab than in other provinces. Once two families, with different cultural backgrounds, come into contact through intermarriage, they have to accommodate the customs and manners of each other. Soon after the birth of children, they have to say goodbye to the idea of cultural and ethnic purity, if they have any. One comes across families in Lahore and other towns of the Punjab where it appears difficult to determine whether they are *muhajir* or Punjabi and whether they are Urdu-speaking or Punjabi-speaking.

In fact, under these circumstances, Urdu itself appears to be undergoing a process of change. During its fifty years in Pakistan, it has assimilated a number of local words and expressions, from Punjabi in particular. At present, this assimilation is at the level of the spoken idiom mostly. But through the mass media, these words and expressions have spread.

I am reminded of a little Punjabi girl, whose linguistic behaviour brought me a pleasant surprise. A young man from Sargodha, who is now my relative through his marriage with my niece, came to see me along with his sister. I noticed with surprise that her little daughter was talking in Urdu continuously with remarkable fluency. Seeing my reaction, her mother laughed and said, 'My daughter speaks not a word of Urdu at home in Sargodha, but the moment she comes to Lahore and meets her cousins in her uncle's house, she begins talking in Urdu, with no recourse to Punjabi.'

It is for linguists to see if this points to some kind of linguistic integration-in-process. What struck me was something different. Noticing the girl's correct pronunciation of *Sheen Qaf*, I concluded that at least one of our linguistic problems was resolved i.e. the pronunciation of the *Qaf*, which had provided the *ahl-ai-zaban* a false sense of superiority over the Punjabis, who said *Kaf*. After all, how could the problem of *Qaf* versus *Kaf* linger on when, in the wake of intermarriages, mixed families were emerging in this society.

Now let me say a few words about food, as culinary dishes, among other things, carry with them a cultural significance. And Lahore has its own food culture. How did the dish of *nihari* infiltrate into this culture and gain popularity among Lahorites? This is particularly remarkable since Lahorites, as a rule, don't relish *bara gosht*, the meat of cows and buffaloes, of which *nihari* is made. Their favourite dish was *siri paay* of goat, which figured prominently in their breakfast. The popularity of *nihari* as a breakfast dish is a post-Partition phenomenon. The credit goes to the *nihari-walla*, who after being driven out from Delhi in 1947, reached Lahore as a *panahgir* and put up his *nihari* shop in a narrow street of Lahori Gate. Soon the Lahorites, who are so fond of delicious foods, developed a taste for this Delhi brand of *nihari*. Now *nihari* shops are as numerous in Lahore as are shops of *haleem* and *kabab tikkas*.

This is how the cultural scene has changed and is changing as a part of every day life, because of the arrival of immigrants in this land. I have simply depicted the scene as I have seen it without trying to give it a twist under the demands of any secular, religious or ethnic ideology. But one thing I must say: that the process of acculturation and integration is never smooth or easy. It brings in its wake so many tensions, conflicts and rifts. In fact, we in Pakistan, are locked in the situation of Sartre's *No Exit*. Migration has landed us in a position where we have no choice but to live together: and no matter whether we love and respect or hate each other, we are influencing and being influenced by each other, without noticing it.

The process of acculturation and integration is going on of its own accord. The process is disturbed only when some unwise politician or pretentious intellectual, posing as a wise man, advises the 'newcomers' in the name of national integration and patriotism to adapt to their new cultural environment. This advice carries with it a veiled threat that unless you oblige, you will be treated as an alien. The preachers of national integration and patriotism fail to see because of their insensitivity, that their uncalled-for, crude utterances have disturbed the integration process. It alerts people's sensitivities; they feel that their cultural identity is under threat and consequently develop within themselves a resistance against a process, which was hitherto going on, imperceptibly.

Patriotism and national integration are high-sounding phrases. The ways of acculturation are subtle. They can hardly reconcile with the aggressive ways of *nasihan-ai-mushfiq*. We have already witnessed their tragic failure in what was once East Pakistan. What they said and did in the name of national integration rebounded on us in the form of the Bengalis' exaggerated assertion of their cultural identity.

What we should aspire to, is the peaceful co-existence of the different cultural patterns we have among us. This can guarantee the long, slow process of their intermingling. Let them intermingle in their natural course. This subtle process can hardly be in harmony with pretentious sermons on national integration and patriotism: what national integration and patriotism demands is the suspension of these sermons.

AQUILA ISMAIL

*R*aised in East Pakistan where her father was posted in the Telephone Department, Aquila Ismail did a University degree in Electrical Engineering from NED, Karachi and is an Associate Professor there. At present she is on leave and living in Abu Dhabi. She has written freelance articles on women's issues for *Dawn*, is a freelance editor and has translated the Urdu novel, *Zinda Bahar Lane* by Fahmida Riaz into English (City Press, 2000).

LEAVING BANGLADESH

It wasn't leaving home as much as leaving a life behind. It was a total shattering of all that one held dear. The coming together of global power politics, greed, avarice, and above all the erroneous premise that two vastly different cultures could live together, forced it. We had no part in the decisions on either side but were merely the cannon fodder that necessarily accompanies such acts by men in power. Driven by force to an alien land with nothing but the clothes on our backs, we were thankful that, unlike many, at least the entire family was intact. It didn't seem possible on that cold wet day, the 4th of February 1972.

For days since 16th December 1971, or thereabouts, when General Niazi signed the infamous instrument of surrender, and with it, the lives of countless innocent people, we had been expecting something terrible to happen. Holed up in our house along with hundreds of neighbours, in the suburbs of Dhaka, there was a palpable sense that we the Urdu-speaking people had been betrayed by our country when the army withdrew, defeated and in shambles. Why they had attempted this foray against their own people is left to be judged by history. All we knew was that suddenly the soil that we lived on, had grown up

on, had called our own, had been 'liberated' and we had become
outcasts. We were left to the mercy of a people who, having
borne the atrocities inflicted on a subjugated race by the
conqueror for months, were looking for revenge. Anyone who
was in any way linked to the now defeated conquerors was to
be humiliated, tortured, maimed, and even killed. This was
carried out in frenzy, notwithstanding the fact that we knew of
no other way of life other than this world that we had grown up
in. Peaceful, simple souls had been turned into beasts, with us
as the grist for their hate-mill. The capacity to hate that came to
the fore was shocking. For them, it was an expression of freedom
from the power, which had choked their identity for years. For
us, it was the surrender of ours to utter desolation and isolation.

When the surrender was complete and the 90,000 'Pakistanis'
had been sequestered in the cantonments for transfer into camps
within India as prisoners of war, the Indian army withdrew
leaving Bangladeshis to deal with their enemies, both real and
perceived. This was the last week of January. The venomous
beast that was unleashed on the non-Bengalis now set about
claiming its victims. All communications to their communities
and even individual houses was cut. Then began the house-to-
house search for 'arms' that the non-Bengalis were supposed to
have cached in large quantities. Stories of plunder, beating, and
even cold-blooded killing began to filter through and we were
absolutely terror-stricken. When our turn came one night at
eleven o'clock the soldiers broke open the door and herded my
father and brothers outside and then locked us up in a room. We
heard a great deal of laughter and singing through the house and
after what seemed like a lifetime we were let out and the
marauding party left. When the men came in, we could feel the
pain inflicted on them by the boots and butts. Mercifully they
were alive. The soldiers had carried off almost all our
belongings. The only things they hadn't touched were our books.
While leaving the soldiers had informed us cheerfully that we
would be dealt with in a 'grand fashion' later on.

Early in the morning on the 4th February 1972, there was
loud banging on the door. We thought another search was to

take place. But from the window we saw hundreds of men, women and children trudging along, prodded by the soldiers, to an open field that lay some distance from our house. Then we knew it was time to leave home. It had started to rain and it was cold. As soon as we went outside the men and boys were separated and made to walk towards the waiting buses. With this came the realization that we may never see them again and our hearts went cold. After that everything was a dazed memory. It was like walking in a trance. There was an old neighbour who was bedridden. The soldiers pushed his family out and then a lone sharp shot was heard from inside the house. From down the street came two friends carrying their old father who was bleeding profusely. He had resisted and had several bullets pumped into him. The girls were dripping in blood and we had barely gone a few yards when the body went limp and the soldiers snatched it and literally threw it by the wayside. Needless to say, the girls wept useless tears then onwards.

Everyone walked on in a dreamlike state. Even little children, mostly girls, did not cry or protest.

It started to rain and grew cold in that open field. No one had anything with them. Suddenly a loud scream pierced the silence. The soldiers had discovered a young man amongst the women. His mother and sisters had dressed him in their clothes in the vain hope that they would not be separated. The soldiers dragged him away, kicking him with their boots, to the open space a few yards away. Then they started stabbing him with their bayonets and everyone looked on as if it was a nightmare and not really happening. How else can one explain the fact that, with so much the stuff that bad dreams were made of, was happening, and yet the mind blanked it out and survived? The mother and sisters were held back by other soldiers and their cry for mercy rent the air, in a loud empty scream. He lay there for a long while bleeding. They had made sure that each time they stabbed him they missed the heart, which would have hastened his end. In the meantime more and more women and girls joined the group in the fields.

Towards afternoon everyone was ordered to walk to the buses which had appeared along the road. These had probably taken our fathers and brothers to wherever they were destined to go. While walking towards the buses we saw a young woman lying by the roadside gasping for breath. She was in labour. Anyone stopping to help was pushed along. God knows what happened to that woman. Did she die on the roadside along with her new born child? Did she die quickly? When all the buses were full, the convoy lurched forward. No one spoke. Each had her sorrow and pain to bear.

The buses began the long journey through the city streets. These were the same streets where one had walked with friends, gone to school. But they were not ours any more. There was a curious detachment from the scenery. It was passing by, but we were not a part of it. The bus went on, leaving the city behind. Towards evening it entered a small town called Narayanganj. We recognized it as we had spent many years of our childhood here. It was a river port town and soon we headed towards the jetties, where river steamers were moored. The bus stopped at the mouth of a jetty and everyone was asked to get off and was herded towards a waiting steamer. There were many photographers and foreigners. God knows what they were told about who we were. Not the truth we were sure, as this exodus from our homes was never reported anywhere in any newspaper in the world. But there are thousands of victims even in this city of Karachi who went through this experience.

It was bitterly cold. Someone whispered that they were going to sink the boat midstream. No one cared though. Of course they were not going to kill us. That would have been too easy. They wanted the women to suffer the ordeal of homelessness, of separation, of hunger and thirst so that they could vent their anger. Inflicting pain on women is the best tool of revenge in times of chaos and war.

Night had fallen and it was pitch dark on both sides of the river. Some women started to chant verses from the Holy Quran. Everyone joined in seeking solace in those words. After hours of going down the river the steamer stopped. It was pitch dark with only the flashlights of the soldiers. Everyone queued up holding on to one another, so as not to get separated in the dark, and walked the slippery plank to the wet muddy ground and on to what seemed in the dark to be a huge building. Everyone was pushed inside a small room and the soldiers left. No one knew where we were and huddled together in the dark each one waited for daylight.

Soon the sun rose to reveal a large broken-down structure and, to our amazement, thousands of women and girls. Children had begun to cry from hunger. Everyone looked at each other. There was absolutely no comprehension as to what was happening. There were hundreds huddled in the vast number of rooms and courtyards of that dilapidated building. Later on, when we had managed to escape that hellhole, we discovered that it was an old borstal, which had been abandoned many years ago. The steamers that had brought us here were no longer to be seen. Nor were the soldiers in sight. It seemed as though we had been left here to slowly die of cold, hunger and deprivation. Slowly as the day went by, some women took the lead and ventured out of doors to see if they could comprehend what was to become of us. All they encountered were more miserable souls.

We do not know what happened to the inmates of that camp and how many survived. Many did not. We were perhaps the only ones who managed to get away within a couple of days. A family friend in the Bangladeshi army took the risk of literally whisking us away at great peril to himself. We informed the International Red Cross of the existence of this camp. The aid workers were, as is usual, staying in the Dacca Intercontinental Hotel. We gained access to them as we were fluent in the Bengali language and could go about the city without being pointed out as non-Bengalis. The Red Cross workers had no clue as to what had taken place under their very noses. They expressed their shock at this mass evacuation. If we had not been able to inform the Red Cross then maybe none would have survived. They showed us a map of the area and we were able to point out the location of the camp. This brought relief to many as they were able to somehow convince the government that such a large body of people cannot simply vanish from the face of the earth without questions being asked. After many days, food and medicine was allowed into the camp in small quantities.

We also asked them to help us locate our menfolk. We later found them, languishing in Dacca Jail, and all we could be thankful for was that they were alive. Many did not make the journey to the jail, as some buses were reportedly diverted to unknown destinations. Many families lived this utterly incomprehensible life of separation, with the women in the camps and the men in the jail until formal repatriation took place around 1973.

No one has ever written about them. There are no records. Doubtless the Bangladeshi Government has the policy paper on the manner in which the non-Bengalis were to be dealt with somewhere in their archives. All we know is that we did not deserve to be treated in the manner that we were. We had no quarrel of identity with anyone. We were targeted because the rulers of that time chose to dismember a country rather than give in to the verdict of the ballot. Such are the ways in which people are made to leave hearth and home. The long journey to Karachi is another saga where new homes are built up never to be left again we hope.

KALEEM OMAR

Kaleem Omar was educated in Nainital, Abbottabad and the University of London. He started writing poetry in the 1950's. His work has been published in British and Commonwealth journals, as well as several anthologies of Pakistani English writing and he edited the much praised *Wordfall: Three Pakistani Poets: Taufiq Rafat, Kaleem Omar, Maki Kureishi* (OUP, 1975). In the 1980s he became a journalist and columnist for *The Star* and is now an editor at *The News International*. He is working on a series of memoirs, *Naini Tal Days, When Pakistan was Young: 1947-1956, Travels in Pakistan*. He is also writing a book-length poem, *Contemporary Notes*.

A LAND THAT WAS LOST TO ME

Memory, in an impersonal world, is like the strands of smoke that drift through our autumn days, the fragments we shore against our ruins. I speak now of that time in East Pakistan many years before it became Bangladesh and was forever lost to me. I say to me, because that green land of yesteryears was no less a part of my inheritance than it was for all my fellow Pakistanis, even for those of us who tend never to think of what we lost. *The land was ours before we were the land's*, says the American poet Robert Frost in 'The Gift Outright.' He, of course, is speaking of his own land, but his words have acquired a special resonance for us in this country, or what is left of it after the tragic events of 1971.

We took that gift outright, that verdant land of ours, and, in our heedlessness, let it go down the tube. Many of us thought that we were well rid of a millstone round our necks. But it was no millstone to me, no millstone at all. To me, that land was as precious as this remaining Pakistan that we now inhabit. Call me a dreamer if you like. But we are nothing without dreams,

less, even, than nothing, mere automatons on the rat-race
treadmill, anonymous digits in a statistical universe—a world
sans everything that makes us human.

In the days of which I speak, Dhaka was still Dacca and still
had a small-town feel to it, with no traffic jams, no pollution
and very few high-rise buildings. The Motijheel commercial
area—a sprawling maze of office blocks, warehouses and
shopping arcades—didn't exist then. Narrow lanes wound their
way through neighbourhoods that really were neighbourhoods,
not faceless concrete horrors. The songs of the river boat people
drifted across the waters of the Meghna. The cries of parrots
filled the sky. Graceful clumps of bamboo grew tall everywhere.
Sporting clubs often got together for friendly games of football
in the stadium.

At one level, it was a simple life, geared to the rhythms of
the seasons. But at another level, life for many was anything but
simple, especially for those living on the economic margins.
For them, each day brought the same set of problems, the age-
old basics of food, shelter and clothing, and how to ensure that
their children got at least the rudiments of an education. Things
were not made any easier by the fact that some fifty million
people were crowded into a land measuring only 56,000 square
miles, and much of that, even, was usually under water during
the monsoon. Through it all, however, people displayed a
resilience that was truly amazing.

Smiling faces greeted you everywhere, though what they had
to smile about was often hard to understand. Dock workers
hauling heavy loads off river barges chanted cheerfully, as
though they hadn't a care in the world. The same attitude was
seen amongst workers at building sites. Their high spirits never
ceased to amaze me, reminding me of Goldsmith's words, *And
still they gazed and still the wonder grew...*

That's my trouble—things always remind me of other things,
setting up correspondences where none seemingly exist. If Colin
Wilson's Outsider, is the archetypal 'hole-in-the-corner man,' a

loner living on a metaphoric island, he still must contend with the correspondences that surround his days and ways. But correspondences can lead the mind into troubled waters, just as the Sirens' song, in the Greek myths, lured sailors to their doom. Better then, to play it safe, think only bland thoughts, I sometimes tell myself. Not that playing safe helps. As the poet Taufiq Rafat says: *The pain, the pain, gets you in the end / One way or another.*

But I digress. I was speaking of life in the Dacca of my youth. In those long gone days, days that now seem to belong to another life, even something as ordinary as going to the cinema was a big thing, an event to be looked forward to. You bought your ticket in advance to ensure that you got a good seat. Then, you could afford to arrive stylishly late, after the ads and the 'Movietone' news. We always watched the trailers, though, making plans with friends to see the upcoming Hitchcock thriller, or the next Pinewood comedy. Some people were perfectly happy seeing the same film over and over again. So what if they'd seen it before? It was a 'fillum,' wasn't it?

Marilyn Monroe films were special favourites. Forget your Sharon Stones, your Michelle Pfeiffers and Demi Moores; Monroe was in a class of her own. Her beauty had a vulnerability that was not of this world. There will never be another like her. The words of the song she sang, all breathy voice and sad, sad eyes, in 'River of No Return' haunt me still: *There is a river / Called the river of no return. / Sometimes it's peaceful / And sometimes wild and free. / Love is a traveller / That has gone away from me*—gone away like that land I loved has gone away from me.

I can hear it calling now, feel that rain on my face. During the monsoon, the rain came down in torrents, drumming like a million typewriters against palm-thatched roofs, turning streets into rivers, flooding everything for miles around, falling sometimes for days without a break. Afterwards, the air would be thick with the smell of ozone, washed clean, the garden a tangled riot of colours. Strangers now live in that house on Mymensingh Road, others now walk in that garden.

And where are my friends that lived in that town? Some, I've heard, continue to live there. Others have moved on. Still others have simply disappeared, their whereabouts unknown to me. They could be dead and I wouldn't know. Or, like me, they could be sitting by themselves in some room somewhere, nursing bittersweet memories of those Dacca days that we, in our innocence, or our foolishness, thought would never end.

Everybody on the social circuit, in that Dacca, knew everybody. This made for a very friendly place, where neighbours could always be counted on to rally round in times of trouble. But it also made for a place where people were constantly in each other's hair and where your business was everybody's business. If you had a few friends over for dinner one evening, the whole town knew about it by the next day and even knew what food you'd served. If you put up new curtains in your drawing room, you soon got phone calls saying, 'So how do the new curtains look?' In this small-town atmosphere, secret romances didn't remain secret for very long.

Like mangoes, gossip was something to be savoured. 'X is having an affair with Y,' one sweet young thing would murmur to some friends over coffee. 'That's old news. He's dumped Y and is now having an affair with Z,' a second sweet young thing would say, stirring her cup with a macaroon. 'Where have you been, my dear? Z cut X dead after Y ratted on him and has now gone off to London,' a third would purr, prompting a fourth to ask, innocently, 'Who's she having an affair with there?'

From which you must have gathered that there were an awful lot of sweet young things about. Dusky belles in saris sashayed through hotel lobbies. Young women in pedal pushers flocked to brunches for the in-crowd. Damsels in Thai raw silk outfits delighted in taunting suitors, leaving long trails of bruised egos in their wake. Visiting beauties from Karachi sneaked off to the tea gardens for naughty weekends. And svelte, cheongsom-clad,

Han Suyin wannabes spoke knowingly of love, insisting that it really, truly, really was 'a many splendoured thing.'

Did any of those lovelies know that the line came, not from the title of Han Suyin's best-selling book of the early 1950s, but from a poem of Francis Thompson's? When I put this question to one, she gave me a withering look and said, 'Of course I know who Francis Thompson is. He's the actor who played opposite Jennifer Jones in the film version'. I was about to tell her that, no, that was William Holden, but then thought better of it. 'You're right,' I said and was rewarded with a dazzling smile.

There were trips to Chakma territory in the Chittagong Hill Tracts, looking out for tigers in the Sunderbands, deer glimpsed fleetingly in the jungles around Kaptai, bonfires on chilly November evenings in the tea gardens, picnics on the shimmering beach at Cox's Bazaar, moonlit boat rides down the Karnaphuli River. The countryside around Dinajpur, to the north, with its miles and miles of lush-green fields of rice, looked like something out of a picture postcard. Jessore, was the starting point for some memorable trips, including one to Calcutta for a New Year's Eve party. Winters in Chittagong were a delight, a heady mixture of balmy days, cool evenings and boisterous parties at the club. Fenchuganj, Ashuganj, Rangamati, Little Feni...how those names roll off the tongue!

Then, when you got back to Dacca, it would be only to find that it was time again (it always seemed to be time again) for more parties, more brunches, more lunches, more of the latest gossip. No one seemed to tire of the routine. And if, perchance, you did tire of it, perish the thought, you could always find an excuse to give another party. It could be any kind of party—a farewell party, a welcome home party, a wedding anniversary party, a party to meet someone visiting town, or a party just for the heck of it. Any excuse was good enough.

This party crowd was a diverse lot. It included young assistant managers from the tea gardens, not-so-young businessmen in the jute trade, steamer company types in town for the weekend, officials visiting from the western wing, bureaucrats, politicians, Britons, Americans, Canadians, Greeks, even an occasional Indian. And then of course, there were the wives and some, it has to be said, were real heartbreakers. And in the age-old tradition of heart breakers, break hearts aplenty they did. In such inconsequential pursuits did our days slide by.

Dacca was a city of trees. My own favourites were the Indian corals around the Maidaan, a park in the centre of town. In spring, they made a beautiful sight, with their brilliant-red blossoms and delicate, upward-curving branches. Filtering through the corals, mellow March sunshine wove filigrees of light and shade on the grass, falling now across the path of an ambling couple, now upon the faces of children at play. No one, in that world, was ever in a hurry.

The same easy pace pervaded the countryside. Fishing boats drifted gently down lazy, brown rivers. 'The Rocket'—an incongruously named, ancient passenger steamer that plied between Dacca and Khulna—would never break any speed records. If you were thirsty, villagers would offer you coconut milk, refusing payment. Jute planting was a leisurely affair. So was the rice harvest. And the night-train to Chittagong—itself the scene of many assignations—frequently stopped in the middle of nowhere, as if nowhere were a station too.

Now all that is lost to me, gone forever. The physical reality of it, of course, is still there, albeit greatly changed in many respects. But it is no longer my reality, no longer my land. Sometimes, the sense of loss is so sharp that it is like acid eating away at the heart. Ezra Pound is right when he says, *What is the use of talking, and there is no end of talking,/There is no end of things in the heart.*

In all the shades of green
Of that green landscape,
One shade
Was nowhere to be seen.
Call it envy-green.
But envy, like hate,
Can breed surreptitiously.

A northwester blew one March.
The wind, a banshee thing,
Stripped all the double-dahlias
Of their flowers, hinting
At what was to come. Landslides
Of a darker brand of air
Began to arrive.
April, May, June—the months
Telescoped into December.
My trouble is that I remember.

MOAZZAM SHEIKH

Moazzam Sheikh was born in Lahore and lives in San Franciso. His short stories have been published in several American and Canadian literary journals, including *The Toronto Review*, *Mobius* and *The Adobe Anthology*. His English translations, particularly of the Urdu writer, Naiyer Masud, have been much acclaimed. He has recently finished his first novel, *Sahab*.

THE IDOL WORSHIPPER

The loneliness inside me, the duality of my person
                                                    – Kishwar Naheed

I

In a recurrent dream, appearing sporadically and nearly unchanged, he would recognize himself, more from the intimacy of the dream than from his own face, in the midst of a prolonged, abysmal fall. Before he could die, he would wake up with a shriek burning in his throat, sit up in bed, soaked in perspiration, panting, and wonder why none of the other soldiers in his barrack had awakened to his scream; just then, or nearly, two dark eyes of a woman would appear and stare at him in the darkness, and as if taking a cue from those eyes he would then turn on his side, afraid, still half-asleep, learning once again, that he had just dreamed a dream within a dream. A scorpion of fear would flex its tail in his heart, forcing him to keep his eyes closed.

II

Naeb Subaltern Prem Lal Singh was of a proven Rajput stock; his forefathers were the Hindu warriors who, under Raja Ranjit Singh *kana*, had held off the British from entering the five rivers. While defending the Punjab, some of his forefathers had, according to family legend, achieved martyrdom, and the knowledge of this profound sacrifice would oblige Prem Lal always to keep his head high with pride. A century later his ancestors once again had proved their mettle, not just in India but in the Middle East and Africa, fighting for the British. The list of martyrs was longer than that of the ones who returned, with missing limbs like his uncle Mukhan Singh *tunda*.

Prem stood out from other non-commissioned officers of the 502 Punjab Corps in the Delhi Cantonment, for his dark bluish-copper, ever-glinting skin, sweat or no-sweat; he also left an image of his face stamped in people's minds due to his unusually high cheek bones, his broad forehead, the slightly mismatched, half-Chinese eyes, but above all for his oil-tweaked, proudly twirled moustache that curled upwards to touch the inward climb of his cheekbones. As a veteran of two wars with Pakistan, once on the western frontier and once on the eastern, his stock would always be high among his peers no matter where he was stationed. One could safely assume that he had seen Dacca; and, yes, indeed, he had even seen the great General Arora snatch the medals off the shirt of the Tiger of Bengal, General Niazi. The shiver he'd experienced in his spine then seemed to have left its memory there, like a permanent taste of poison.

In the service of the Indian Army he had been stationed all over the country, east west north south, you name it, and yet there were only a handful of places he considered worth remembering, Lucknow being the best, closely followed by Hyderabad of the Nizam. The worst was Calcutta, he would tell an acquaintance snidely, but when asked why he thought so, he would admit, reluctantly, that it was more of a feeling perhaps than any particular experience; it's like not being able to breathe easily, he would say, or sleep well. But, ah! he would sigh

deeply, 'I'll always remember, *wah*! Lucknow and the delicate
balconies of the houses there...and the women...' He would also
recall, though fleetingly, the intermingling of Urdu and Telegu,
the Chaar Minar, the Nampally Station, and the malignant tree
shadows in the sweltering heat of the notorious Hyderabad
afternoons.

Since adulthood he had been drawn to classical music,
probing into the mysteries of *raags* and *thumris* and *ghazals*,
which was quite unusual for a person of his rugged background,
the son of peasants who traditionally loved *bhangra*, sang *joogni*,
or listened to *qawwalis*. After all, he was only a senior Naeb
Subaltern, a man without a college degree. He became the butt
of jokes behind his back for this obsession with *raags* and
raagnis; to add yet another shade of ridicule, it was known in
the vicinity of the Cantonment District that he carried with him
a small transistor radio day and night, rain or shine. It couldn't
be seen, but everyone knew it was hidden inside his pocket. A
friend had even joked once, '*Oe-hoy*, do you take your shower
too with it, *enh*? Bhai Saheb?'

'I'm a religious man, Mian ji; this is my pocket-sized Gita,
made in Japan,' he had answered with a smile.

But Mian wasn't the kind whose hair had gone grey from the
sun alone, and his kind knew precisely when to lash back; as
expected, he retorted, 'Bhai Saheb, the Gita-*shita* is fine I agree
one hundred percent, but *kabhi kabhi* one should, I say, step
inside a temple as well, *naheen*? and offer a *pranam* to the gods
made in Hindustan with Hindustani material.' There had
followed a roar of laughter from the bench-sitters, tea-sippers.
The sister-fuckers! Prem had bestowed them with the appropriate
appellation, silently.

'What can I do, Mian ji? Your gods won't let me inside their
home,' he'd replied. 'Their scorn checks my feet at the door.
Besides, I'm a lover, not a worshipper; my sins are too heavy
for any god to forgive.'

One tea-sipper had shaken his head and exclaimed: 'Premji,
you're a lost soul, lost.' Another man, aged and toothless, had

added, as he constantly picked at his teeth, though good-humoredly, 'Go, go listen to your *ghazals*, *Mussla bhaenchod*!'

Walking away, smiling, he repeated, 'Not a worshipper... *Mussla bhaen...*'

III

With the greyness of four decades in his hair, Prem remained a bachelor, such an oddity in this culture for a man with a steady income and government privileges that it lent tongue to spicy tales of impotence, betrayal, and unrequited love. One rumour was that ever since he'd seen *Bhoomika* he had been in love with Samita Patel, who had recently died in labour; another version had it that their distracted subaltern adored Shabana Azmi because she was not only an actress but also a social worker and a poet's daughter. A young *chaiwalla* went so far as to claim that he had actually spotted a Shabana Azmi poster on his wall with all the faces of the male actors scissored out. But then frequent stretches of imagination of this sort are, in a sense, what Hindustan is all about.

The reality, however, was quite different from what entered idle ears: Prem Singh had been born in Lahore, and while only a year old had lost both his parents to the madness of Partition. He and his relatives somehow managed to reach India alive as beggars, uprooted like trees in a storm, some half-insane and a few beyond recovery. Orphaned, he managed to finish high school somehow and then joined the army as a corporal. In the beginning he would hide his face under the bed sheet and cry, missing his estranged half-insane relatives, while the other soldiers slept soundly in the same barrack, a few snoring occasionally. He especially missed his younger uncle, Makhan Lal Singh *tunda*, who'd gone insane after the Partition and hung about the neighbourhood during the days, by turns chasing after stray dogs and being chased by them. Sometimes Prem would have to go two neighbourhoods down to find Makhan sleeping by the roadside with his mouth ajar for the flies' inspection, the dried snot blocking his nostrils. Prem would wake him up, dust his clothes, and lure him back to the house. The two wars took him farther and farther away from his family, and now he would only receive the occasional letter written by a relative usually announcing the death of a family member. Replying, he would pay his condolences and add: *I am deeply grieved to hear about...I am sorry to say that I cannot get to attend the chitta burning. Yours obediently, Prem.* And as time went on he finally lost the sense of ever having had a family, and soon became quite disenchanted with the idea of getting married and forming his own little nest.

Many years ago in Lucknow, however, he had had a short, bitter-sweet love affair with a Muslim school teacher. She taught at the Cantonment High School, inside the military compound, and while coming inside and on her way out to the street she walked past the window of his office twice a day, five days a week. The steady and determined click-click of her heels against the pavement alerted the men, distracting them from work. Along with the other soldiers, he admired her youthfulness; as discreetly as possible, his eyes, too, ravished the cut and trim of her figure. He couldn't behave vulgarly the way others did, with their whispers and moans, straight out of the Hindi movies, of *wah ji wah*! or *hai ram*! *margya ji*! Nevertheless, she had caught him looking with the subdued flame of longing in his eyes. Each time, his blood had burned from embarrassment. Still, the next day, as soon as he recognized the strike of her heels, his head turned to her in defiance of his shyness. This game of looking and not looking, of averted glances and hesitant invitations, of curved lips, the beckoning of her curves written in the ancient language of loneliness across the screaming blackboard of his desire went on for a few months, and then on one of those rainy days when the streets of the old city become small rivers and clouds pump in continuously, our Prem Singh in the best of Lucknavi attire, his moustache freshly oiled, curled, and pointed, found himself standing outside her door on his two shaky feet, distractedly gripping an umbrella, suffocating in the push and shove of whether to knock or still turn away gracefully.

Then a few years later in Hyderabad he had seduced with his manly persistence a Christian woman with big dark eyes, eyes that cut and healed at the same time. Her eyes were the knife, he believed, that entered your flesh with a dash of balm on its tip. She was the wife of the gardener who tended the grounds of the premise. Prem once brought her silver bangles from Agra, and a pair of silver anklets from Jodhpur; she would wear them only when she came to visit him. During one monsoon he slept with her almost every day for a whole month, still he felt alone and lonely at nights. While the husband mowed the grass, tilled the small patches of earth, and watered the mulberry trees close to Prem's window, Prem would lie beside her, dissolved in her presence, hearing the swish-swosh of the lazy sickle. He would examine her dark skin for long moments, like a soldier mapping out a dangerous territory at night, and savour the clove-like odour of her back. He was mesmerized by the colour's absorbency. Is it the colour of nothingness? Is there such a thing as nothingness? Is death nothingness? he would . . .

Only from time to time now did he think of the Muslim schoolteacher, her voice and its sadness echoing in his mind. Then he would remember how much he had enjoyed the sight of her narrow waist and small, shapely hips as she would get up in the morning to bring him tea, and often the *ghazals* of Ghalib, Dagh or Momin, to recite in bed. But strangely enough not much had remained of the Christian woman's memory, and every time he tried to conjure up scenes of the sweltering Hyderabad afternoons when their bodies lay locked like mating snakes, all he could muster was a nostalgic whiff of her odour in his nostrils like a scent of death. If this thought came to him while he tried to sleep, he turned on his side, then shifted to the other, from the heaviness of the memory. Or from the lack of it. Yet, when asleep, he would dream of her dark eyes.

IV

Premji, or Premiya, or Premi, as he was sometimes called, received the transfer order one day as he was sunning himself outside his barrack in Delhi. Holding the paper in his hand, he felt an unfamiliar tinge of melancholy; the lower lid of his right eye fluttered a few times, as it did when he had something on his mind. He wasn't afraid of going to Kashmir, nor was he afraid of death. He traced the restlessness of his heart to the young prostitute, Baby Madhubala, to whom he had been growing quite attached. If he had been married in time, his daughter would have been her age, but this thought did not bother him. The young prostitute had auditioned for All India Radio twice and failed accordingly, yet it was her determination that had impressed Prem, along with her succulent lips and her openness to planting a kiss wherever he desired. When a little drunk, our subaltern would ask her to sing a *ghazal*; but, alas, she was not classically trained and could not sing *ghazals* or *thumris*; her voice did not know the contours of nostalgia the way, he recalled, the Muslim teacher's had. At the most, she could sing songs from the films *Pakeeza* and *Mughal-e-Azam*, acting out the lines, also, from her favourite films. Once she startled Prem as she'd spoken, 'I am not a phantom, but a reality,' with such seriousness that it took him a full moment to realize that this was a famous line from the movie *Mahal*. She could be Meena Kumari one minute, the other Nootan. This acting business of hers bothered him, though he pushed the thought to the periphery of the zone of comfort in his mind.

He had moved out of women's lives before, and would again, without an apology or an excuse, with no promises to return or write a *prempatr*, without regret, even guilt. He steeled his heart, reprimanding himself silently: '*O bhaenchoda*! You can't lose your heart to a bazaari woman. Snap out of it, *o bubber shera*! Move on. *Hulla hulla hulla*!' In a week he had packed up and was off to the Valley, in the back of a jeep with two full subalterns, Anand Hira the *pakora*-nosed and Ranbir Malik the chinless, one stiffer than his uniform and the other a sagging quilt, neither with the slightest taste for Hindustani classical music or courtesans—now followed by a caravan of mud-green trucks bearing the five hundred strong men of the Five-O-Two Punjab Regiment.

For some days after his arrival, he felt unsettled by the impossibility of holding anyone's gaze on the streets for a decent minute; their downcast or averted eyes made him want to approach them and order, 'Look up! Look at me, *saley*!' Initially, it made him want to strangle them. But that cold anger had dissipated in a week, leaving an iciness behind in his fingers, and now he too kept his eyes wandering, a restless pair of hawks, as if searching for the lost childhood of his innocent memory. People emerged from the masjids and mandirs, shops and houses, with faces devoid of any impulse to offer salaam or namastay. It was as though he had been stationed in a graveyard full of wandering ghosts and shadows. The shuttered windows frightened him. Looking up at the balconies where clothes dried on a string, fluttering in the wind, he was reminded of the people missing from those clothes.

On his day off he would venture outside the barracks in the afternoon and look up at the famous sky of the Valley, which now appeared colourless to him, and feel that people had polluted the sky as well. As he walked back to his room, plucking a flower here and a leaf there, the air he breathed stifled him as though evacuated of its fragrance and music. He was a man who kept his thoughts to himself for the most part, and only conversed with his own demons during his long nights alone. He had been ruminating on how to meet a tribal woman, if there was such a thing here, from the nearby hills, Hindu or Muslim or Buddhist, anyone with firm thighs and breasts and a pussy that's from *swarg*; religion was nothing to him but a hurdle to getting in bed with someone, a potential deterrent which he desperately tried to avoid. Every evening, he would trim, oil, and twirl his moustache to his heart's content, and once done go out for a lazy stroll, listening to the little Gita. Early the next morning he would be patrolling the streets and city outskirts with fellow soldiers, sometimes in an army jeep, leaving behind, at sudden turns, an agitated ghost of dust. Sometimes he was ordered to maintain a tight checkpoint at a certain fork of streets where one of his men stood behind a machine gun inside a bunker, his helmeted-head visible through the hole like a turtle.

V

One very hot afternoon as Prem fought off the suffocating heat by drinking a glass after glass of lemonade, sucking on pieces of ice while listening to Begum Akhtar sing a *thumri* in the *Raag Mishra Kafi* '*Jab se Shyam sidhare, ho...*' his thoughts were interrupted by the sudden arrival of the short, stocky corporal Subhash Thakur, whom a few soldiers had nick-named *gol-gappa*. He turned down his radio. Subhash, from a Bengali peasant background, had tremendous respect for Prem Singh because the son of the Rajput had been promoted twice since he had known him. He had on a few occasions earnestly attempted to strike up a friendship with his Premji, but nothing had ever materialized; they remained no more than acquaintances. Undoubtedly, Prem was to blame for this failure, as he was extremely cautious by nature except for his propensity to yield to the needs of flesh. Also, he had unconsciously adopted certain prejudices, beliefs not informed by direct experiences. All Bengalis, to him, were brainy and intrigue-driven; were cowards and not hard-working, and even when he saw Thakur sweating under the sun digging a trench or carrying a heavy sack, he could not bring together in his mind Bengalis and hard work. But Subhash had his own analogy for the unrequited friendship: he ascribed it to Prem's inability to appreciate the river song aesthetic of Bengali poetry. Subhash assumed, discomfittingly, that Prem thought of him nothing more than a *bong*, a simpleton.

Now Prem Singh smiled. 'Aao, Bhai Subhash ji, *ki haal haye*?'

'*Durga maa's* grace, Bhai Shaheb. *Accha* ji, lishtening to *gojols*?'

Prem Singh, embarrassed, shrugged his shoulders as he clicked off the sound. Then he asked, 'How's family-*shamily*, Thakur?'

'*Durga maa's* blesshing, Shaheb.' Then he added, 'Wife's letter arrived today; all is fine, ji.'

'Well, what brought you to my humble abode, Bhai?'

'Oh ji, Naeb Shaheb, *tushi ko Caapitan* Khana Shaheb is calling, ji,' said Thakur.

Prem Singh went to his room and changed into his uniform, took one quick look in the mirror, chiefly to assure himself of the stiffness of the moustache, then hurried to present himself to the newly arrived Captain Khana. Dank and dimly lit, the new Captain's headquarters was a temporary office, situated on the other side of the Mess Hall, which Prem visited, to his acute displeasure, twice a day. He preferred eating out in the mixed company of civilians, as the rare sight of a woman late in the evening pleased him immensely. As he now crossed the untended garden which separated the two pale-yellow-bricked buildings, his eyes scanning the overgrown grass and weeds and dried hedges, he caught the incipient sound, in the depth of his mind, of rusty scissors going swish-swosh, swish-swosh. But instead of the image of the scissor-blades, his mind conjured up the misty memory of the Christian woman's dark legs curling around his. As he ran up the entrance steps, he felt somehow that he was carrying the extra weight of someone else's existence inside him; he shook his head to clear it of any distraction, then opened the door. At least for the next hour, his country needed him, and the Captain must have his attention.

A young, handsome Captain Khana sat behind the desk with files on one side and an ashtray on the other. Prem Singh halted on entering the door and saluted. Khana motioned him to stand at ease and he reluctantly relaxed. The red glow ringed by ash at the burning end of the cigar between the Captain's teeth cast a sudden bright circle on his face. Prem Singh then realized that Subedar Malik and Hira were also present in the room; noticing that he was about to salute them, the latter shook his head and winked at him. The Captain stood up, leaving his cigar slowly burning in the ashtray.

'Our country needs us again, Singh Saheb,' said Khana.

'Yes, sir,' answered Prem. He stole a glance at the other two men in the room. The weakly lit room resembled a hospital ward. Captain Khana informed him that five experienced soldiers of different ranks had been selected by the High Command; under Prem's leadership, they were to leave the following evening for a highly strategic point near the Kashmir border in an attempt to capture, dead or alive, a band of infiltrators trained in Pakistan about whom the Indian authorities had been tipped-off. Captain Khana scrutinized his face for any reaction; there was none, and satisfied by Prem's stolid expression he then spread across the table a large map, detailing the zones of activity. Holding the mahogany cane, he tapped with its pointed tip crucial points of intersection as he invited the other two subalterns over for a look. A dust-covered light bulb above their heads shed a dismal light on the map of two Kashmirs. Prem's eyes travelled with the tip of his Captain's cane along the curvy red lines, and he nodded whenever he felt Khana's eyes fix upon him. Throughout the briefing, Singh remained focused and silent except for once when he caught himself sniffing rather unconsciously; at that moment a sudden faint but sad giggle of Baby Madhubala of Dilli had burst into his mind. Was she doing her Sharmila Tagore routine? He sniffed it out, hunh!...hu...! and then rather comically squinted his brows which no one in the room noticed.

'Is everything clear, Naeb?' the Captain asked, concluding.

'Yes, sir.'

'Good luck then.'

'Thank you, sir.'

As he stepped out into the harsh light of the day, he felt mildly perturbed for no clear reason, and as he walked off he decided the scorching heat must be responsible for the sudden discontent in his heart.

VI

The next day just at sunset an army jeep picked up the six men from the Intelligence Headquarters and after a long journey of countless zigzags dropped them off at an abandoned looking check-point bunker. But soon two soldiers appeared and saluted them. The six men returned the salute. The jeep made a U-turn, awakened an another agitated ghost of dust, and soon disappeared before vanishing.

Within minutes the five commandos and Prem were walking southward in search of the desired trail; they walked for more than three miles, zigzagging along the waists and hems of the hills to arrive at the edge of their mission zone. All six of them kept a ready finger on the strong spring of the trigger, holding their guns tightly on the uneven paths. They knew they could be finished off here, ambushed in the dark by an already alerted enemy. Two hours later they reached the spot taken as their main compass-point. Under the glow of a mini torch held by a Tamil soldier, Prem Singh unfolded, on a fairly flat rock, a map showing hundreds of thin black and red and green lines cancelling each other all across the crumpled surface. Twenty minutes later, their precise mission set and memorized, the five strong men branched out in five directions like a trembling human hand only to criss-cross each other every forty to fifty yards. The men were under order to return before sunrise. The five soon disappeared behind the trees and bushes, into the jaws of the night. Subedar Singh, with a mild pang of guilt, looked at his wristwatch, and sighed, 'An hour still!'

An hour later he pulled out his transistor radio from the inner pocket of his green-khaki jacket. In one movement he flicked it on and brought it extremely close to his right ear, running his finger meticulously over the black dial. It was a Wednesday night, and Islamabad Short Wave One transmitted a two-hour long programme of *ghazals* every Wednesday and Friday night. The stations from across the border were hard to pick up in the Valley, but back in Dilli the sound poured in like a stream of clear water, even during the monsoon. After he had arrived in

Srinagar he had asked a dozen or so intimidated people if they
knew of a local station that played *ghazals* or classical music
sometime during the week. It was like trying to engage ghosts
in a conversation. But one night, as he was sipping Kashmiri
chai at the Sheikh Bhai's stall, Sheikh Bhai raised his hand
automatically to the big radio set into the wall to change the
station where a few tired voices were discussing the political
calamity in Afghanistan. Sheikh Bhai himself liked *ghazals*, but
settled for what Prem would call the pseudo *ghazal*; still it
owed to Sheikh Bhai's restless hand that Prem discovered the
local station that played them. Islamabad Short Wave One—
which he was now trying to tune—he had found by keeping the
radio on for long hours, fiddling with the dial as he strolled
along the verandah, fending off the boredom that always
threatened to overwhelm him in the absence of a woman's
intimacy. He hated modern Hindi film music, which one heard
at every shop, and it depressed him to reflect on the kind of
music people had fallen prey to. For this reason alone he would
always remember his time with the Muslim school teacher, her
impeccable taste in music and poetry; he would always
remember the love with which she sang Mir, Ghalib, Dagh,
Faiz, Munir, Kaifi Azmi, the way she would explain a verse
from Kishwar Naheed, *with wounds it chisels the figure of
decline* . . .

He had learned to ignore the constant hissing, that tended to
underlie the music here, as a form of curse of sins from the past
lives of the listener. Only on rare occasions, when the sky was
clear and the wind was quiet, did the radio capture the clear
sound of a voice. Even then the sound would suddenly warp
and wave, fading in and out. The vanishing of the voice in the
midst of things made him pull at his hair; he would imagine
crushing the cockroach of a radio under the wrath of his heel.
But he would think twice, and the sanctity of his holy Gita
remained untouched.

Now he moved the dial forward with his index finger and
waited, then ran it backwards. He repeated this a few times at
different speeds, but without luck. He had to keep the volume

extremely low. He recalled the second time he had gone to the teacher's house in the evening for tea and had stayed the night; they had had to speak in whispers because she lived with her grandfather who in his old age was going blind but not deaf. No matter how carefully and slowly he moved the dial all he got was a crackling sound, as if the enemy was mocking him from inside the radio. He grew flustered, shifted the radio up and down around an imaginary axis, tilting it left, tilting it right. He had to suppress again the urge to smash the radio against the jagged edge of a rock some ten feet away from him. He remembered that it had begun to drizzle towards the end of that evening, and as he observed the light rain through the fluttering curtains she had asked him if he would like to see her room; they could talk in their normal voices there she had added, and giggled softly. Her mouth at that moment had made him think of Punjabi rosebuds. Since then, he had addressed her as Gulab, or simply Gul, in his mind. He had stayed the night. It had been the most fulfilling night of his life. Yet he'd never fallen in love with her. But he would often recognize the red-tiled verandah of her house in his dreams, and sometimes felt her presence behind his ear, as if whispering *Gulab...*

He clutched the radio tightly in his grip. He realized he was beginning to sweat, and then, as he shifted the radio to his left hand the tip of his thumb slipped off the dial and he fleetingly caught the sound of a human voice, sending a jolt to his heart. His body tensed with heat, as though engulfed in a *chitta* burning. This time he caught the voice and did not mind the devil-sent crackling which wounded his heart more than his ear. Mehdi Hassan—he recognized the voice instantly, a voice so deep and tranquil he thought he would weep. There must be some truth to what Lata had said, he reflected, that Bhagwan's chariot had passed through his throat. To him the voice seemed to emerge from the depths of the Indian Ocean in the shape of pearls. What if he were caught with the radio up to his ear? He would certainly be court-martialled; a sweat of worry pearled on his forehead. But he had hardly lowered his hand when the singer's voice, smooth as the morning breeze, reached the end of a famous verse with a nascent tremor, then rose like a wave, drowning every other thought in him. The fear of getting caught, or having his head blown off by an enemy bullet, dissipated. The hand clutching the radio moved back to his ear.

'I like your skin, I'm fascinated by its deceptive shades,' she'd whispered into his ear after kissing the lobe. The memory almost made him move the radio away. Getting out of bed, she would involuntarily hum a half-forgotten *ghazal*, and her voice in its morning huskiness would waft like smoke to his nostrils as though he could smell the voice, the words, even her moments of silence.

He recognized the notes of the *raag* in which the *ghazal* was being sung: *Basant Bahar*, a night *raag* of the *Purvi tthaat*, sung slow and in lower notes, with a long *alap*. *Basant Bahar's* dominant note was *pa* with *ma komal* with *ma ga ma ga* in the ascendant and the addition of *ra* in the descending scale; the *raag's* primary concern, if he recalled it correctly, was to heighten the sense of longing with a tinge of joy. He noted that Mehdi Hassan was throwing the *sam*, the cyclic stress on the word '*andaz*', making Prem's entire body react at that point, as if in a spasm, to the *sam*; a pair of invisible hands was playing the set of *tablas* inside his mind.

   umr to sari kati ishq e butaan mayn, Momin
   akhri waqt ab khak mussalman hongey

'All my life I spent adoring idols, Momin!' Prem remembered explaining this particular couplet to Subhash Thakur and Kashi Nath one night. 'At the last hour, I cannot pretend to be a Muslim.' Thakur had nodded his head and Kashi Nath swayed his torso, though Prem had thought that both had failed to grasp the essence of the couplet. Now Prem Singh suddenly found a new meaning within the meaning; such was the world of *ghazals*, and so much, he mused, depended on how long one had known the couplet and how deeply or crudely, the singer interpreted the verse. He was drowning in his own universe of music. The combination of the voice and the harmonium was like two ancient rivers falling into an embrace. Oh! this would leave him drunk for days. In the singer's voice resonated a unique relationship between the consonant notes of *Basant Bahar* and the soul of the couplet. The voice, he felt, poured from a silver decanter filling the goblet of his solitude.

Big, dark eyes, silent and forgiving Christian eyes; he often called them the eyes of Jesus, and sometimes the eyes of Mariam. He hated her shyness though, her stubborn refusal to sing—even *Bande Matram*. When she lay next to him she would suddenly close her eyes, as if she were closing the doors and windows of her house to him. And her silence on the day of his transfer was like cobra fangs suspended an inch from his heart. The fact that he never felt any remorse for lying to her, telling her that he was leaving on a temporary assignment, in fact, surprised him. But her silence, he knew, would hurt him once he had left; yes, her silence: he would scream *bhaenchod ki batchi*! silently, knowing those dark eyes knew his lie.

It was past midnight. He had drunk in an hour of *ghazal* music like an addict who needs his hit of hashish; the radio was back in his pocket. He looked at his watch, then up at the sky, finally resting his gaze on the thin crescent sleeping in the dark. The weak moonlight had added a thin coating of silver to the earth, the distant landscape, the tree tops; the peaks of the distant mountains were mysteriously visible and if a wild animal had climbed up there now and howled, Prem considered, he would be able to make out the beast's silhouette. He glanced casually at his rifle, which he had left leaning against a tree a few inches from his feet. The bayonet had dug into the wood, leaving a shallow cut. He grabbed the rifle and gripped it as if ready to ambush. The absurdity of this urgent stance brought a soft smile to his face. He let go of the weapon with one hand and lowered its butt onto the ground. '*Taab e nazara hi naheen, aayina kya dekhney...*' the words of the *ghazal* flowed back to his consciousness, then slid down to his lips. 'You cannot bear the sight, how can I let you see the mirror; you will become a portrait struck with wonder.'

'Take me to a mandir someday, Premu,' she had asked him. 'Diwali is coming.' They stood under the tin-roofed shelter on the back verandah of her house. It was dark except for the faint glow from the lantern hanging by the door frame; the smell of kerosene oil hung in the air. Holding her face in his strong hands, he had tried to read her eyes, their past, their many mysteries, as they stared back at him without shyness. 'I don't go there, haven't been to one in such a long time I wouldn't know the difference between a mandir and a gurdwara,' he had answered with neither guilt nor contempt. 'Why?' she had asked. 'Why? Because I hate gods, or perhaps I'm scared of gods and goddesses, scared of their stony eyes. Those hardened stares stifle me.'

It was then, after a long silence, that she told him that she had been married once, that now she was a widow, a young widow. His hands had slid down to her neck, her shoulders, and then he had hugged her, and the limp embrace of her arms around him made him ask how her husband had died. She had remained silent. He had insisted on knowing; her husband, she told him then, clutching his shirt fabric, had been a journalist who worked for *The Hindu*, and she had loved him. Hearing this, he had released her to hold her face in his hands once again; she continued, 'He was killed as he was returning home from work on the 10th of Moharram when he ran into a Hindu mob', which had clashed earlier with a Muslim one at the other end of Umeed Street. 'Someone had recognized him and his scooter,' and the shouts had erupted: 'Catch that *sala harami*, that son of Babur; get the Mughal bastard!'

By the time Aurangzeb died, Rajput blood had already claimed Mughal veins: Prem had read that in a book. She had stopped crying at the memory of her husband a few years back; she believed in life, not death, she had told Prem. In the slightly pungent smell of the kerosene, he uncupped his hands from her face. Perhaps he should have held her, comforted her, planted a caring kiss on her half-moist lips, he had thought hours later, but he hadn't been able to muster the desire. That moment of apathy gradually had turned into a memory of cowardice that tugged at his conscience from time to time.

It was two in the morning now, and he glanced up at the moon, which seemed to be growing. '*Navak andaz jidhar ...*' he caught himself singing quietly again. Midway through the *ghazal* he thought: what kind of a soldier have I become? He was seized with a sudden uneasiness, an unpleasant sensation of having been used, or cheated by a higher authority. Governments? Gods? Fate? Who? Whom could he blame? He questioned himself quite loudly in his mind. Whom could he blame for this inertia of his soul? All his life, it seemed, had been put to useless goals, and all he was left with was his loneliness and the heaviness of being. The fact that he had never said good-bye to Qurrat-ul-ain, the teacher, weighed on him now. He gazed into the distance, then blinked and breathed deeply, having learned from experience that deep breathing always drove his thoughts away. He spat on the ground in mild disgust and began to pace back and forth, keeping a vigil in the pale darkness as he strove to avert the thoughts that poisoned his mind, to re-focus on his soldiers, his precious men who would be returning soon. He even brought his fingers to his moustache to give it a stylish twirl, but his hand lost the desire midway.

The thought of not being able to go to Pakistan, to go and visit Lahore, the city of his birth, to walk through the Anarkali Bazaar or sit by the bank of the river Ravi crept over him with sadness. Looking at his boots, quite visible under the moonlight, to which his eyes had grown adjusted, gave him a sudden feeling of nakedness. Uncomfortably, he shifted his gaze to an unfocused spot on the earth away from his boots.

Prem Singh realized that he had been staring at a crawling insect as it inched ahead with remarkable slowness. He watched the insect with the seriousness of a thinker, and in that moment of absorption he noticed that the insect was carrying a smaller insect in its mouth. Prem considered for a minute the kind of fight the victim might have put up. Could it be still alive, and in fact struggling to get out of the bigger insect's mouth? Before he knew it he had lowered himself almost to a squatting position, observing the hunter and the hunted. He had put one knee on the ground to stay closer to the insects when his ears pricked up at the sound of a faint rustle. He froze, his neck tensed; an invisible lump formed in his throat.

He gripped his rifle with both hands, ready to fire instantaneously at the slightest danger. His eyes darted frenetically in the darkness, suspiciously interpreting every ambiguous pattern of light and shade. He breathed slowly. One knee glued to the ground, he stayed where he was. He heard the soft rustle again, shorter in length by a fraction of a second this time, so that even by concentrating he was unable to detect the direction from which the sound had come from. Suddenly Prem was gripped by a fear of being killed by the enemy before he could even spot him. He felt the sweat break out on his forehead; a drop actually slid down the side of his nose and disappeared into the abyss of his moustache. His ears caught the sound again, and for a second he thought he'd caught a subtle movement somewhere quite a distance off, but he couldn't be sure. Holding the rifle in his hands, closing one eye, he sighted through the target-lens. He narrowed one half-Chinese eye, keeping the other closed, penetrated with his burning gaze the fabric of night, and detected a form resembling a human lying flat on the ground. His heart began to pound, matching a particular *tabla* rhythm *bhoom bhoom babhoom*... He squinted harder. There! He spotted the half luminous head of a man, then witnessed the entire body stealthily crawl up the side of a hill like a maggot. He surveyed the landscape around the man, hoping to catch sight of his fellow infiltrators, but he spotted none. Swinging the cross-hairs back to the man's head, Prem adjusted the rifle's aim to a perfect bull's-eye.

He wanted to wait for the enemy to finish his climb, arrive at a little plateau-like area, and be more exposed to the bullet; that way he would have a better shot at capturing the bastard alive. He waited with a tortoise's patience. Is my enemy Kashmiri? A strange thought at a very inappropriate time. If he is one from our side, then...? Humh! Then the bastard is my countryman, isn't he? And what if the *harami* is from Muzzafargarh, or Pakistan? Oh, Babur's son is still an enemy infiltrator and a big

mother*chod* on top of that. Prem was aware of an unsettled
sense of happiness at knowing he had the fool pretty much in
pocket. Suddenly he aimed the muzzle to the sky, catching the
moon in the cross-hairs, but quickly brought the weapon back
to the crawling head. What if he is Punjabi? The thought amused
him, but as it faded it left an unsettling trail. 'He could be a
Rajput, or a Mughal with Rajput blood in his arms, his legs, his
head.' Prem shook his head to derail the undesired train of
thoughts. '*Navak andaz jidhar deeda e* ...' Mehdi Hassan's
voice awoke in his mind without any warning, curving and
rising with every other syllable, and Prem noticed that his hands
shook a bit. The voice, in his mind, was throwing the *sam* on
the word '*andaz*'—splitting it, *an'da'aaz*—and the fingers of
the *tabla* player were following him like a maddened snake.
This sudden intrusion vexed him.

The thoughts he had tried to banish earlier found their way
back into his mind again. So what if he is a Punjabi, so what if
he is a *kanjar* Rajput, he's still a *bhaenchod Mussla* and a
murderer of innocent Hindus. *Bham! Bham!* His mind fired two
bullets. Didn't they colour their hands with our blood? With a
surging pain the thought which he had tried to bury a thousand
times resurrected in him: the vague memory of his parents whose
lives the conflagration of Partition had consumed. 'Look,' he'd
pointed to his eyes, 'look deep into my eyes, Qurrat-ul-ain
Begum; do you see the flames way back in them?' She had first
nonchalantly looked into them, narrowed her eyes, then as if a
little frightened she had withdrawn from him, though still staring
at his face, obscurely understanding the depth of his pain. He
spoke again, 'Those are the fires still burning from my
childhood. Bhagwan is my witness, I have tried to put them out,
I have tried and tried and tried..., but they keep flaring up
again...I am a live volcano, Qurrat-ul-ain.'

Prem saw the man approach the plateau and tightened his
grip on the rifle. He prayed, 'O Bhagwan, give me *shakti*!'

The infiltrator seemed young from the distance. Prem tried
guessing his age. Unlucky *bhaenchod*! Prem felt a moment's
pity for the wretched soul.

'Freeze! whoever you are, or you'll be shot.' Prem took a few strong steps forward, then heard his own echo talk back to him. *Freeeeeze*! *Whoooo*...The man froze instantly.

'Now put your hands up and stand up slowly. *Now put yourrrr...* No smart move, you hear me?' he yelled. '*No smart moooo...*'

The man put his hands up in the air, as he half stood, but then, as if judging the direction and distance of Prem's voice, he started running downhill, veering away.

'I said, *Freeeeeze*!' But the man kept running. Prem ran out from behind the bush, craning the muzzle to follow the running head. Bending his knees a bit, he curled his index finger on the cold trigger, then pressed it. *Bham*! A Rajput, a warrior, an excellent marksman, he had awakened the night. His finger still pressed against the trigger, he felt as if the bullet had pierced his own lungs. His body was suddenly made of holes, drenched in a monsoon of sweat. A maddening violence was about to explode somewhere in him and he would be a man in thousand pieces. Yet in the midst of the fury inside him he detected a dim voice singing, singing something in his mind... Qurrat-ul-ain's voice?... mingling with the vicious pounding of his heart... he noticed the smoke still oozing from the end of the barrel, a crack in the mirror of night. And as he peered straight into the night, he felt he was staring straight into the Christian woman's dark eyes. Into Mariam's eyes. He was suddenly afraid that she would close them, shutting the doors and windows of her house of memory on him. A burning howl was lodged in his throat and he wished it were only a dream within a dream.

FAHMIDA RIAZ

Fahmida Riaz is a renowned Urdu poet and writer, as well as a feminist and human rights activist. In 1997, Human Rights Watch gave her the Hemmet Hellman Award. She has published 13 works of Urdu prose and poetry, including *Badan Dareedah*, (Maktab-e-Danyal, 1973) which was Pakistan's first volume of feminist poetry. Her work has been extensively translated into English including *Zinda Bahar Lane*, translated by Aquila Ismail (City Press, 2000). She wrote her only English novel, *People*, while living in exile in India. She now lives in Karachi, where she runs a publishing house, WADA, for women and children.

AMINA IN HIGH WATERS[1]

Amina came to Karachi from London in 1972 and then completely lost track of time. Much as she tried, she could not correctly recall when she obtained a divorce from her husband, who lived in London (*soon...soon after I came back, she would lamely mumble to herself*), nor could she remember when she re-married, or when a child was born to her. She had to count backwards to get at the exact year of its birth. *The child is four and it is now '83; in '82, it was three; in '81 it was two...*and then she quickly forgot it again. *Why? ... Why can't I recall dates? What year was it?* ... she thought and cried helplessly.

Amina sat alone in the vast and vacant backyard of the University guesthouse. Not in Karachi, not even in Pakistan. This was Delhi, in the grip of a roaring monsoon. Fascinated, she watched the downpour, the pink, forked lightning and thunder. Suddenly vast expanses would light up before her eyes revealing tall, slender, Asoka trees tossing in the howling wind. She was both thrilled and miserable, drenched to the roots of

---

1. From an unpublished English novel, *People*.

her hair, wishing with all her heart the rain would never cease—
and grappling with a hopelessly befogged memory.

In the past, Amina did not care for chronology. She never
looked back. (Well yes, she did not look back). Ever since she
returned to Pakistan in 1972, the only year that mattered, she
had been preoccupied with doing things. She did not envision
time as passing away, but rather saw it coming straight towards
her, as one feels water, while swimming upstream. She had set
the course of her life with clarity and was free to do whatever.
But what kind of clarity was it, that so befogged her memory?
Now when she looked back, when she had to look back, she
could see no landmarks. Ahead of her, there lay only a blank.

*Have I been sleepwalking all these years? Deluding myself
... walking in a thick, milky fog? It is now unbearable. Anything
is better than this.* She wrung her hands and wept.

Why did she yearn to cut out the fog? Why now? Murad had
been unfaithful to her for years, perhaps since the very first
months of their marriage. In the past, he had denied it
vehemently. Suddenly, one day, when she questioned him,
pathetically, about her suspicions, he made a confession: he
brutally smashed her tremulous white world of cloudy delusions,
leaving her with no choice but to face the truth.

Amina broke down.

When they were living in Karachi, Amina had fitfully noticed
her own odd behaviour, her irrational fears, their inability to
make love happily. She never went to a psychiatrist. Psychiatry
in Pakistan is not even a fashionable pastime. Magic charms
from darvaishes are held in a far higher esteem. Perhaps it was
really more sensible to visit a darvaish. Saints and darvaishes
asked no questions and you did not have to strip your soul
naked before a stranger. They understood that you were suffering
and simply wrote down a charm, promising peace and
fulfillment. The small piece of paper, with mysterious,
undecipherable graphs, memorials and letters, gave you the gift
of hope.

Amina did not believe in darvaishes, or their charms, yet she
would have laughed in derision had anyone suggested

psychotherapy. Like all writers, she was convinced that she knew better psychology than the professionals.

Amina was a poet. She was editing a politico-literary journal in Karachi when the Generals suddenly overthrew 'B'. The events that followed had at last forced Murad and her to seek asylum in India, accompanied by the child. And here, in Delhi, where they had no one to depend upon but each other, Murad had chosen to first betray her and then make a confession. Amina was stunned. In the blur that was now her mind, there would come the thought sometimes: *imagine we are political refugees here*!

Murad's betrayal and their political stand appeared to her as two pieces of a jigsaw puzzle that did not match. Or were they pieces of two different pictures perhaps? The 'inward' and the 'outward'? What was the relation between the two? And why was the 'outward' so incongruous with the 'inward'? These were two lines that did not even run parallel to each other. Perhaps they were more like the twin Indian rivers, Ganga and Yamuna. Both have the same source, but when the glaciers melt, their waters traverse different courses on very different terrain and even their myths are set in different areas of history. But before they flow down to the sea, they merge with each other at Allahbad.

To the Indian mind, an elemental union is always of great significance. The confluence of Ganga and Yamuna is the holiest place of worship in India.

While Amina was sitting in the rain, weeping and trying to face the truth, half of her mind was marvelling at the awesome monsoon downpour. The first shower! She had been intrigued to read in the newspaper, what had appeared to her to be a wishful astrological prediction: *Rain will come to Delhi on the 29th of this month.* Nonsense! She had thought pragmatically. Since Pakistan does not lie on the Monsoon Belt, Amina had no idea that the onset of rain can be easily calculated.

Amina lay down prone, on the wet earth, let the water seep into all of her body. Confident that no one could see her antics and laugh at her, she could do whatever she wanted. *Rarely does the rain meet you when you are alone*, thought Amina. She nearly called for Murad. This was fatal. Because now she would weep again and ask herself exactly how long she had deluded herself and try to make a correct count of years and months. It was as if this chronology held an important secret, the key to a certain solution. She could then perhaps arrange her life that had rambled into too many directions.

What is to be done? Where to begin? She thought. *Shall we go one step forward and two steps back?* This was somewhat like the course of Amina's life, the self-professed poet who had sleepwalked through her thirty odd years, only to wake up occasionally when she had a particularly steep fall, to survey her wounds and weep bitterly. She imagined her life to be a journey, perhaps a pilgrimage (that's more like it!) through green mountains and grey sea shores. While all the time, she was walking in the middle of oncoming traffic, oblivious of the honking horns of buses and cars and scooters, jostled and pushed by the crowd and often trampled over. How was she equipped for this journey of delusions and falls? All she had was a vague resolve, so shapeless and ephemeral that it might as well be a mere phantom, and she was no longer sure if that was enough to carry her through.

When Amina nearly called for Murad and wept, a voice had whispered to her, *You may eat many almonds but remember only the bitter ones*. This sing-song voice came from a chatterbox of Urdu aphorisms and proverbs buried deep in Amina's memory. Urdu is a language riddled with aphorisms and adages. Besides swarms of Arabic and Persian proverbs, it has a bewildering multitude of sayings from the hundred and seventy six languages and the four hundred and ninety eight dialects of India, enabling her people to sometimes converse with each other, only through axioms for days on end.

Amina was not inclined to listen to proverbs for fear of falling into the same trap of make-believe again. The good moments she shared with Murad now lay revealed. Besmirched with lies and deceit, they were now repulsive to her, even their first night together in Delhi, when she lay in the cool Indian night and sighed with relief 'So we have really escaped, the three of us … at last!' What was Murad thinking then? Was he laughing at her foolishness secretly? Planning his escapades already?

No, she would not be taken in again. She must make a decision.

Amina was so lost in her thoughts that she did not notice when the rain stopped. Heavy clouds still hung overhead but there was no breeze. It was growing hot and humid. She walked into her room. She could hear the wheeze of the electric fan and the sleepy breathing of Murad and the child. In the dark, she felt her way to the bed and lay down. Her eyes were dry, and ached. Tomorrow would be a different day. An answer would be revealed to her tomorrow, she hoped, and fell asleep.

When did Amina first see him, this friend of hers, this Darvaish, who was to remain her companion, for years to come? Was it while she walked alone and taking a turn, suddenly came upon him? Or was she lying in her bed in a daze, when he first made her aware of his presence? She could not be sure. All she remembered was that he was certainly there, almost like a ghost: a tall figure, long grey tresses and a flowing grey beard on a plump, unwrinkled face, a kind of Santa Claus, without the sleigh and reindeer. He wore a long robe of deep orange.

'I have come to lighten your burden and show you the way,' he said.

'Oh?' said Amina. 'You know very well that I do not want to lighten my burden, or to see the way. Leave me alone! Please…'

The old man changed his expression so fast, that Amina was taken aback. He looked at her fiercely.

'You want to see the truth of your situation. And you want to take the right step,' he said sternly. 'The right step, even if it kills you. You know what should be done now. Think of what your mother would have done... your grandmother, your great-grandmother.'

Amina had stopped listening.

'Divorce!!' said Amina and heard herself say it loud and clear. 'Take the child and leave Murad...'

She had repeated this to herself often enough. What made her hesitate?

The Darvaish brought out the single stringed instrument from under the folds of his robe and began to play softly.

'You won't be able to help me, Sain Baba,' she said.

She picked up a book and tried to read. She heard the soft pitter-patter of raindrops on the windowpane. Outside it was drizzling again. Inside, Kalidas was singing of love.

The Darvaish began to laugh.

In the dark monsoon night, live with whispering raindrops, softly whirring night insects and swarms of earthworms crawling in the slush, Amina lay awake, listening to the Darvaish's liquid laughter, slowly turning into steam and cooling into millions of beads on the glass window.

'*Pia ... Pia ...*' the night bird of the monsoon, wheeled and called out loud. 'Where is my love? Where is he?' it asked the laden skies.

Heat and moisture, moisture and heat, they did not make a suitable culture for brooding. (They were only suitable for breeding). That could be the reason why no great tragedies were written in India. The climate is not conducive for tragedy. Only in the colder climes of Europe or Scandinavia, could one really brood heavily. The Indian climate only inspired the creativity of expedience. While the European intelligentsia drafted gloomy verdicts on the finality of impending doom, on some dismal wintry evening, their Indian counterparts contemplated ways and means to balance the partner on a single prop, without the rest of the body touching, in these terribly humid nights.

Amina who had not been able to walk a block alone for months (her paranoia had grown that acute), was now going to see a lawyer. How would she make it at all?

There was only one bus route she knew of, on which she had travelled half way with Murad. Taking a cab all alone, was out of the question: to her the mere thought was more dreadful than standing blindfolded before a firing squad. In the tightening grip of fear, which was increasing by the minute and hurting her near paralyzed body, what could she do?

She dragged that near paralyzed body to the bus stop and bussed half way on the route familiar to her.

Alighting from the bus, she walked to and fro, for a while. Then she suddenly remembered that a journalist she knew lived close-by. Straight away she walked into his house. *I will ask him to take me to the lawyer's office*, she thought.

The journalist was pleased to see her. He welcomed her with delight. 'Amina ji, how wonderful to have you here!'

They talked of pleasantries, then of politics and what was now happening in Pakistan. He had written a heart-warming piece on her tug with the army regime. Looking at her with admiration, he said 'Amina ji, you are brave. We really envy your courage!!'

Amina was dumbfounded.

Now she could not tell him she dared not travel alone. She could only look at him more and more intently. The journalist took her back to the bus stop and went away to his office.

The bus stop was close to several newspaper and magazine offices. Soon there were others recognizing her. They waved, they smiled. They came to her for a quick chat. People coming, waving and going away and Amina standing there, rooted to the spot, pretending to be waiting for her imaginary bus...

There were those who were known to her, and therefore she could not ask them to escort her, because she was ashamed. Then there were those who were not known to her, and therefore she could not ask them to accompany her, because she was sure they would take her to a deserted lane, where something would happen to her, something as terrifying as it was vague.

The drowning man catches at a straw. A woman! Amina realized that she was not afraid of unknown women. If there was a woman cab driver, Amina had nothing to fear. The woman cab driver would pass by the turn to the deserted lane and drive her straight to her destination. On the way she would even chat with her. 'How many children to you have?' she would ask. Women constantly ask this question, perhaps to gauge the extent of each other's exasperation.

So the first familiar face of a woman journalist rescued Amina. Amina not only asked her to accompany her to the lawyer's office, she poured out her whole story. Amina made another discovery: she was not ashamed before other women.

The journalist was a young firebrand and she was beginning to flare up at the injustice. She first took Amina to the office of a woman's journal, which was grudgingly accepted but still ridiculed for its feminist ideology.

In the magazine office, Amina sat surrounded by eager young girls, each almost a decade younger than her. So raw, so inexperienced in life, they reminded her of her young niece in Karachi, whose face she had held tenderly in her cupped palms, given her good advice, told her the secrets of life.

But these young things were holding her hand, advising her, asking her to take courage! Amina felt she was living through a very unreal moment of her life.

They told her of their work. Not long ago, they had held a day-long *dharna*, a sit-in outside the house of some Mr Joshi who beat his wife regularly. A large crowd had gathered and Joshi was so nonplussed, he had spent hours fiercely whispering through a crack in the window, a thousand unintelligible promises and apologies. He was ready to do anything, if only they would go away and not make a spectacle of his 'private' life before his perversely curious neighbours.

Amina laughed 'Really?'

How light she felt already! She had not remembered that 'people' included women also. These chatter boxes! What seemed impossible in the 'inside' did not look so unattainable on the 'outside', where there were other people like her. Outside, a new wind was blowing.

Where was the Darvaish when Amina was coming back from the lawyer's office? Not very far. He caught up with her as she walked quickly to her familiar bus stop in Connaught Circus. He was annoyed, hurt.

'So you never heeded me?' he said accusingly. 'Will you never trust him completely? Never? Do you think a lawyer can win you a man's love?"

She kept walking, hurrying to the bus stop. She turned her face away, because her eyes were brimming over. She was almost running and crying and the passers-by were beginning to be intrigued.

'No, no, Sain Baba,' she whispered. 'You don't understand.'

The Darvaish strained to hear. She was mumbling something about a rope, a thick strong rope...

Then it happened. Her worst fear, her most dreaded premonition came true. The bus stop vanished. The familiar bus stop! Where was it? Wiped clean off her memory!

She turned to the left...

Then to the right ...

She turned around.

...*Bia janna ... Bia janan*!

...*Come my beloved ...*

...*Tamasha kun*

...*Behold the splendour*

...*Ki dar ambohe janbazan*

To the left? To the right? If only her tears would let her see clearly! People were giving her odd looks. Again she turned around.

...*Sare bazar me raqsam*

...*I am dancing in the market place*

...*The joyous dance of my disgrace*!

PART II
GO WEST!

JAVAID QAZI

*B*orn in Sahiwal, Javaid Qazi was educated in Lahore at St. Anthony's School, Aitchison College and Government College. He went on to the University of Michigan, the University of Chicago and did his PhD in English Literature from the University of Arizona, specializing in Shakespearean drama. He has published a collection of short stories, *Unlikely Stories* (OUP, 1997) and is working on a second. His fiction, non-fiction and critical work has appeared in anthologies and literary journals and he has written extensively on Thomas Pynchon. He lives in California, translates Urdu fiction into English, teaches English Literature and paints in water colours.

GO WEST YOUNG MAN![1]

> *Come my friends,*
> *'Tis not too late to seek a newer world.*
>
> – *Ulysses*, Alfred Lord Tennyson

Raza lay in bed feeling weak and queasy. He stared at the ceiling and made an effort to access some memory banks, open old files in his brain to figure out what the hell happened. Not just yesterday, or the day before, but way back. What happened to the whole bloody program? How did it get so full of bugs? When he left Pakistan to come to the States, everything had looked so rosy, so full of promise. He remembered the scene on the day of his departure. It flashed across his mind like an old silent movie, all scratched and jumpy, but a movie in which he had played the leading role...the role of the hero.

The day he left, a large crowd gathered to see him off at the little airport in Lahore. Friends and foes—kith and kin—relatives and family friends and even servants. They all came to witness

---

1. From an unpublished novel, *The Adventures of Raza Sahiwal*.

the Big Moment—his departure for America. Everyone considered this a miracle, really: the Sahiwal boy getting a scholarship to study engineering at an American university. Who would have thought it? So, they all gathered to see the drama, be a part of the miracle. His father and mother were on hand, along with Billoo, his younger brother, and Fawzia, his older sister. Uncle Masood, his favourite uncle, had come and he had even brought his wife, a reclusive lady who seldom emerged from the seclusion of her home. A dozen other aunts and uncles also showed up bringing with them a small army of cousins. Even some friends of the family and neighbours were there to share in the excitement.

In the oppressive heat of a June afternoon, the crowd pressed and jostled around him, making it difficult to breathe. His closest friends, Shams, Jaydee, Faiz and Mohsin lurked at the periphery of the family cluster, pacing restlessly like pariah dogs, chain-smoking Capstans and cracking off-colour jokes, while the rabble of cousins milled about aimlessly, smirking and snickering.

At the time, only one thought dominated Raza's mind-scape. He just wanted to get the hell out of there. Quickly. Without tears and embraces or last minute words of advice. He wanted this painful and needlessly long ceremony to be over with. He worried about last minute hitches, the formalities with passport and tickets.

His uncles stood around, gesturing and talking in loud voices:

'Great country…America.'

'Best place for engineering.'

'Far ahead of the Russians.'

'Hollywood…smashing films.'

'Robert Kennedy…how tragic.'

'Riots…Martin Luther King.'

They talked knowingly about the United States but they only knew the place from a distance, through Hollywood films, news reports, public scandals. His aunts stood in a colourful huddle of flowered chiffon, crepe and voile, protecting and supporting his mother, who held herself stiffly, her lips clamped in a tight smile. But he could see her chin tremble and the tears lurking in her eyes.

In the midst of this hullabaloo, his father grabbed him by the arm and pulled him aside. He led him to a quiet corner of the main hall, put a hand on his shoulder and said: 'Son, you are going to a distant country. You will be living among strange people with strange customs. Only Allah knows if we will ever meet again in this world...' He paused. His voice trembled and his eyes filled up with tears. Then he spoke again: 'Son, I want you to remember three things—never drink alcohol, never eat pig meat and never touch one of those foreign women. Islam forbids alcohol and pig meat, to good Muslims because those things bring madness, immorality, and sickness. And above everything, keep yourself chaste, free from the defilement of unlawful sex with corrupt foreign women. When you have finished your studies and come back to Pakistan, your mother and I will arrange your marriage with a pure and innocent Pakistani girl who will make you a loyal wife. Those foreign women, son, are like crazed bitches in heat. They go indiscriminately from man to man, spreading disease and confusion. Stay away from them and you will be happy. Run after them and you will suffer the pains of hell. This is my advice to you. Now go to the West, learn all about science and bring honour and glory to the Sahiwal name.'

Raza listened to his father's words with a downcast head.

'Yes, Abba-ji,' he said. 'I will do exactly as you say.'

A vague dread filled his heart and he wondered what tests and torments lay in wait for him in America. But deep in his heart he made a silent vow to never break the three commandments of his father.

He checked the time on his wristwatch and scanned the crowd looking for a certain face, a face that had obsessed him for a long time. Finally he saw her, the prettiest girl among them all. He'd yearned for her, mooned over her, fantasized about her for months, years. But Sameena hardly ever acknowledged his existence. She had not come to the airport on his account, but because she liked public spectacles where she could display her good looks. She stood aloof and detached like a sleep-walker, savouring the caressing glances of the men and the snake-eyed envy of the women. Suddenly, he felt a tremendous urge to walk up to her and slap her. But even as he started to move towards her as though he were being reeled in by an invisible line, the public address system began to squawk and a cousin grabbed his arm. Too late. It was time to board the plane. Confusing shouts rose up all round him:

'May Allah protect you my son.'

'Send us a telegram when you get to Missouri.'

'Send me a colour TV.'

'Send me an American chick.'

But he barely heard what they said. Jet engines were roaring in his ears, revving up, getting ready for take-off, preparing to carry him to faraway regions, higher altitudes.

He climbed the metal ladder that led up to the plane as if in a dream. When he reached the top, he paused and turned around grandly like a movie star. Bright sunlight spilled into his eyes, blinding him. He could vaguely make out a dense crowd of people pressed up against a wire-mesh fence. They all looked small and insignificant. He could no longer distinguish his friends and relatives from the mass of nameless strangers. He waved. This was a symbolic gesture. His goodbye to friends and family. He was leaving behind all the old loves and lusts, the cancerous hatreds and jealousies, the dreams and delusions. This was his farewell to the dusty plains of the Punjab, the blistering, fly-blown summers, the malarial monsoons, the typhoid winters. He was leaving the crowded towns and mud villages. Goodbye Lahore, goodbye Suddur Bazaar and Anarkali and Mozang Chungi and Bhatti Gate and Gulberg and Government College. Goodbye all you bastards who made me miserable. Goodbye filthy-rich college-mates with your imported colognes, shiny cars and tawdry bungalows. Goodbye civil-servants and uncivil bureaucrats and government officials. Goodbye Generals and Chiefs-of-Staff. Ta-ta President Sahib. You can take your Martial Law and shove it up your hairy nose! I'm breaking free. I'm the One-Who-Got-Away.

I'm through with your Islamic fanaticism, your sex phobias, your oppression. To hell with all of you. Amen.

He turned his back on the assembled throng and ducked inside the plane. Then even as he settled into his seat and the first currents of cool, air-conditioned air played about his throbbing temples, he felt a heavy weight lifting from his back, the wings sprouting from his shoulders....

The journey westward unfolded like a dream. Raza slipped in and out of reveries, memories, images from the past and scenes he imagined of the future, which lay before him. The plane landed in London—Heathrow Airport—a marvel of steel and glass which impressed and scared him. He stayed close to the other passengers as they changed planes, afraid of doing something wrong, of being left behind. Then began the long haul across the Atlantic. For hours and hours nothing to see but the pale sky above and a cobalt blue ocean below. An eternity of blue. He ate and slept, then ate some more, trying not to let his anxiety overpower him completely. He tried to think of what America would be like, but he couldn't visualize anything except for an image of the New York skyline all lit up at dusk, like an Ethiopian bride decked out in glittering diamonds and pearls. People owned long, elegant cars in America—Cadillacs, Chevrolets, Fords. They had tall buildings—skyscrapers—and superhighways and everywhere there were pretty girls who didn't mind being kissed. You took them out on 'dates.' Then you screwed. Really. That's the way it was—a free society. Uninhibited. Yes, that's the word.

In Pakistan it was impossible to meet girls, talk to them or be friends with them. Women were kept behind black veils, high walls.

It was only when he finally got into the Government College in Lahore that he actually began to associate with some girls. Oh the hidden, forbidden princesses of Lahore. How he had yearned for them, wanted them, madly, passionately. Girls like Sameena, the russet-haired beauty with skin so fair that she'd get freckles from the summer sun; Scheherezade of the big boobas and dreamy eyes; and Shaheen, so graceful and charming but so utterly unapproachable. They were all unapproachable. You saw them around the campus of Punjab University everyday but you couldn't talk to them, get close to them. They swished and fluttered past you in their georgette sarees and flowered muslin *shalwar-kameez* outfits, leaving trails of perfume behind: Ma Griffe, Patras, Joy, Madame du Barry, Chanel No. 5—odours that drove you mad with desire....

Suddenly it was time to land. The plane tilted its nose as it approached Kennedy International Airport. America at last. Raza's heart jumped and throbbed in his chest as the plane touched down and he began to worry about complications with his papers. Almost quaking with anxiety he hurried along with the other passengers as they made their way down various corridors and chutes to the vast hall where the immigration checks were underway. A uniformed official looked at all his documents with a grim thoroughness: passport, visa, admission forms, scholarship papers. Then he smiled and said: 'Welcome to the United States.'

'Thank you,' Raza stammered.

He was in at last, worn out but happy. But he still had to get to Columbia, Missouri where the university was located. He wanted to explore New York City but he only had a tiny hoard of US dollars and squandering them on sightseeing did not seem like a good idea.

He could barely keep his eyes open from fatigue but pure excitement kept him going. Again he changed planes and up they went zooming through time zones and endless sky, flying over towns and cities, farms and highways. Silver lakes glimmered below him in the mellow late afternoon light like newly-minted coins. The countryside looked green and lush like someone's well-watered lawn so different from the beige dusty plains of the Punjab.

When he got to St. Louis it was late in the afternoon and he had to catch a bus for the last leg of the journey to Columbia. He recognized the leaping greyhound emblazoned on the side of the shiny new coach and the red, blue and white stripes. The seat tilted back—ah! luxury—and cool, air-conditioned breezes ruffled his hair. America from ground level proved to be a new thrill. Everything was so different from the way it was in Pakistan: buildings, roads, houses and shops—they all looked so clean, so uncrowded, so new. The bus cut through downtown St. Louis, past glass-sheathed towers. Raza caught a glimpse of the silver crescent of the arch, and he recognized it instantly from the photographs that he had seen. He smiled with satisfaction. He was indeed in America. This was no dream.

The bus went around the sweeping curve of an on-ramp and came up onto a six-lane superhighway. Three lanes of traffic were going east, three moving westward. Cars and trucks whizzed by at fifty, sixty, even seventy miles per hour. This is something! he thought, this road, smooth as glass and straight as an arrow. He gazed out of the window, at the rolling hills and farmland, the red barns and cylindrical silos. He looked at everything with hungry eyes, wishing his friend Shams was with him, to see all this, share it with him.

An old negro lady, sitting next to him, engaged him in conversation but he had a difficult time understanding her pattern of intonation. Her accent sounded strange to his ears, probably as strange as his sounded to her ears.

'Way you fum?' she asked him.

'Pakistan.'

He didn't think she knew where that was.

'How long has you bin here?'

'Twelve hours.'

She smiled, as though she did not believe him.

'Where you headed?'

'Columbia. To the University there.'

She nodded her head wisely.

'You gome laak it there, honey.'

'Yes,' he said. 'I'm sure I will.'

By the time the bus pulled into Columbia, it had gotten very dark and a steady rain had begun to fall. The road streaming with water reflected all the lights: the flashing neon signs, the headlights of the cars, the gaseous globes of the street lights and made them look as though they had melted on the wet blacktop.

Raza collected his bags and asked about a hotel. He was told to go the Daniel Boone, which luckily happened to be right around the corner from the Greyhound bus station. He lugged his suitcase through the rain, checked in and wearily fell into crisp white bed sheets. As he drifted off to sleep he made plans to get in touch with Professor Wilson who was the Head of the Engineering Department and his only contact in Columbia. Yes, he sighed, I'll do that tomorrow. Tomorrow is the first day of my new life.

Raza woke up with a start, suddenly very anxious and afraid. Where am I? he thought. Everything in the room lay steeped in quiet darkness. The glowing numerals on his new clock-cum-radio indicated twenty-to-six. Then he suddenly remembered. He was in his dorm room. He switched on the lamp and the radio. Sounds flooded the room, music, songs, the voice of the announcer. He forced himself to get up and collected his shaving kit, a towel and clean underwear. He wanted to get to the bathroom before the other guys took over the whole place. But when he got there, plenty of guys were already standing around shouting and laughing and joking with each other. They walked about naked, flicked wet towels at each other's butts or stood primping in front of the mirrors. He turned red with embarrassment at the sight of so many pale bottoms, hairy legs, and pink, drooping penises. He tried to avert his eyes and concentrate on shaving.

   The whole dorm experience was a first for him. In Lahore he had lived at home with his mother and his younger brother and sister. And, of course, the servant who was always ready to fetch a glass of water, polish his shoes, or iron his clothes. Old Ahmed Dean, would knock on his door every morning with his bed-tea on a tray. 'Wake up Raza Sahib, time to get up now,' he'd say.

   In the dorm, he is no longer 'Raza Sahib.' He is just another body packed into a six-storey concrete structure. His room which was on the third floor, had been designed for two people. There were two beds, two desks, two chairs, two table-lamps. A sealed plate-glass window looked out onto a huge parking lot and beyond that he could see the girls' dorm.

He opened the drapes, wondering if he'd catch sight of something titillating: rosy nipples, creamy thighs, lacy underthings. He'd heard a lot of talk about the naked girls one could see. But most likely they were made-up stories. He'd never seen anything even vaguely erotic. He opened a new pack of Benson & Hedges, lit a cigarette and paced up and down. The dorm room made him feel cooped up, claustrophobic.

Suddenly there was a loud knock on the door. It sounded like the opening notes of Beethoven's Ninth. Tah-Tah-Tah-Tum. Who could it be? Raza wondered. When he opened the door, he found a guy standing there with a huge canvas backpack slung over this shoulder. Beneath a mop of curly black hair, his brown eyes twinkled mischievously.

'Hi,' he said, 'I'm your room-mate.'

Not knowing what else to do, Raza shook hands with him and introduced himself.

'The name's Tony Kouros. Born and bred in Brooklyn. But—fortunately—my parents were from Greece.'

Raza's eyes lit up.

'I've never met anyone from Greece,' he said. 'Do you speak Greek?'

'Naaah,' Tony said and grinned impishly. 'It's Greek to me.'

Raza chuckled, grateful to have a room-mate with a sense of humour.

'Too bad,' he said. 'I would have liked to hear you say something in Greek.'

'Hey, this is the US of A, man. The Melting Pot. Everyone's supposed to melt into a WASP.'

'A what?'

'WASP. White Anglo-Saxon Protestant.'

Raza nodded his head as if he understood, but the term, the concept had no meaning for him. But he didn't want Tony

Kouros to get a bad impression, think that he was naive or uninformed about the United States.

'Can I help you with your luggage?' he said.

'This is it,' Tony said, flinging his backpack to the floor.

'Last year…brought two suitcases full of fancy junk. Clothes. Shoes. Heavy as hell. A real pain to lug around. Never used half the shit. So this year, I thought…just the essentials.'

Tony spoke very fast with a nasal tone to his voice in brief, telegraphic phrases as though he had a lot to say and was in a great hurry to say it. Turned out he was majoring in Poli Sci, wanted to be a lawyer and then go into politics. Right away he wanted to know what Raza thought of the United States.

'It's wonderful,' said Raza. 'I always wanted to come here.'

Tony smiled and shook his head.

'It's all fucked up, man. Don't you see? It's a mess.'

'What do you mean?' said Raza.

'First that Vietnam business and now Nixon and his shenanigans. Believe me we're headed for a crack-up.'

Raza tried to grasp Tony's meaning, to not look vacant. He knew next to nothing about Vietnam or American politics. Where was Vietnam? All he could think of was a vast swampy region somewhere between East Pakistan and China, a part of the world which meant nothing to him. The only Far Eastern country that had any importance for him was Japan, the source of highly-desirable transistor radios and Toyota cars. But Vietnam was just a big blank space in his mind.

All he knew of the war was what he had read in *Time* magazine and he was fuzzy about the reasons why America was involved over there. Basically he hated war because it frightened him. He had been very young when Pakistan and India had gone to war with each other. Thousands died, thousands were wounded and maimed. In ten days it was all over. The Government handed out medals, politicians made long boring speeches, talked about 'martyrs'. But in a few months people forgot all about the dead heroes.

Tony said something about US imperialism.

Raza nodded his head vigorously. Yes. He knew all about imperialism. India used to be a part of the British empire, a conquered and enslaved nation. But how could America be imperialistic? America had always stood for Freedom, Justice and Equality.

'Bull-shit!' Tony said.

Raza opened and closed his mouth, trying to say something profound or meaningful but nothing came to him.

'Don't believe all the *Reader's Digest* crap. The Government never tells us the truth. All we ever get is lies and still more lies.'

Raza kept quiet. He didn't want to get into an argument with Tony, who obviously knew more than him about what was going on. Moreover, Raza began to like Tony. There was an appealing frankness and honesty about him.

'Oh, fuck it,' said Tony suddenly. 'Let's go get a beer.'

Raza hung his head, slightly ashamed over what he had to tell him.

'I don't drink alcohol,' he said in a small voice.

Tony shot him a peculiar look but then his face lit up.

'I suppose you smoke hashish?'

'No, no,' Raza said hurriedly. 'In Pakistan very few people drink alcohol. It is forbidden in Islam. Of course, hashish is available but only the illiterate—the lower classes—use it.'

Tony's eyes narrowed as he digested this for a moment. Then he grinned his characteristic grin and said: 'Oh, shitsky! Come, I'll buy you a goddamned coke.'

S Afzal Haider

Syed Afzal Haider was born in Jhansi, migrated to Pakistan in August 1947, graduated from DJ Science College, Karachi, and did degrees in electrical engineering, psychology and social work, in turn, in the United States and worked in those respective fields. He started writing in the 1980s, is co-editor of the *Chicago Quarterly Review*, and his fiction has appeared in various literary magazines and anthologies. He lives in Illinois and is married to a Japanese American.

TRIBES

I was nineteen then, a sophomore at Oklahoma State University, just one year in the United States; I lived at 786 Knoblock Street in Stillwater. Those were my days of the pursuit of education and learning, my days of being a foreign student, my days of being in love with Paula McKeever, a Ponca City woman, my Marilyn Monroe, my American Madhubala. I watched Paula an entire fall semester while I served food to her in Scott Hall Dining Room. She had golden hair and deep green eyes. Until Paula, I don't remember any green eyes.

On the first day of the spring term, she walked into my American History class and sat down next to me. All that semester, while the lecturer droned on, I wrote love letters to Paula which I never gave to her. She was pinned to Max Reagan. Max played football for the OSU Cowboys and lived in a fraternity house. Max was big, beautiful, and wore a crew cut— he looked like a football player. I didn't like him much. We treated one another courteously. I don't think he understood my relationship with Paula. I don't know if Paula understood my relationship with her. I never told her how I loved her.

Paula worked at the library from seven in the evening until closing. I used to go to her section to study. After our meeting in American History, I would occasionally run into Paula during breaks, and we would have coffee together. I fed coins into a juke box: Joe Dowell singing 'Wooden Heart,' Peter, Paul and Mary's 'Lemon Tree.' Sometimes, playing three for a quarter, I'd invite Paula to choose the third selection. She always pressed L-23, the Shirelles, 'Soldier boy, I'll be true to you....'

Again, just by change, I'd run into her as the library closed and walk her to Scott Hall. I told her about my life back home in India. I confided that I was learning to be an engineer so that I could return to India and build bridges, how one day I expected to marry a woman of my mother's choosing. Paula listened to everything as though fascinated. She explained American lifestyles, that she wanted to be a writer and to have many children. Once when Max was away playing football, Paula and I went to see *No Exit* at the University Cinema.

During our coffee break just before the Thanksgiving holidays, out of the blue, Paula told me that she'd throw Max's pin in his face if I would marry her and have children with her. I sat there adding sugar to my coffee, saying nothing. It was not practical, I thought. You don't marry a blonde American if you're planning to build bridges in Jhansi, India. That night, walking Paula from the Memorial Library by Theta Pond, she held my hand and kissed me. With much hesitation and great anticipation, I kissed her back. But I did not say how I adored her.

That was thirty years ago. The death of a romance, the betrayals of a man. I live in Waukegan, Illinois. I'm a civil engineer with the city sewage department.

I have a lovely wife, Joan. She's a redhead and she teaches fourth grade. I also have two lovely boys. Arman, from my first marriage, is a freshman at the University of Nebraska. Junior, who'll turn fourteen in March, from my current marriage, is a regular all-American jock. He plays baseball, and he plays it very well. I am proud of him. He's going to speak at his school's Thanksgiving Assembly. We all have a lot to be thankful for, living in America. It's a great country, and there are no drugs in my son's school.

I arrive late to the Thanksgiving Day Assembly. Rushing through the hallway, I can hear Junior's voice: 'Thanksgiving is now celebrated on the fourth Thursday in November.' I enter the auditorium in the middle of applause, as my son is leaving the stage. I look around to find a familiar face and an empty seat. I see Tom White, the father of one of Junior's friends, sitting next to a vacant chair toward the back. I sit next to him. Tom stops applauding. 'You missed a great delivery,' says Tom.

'I had to finish a report,' I say. Tom is all dressed up. I like his tie, green mallards on a maroon background. 'Buy yourself a watch,' says Tom, smiling. I remove my raincoat and look around. Junior is invisible in the front row, but his home room teacher, Miss Powers, occupies an aisle seat toward the front. I think she smiles at me. She is sitting close enough to see, but too far away to tell for sure.

Next on the programme is an educational film, *Native American Influences in the United States*, by some Joe Shmoe, PhD. I learn how place names like Manhattan, Chicago and Milwaukee originated in Indian languages. I am comforted to hear that I live in an Indian city. The movie further explains that many highways, such as our local Sauk Trail, were once Indian trails. Once upon a time, in the not-too-distant past, Indians travelled on these trails, trading with Indians of other tribes.

One such trail brought me to Ponca City on a rainy Thanksgiving Day in 1961. I got off a bus at Ponca City Bus Terminal to wait for another bus to Tonkawa. The only people in the terminal were a few Native Indians and me, a foreigner, all of us nonwhite folks. I sat on a dark mahogany bench looking down at the green-speckled concert floor. Suddenly I heard a drunken voice say, 'Don't look down, son. You're as good as them.'

'Yes, I am,' I replied quietly, not believing what I said. I looked up to see a Native American Indian standing before me. I thought that he must have taken me for one of his own. 'I'm not from here,' I said.

The Indian's hair was cut short, but so thick that it stood up like fur. There was a lot of grey in it. He dropped onto the bench next to me. 'But I am an Indian,' I explained. 'I was born in India.'

'I am an Indian,' he replied, smiling. 'I was born here.' The native had a pleasant, weathered face. He reminded me of my Uncle Aftab. Showing a tourist's interest in a national monument, I asked, 'What is your tribe of origin?' For a moment he looked at me as though he hadn't understood the question. He took a pack of Lucky Strikes from the pocket of the cowboy shirt he wore under a grey cowboy jacket that matched the colour of his skin. 'We're the children of the Trail of Tears and broken treaties.' He pronounced each word deliberately. He offered me a Lucky. I declined. 'In Oklahoma,' he continued, 'We have Cherokee, Choctaw, Chickasaw and Seminole.' He tucked the pack of cigarettes back into his pocket.

'What tribe did your forefathers come from?' I insisted.

He removed the unlit cigarette from his lips and let out a deep sigh. He stared at me, his eyes exhausted and haunting. I looked away. 'Can I buy you a drink?' he asked.

'I don't drink, thank you. I am a Muslim.'

'I pity the white man,' he said, 'for having no pity on me.' He slapped at his pockets, searching for a match. 'I have to adopt the laws, religion and customs of aliens.'

I didn't know what to say. I felt like an alien all the time. The native smiled at me sadly. 'What I can't stand is being treated like an outsider in my own land.' He finally located a box of matches in his jeans. As he pulled it from his pocket, a coin popped out with it and plinked onto the floor. I bent to catch it. As I handed it back, I saw that it was a buffalo-head nickel. The native exhaled smoke through his nose and stared at it. 'In years to come in this land of ours, there'll be no more buffalo and no more Indians.'

'Maybe we Indians should start a rebellion,' I suggested seriously.

'It's been tried,' said the native. 'The oppressor won. They prosecuted and persecuted and slaughtered most of us.' He slipped the nickel back into his pocket. 'The rest of us live in concentration camps.'

We sat in silence until I heard my bus announced. The native asked me where I was going. I told him I was on my way to Tonkawa for Thanksgiving dinner at the home of Reverend Freeman, arranged for by the foreign student advisor. I stood up, looking down at the green-speckled floor. 'Do you celebrate Thanksgiving?' I asked.

'I am an Indian,' said the native, rising to his feet with me. 'I have little to be thankful for. It's just another Thursday in November.'

I wanted to hug him. Instead, we exchanged the white man's gesture of leave-taking, a handshake. It felt awkward. 'Goodbye, Indian,' I said, looking into his grey face. He put his hand on my head and rubbed it gently. 'Good luck, Indian,' he said, grinning.

I walked to my bus, looking down.

The movie is over and the lights come up. Mrs Tate, the school principal, is an attractive middle-aged black woman. Today she wears a blue suit over a white blouse. There is a red rose pinned to her lapel. She commends the boys and girls of Mohawk Middle School for a great Thanksgiving Day programme. She invites the parents to stay for fruit punch and a taste of sweet Navajo fry bread prepared by the eighth graders.

'Join us for this American occasion of thanks and giving,' she concludes. In the background, music swells. I hear Indian drums, like in a cowboy movie. The crowd is in motion. Tom and I get up at the same time and move towards the punch. On the stage a few parents seem to be dancing. It looks suspiciously like the Watusi of my college days.

'So how are you celebrating Thanksgiving?' Tom asks. I am watching an attractive blonde, blue-eyed dancer. I say, 'I'm an Indian. I have little to celebrate.'

Tom dips his Navajo fry bread in honey. 'We're all chiefs here,' he says. 'We have no Indians.'

Looking down at the polished yellow oak floor, I agree.

Where are the natives? I wonder. What's my tribe of origin?

TARIQ ALI

*T*ariq Ali was educated at St Anthony's High School and Government College, Lahore. He left Pakistan for Oxford University, because his political activities had earned the ire of the government. He has lived in exile since. He played a pivotal role in the 1960's student revolution in Europe and served as a member of the Bertrand Russell War Crimes Tribunal, visited Bolivia, Kampuchea and North Vietnam, which he has described in *Streetfighting Years: An Autobiography of the Sixties* (Collins, 1987). He was the editor of two magazines, *Black Dwarf* and *Red Mole* and his non-fiction includes *Pakistan: Military Rule or People's Power?* (Cape, 1970), *1968 and After* (Blond and Biggs, 1978), *Can Pakistan Survive?* (Penguin, 1983), *The Nehrus and the Gandhis* (GP Putnam, 1985). In the 1980s he became a film maker and has his own film company, Bandung. He has written several plays including *Moscow Gold*, which he co-wrote with Howard Brenton (Nick Hern, 1990); *Ugly Rumours* (1998) *Collateral Damage* (1999). He has written five novels, *Redemption* (Chatto, 1990), *The Hall of Mirrors* (Arcadia, 1999) and three in a historical quartet about the encounter between Islam and Christianity, *Shadows of the Pomegranate Tree* (Chatto, 1992), *The Book of Saladin* (Verso, 1998) and *The Stone Woman* (Verso, 2000). *Shadows of the Pomegranate Tree*, about the 1492 Fall of Granada, was translated into ten languages and received the Archbishop San Clemente del Instituto Rosalia de Castro prize in Spain.

THE LAST YEAR IN THE LIFE OF ERNESTO 'CHE' GUEVARA: 1967[1]

> *In my time streets led to the quicksand.*
> *Speech betrayed me to the slaughter.*
> *There was little I could do. But without me*
> *The rulers would have become more secure. This was my hope.*
> *So the time passed away*
> *Which on earth was given me.*
>
> — *To Posterity*, Bertolt Brecht

---

1. From *Streetfighting Years: An Autobiography of the Sixties.*

12 October 1967

It was a crisp and clear autumn day in London. We were in the midst of preparations for the first of the big Vietnam demonstrations. I was due to speak at two meetings that day. *The Guardian* of that morning had published the news of Che's death in Bolivia, together with a photograph of the dead body and a despatch from Richard Gott. There was no longer room for doubt. I sat at my desk and wept. The sense of loss and grief was overpowering and there was nothing else one could do but cry. Nor was I alone. On every continent there were many others who felt and reacted in a similar fashion. Everything associated with that day became unforgettable. I do not remember, if the truth be told, what I was doing when Kennedy was assassinated. But I can recall every small detail of the day that Che died. The conversation with Clive Goodwin. The speeches I made at the two meetings. The suggestion to Pat Jordan that we organize a memorial meeting at the Conway Hall. The long wait for the response from Havana. The anger I felt both at the manner of his death and our collective impotence. What made it marginally worse was that a number of us had been in Bolivia not so long ago in the region where Che and his tiny band of fighters were surrounded and trapped. I had not realized that his death was so close. The very thought had been inconceivable.

The secret of Che's appeal is not difficult to fathom. He was a successful revolutionary leader in Cuba, where he held high office. Yet he had left the relative safety of Havana to resume the struggle in other lands. In his person, theory and practice were in complete harmony. Such a display of internationalism had not been seen since the twenties and thirties, but even then none of the central leaders of the Russian Revolution had left their posts and departed for other storm-centres in Europe. It is true that at one stage the German Communist Party, deprived of Rosa Luxemburg and Karl Liebknecht, had appealed via the Comintern for Trotsky's talent to be made available to their party. Trostsky had been willing, even eager, but the demand had been rejected by the Soviet party on the grounds that Trotsky was needed more in his own country. In Cuba, too, Castro had been extremely reluctant to lose Che, but the veteran Commandant had insisted that in order to help Vietnam concretely it was vital to open new fronts and distract imperialism from Indo-China. His departure from Cuba led to a great deal of speculation. His presence was at various times reported in the Congo, Vietnam, Guatemala...everywhere, but where he was, deep in the heart of land-locked Bolivia.

The Che myth began in Latin America, but spread rapidly to North America and Europe. He was called a murderer and a pyromaniac by the oligarchies, but to the poor he was a Robin Hood, a modern Christ, a Don Quixote. He was not unaware of the mythology that surrounded his name. In his last letter to his parents in mid-1965 he bade them farewell, warning them that 'perhaps this will be my last letter. It is not my intention, but it is within the realm of logical probability. If so, I send you a last embrace.' He had begun the letter by a reference to Cervantes and a light-hearted identification with the fictional hero: 'Once again I feel Rocinante's bony ribs between my legs. Once again I begin my journey, carrying my shield...' He was not universally popular on the Euro-American Left. The Maoists and sectarians of every hue united in their chorus of disapproval. 'Adventurer!', they screamed in unison, angry at his popularity. Guevara had foreseen such a charge and had replied to it in advance. 'Many,' he had written, 'will call me an adventurer, and I am, but of a different kind—one who risks his skin in order to prove his convictions.'

The choice of Bolivia was not so foolish. The country had a strong revolutionary tradition; in the tin miners, it boasted one of the best organized trade unions of the entire continent; and the military oligarchs were corrupt to the core and racist in their attitude to the predominantly Indian peasants, who were the victims of super-exploitation. The fault did not lie in the country or its people, but in the form chosen for the struggle, without the existence of a strong and reliable urban network.

News of Che's presence in Bolivia had begun to circulate freely in Latin America within the ranks of the Left, but it was not until Regis Debray's arrest that we obtained confirmation that this was indeed a fact. Debray, referred to as Danton in Che's *Bolivian Diaries*, was captured in May 1967 in the main street of a tiny town, Muyupampa. He was in the company of George Roth, an Anglo-Chilean photographer, and Ciro Bustos, an Argentinian painter. Debray had been lecturing in philosophy at Havana University and living in a room at the Hotel Habana Libre on the 21st floor. It was here that he received word from Che asking him to rush to Paris, where an urgent message awaited him. The place of assignment was a left wing bookshop in the Latin Quarter, 'La Joie de Lire', owned by the radical publisher, Francois Maspero. Che had chosen Debray to be the first journalist to report first-hand on the establishment of a guerrilla base in the Andes. Debray's book-essay, *Revolution in the Revolution*, had been widely acclaimed in Cuba as a primer for extending the Cuban experience to the entire Latin American continent. Che offered the young Debray (he was twenty-six years old at the time) the opportunity to write on how these tactics were being deployed in Bolivia. The attraction of the offer was obvious. Debray returned to Paris, where a messenger handed him his instructions. He was told to proceed to La Paz, the Bolivian capital where, at 6 pm every Tuesday, a courier named Andres would wait for him outside the Sucre Palace Hotel. Debray travelled under his own name, armed with official papers confirming his status as a writer and journalist from Maspero and the Mexican magazine *Sucesos*. These credentials were duly validated by the Bolivian authorities, as was his passport.

Debray duly met Andres, who took him to an underground guerrilla using the name 'Tanya'. She travelled with him by bus (a journey and vehicle that has few equals anywhere in the world) and eventually they arrived at the Hotel Grande in Sucre. Here they met Bustos and on the following day continued their travels till they reached the tiny oil town of Camiri. After a day's rest they proceeded northwards into the dense jungles until they reached an isolated ranch in the district of Nancahuaza. Up to this time there had been no clashes between the guerrillas and the troops of the Barrientos military dictatorship. In fact,

Che's plan was to wait another six months before undertaking any action. While Debray was waiting for Che in the ranch, a military patrol was sighted heading in its direction. An oil engineer had reported some suspicious movements to the army. The guerrillas ambushed the patrol, killing three officers and capturing 15 soldiers. It now became impossible to stay on at the ranch and Debray and Bustos were taken to the mobile units in the jungles.

It was here that Debray met Che and interviewed him, but since the latter was more involved in commanding units, which found themselves suddenly at war, there was not much time for prolonged discussions. By early April, Debray had accomplished his task and both he and the painter attempted to exit via Gutierrez, but found that city was already under military occupation. They marched with the guerrillas for another 14 days. Here Debray must have pondered on what he had written two years previously: 'Bolivia is the country where the subjective and objective conditions [for armed struggle] are best combined. It is the only country in South America where a socialist revolution is on the agenda...' There was little sign so far of the ripeness of subjective conditions. The peasants, destitute, but not stupid, remained unconvinced of the need for armed struggle. Che had realized that contact with the miners was critical and was attempting to achieve this objective, but the unforeseen discovery of their movements had made everything very difficult.

While the guerrillas were camped near Muyupampa, George Roth rode into the camp on a horse. Che was now seriously alarmed and felt that all three outsiders should leave as soon as possible since their presence was adversely affecting the capacities of the guerrillas. They walked into the town, unarmed except for cameras, where they were arrested by the local police. Fortunately for them they were seen by a Bolivian journalist and a French Dominican missionary. They might all have been released had it not been for the fact that a deserter from the guerrillas told the police that he had seen Bustos and Debray in the camp. The police panicked and informed the army. A military helicopter arrived and transported them to an army barracks. Here all three were badly beaten up. Debray was virtually unconscious when inspected by a doctor. Within days of the capture, an officer showed Debray his obituary which had been published abroad and taunted him with the words: 'The world already believes you're dead. Now it's easy for us to just shoot you.' More sinister was the fact that Debray was endlessly interrogated by CIA agents, and Cuban exiles from Miami. Their logic was faultless: if Debray was there, could Che be far behind? Four days after the Frenchman's arrest, two American military men booked into the Hotel Beirut in Camiri. A few weeks later, they were joined by others.

Debray was tortured regularly. His interrogators wanted information as to Che's whereabouts. He was often threatened with execution. What saved him was the worldwide concern. His father was a conservative Parisian lawyer; his mother a staunch Gaullist, well-known in local Parisian politics for her right-wing views. They moved into action rapidly to try to save their son's life. On 6 June, an American prelate, Monsignor Kennedy, a distant relative of the famous American clan, was permitted to see Debray in his cell. Kennedy told the outside world that he was alive and would soon be tried in a public court as a guerrilla-collaborator.

This information had reached us while we were busy preparing the Tribunal. Sartre had suggested to Russell that the Peace Foundation should despatch a team of observers with the aim of ensuring Debray's safety and attending his trial. A few weeks later the Cubans had approached the Foundation with a similar suggestion. They were now concerned for Debray as well as Che and the others, whose whereabouts had been prematurely revealed. I was asked by Ralph Schoenman to purchase up-to-date camera equipment and take a large stock of film. He suggested that we, too, might have to establish contact with Che's units and therefore security was a prime consideration as far as the nature and circumstances of this trip were concerned.

The team was to consist of five people. Apart from Schoenman and myself, there were Perry Anderson and Robin Blackburn. Both were described in a Sunday paper as 'two young British dons', which was technically accurate, but very inappropriate. Anderson was editor of the *New Left Review* and Blackburn one of his closest comrades-in-arms on the editorial committee of the magazine. I had met both of them at social gatherings, one of which had been a party organized by Blackburn's Chinese wife, Fei Ling, at their Ladbroke Grove flat. I had been extremely impressed by Perry Anderson's frenetic dancing style, which went well with the music of the Stones, but my knowledge of his work was limited to his introduction to the Italian Communist Party documents which I had read while in Pakistan. I still had not at that stage studied the much talked about polemical exchange between Anderson and EP Thompson on the historical roots of the crisis in Britain. The debate had covered a wide range of subjects, including the nature of the English Civil War, the function and role of the land-owning aristocracy in Britain, the effects of Protestantism and Darwinism on English culture and history and finally the development of Marxist thought in this century. Thompson and Anderson were both experienced in the art of polemics and the rapier-like thrusts and counter-thrusts became the most celebrated and important battle of ideas that the Left in Britain had ever experienced. I had, of course, noticed both Thompson's essay in the *Socialist Register* and Anderson's response in the *New Left Review*, but since the terms of reference were limited to Britain, I had simply not been interested, a philistine response which I was later to regret. Apart from anything else, it would have enabled me to understand the complexities of Anderson's character much better while we were in Latin America.

I had first encountered Robin Blackburn through an article of his in defence of the Cuban Revolution. He was also a co-editor of *The Week*, though I do not recall ever reading anything by him in that tiny, but influential, magazine. His hair had turned white prematurely, but whereas others might have panicked, Blackburn converted this biological accident into a much envied sexual asset. I knew Fei Ling a little better since she was active in the Vietnam movement and was an enthusiastic partisan of the Vietnam Solidarity Campaign. In fact I first met Blackburn via Fei Ling and subsequently at one of Clive Goodwin's soirées.

The fifth member of our expeditionary team was a German leftist, Lothar Menne, who was camping at the time in Ladbroke Grove, together with Angela Davis and a few others including his lady-friend. It was felt that we needed a more mainstream Continental representative, so Menne's amorous activities were abruptly terminated and he obtained credentials from the German magazine, *Konkret*, to cover Debray's trial.

We spent a day and a half in Rio waiting for a connection to Lima, since there were no regular flights to the Bolivian capital. Ralph Schoenman and Perry Anderson disappeared for the best part of the day. Both had friends in town and were keen to re-establish direct contact. Robin Blackburn and I spent the day on Copacabana beach, observing the sights and reading newspapers. It was a slightly surreal interlude. I could not enjoy the sea. My mind was fixed on Bolivia. I wondered how long victory would take in the Andes. Cuba had taken four years, but Washington had been unprepared for Fidel Castro. They were now far more alert and I had direct experience of their technological skills from Vietnam. The struggle would never be as easy as in Cuba ever again. One could not afford to be sanguine, but the thought that Che could be defeated did not even enter my head.

We left for Lima the next day, but our flight was late and we missed the only connection to La Paz. The others had American, German, British and Irish passports, which did not require a transit visa to enter Peru. I still had only my Pakistani passport and I don't think that such a document had, at that time, ever been seen in Lima or La Paz. I pleaded with the airport authorities to issue a temporary visa. They declined. There was no Pakistan Embassy in the country and so no consular appeal was possible. There was no other flight out of Lima that day. I was a prisoner of the Lima airport immigration authorities. So I parted company with my European comrades and we agreed a meeting place in La Paz. The night was extremely cold and there were no facilities of any sort at the airport. Fortunately there was the equivalent of a change of guard at 2 am or thereabouts and the new team was much more friendly. I managed to explain my predicament and was, to my surprise, provided with a bed in the police room. Next morning they gave me breakfast and I caught the first flight to Bolivia:

La Paz, the highest capital city in the world, has an airport which is situated at a staggering altitude of 13,358 feet, more than two and a half miles above sea-level. As the plane was circling the airport, I suddenly became very alarmed. There were no buildings in sight and it felt as if though we were going to land in the middle of a moon crater. Everything seemed unreal. The plane did land and, yes, there was a runway. As I stepped out of the plane and breathed in the Altiplano air, which was crisp and thin, I looked anxiously for the airport building. There was none to be seen. Finally we followed the stewardess and the more knowledgeable travellers. There in the distance was a tiny wooden shack. Inside was a makeshift desk, behind which sat the immigration officer. My passport was closely inspected. 'Pakistan? Pakistan?' The man looked genuinely bewildered. I explained that it was a new country near India. They knew where India was and since my visa from the Bolivian Embassy in London was genuine, I went through without any problems. Customs, when the luggage finally arrived, was even less of a formality. I shared a taxi to La Paz with some fellow passengers and caught my first glimpse of the bowl-shaped valley that lay below. There at the very bottom was the capital city of Bolivia. On the way I saw the hovels clinging to the side of the mountain in which the Indian population lived. These homes were made of mud, like in large parts of India, but even from a taxi the poverty seemed much worse.

I booked into the Sucre Palace Hotel on the Avenida 16 de Julio. It was a large white building, probably constructed in the forties. The rooms were spacious and clean, but unfortunately there would be none available for the others when they arrived. I bathed, rested and then went for a walk on the streets. This was an Indian city in a country where a majority of the population consisted of Quechua and Aymara Indians. The former claimed descent from the Incas and the latter were the heirs of the pre-Inca inhabitants of this region. The Spaniards had conquered and occupied, but had not been able to either assimilate or destroy the indigenous population. The country was run by the mestizos, who are very proud of their Spanish blood and one of the more racist ruling groups in Latin America. They treated the Indians with contempt. The President of the country, Rene Barrientos, was a General who had toppled the civilian regime. He had been trained at Randolph Field, Texas, and his cowboy flying style ultimately led to his death. Interestingly enough, however, Barrientos was half-Indian and spoke better Quechua than Spanish. This enabled him to communicate directly with the Indians, but did not lead to any fundamental changes. I wandered round the streets taking in the colours and the smells and testing the street-vendors' cuisine. The quality of a country's food can always be judged by what is being served on the streets. The best food is, more often than not, to be found in cheap eating-houses or cafés rather than the expensive restaurants. I am talking now of most countries of the Third World, though probably the same could be said of some in Mediterranean Europe.

When I got back to the hotel, I was told that someone had arrived to see me. This gave me a jolt as I was not expecting anyone. A man was waiting for me in the corner of the lobby. He did not look like a plain clothes cop so I felt a little less uneasy and went up to him. He introduced himself, but spoke no English. I took out my Spanish phrase book and a painful conversation ensued. After an hour I realized that he had been expecting all our party to arrive that day and that he was one of Schoenman's contacts. Every time I asked who he was and what he did, the only response was laughter. Embarrassed by my inability to communicate I gave up. We sat and smiled at each other for another half an hour or so and then he stood up, shook hands and departed, leaving me bewildered.

We had been warned not to carry reading matter which might betray our political proclivities. This meant no Marxist literature, only novels and plays. That night after a lonely supper I retired to bed with Aeschylus' *Prometheus Bound*. A friend had happened to remark that it was the only play that Marx himself read at least once a year. I had always wondered what had attracted him to the Ancients. That night in the Sucre Palace Hotel, I read, reflected, read again and understood. Previously, Greek mythology, which had been a childhood favourite, I had always read as adventure yarns. Mars and Athena had been teenage idols. Now I read of how Zeus had punished Prometheus for stealing fire from heaven and imparting its secrets to the mortals. Prometheus' natural sympathy with the underdogs resulted in his excommunication by the Immortals. Marx must have identified his own situation with that of the deposed Greek god for had he not, too, given the wretched of this world the means to liberate themselves from the new deities of Capital. And that night it also became clear that the myths of Antiquity must have been related to class struggles on earth. The dynastic factional struggles of mythology must have been a reflection of real turbulence in these societies.

The rest of the gang arrived the next afternoon and booked into the much grander Copacabana Hotel a few blocks down on the same street. I went to meet them and there in the foyer I ran into my strange visitor of yesterday, deep in conversation with Ralph Schoenman. He was a trade union militant and from him we obtained an account of what was really happening in the country. We set about making plans for our trip to Camiri, but discovered that we needed a special pass signed by General Ovando, the second highest figure in the oligarchy, before we could be allowed to enter the 'military zone'.

The others had come well armed with the required credentials. Between them, they monopolized the handful of Left magazines in Britain. I had come with my membership card of the National Union of Journalists, which did not count. What was to be done? Our Bolivian friend had a suggestion. I went with him to a tiny left-wing printshop in an even tinier backstreet in La Paz.

Here I designed some notepaper with some skill, I might add, and the printer dug around for his best quality type-face and paper. Then before my very eyes I saw the sheets with *Town* magazine emblazoned boldly on the top with correct address and telephone number come sliding down the press, which must have been an antique captured during the Chaco Wars against Paraguay. We then went to the offices of a local daily, *El Diario*, borrowed their best typewriter and I typed out my credentials as a 'Special Foreign Correspondent' assigned to Latin America. I then paused to work out whose signature I should forge and decided on Michael Heseltine's. He was, after all, the publisher and deserved this privilege. An intermediary organized by Schoenman then began the process of getting us official permission to travel to Camiri. We had to wait two days.

One evening our Bolivian friend suggested that we go with him to a fiesta organized by various groups in the Indian quarter of the city. We were promised songs, music, dancing and an opportunity to see the district where the bulk of the population lived. This was the highest section of the town and on that cold night we ate at a local café and then went to the hall where the fiesta was in full swing. This was the real Bolivia. I felt both moved and elated by the sight of a largely proletarian and sub-proletarian assembly which was full of confidence and laughter. We joined in the celebrations. Later, in circumstances that I do not fully recall, some speeches were made. I felt the urge to say something to such a unique gathering. On the way to the quarter I had seen anti-Vietnam war graffiti and I thought that I must tell the Indians of what was really happening in Vietnam and how the NLF forces were fighting back. Unable to speak their language, I decided to explain my points in the form of a mime. There was complete silence as I enacted the war in gestures and body movements with the odd explanatory word. By the time I ended the entire hall was chanting *'Vietnam Si, Yanqui No!'*. This brought a few policemen to the scene, at which point our Bolivian friends discreetly took us out by another exit and we made our way back to the other city. There was no time for Aeschylus now as we talked late into the night. I realized that my outburst at the fiesta had represented a deplorable breach of security, but interestingly enough none of the others reprimanded me and the Indian faces of that night accompanied me everywhere I went in Bolivia.

The next morning as we were on our way to collect our credentials from General Ovando's office, I noticed the Bolivian army on parade in full gear and with band. We all stood and watched in amazement. The soldiers were dressed in Prussian outfits, which was bizarre enough, but the tune being played by the band was distressingly familiar. It was the 'Horst Wessel Song', a favourite Nazi anthem. There could be no doubt at all. Later when we asked a local journalist about this, he acknowledged the fact and told us that one of the Germans who had helped to train the Bolivian Army during the thirties was a Captain Ernst Rohm! What a strange ruling class possessed this unfortunate country, which Queen Victoria once had erased off every map in Britain after her consul had been stripped naked by the then dictator and forced to ride through the streets on a donkey—a cross between Lady Godiva and Lord Christ.

We finally obtained our papers and rushed back to pack our bags. There was no flight to the tropical zones that day, but Schoenman was insistent that some of us had to get there immediately. No further delay was possible. I volunteered and Schoenman hired a twin-engined Cessna and a pilot to fly the two of us to Camiri. The deal was struck, though the blood-shot eyes of the pilot did not inspire confidence. The journey was sensational. Flying low across the Andes to the tropics, we had a unique view of the country. I wondered as we approached our destination where the guerrillas were based and Schoenman and I would often point down and exchange knowing winks. There were no disasters *en route*, not even when the pilot handed me the controls, only taking them back when the plane began to nosedive a bit. We landed on a tiny military airport. Just as we were disembarking, a military helicopter landed and an officer stepped out to be immediately surrounded by soldiers. He stared at our plane, then at us, and with a wave of his hand summoned us to his side. We walked towards the helicopter slowly. Colonel

Reque Teran asked to see our papers, inspected them closely and asked why we had come to the war zone. We explained that we were there to observe the battle and report back to our respective journals. He appeared somewhat bemused, but gave us a lift to Camiri in his jeep, but this was only after he had posed for several photographs in front of his helicopter. Later he would pose for me with his stretched out arm pointing a revolver at the horizon. The Colonel wanted to become famous.

Arriving in Camiri escorted by Reque Teran meant that no one else asked us any more questions that day. We booked into a hotel and then walked down the main street. Camiri was surrounded on all sides by mountains and only a single dusty trail led to the town. It could easily have been the set for a Hollywood Western. The single-storey houses, rectangular streets and the saloon bars gave this small oil town a very odd character. That night in a restaurant we were told that the last civilian mayor was fond of firing shots into the air when the waiters were slow in serving his meal. So it was not just my imagination which insisted on these images of Dodge City. After dinner, Schoenman and I walked outside the prison where Debray was being held, talking loudly in English in the hope that he would realize that there were friends in town.

The next morning we registered our presence with the local police chief. He stared at me for a long time and then nodded knowingly. He then muttered some insult which neither Ralph nor myself understood, but which had his cohorts roaring with laughter. We stared back silently till he returned our papers and then walked out quickly. Reque Teran was free that morning and agreed to talk for the record. He spoke good English. He had been trained in Georgia and had served as a military attaché at the Bolivian Embassy in Washington from 1964-66. He was in command of the Fourth Army Division's anti-guerrilla campaign and he confirmed much of what we already knew, though he was disturbed by the fact that 'there is contact between the miners and the guerrillas. Some of the people we kill are miners.' We questioned him about Debray and the other prisoners. He admitted that Roth was a genuine journalist, but

'Bustos is an agitator from Argentina. He came here to receive some instructions from Guevara. He knows many things about the guerrillas. He knows more than he says...' And Debray? 'Monsieur Debray is a well-known communist, an admirer of Guevara, a friend of Castro. I've read Debray's book. It is a good book for guerrillas. I would recommend it to you. Mao Zedong doesn't work here. He wrote for a country with a big population, though some principles can be used here, of course. But, Debray came to help the guerrillas and we caught him. I hope it's death. Not just thirty years. If you have a snake you kill it immediately.'

It was a tremendous strain listening to talk of this sort without being able to reply in kind and since self-control was not a virtue for which Ralph Schoenman was best-known, we decided that it would be best to continue the interview on another occasion. As soon as we were out of the Colonel's earshot, Schoenman exploded and the bile poured out without restraint. That afternoon the remaining three members of our party arrived and we briefed them on the special qualities of this zone.

Our aim was to see Debray in his cell so as to reassure ourselves that he was alive and to make him feel that he was not alone. He had met Robin Blackburn in Havana and it was therefore essential that Blackburn was one of the visitors. I asked Reque Teran whether I could go in and photograph Debray. Surely, I pleaded, it is in your interests to let the world see that he is alive and permitted to receive visitors. The Colonel said that this was too important a matter for him to decide, but he would make the request known to higher authorities. In the meantime he advised us to be patient and invited me to accompany him on one of his missions to Langunillas the following week. The very thought filled me with nausea, but there was no way out and I agreed with a fake enthusiasm. He promised that he would let me photograph captured guerrillas that day.

Meanwhile, all that we could do was wait till La Paz sanctioned permission for us to see the prisoner of Camiri. The town was full of officers, soldiers and, increasingly, US officers,

who refused to speak to us. We must have seemed a pretty odd
bunch to the Bolivians. We certainly did not behave as
journalists are supposed to in these circumstances. If they had
decided to spy on us or place hidden microphones in our hotel
rooms, the Bolivians would have received a serious shock. For
in private we talked endlessly about world politics, Marxist
theory, the fate of the Russian and Chinese revolutions and
similar topics. One of the most heated exchanges took place
between Schoenman and Anderson on the practice and nature of
Stalinism. Perry Anderson insisted on putting the record of
Stalinism in some overall perspective. Both he and Robin
Blackburn, who, much to Schoenman's great annoyance, tended
to agree with each other on most questions, were sympathetic to
the positions of the pro-Moscow CPs in Western Europe. This
was, in Anderson's case, moderated by a particular interpretion
of Isaac Deutscher's writings on the USSR. Schoenman was, I
suppose, a libertarian Trotsko-Marxist slightly infected by
anarchism.

My own political formation was in a state of flux, but having
recently read Deutscher, I was fascinated by our debates. It is
difficult to describe Lothar Menne's orientation at that time. He
said very little and tended to become passive when the political
temperature rose in our small rooms. He did, alas, chain-smoke,
thus breaking the united front against tobacco in our group. At
one stage the noise of debate reached such a crescendo that the
guests in the neighbouring rooms complained by knocking on
our door. We had been discussing the scale of the repression in
Stalin's Russia. Schoenman had the facts and statistics at his
fingertips, but he also insisted on describing the most gruesome
tortures inflicted on political prisoners, who included tens of
thousands of veteran Bolsheviks, by the torturers of the NKVD.
At the end of his peroration, he stared hard at comrades
Anderson and Blackburn as if challenging them to reply. Perry
Anderson responded by reprimanding him for reducing
everything to 'a moral question'. At this point Schoenman
erupted, 'Stalin killed millions including the majority of old
Bolsheviks and you say this is a fucking moral question. We're

talking about one of the biggest crimes against socialism this century.' Robin Blackburn and myself acted as responsible seconds on that occasion and took our respective pugilists back to their chambers.

I was much more sympathetic to Schoenman during these battles and the arguments that underlay his freak-outs appealed far more than the icy logic of Perry Anderson. There was one time, however, when both men backed each other up against Blackburn and myself. The argument that night was on the events which led up to the success of the Chinese Revolution. Both Schoenman and Anderson dismissed Maoist pretension and the cult around Mao far too brusquely as far as I was concerned. Anderson then suggested that if there had been no Japanese occupation of China, the Maoists would never have succeeded. I responded by saying first that the argument was somewhat pointless since it could be argued that without the First World War there might not have been a Bolshevik victory in Petrograd in 1917. 'Not so,' said Schoenman, 'because Lenin's party had the correct ideas and understanding and would have won in the end. That cannot be said of Mao. He was a total confusionist.' We defended Mao vigorously, but the discussion ended as all such things do, not because we resolved anything, but because it was time to retire.

There was no food of any sort at the hotel. We used to breakfast on large helpings of fresh fruit juice at the various juice-bars and then sup at a rather good Italian bistro without a name, owned by a Sr Giuseppe. The only other eating place was a pretentious café, which served unrecognizable chunks of meat and charged a fortune. There were, alas, no street-vendors as in La Paz, so our choice was restricted. One night, the owner of the Italian restaurant joined us underneath the big tree where we normally ate. Small talk flowed as freely as the wine. Then we asked why he had left his native Italy and settled in Bolivia. It was a long story. Sr Giuseppe had been a leading fascist in Mussolini's party, had fought hard and well for the Duce, but rather than face arrest afterwards he had fled to Latin America and sought refuge in Bolivia. We became silent. So our jovial host was part of the postwar fascist emigration from Europe. I wonder what crimes he had committed. They must have been fairly horrendous for him to hide in this particular hole. He left our table after this, not realizing the terrible moral dilemma we now had to confront. A discussion followed his exit. Could we carry on eating there? I was in a minority of one. The others decided that Giuseppe's had to be boycotted. I accepted the status of a 'loyal minority' and trailed behind them the next day as we made our way to Café Rubbish. One meal there was sufficient to enable me to reopen the question. The previous day's decision was unanimously reversed. The boycott was over.

Every day after supper we would stroll down the main dust track of the town. As we passed the prison quarters we would whistle the 'Internationale', hoping that Regis would hear and recognize the tune. One morning permission arrived, but only for a photograph and not any interviews. This posed a problem since the local authorities knew that it was *I* who was the photographer. I insisted that I needed someone to carry my camera bag and telephoto lens and, much to my amazement, this was agreed. Robin Blackburn followed me in to Debray's cell as an assistant. Debray recognized him immediately and acknowledged him with a nod. The look of relief on his face had made it all worthwhile. During the time I was photographing him, I managed to mutter that more and more people were arriving in this country and there was no way they would kill him. He nodded again and we were then ushered out.

In the square that day I began to photograph every military officer in sight. I did so with a powerful telephoto lens. Unknown to me, I was being watched by another Colonel from the Fourth Division. As he walked out of his office I took several photographs of him as well. When I saw him striding towards me, I took the roll out and put it in my pocket. He marched straight up to me and demanded the film. I showed him an empty camera. He pointed to my camera bag. I put my hand in blind, took out an exposed roll from the very bottom and handed it over to him. He grunted, said he would have it developed and if his image was on it he would return to have a word with me.

He then took out a revolver, pointed it at my chest and warned me that if I took any more unauthorized photographs of military personnel he would not hesitate to shoot me dead. He was not joking. In fact he appeared to be suffering from rabies, since he was frothing at the mouth. In any case I agreed. The next day Colonel Juan Delgado Molanoz, for that was his name, returned the developed film. As luck would have it, the roll had only contained some scenic views of the Andes photographed from the air.

The next morning I accompanied Colonel Reque Teran on one of his helicopter missions, hoping against hope that I would not have to witness any brutality against the guerrillas. Once or twice the helicopter swooped down at the sign of some movement, but they were false alarms. We landed at Lagunillas, a village where the guerrillas were known to operate. Reque Teran was saluted by the officer in command of the local military post. He was not wearing insignia. I asked him for his estimate of guerrilla strength. 'Those who serve a foreign interest,' he replied, 'are called bandits not guerrillas.' It was an interesting distinction, but I could not help replying that if that was so then the Bolivian Army could be characterized in the same way given that some people said they were operating in the American interests. He hurriedly changed the subject and reverted to my original question. He forgot his earlier strictures and used the forbidden word. 'The guerrillas have suffered serious losses, but we can't reveal this as yet.' Reque Teran interrupted him with an odd aphorism: 'If you want the fly to enter your mouth, you mustn't close it too soon.' Both officers roared with laughter. Then the junior man explained that there were lots of little groups of guerrillas, but no fixed force. He spoke, too, of 'Operation Cynthia', which he described as a mopping-up exercise. He told me that Che was 'somewhere near here, but we cannot tell you the exact location'.

While he had been talking, Reque Teran had wandered away to speak to some local soldiers. I could see them pointing at me from a distance. I did not pay much attention since my appearance—very long hair and droopy moustache—often excited adverse comment. The day before, a fat, fascist comedienne, who had arrived from Sucre to entertain the troops had shouted: 'You need a haircut, you...' I responded in kind. 'You badly need a diet, fat lady ...' There was a great deal of nervousness about the guerrillas and long hair was viewed as an insignia of rebellion. Suddenly Reque Teran sent a messenger to get me. I walked over to him. The two soldiers stared at me. Then the Colonel asked if they could see my watch. I rolled up my sleeve and allowed them to inspect it from every angle. Reque Teran then asked me some trivial questions and I gave equally trivial answers.

Reque Teran was planning to stay there overnight, so I returned to Camiri in a jeep. As the vehicle entered the town, we were stopped. Two soldiers asked me to get out and accompany them to their office. I did so and was taken to a tiny room, without windows. Inside was a chair and a table. They asked me to wait and locked the door, leaving me in total darkness. I don't remember how long I was left there alone, but it was definitely over an hour. As I sat there I tried to work out the possible reasons for my arrest. It was unlikely to be the fake credentials. Perhaps they had discovered that we had been sent by the Russell Foundation, but if so why pick on me alone? To say that I was scared would be an understatement. After a few weeks in the 'war zone' I had no illusions as to the capacity of the Colonels to do whatever they liked. The rabid Colonel had said as much during the fracas in the square.

At last the door opened. Two men walked in, sat opposite me and started asking me questions in Spanish. I repeated several times that I did not speak the language. One of them spoke English and muttered in classic B-movie style that 'we have ways of making you talk Spanish'. I replied calmly that I did not speak Spanish, but if he was suggesting that a few days of torture might lead to my acquiring a new language, then I would be eternally grateful. The sarcasm was not totally wasted and the man informed me that I had been recognized by two soldiers at Lagunillas. These men had been captured and then released by Che's group. I was amazed, and the incredulity must have convinced them to some degree. 'Are you saying,' I shouted, 'that I am a Cuban guerrilla?' Both men nodded. 'Then why in heaven's name should I travel on a Pakistani passport? Surely it doesn't make sense, does it?' The English speaker actually smiled and I sighed with relief. 'You are not any Cuban guerrilla,' the inquisitor continued. 'You are Ponbo, Che Guevara's bodyguard.' At that point I wished I had been Ponbo somewhere in the jungle. To their faces I simply grinned and told them that if they were foolish enough to charge me on that score they would make a laughing stock of themselves since it would not take me long to prove my identity.

Outside, unbeknown to me, Ralph Schoenman was mobilizing support. A stringer from the *New York Times* had filed a despatch claiming that another journalist had been arrested and the military were incredibly stupid. The local censor had not permitted the report to be filed, but my release was ordered. I was told to report to the police the next day. When I went back in the morning I was made to walk past all the guerrillas held prisoner including Bustos. Slowly they all shook their heads in the negative. Later that day we went to see a Captain Reuben Sanchez, who had been captured and released by Che. He had made sketches of the guerrilla fighters. When we went in, he showed me his drawing of Ponbo and there was a certain likeness. Sanchez had clearly been impressed by the conduct of his captors, even though they had released him without any clothes and he had been found naked. Even at that time one felt that this officer had been won over by Che. Five years later he fell resisting the Banzer dictatorship. Prior to that he had announced his defection to the ideas of Che Guevara.

Later that night Schoenman insisted that I return to Europe. He was worried that this incident might not be the last and the fact that the military had blundered might provoke some young blade to take individual action. As Debray's trial had been further delayed, I agreed, albeit reluctantly. Schoenman accompanied me to Cochabamba. We spent a day there and in the evening watched *Cat Ballou* in the local flea-pit. It had no subtitles in Spanish, let alone Quechua, even though the audience was largely Indian. The next morning I said farewell to Schoenman and flew back to La Paz. I had to wait a few days before I could get a flight out of the country. The Sucre Palace was booked out, so I stayed at the Copacabana. As I was waiting for the lift, I suddenly saw Richard Gott. We embraced and I told him my tale. He was off to tea with some other journalists, including a man from *The Times* at the British Embassy. I was dragged along and the jovial diplomat happily conferred honorary citizenship to me for the occasion. Richard asked about the real situation of the guerrillas. I said that the Colonels were fairly confident that they had Che cornered and repeated Reque Teran, who had told me that 'It is difficult to leave the country when the whole of Bolivia is hunting for Che Guevara'. This was rubbish, however, as Ponbo and two other Cubans did escape the dragnet and reached Havana safely many months later. Che had refused to leave the field. We talked in the night and he regaled me with the latest crimes of the Labour Government. The next day he left for Camiri. Little did we know that in a few months he would be asked to identify the dead body of Che, whom he had met in Cuba. I also met Regis' mother, Madame Janine Debray in La Paz and told her that I had seen her son with my own eyes and that he was safe. She had brought an appeal from De Gaulle and the Pope to Barrientos, asking for his release. It was a strange experience for her, a right-wing Gaullist, being compelled to hobnob with the left-wing mafia, who were the only people actively and systematically campaigning for Debray's freedom.

On my last day in La Paz, I witnessed the arrival of the left-wing Italian publisher, Feltrinelli, with a lady friend. They had been in town for only a few days but had already created a scandal in Rome. Feltrinelli's companion was photographed with him and the newspapers captioned her as his wife, upon which the real Signora Feltrinelli had raised a tempest back home. When I went to greet him in the lobby of the hotel, Feltrinelli was attired in a large fur coat. He was poring over a large map of Bolivia and had marked the guerrilla zone with red stars. He told me that he had come with money, lots of it, to help buy arms and medicines for Che's fighters. This was said in a loud voice. His bejewelled lady friend seemed oblivious to the world. Within 24 hours both of them had been declared *personae non gratae* and expelled from the country.

Some ten days after my departure, Ralph Schoenman devised a plan to hire a jeep, buy food and medicines and locate Che's camp. He had bribed some officers to discover the region in which the veteran revolutionary was meant to be operating. I have often wondered how I would have responded to such a plan. I have a feeling that one's heart would have overridden reason. This was also Robin Blackburn's secret reaction, but Perry Anderson's intellect was in command. He realized that it was a madcap adventure which might get them all killed. Schoenman was now in a minority of one. He ran after the jeep transporting Messrs Anderson, Blackburn and Menne to the airport, on their way home, waving his fist in anger. He did carry on regardless, almost got himself killed but was finally deported. The Labour government declared him an 'undesirable alien' and prevented him from returning to Britain, presumably on instructions from the State Department.

I reported to the Peace Foundation, gave them dozens of rolls of film, which they certainly used, but which mysteriously disappeared. One set went to the archives in Havana. There is no trace of the others.

ZIA MOHYEDDIN

Zia Mohyeddin is a well-known actor, director, producer and was with Central TV in Britain from 1980-94. He graduated from Punjab University, worked for the Pakistani stage and for Australian broadcasting and went on to The Royal Academy of Dramatic Arts, London. He has appeared on stage in *A Passage to India* (1960), *The Merchant of Venice* (1966), *Volpone* (1967), *Film, Film, Film* (1986) among others and in films such as *Lawrence of Arabia* (1961), *Khartoum* (1965), *The Assam Garden* (1985), *Immaculate Conception* (1995). He created the Channel Four television series, *Asian Pride* (1990) and his extensive television performances range from *Jewel in the Crown* (1983), *King of the Ghetto* (1986), *Mountbatten* (1988), *Shalom Salaam* (1989). He was Director General of the Pakistan National Performing Ensemble in the 1970s and for the past few years he has been writing a weekly column for *The News International*, in Pakistan.

LEELA LEAN

I

Nobby Brabham had a bad leg and he tottered as he walked, much in the manner of West End actors simulating the gait of gout-ridden aristocrats. Nobby was not an aristocrat, but he dressed, talked, and entertained like one. He was a charming host who could have become a little too fond of his own assets but was kept in check by his plain and sensible wife, Esther who was an aristocrat, but was extremely down-to-earth.

The Brabhams lived in a smart town house near Lancaster Gate. They were childless and they entertained frequently. I was introduced to them by a successful West End actress—I shall call her Henrietta Ince—who had made a reputation for playing suave ladies in drawing room comedies. Henrietta had befriended me when we were both appearing in Oxford in different theatres. When our respective plays were transferred to the West End more or less simultaneously, we began to see more of each other. She had known Esther since the time when Esther, in an effort to de-class herself, had accepted the job of a wardrobe assistant in the same theatre where Henrietta was playing the lead in a Lonsdale comedy. Esther became Henrietta's dresser for a while. Rumour had it that Nobby went backstage with a bunch of roses to pay court to Henrietta, but was so smitten by Esther, when he encountered her outside the dressing room, that he gave Esther the flowers and asked her for a date.

Apart from Henrietta, who was a regular, and for a while myself, Esther's chic dinner parties were attended by a rich variety of people: diamond merchants from Antwerp, Central European counts (Esther's parents were from Austria), art critics, county judges, dress designers—and Lofty Wickham-Flint, a cherubic, wavy-haired man given to wearing flamboyant socks, who always had an appropriate remark for every occasion. He was Nobby's business partner in some ways.

I don't think I ever met a more amiable man. Lofty was not a politician but his perception about politics and political personalities was astute. It was through him that I first learnt about the shenanigans at Cliveden. He told me that the Pakistani Field Marshal never frolicked in the pool with Mandy Rice-Davis simply because he wasn't a good swimmer. The President was enamoured by Christine Keeler though, but then, so was everyone else.

Wickham-Flint invited me (and the Brabhams, of course— Henrietta was on tour) to spend a Sunday at his place. He lived in a beautiful Georgian house near Amersham. We were greeted by four or five friendly dogs who accompanied us into the hall, but then not finding us very interesting, disappeared. We walked through the spacious hall into the morning room with lovely French windows which revealed the lush green undulating Buckinghamshire landscape. There were comfortable chairs all around, but the main feature of the room was an exquisite Regency *chaise-lounge* on which sat, cross-legged, like a high priestess, Leela Lean with a golden ring in each one of her toes. One or two guests sat close by, listening to her with rapt attention as though they were receiving benediction. There was a pause as we were introduced. The spell was broken; positions were shifted; courtesies were exchanged. Leela Lean did not move an inch. After a few minutes a different circle formed itself around her.

She had been the legendary Leela Madkar. It was said that apart from the Khajuraho temples, the only other thing worth seeing in India was Leela Madkar. Her long hair that reached well below her waist, her Mogul-miniature eyes and her perfectly sculpted nose had made her into the darling of portrait painters. David Lean, the great movie director, on what he used to term as a 'spiritual work-out' tour of India must have been taken in by this quintessence of oriental femininity. He wooed her, pursued her (Leela would later confess that he hounded her, but the remark was made when she had become embittered), allowed himself to be photographed everywhere, Leela ever so slightly reclining upon his arm, and soon the fabulous Leela Madkar became Leela Lean.

All of this I had heard from friends in India and England, including contradictory stories about Madkar: the wealthy businessman who was callous and never gave Leela the care and succour that she needed; the Maharashtrian gentleman who was heartbroken when he heard of his wife's waywardness and took refuge in an *ashram*. It was generally believed that Leela swept Lean off his feet and that well before he took his return flight from Bombay he had knelt and popped the question.

When I got to know Leela, I realized that it was not Leela, the flirt, who used her wiles to 'make a catch of the century' as one Indian newspaper put it. David Lean was an unusually handsome man with ascetic features and a winning smile. He had gone through a couple of marriages which had turned him into a bit of a misanthrope. He needed a new experience, an Eastern lady who would not assert her individuality, a decorative woman who would be submissive and stay content wherever he chose to lodge her. It was Lean who swept Leela off her feet, brought her over to London, parked her at Basil Street Hotel in Knightsbridge and then went about his work.

David Lean was a big name in those days. He was in New York or else he would have been there that afternoon. The Oscar he had received for his *River Kwai* had meant that big American money was now at his feet. He had not yet embarked upon his career of reclusion and visited the likes of Wickham-Flint in his wife's company (a practice he was to discard within a few years). People naturally flocked to meet the great man's wife. Leela seemed to revel basking in his glory.

She talked hurriedly with a very slight stammer; at times it was difficult to understand what she said because she ran some words together like 'Davidhateslondon'. She had the kind of accent much sought after by stand-up comics. Nobby and Esther stood around her, their newly acquired fascination with the East became reinforced. When luncheon was announced she asked me to sit near her. She wasn't going to be hurried.

She spoke to me in chaste Hyderabadi Urdu. It was an agreeable surprise to learn that her Urdu was devoid of any trace of Hindi. When 'DavidandI' were in India every movie star had asked her to introduce him to David. It had become quite tiring for him. Even the great Dilip Kumar had approached her. She would like me to meet David. She had seen me in the play that I was appearing in at the time, but wanted to see it again because David hadn't. I felt flattered, naturally. She was dressed in a smooth grey saree. The rings on her toes glistened. She had liquid eyes with long, natural eyelashes.

II

Lunch was a long drawn-out affair. Wickham-Flint was renowned for his excellent cellar. The lull between courses was filled with conversation brightened by some excellent vintage stuff. Leela left before the dessert because she had to go and meditate. Everyone tried to persuade her to stay on but she was firm.

A few weeks later true to her promise, she came backstage with the great man. He was courteous; she chattered and he listened, smiling benignly. I stood, a towel wrapped around my neck, until David Lean insisted that I sit down and stop playing the host. The gist of Leela's talk was that David had been interested in filming Forster's masterpiece for a long time. Lean suggested that I approach Forster about it. I mentioned that as far as I knew Forster was deeply suspicious of Hollywood and its output. Lean said he had heard about it, but Leela insisted that Forster's reservations would 'become ill-founded' once he knew that David would be tackling his work. 'Whydon'tweaskhimtolunch?' she enquired.

Lean, in a tone of voice used for recalcitrant children, explained that one did not invite an eighty year old, secluded Cambridge don to lunch. I became familiar with that tone later on, because he adopted it whenever actors dried, or an over-zealous assistant did something wrong. Leela, suitably chastened, sighed and said the ways of the West were strange. This pleased her husband because it fortified his notion of Indians as an unspoiled, slightly muddled, deviously spiritual people. I remember I was on guard all the time. I wanted to know what Lean thought of me as an actor at the same time as I wished not to appear too overwhelmed by his presence. I had spent sufficient time in penury and wasn't, therefore, susceptible to accepting the newly bestowed status of a celebrity without being wary. Also I had become disillusioned with people who imitated an Indian accent in the belief that they would thus befriend me sooner. David Lean at least spared me the ritual of saying 'Goodness gracious me.'

Leela Lean with her unique status of 'protector of all Indians in David's domain' as well as being his chatelaine, understood that I was in awe of her husband and was unable to give her the attention she commanded. She turned the conversation to the Pinter play which had just opened and how hard she found him to swallow. Her husband interrupted her. 'Come on,' he said, gently. 'We can't stay here all night. The man has things to do.' She got up, but not before inviting me to lunch. 'Can we?' she asked him. 'He is not a secluded don.' 'Yes darling,' he said with a winsome smile.

Lean's visit created a bit of a stir in the theatre. Everyone wanted to know what he was like. Did he say when he was beginning his next film? People assumed that because of his (beautiful, they all said) Indian wife, my connection with David Lean was firm and solid.

It took a long time for the lunch to transpire. In between I had a chance to see Forster. I told him about Lean's visit and interest, but Forster good humouredly said it was simpler to say 'No'. He had already told me about the overtures Hollywood had made towards him and how he had found it difficult to tell them he was not interested. He was sure his work would be distorted and he didn't want that.

The invitation for lunch came through Maud Spectre, who was David Lean's casting director. When I arrived at the Lean's hotel suite, Leela opened the door and greeted me with a Hyderabadi salaam. She apologized for the delay; David had to go to all kinds of places in Europe and America and, much against her wishes, she had to tag along. As usual, she spoke breathlessly.

She was dressed in a *farshi gharara* and a short sleeved, fitted *kurta* which showed her excellent figure to perfection. The *dupatta* was an accessory, flung across her neck. Her long hair hung loose; a tiny diamond sat upon her nose. She was barefooted; this time only two silver rings shielding her toes.

She perched herself on a big settee for a moment before settling down, cross-legged, as she had, at Wickham-Flint's house. She said she couldn't relax if she sat like an *Angrez*. Ideally, there should have been a *takht* with bolsters all round. 'That's the style I've been accustomed to,' she said in a subdued voice.

'And a *paandaan*?" I said jokingly.

'Oh yes, yes, yes,' she perked up. 'I have one, but it is only a travelling *paandaan*, given to me by Nawab Sahib Chhattari. I had such beautiful proper *paandaans* in Hyderabad.'

I tried not to look at her, in case I betrayed my infatuation.

There was a small *tanpura* resting in a corner. She told me she carried it everywhere. She couldn't live without her morning practice, her *riyaz*. We talked of music and *ragas*. She talked of the great musicians she had hosted in her house in Hyderabad. She interspersed her discourse with a few well-known Urdu verses.

David was nowhere to be seen. He was doing preparatory work on *Lawrence of Arabia* in those days. He must have been held up in a script conference, she thought. When David worked, he forgot all about his appointments. Lunch was ordered; she was a vegetarian but I could have whatever I fancied. I declined politely and had to make do with an insipid celery and carrot cutlet.

The afternoon lingered 'as it malingered.' She was now reclining on the settee on one elbow. I was still expecting David Lean to turn up any moment and so, exercising a great deal of self-restraint, refrained from any flirtatious remark. She sensed that my self-composure was hollow and, with a deep throated laugh, got up to announce that it was time for her meditation.

I took leave of her. She told me that David was going to cast me in *Lawrence*. She had suggested this to him but David had taken the decision not because of her recommendation. David never listened to *sifarish*, she said. I mustn't become hoity toity and turn it down. I needed to work with directors like him. She asked me to promise that I would accept whatever I was offered.

I saw her only once before I arrived in Akaba for the filming of *Lawrence*. This was at a premiere to which she had invited me. She never spoke to me on that occasion. She and David were surrounded by movie moguls and films stars. The starlets stood around her as though she was royalty. She was decked up in jewels. She wore a black velvet cloak over her saree; her hair fell over the cloak like a silken waterfall. She looked gorgeous.

The filming had not yet begun when she landed in Akaba. We were all living in tents. There was only one bungalow other than a few ramshackle army barracks, and that's where the Leans were lodged. A big marquee had been installed not too far from their bungalow as a kind of mess. We all ate there together in the evening. The Leans would sometimes deign to join us. Leela had given up wearing jewellery. Instead, she wore flowers. The flowers were flown in specially for her from Amman and her maid threaded them into bangles and ear-rings. People bowed to the majesty that she invoked and she bestowed gracious smiles on everyone.

When I developed a virus of some kind, she prevailed upon David to have me moved to the spare room in their bungalow. She tended to me, caringly. I learnt a bit about her. Her devotion to religion was absolute. She had been hungry for love ever since her childhood but she had never got it. People professed to love her but that was not the kind of love she hankered for. Her mother was an extra-ordinarily beautiful woman; compared to her she was a plain Jane.

Soon we all moved to a gruesome location in the middle of the desert. Leela went back to Amman. David was now fully immersed in his work but in the evenings he was spending more and more time with his continuity girl, who assumed a new authority within days. Previously, she carried her own portable stool; now a prop man carried it for her.

After a few gruelling weeks of work I, along with two or three other actors, were sent to the only hotel in Amman to recuperate for a weekend. Leela got to know of our visit. She was staying with some American friends in a luxurious villa. I was invited over and the American hostess never allowed me to return to the hotel. Leela was back to wearing long earrings, silken sarees and golden rings on her toes, but there was a pinched look about her, and her eyes remained hooded most of the time. She began to say something in Urdu once or twice but the hostess intervened, 'Hey, no shop talk.'

I wasn't able to talk much to Leela during that weekend, because the hostess monopolized me. She was one of those ebullient Americans who thrive upon hobnobbing with people from, what they consider to be, the artistic world. Leela may have regretted inviting me over because her eyes were sad when she said goodbye to me the next morning.

I learnt from a postcard sent to me by the American hostess a few days later that she had gone to India, indefinitely.

III

Three eventful years rolled by very quickly and I found myself in New York preparing for a show which took me to the library a good deal. As I left the library one late afternoon, it began to pour. Everyone knows that it is easier for a camel to pass through a needle's eye than for you and I to find a cab in Manhattan when it rains. I cursed myself for not carrying a mac and for not wearing a hat. My hair was dripping wet as I waved frantically at every passing yellow cab. A taxi eventually pulled up near me; the door at the back opened and I heard someone say, '*Ah-yea*, I'll drop you.' Murmuring thanks I got in quickly. He was a thick-set man with a round, chubby face and darkish, tortoise-shell glasses. He introduced himself, 'I am Aslam Khan, the brother of Dilip Kumar.' He knew who I was. He would drop me wherever I had to go, but if I wasn't too tied up could I not come up to his apartment, which was very close, and take some refreshments. He was civilized and persuasive.

His younger sister, Faridah and his brother, Ahsan (both of whom I was to meet frequently in Bombay in a few years time) were also staying in the apartment. I spent an agreeable evening. All three of them came down to find a cab for me. 'By the way,' said Ahsan, putting his hand on my arm, 'I met a lady here who talks very fondly of you. Her name is Leela.' Faridah remarked impishly that ladies were bound to be fond of ZM. 'I didn't know that she was in New York,' I said, embarrassed, for no reason whatsoever. We agreed to meet soon, as we parted.

It gave me a bit of a start when I received a phone call from Leela Lean a few days later. Why had I not been in touch with her? Had I forgotten her? Had I become too important? She knew I had been in Manhattan for quite a while. I had seen the Khan clan who had told me her whereabouts. She had swallowed her pride and was ringing me up herself. 'Cometomorrow.'

She was living at the Hamilton, a small hotel off 5th Avenue. It had a narrow, dark lobby, not too unlike the Basil Street Hotel in Knightsbridge. David was obviously partial to a bit of gloom. The suite she had been installed in was comfortable though not plush. The *tanpura* rested in one corner, the silver-framed photograph of her Guru, the late Maharishi someone stood on a tallboy. She was dressed as ornately as I remembered: bracelets, diamond-on-the-nose, toe-rings, earrings, all complementing a burgundy and cream saree. 'You look ready to be painted,' I said.

In between cups of coffee and stale pistachios, she rambled about her long stay in India, the trips she made from North to South. At times she felt she found a meaning to her life—when she woke up and walked barefooted on the grass or when she sang a few phrases to herself as the sun was going down, but most of the time she felt uncomfortable; she no longer felt at home with friends she had known for ever because they had begun to distance themselves. She belonged to the glamorous world of Hollywood and 'showbiz'. She wanted to be accepted for what she was, but this was not possible. They wanted to hear scandals about Rock Hudson and William Holden, and she couldn't tell them any.

It was Sam Spiegel, the arch manoeuvrer, the real force behind *Lawrence*, who plotted her return. Spiegel knew instinctively that Leela would fit in well with his plans for the grand opening of the film in America. A bedecked oriental beauty on the arms of Lean was exotica of the highest order. He began to make phone calls to her. When, eventually, she asked David whether it would be a good thing for her to return, he said, 'You know what a farce these openings are. Come if you can stand being monkeyed around.' But Spiegel insisted; in fact, he said he would come and drag her out personally if she became silly. 'And don't worry about David, he is English-shy. Of course he wants you to be here.'

It had been a long, unending spree; days spent in getting dressed and browsing in antique shops, evenings taken up with sitting on silken settees, her feet tucked under her, soaking up the admiring looks of men and women. And then the night of the Oscars, 'the fanfare, the ballyhoo, the limousines, the Spencer Tracys, the Pandro Bermans, thejingbanglot.' The glitz

of the Oscars and the openings had worn off. David was away;
he didn't show up for weeks.

It was not till our second meeting that I told Leela why I had
been hesitant in making contact with her. I didn't want to run
into David who, I felt, was sure to imagine that I was after a
job. 'I might as well tell you,' I said, 'My visit to you in Amman
must have caused him some displeasure because he cooled off
towards me and I stopped getting the nod from him to join him
at his table for dinner.'

She laughed bitterly. 'He was muchworsetome.' She had
tried to plead with him, tried to explain that it was her friend
Lueen who had insisted upon my stay in her house, but David
was convinced it was a conspiracy to undermine him. 'Davidisa
big sulker.' And he could be sadistic.

I saw quite a bit of her during that autumn. Usually it was
mid-morning. She did not finish her toilette till then. When I
suggested we go out for a meal, she declined. Later on I realized
that she was being cagey. She had the comfort of staying in a
hotel but that was it. The modest stipend given to her through
one of David's secretaries was barely enough for the special
dry-cleaning of her sarees. If she wanted extra money, she had
to ask the secretary who bluntly told her that she would have to
check it with David first. She didn't like doing that. The same
secretary probably kept a record of who she went out with. She
could get a limousine, but she would have to inform the secretary
where she was going. Sometimes she would be so overwrought
that she would sit cross-legged on the floor and quote Ghalib:
Kis din na hamarey dil pe aarey chala kiya. She always
murdered one of his most poignant lines.

Once or twice, upon my insistence, she picked up the *tanpura*
and began an *alap* of *Asawari*, a difficult *raga* at the best of
times. It was evident that she was tone deaf for she repeatedly
went off key. She had a passion for music, a deep-throated
voice like Gangu Bai Hangal, but no musical sensibility. I
admired her absorption though. She would flick off an imaginary
tear as she put away the instrument.

IV

Leela had become enmeshed with a few well-heeled Jewish doctors and stockbrokers and their heavily bejewelled wives who all lived in individually designed homes in Long Island. They were all anxious to learn about the real significance of *mantras*. She was the ideal person to satisfy their curiosity. Besides, she could tell them tittle-tattle about William Holden and Anthony Quinn. Oddly enough, the wives didn't resent their husbands' unconcealed fascination for her. They adored her because she was totally unaffected by American opulence. The husbands doted upon her because she didn't wear her femininity as a weapon. Leela was their icon.

She never talked to me about my work or myself so I never discussed it with her. Usually, she chattered, desultorily, about Nawab Sahib Chattari and Bahadur Yar Jung, She was not daft and, often, her opinions of plays and personalities were astute. She would stop abruptly and sigh as a mark of full stop. If, at such moments, I got up to take my leave, she didn't try to stop me, but looked at me with those hooded, lambent eyes. She could fall in love with me, she would say teasingly, but it would only make me run away.

This always made me a little uneasy because she saw quite a few other people to whom she was equally attached. Did she say this to all the others? She was not promiscuous by nature; it was just that she gave herself wholeheartedly to anyone she thought would love her with all his spirit; bodily love stayed in the inner crevices of her soul as something shady and an act of darkness. Once when she snuggled close to me, as I parted, I found that her bracelets and rings and ear-chains were like pincers cutting into my flesh. I observed (in jest, I thought) that it must take her hours to remove her armour plate, and tears rolled down her cheeks. There was a time, she said, when she never had to do it. Her Indian maid would, slowly and gently, undo each ornament—and massage her feet while doing it.

I returned to New York after more than a year to learn that she had been removed to a single room. David had rented a place for her in Los Angeles. She had gone there but had felt miserable. People had been nice to her; at least two of Lean's admirers, George Cukor and Fred Zinneman, excellent directors both, had invited her over a couple of times which restored her dignity for a day or two; otherwise she just sat around waiting for the sunset. At last she became defiant and insisted that she be moved back to New York, but this time a different minion could only arrange for a single, poky little room.

She had begun to neglect her appearance. She had become moody and languid. Sometimes I could see that her brain was drumming its fingers and looking around for something to do, but then apathy set in. She looked an ex-B-movie star, sliding across her room in a faded, chenille housecoat. It was her rich, dark brown, shimmering hair and her mysterious eyes, which prevented her from looking frumpy. The once pampered lady of leisure, who had spent her life cruising antique shops and enjoying long, sumptuous dinner parties, was reduced to eating yesterday's potato salad. Her *pooja* brass gods and goddesses occupied the windowsill. She was anxious to peel off life's accessories, but was torn between living and not living. David only spoke to her through one of his assistants. After years of pain and disillusionment she was teetering at the edge of despair, but she didn't moan. 'Why don't you go to India?' I said. But India only meant a daughter who was married with children. The thought of living with her daughter in a tiny two room flat and playing grandma, sent a shiver down her spine.

Why did she choose to exist as a more or less discarded mistress? She must have known deep down that David was never going to come back to her. There had been gossip about his dalliance with a new secretary. I think she hoped that there would be a large enough settlement to enable her to live in the style and manner to which she had become accustomed—a hotel suite with room and maid service. She didn't want a home; she wouldn't know how to run it. She didn't know how to get into a subway or drive a car. There were people still willing to pick her up and drop her back, but she did not go out as she used to. Perhaps she didn't want word to reach David that the abandoned, suffering wife was seen cavorting or socializing.

Her stammering had become a bit more pronounced, but she was determined not to become morose or religious. A new devotee, a part-time teacher in the Bronx, brought her freshly cooked vegetarian food three or four times a week. He was a shiny looking man with a balding head and he was quite content to worship her from afar.

It was during a rehearsal in the late 70s, nearly fourteen years on, that an actor I normally avoided because of his feigned uncouthness, informed me that he had a message for me from Leela Lean. She had invited him that evening and she had asked him to bring me along.

It was an agreeable surprise to see her ensconced in a lavish suite at the Grosvenor House Hotel. Had a settlement been made? I wondered. The large sitting room was full of young people from the sub-continent: long-haired painters, plain, earnest looking girls, research students probably, out-of-work actors and an erstwhile Maharajah who was having his palm read by a bull-doggish woman. Leela hadn't lost her knack of drawing people to herself.

I went looking for her in the pantry. She looked at me and shut her eyes as if I had betrayed her in some way and she couldn't bear to see me. She looked wrinkly and frail; her hair had greyed and her once moist lips were partially cracked. Then she took a step towards me and held my hands; her fingers were gnarled. She was dressed in all her finery.

It was not a setting I cared for, so I left soon after. As always she didn't try to stop me. She looked perfectly at ease with her surroundings. 'Come again,' she said, 'and bring your wife along. I've heard a lot about her,' she stuttered slightly, 'b..beauty.'

I never saw her again. The cruellest blow she was dealt with was that she was evicted from her Grosvenor House apartment, I heard. The settlement may not have allowed for a large suite in a posh West End hotel. No one knew her whereabouts, not even the actor who kept tabs on everyone. Where had she gone? Which county? Which town? The lady who evoked lush, exotic landscapes had simply vanished.

Only last week I was walking along 5th Avenue when I thought of looking at the narrow facade of the Hamilton. It doesn't exist any more; there is a new plaza in its place. I felt a strange pang as I stood for a while looking at this glass and steel structure. I could have sworn I heard a few resonant notes of *Asawari*, albeit, slightly off key.

SARA SULERI

Sara Suleri Goodyear grew up in England and different Pakistani cities. After graduating from Kinnaird College, Lahore, she went on to Punjab University and then the United States for higher studies. She is now a Professor of English at Yale University. The first chapter of her memoir, *Meatless Days* (University of Chicago Press, 1989), was selected for the 1987 Pushcart Prize. She has also written a book of literary criticism *The Rhetoric of English in India* (University of Chicago Press, 1992) and is now working on a novel, set in Pakistan.

WHAT MAMMA KNEW[1]

My mother could not do without Jane Austen. This I had always known, long before I watched her face wear like the binding of a book, that creases its leather into some soft texture and acquires a subtle spine free of gilt, knowing better than openly to announce its title. For her preferences were there in every room, putting words into my mouth before my taste buds had acquired a means to cope with their suggestion: I had conducted a steady parlance with the names of books years prior to my reading of what those names embraced and held as secrets from me. Titles with a proper name in them were easiest, so I never had much difficulty with respecting the privacy of *Tom Jones, Madame Bovary*. I next felt reassured by every definite article that came my way, because even my own books—storybooks— knew how to tell me in an uncomplicated fashion what it meant to read upon a printed page 'The End'. So I did not mind when I spelled out to myself *The Mystery*—even when it then became the possession of such a haunting name as Edwin Drood—as

---

1. From *Meatless Days*, a creative memoir, at the heart of which are the deaths of the author's mother and later, her sister Ifat, both victims of hit-and-run accidents.

long as mystery was contained by a *The* that declared some
mastery of narrative. The titles that eluded context were the
ones that troubled me: *Persuasion*, I would read—a whole book
about a single word!—or *Beyond the Pleasure Principle*—what
did it mean, to write a book beyond what it was about? Troubled
and entranced, I was pleased to have my mother lead me through
those shelves and see the pleasure it conferred on her when she
told me, contemplatively, 'Yes, now you're old enough to read
Jane Austen.'

Afternoons were reading time, since the obligatory siesta of
the East, constructed to appease a summer sun, barely changes
character during those brief winter months when the brilliance
of the sky brings cool pleasure. In every season each day was
built around the expectation of a secluded afternoon, it being
useful for a day to know that a space of time will arrive when
the hours need not behave as day but can lie down, abstracted.
My mother's children would retire to their various beds with
books: each afternoon the house was quiet with reading. Then
the day could rise again, inspired by the prospect of the night
and ready to resume the task of company. I liked this segmented
quality to time, this pause—surely something on each day should
give it pause—the reintroduction through which day gave way
to evening and then to the workings of the night. But we had to
rise early, start thinking early, in order to enjoy those afternoons:
I begged to be allowed to sleep as long as possible, savouring
each minute of my sleep. Finally my mother would go out into
the courtyard and call up my name, which would reach me
reluctantly, breaking through rest's liquidity to say, 'Mair Jones,
your mother, is standing outside and calling up to you, asking
you to wake and become this thing, your name.' An
overalliterated name, I thought as I got up, this thing that I have
to be.

I liked the old campus of the university where my mother
taught. Its crazy commingling of Victoriana with the kind of
architecture the Victorians thought we Indians liked was pleasing
to me, with its curious lion-coloured stone and vast, aging
interiors. Those massive dams and courtyards sit opposite the

red museum and the court, just at the point where the Mall is about to trail off toward the Ravi River, making the transition from British Lahore to Mughal Lahore. The university intersects the two, looking out at Kim's Gun and the museum where Kipling's father worked, turning its back on the intricacies of the Anarkali Bazaar, named after the dancing girl that Jahangir is fabled to have loved. She was bricked alive into her grave as punishment for having solicited a prince's love, but at least it was not a lonely grave, lying at the heart of the getting and spending of Lahore's busiest bazaar. When I first entered the university, the thought of being—in such a literal way—my mother's student was strange to me, putting us both in a novel setting, over books. She seemed subdued to see me sitting in her public world, as though one had leaked into the other in some dreamwork, and, to the voice that had roused me an hour earlier, my name became an intensely private thing: 'Yes, Fawzia?' 'Yes, Huma?' she would say, and then, looking at me, 'Yes?' But she forgot my presence once, thus teaching me the rare pleasure that can attend a mother's forgetfulness. For she was teaching Jane Austen. Whenever was there such a perfect match, I thought entranced, between a teacher and the task? Task and teacher seemed wedded as a voice marries thought, making it impossible to discern at which point one revealed the other's reticence. I was working at the theatre in those days, dropping in at the university only when I had a chance, but now had quickly to reschedule all my rehearsal hours to accommodate Jane Austen. 'What,' I exclaimed, 'rehearse right now, and miss my mother teaching *Emma*?' Then, as I watched that face light up, a smile quickening its voice even when she was not smiling, there was curious recognition in her familiarity of face. 'Oh,' I realized, 'so it's not just Emma. Mamma's daughters also bring her joy.'

I recalled the posture of that discourse, its reserve, when last summer my sister Nuz turned to me and said, 'Mair was *To the Lighthouse* for me—she was Mrs Ramsay.' Nuz loves to pay a compliment, although it is a love fraught with risk to her: her eyes watch anxiously the unfolding of her praise, saying—even before it's done— 'No, I have not said it: this is not enough.' I smiled at her analogy, which pleased me, but told her that somehow I would say my mother was more invisible, more difficult to discern. 'Mair was beautiful!' Nuz answered, bridling. I laughed. 'So much so that she never wore it or anything upon her sleeve—did you notice that?—Her sleeves were always empty.' This was true, there always being around my mother hints of the capacity of space, as though each time she moved, she made interstices, neutral regions of low colour quite ravishing to anyone who, as daughter, was observer. For she moved in observation to a degree that caught my breath, made it draw back to create more space and murmur, 'I am observing what it means to be in observation.' During the years of her existence, I did not altogether understand this gravity, this weightlessness, she carried with her. But then, I did not teach. Now that I do, I know that great sobriety of tone betokens the bearing of a stately teacher whose step is always measuring out what she sees as the edges of this great impossibility, of what it means to teach.

Sometimes, when I feel burdened by this baldest prose—I lived too long with the man of the hairless head—and tyrannized by the structure of a simple sentence, it does me good to recollect how quietly my mother measured out her dealings with impossible edges. What can I do but tell the same story again and yet again, as my acknowledgment of how dangerous it is to live in plot? What else was Mamma teaching when she passed me with a story that was always falling short? For something has to fall, as a day writes itself out into the more hectic writing of the night, and I am glad to be imbecile enough to wish it had been mine and not my mother's head. 'You can't change people, Sara,' she once told me, watching with compassion my crazy efforts on that behalf. How she would smile and shake her head, to see my complete regression into a woman who does to care for character at all and wants to change only the plot. Was it because she had so many children that she exempted herself from similar pedantic tricks, preferring, of necessity, to configure her mind around what need not be said, much as she congregated all our fussy eating habits around a meal? I would not like to be responsible for the way so many people choose to eat and not to eat, for even when I teach I sometimes think I fall into a lazy way of talking as though there were simply a bunch of equally fed bodies in front of me, not stopping in my haste to listen and to differentiate. It makes me realize something of my mother's concentration in her home, of her perpetual attention to the assembly of our stories, which let her learn the limits of our private tastes, what each of us could and could not eat. She was too courteous to write as I am writing now, thrusting down the gullets of my intimates each day the selfsame meal!

'You learned to talk very early, Sara,' Mamma told me of my forgotten past. 'You were so interested in sentences.' It made me the quaintest baby that she had—as an infant I was absorbed with grammar before I had fully learned the names of things, which caused a single slippage in my nouns: I would call a marmalade a squirrel, and I'd call a squirrel a marmalade. Today I can understand the impulse and would very much like to call sugar an opossum; an antelope, tea. To be engulfed by grammar after all is a tricky prospect, and a voice deserves to declare its own control in any way it can, asserting that in the end it is an inventive thing. Think how much a voice gives way to plot when it learns to utter the names of the people that it loves: picture looking at Peter and saying, 'Peter'; picture picking up the telephone to Anita's voice and crying out, 'Nina!' How can syntax hold around a name? Picture my mother on the beautiful old campus of the Punjab University looking straight at her daughter and saying, 'Yes?'

During my years at the university, I became quite accustomed to the way people would walk up to me and say, 'I love Mrs Suleri!' 'I understand the sensation,' I'd smile in reply. And the reason that they loved her made me smile further, for Mrs Suleri's demeanour was most enchanting to the world at precisely the moment when it announced, 'It is not necessary to be liked.' Her composure held this compelling thought at bay, as though the greatest lucidity she could conduct was to say silently, 'Leave it, let it go away, the grammatical construction of what it is to like and be liked!' She looked lovely with announcement: 'Think what you will liberate—your days to extraordinary ideas—if you could cut away the sentence with which you wish to be liked!' Without even knowing what they had heard, her students' faces would suffuse with gratitude, conscious that some kindness had occurred while their understanding was elsewhere. And so with devotion they would leave her presence; with devotion they'd return. Mamma, who was always irritated by the unthinking structure of adulation, would smile a little absently at them, concealing her annoyance in something else, some slight gesture of vagueness or distraction. For trying to make people think beyond devotion made of her a particularly absentminded woman, one who hid the precision of her judgment in a dispersed aura that spread throughout each room she inhabited, so that finally her students were not to blame for breathing happily in such lucid air. What lesson could she hope to teach, when she was sitting there before them, her face ravishing with some forgotten thought?

It was always hard to keep her in one place, make her stay with you in a way that let you breathe, 'Now she has no secrets.' She seemed to live increasingly outside the limits of her body, until I felt I had no means of holding her, lost instead in the reticence of touch. I could tell that she was still teaching me, I sensed throughout a day the perpetual gravity with which my mother taught, but I was baffled by her lesson: if I am to break out of the structure of affection, I asked her silently, then what is the idiom in which I should live? She would not tell me, but even today—as I struggle with the quaintness of the task I've set myself, the obsolescence of these quirky little tales—I can feel her spirit shake its head to tell me, 'Daughter, unplot yourself; let be.' But I could not help the manner in which my day was narrative, quite happy to let Mamma be that haunting word at which narrative falls apart. Like the secluded hours of afternoon, my mother would retract and disappear, leaving my story suspended until she re-emerged. I think it was a burden to her to be so central to that tale: she certainly seemed most full of her own quietude when we let her wander by herself up and down the garden, picking up a pebble or a twig to murmur, 'Look...' I so loved to watch her when she was alone and also so much liked to be her companion on those strolls that it always wrenched me, as though some great pleasure had to be renounced whether I watched or walked. 'Mamma,' I once asked her tentatively as we walked up and down an evening garden, 'Do you need to spend more time away from us, from this?' gesturing at the house and all the duties it implied. 'No,' she said judiciously, 'all of you are quite sufficient to me,' adding with a slightly rueful smile, 'you keep me entertained.' It brought quick guilt to me, when I could suddenly sense how many stories sat around her secrets, clamouring for the attention of her face. There were the five of us, and Dadi, and students, and the cook, and Halima the cleaning woman with her sick son. And then there was also my father.

How can I bring them together in a room? My plot feels most dangerous to me when I think of bringing them together. Can I even recollect how they sat together in a room, that most reticent woman and that most demanding man? Something in me wishes to recoil, to say let it be hid, the great exhaustion of that image. Papa's powerful discourse would surround her night and day— when I see her in his room, she is always looking down, gravely listening! They were rhetorically so different, the two of them, always startling each other with the difference of their speech: no wonder their children grew up with such a crazy language; words that blustered out their understatement, phrases ironic of their scorn. To Papa's mode of fearsome inquiry we married Mamma's expression of secret thought, making us—if nothing else—faithful in physiognomy. For we were glad enough to sing epithalamiums for the way that history wed silence, almost freshly, every day. Oh, of course there was dignity in that incongruous union, in the lengthy habit of that unlikely pair, reminding me of how much they must have lost and suffered in order to become habitual. I could sometimes see it on my mother's face: not judgment but a slightly sorrowful acknowledgment that said, 'It was for this,' as she watched my father talking; 'For this,' as we came bantering into the room.

She found him moving—his very doggedness, committedness, a
moving thing—long after she had glided off into a realm beyond
the noncommittal, a creature of such translucent thought that
my father could not follow, could not see. But he respected her
almightily, fearing the ill-judgment she was far too courteous to
give, so that daily he would watch her finish his latest article to
ask her anxiously, 'How does it read?' 'It reads well, Zia,'
she'd say, which—once one had pushed through his baffling
single-mindedness—it very often did. I was bone-tired after ten
years of reading articles in galley proofs and needed to put
continents between newsprint and my mind: my mother lived
through thirty years of the daily production of that print, the
daily necessity of sympathy.

'Mairi,' said my father to my mother, 'what is the greatest
thing you've done in your life?'—Hardly my mother's favourite
lingo, but Pip was in a chatty mood and liked to talk of greatness.
She looked at him, restrained. Her restraint said clearly: 'Why,
enduring you, you impossible, you moving man!' But to protect
him, she added, 'Oh, my children, I would say.' 'And I—I have
not done one great thing, but I saw greatness, during the struggle
for Pakistan.' And then he launched off into one of his familiar
rhapsodies—not too different in tone, I'd hazard, from the ones
that felt so strange and moving to her in post-War London,
when she was a girl. I saw the crossing of patience on her face,
making her at once abstracted, far away. To mock him would
be too simple: he demanded to be mocked, and had enough
detractors as it was, proliferating through his day. So my mother
gave him the seriousness of her concern, following the self-
interruptions of his talk to say, 'I see, I see.' I think she had
expected him to age out of defiance, as had she, for in her
defiance dropped away to leave her in some new simplicity:
when it did not in her husband, she took note, and said: 'I see.'
As I watched their conversation, I was struck. No wonder my
mother sought to teach me, with oblique urgency, the necessity
of what it means to live beyond affection. No wonder she said
to me—startlingly, incongruously—'You can't change people,
Sara.' For when her sympathy was in its bloom, I saw, how

hard its fresh-faced patience must have worked to compensate for each bad dream! Why, she had tried to change my father, I realized; she tried, until she could not try.

But now I am dejected, as though I had been commissioned to write a piece of melancholy music for which the only payment was my own melancholic chords. Somehow it will not grip me, the telling of this tale, not with my mother's aura hovering nearby to remind me of one of her most clear announcements: 'Child, I will not grip.' Intensity of any kind made her increasingly uneasy, and as a consequence she worked at all hours to keep her connection with her children at low tide—still a powerfully magnetic thing, but at an ebbing tide, so that there was always a ghostly stretch of neither here nor there between her sea and our shore. 'Mother,' I would sometimes exclaim in raw exasperation, 'You are too retrograde, you have no right to recede so far!' 'Would you have me possess you, then?' her manner quietly replied. 'Shall I stay close till you are in the marshland, admiring the bulrushes sprouting from your brains? Must I search among those bulrushes for some baby Moses of my children's minds, when surely I by now have seen all that I should of similar labour?—No, child, I will not grip.' And so today it saddens me to think I could be laying hands upon the body of her water as though it were reducible to fragrance, as though I intensified her vanished ways into some expensive salt. Flavour of my infancy, my mother, still be food: I want my hunger as it always was, neither flesh nor fowl!

So let me tell us all some happy story. 'But does she spend too much time alone?' I heard my mother wonder to my father as I walked unexpectedly into their London bedroom. My father was in bed, at bliss, lying in bed surrounded by newspapers. He turned to me with huge concern, holding my seven-year-old shoulders to exclaim aghast, 'Sara, Mamma tells me that you have no friends!' My mother looked pained in her tact. She shook her head and sighed; then she looked down. 'Ifat has so many friends!' he added. It was true that my sister was radiant with company, and so I thought about his analogy, until a happy formulation crossed my mind: 'It's because Ifat's white, and I am brown,' I suggested brightly. I knew that I had given him, essentialized, a scrupulous rendition of school-ground politics, but Papa the politician was outraged. Ifat, who could pass as English, had one hurdle less to cross than I did in our Chiswick school—she and I had talked about it many times. But Papa could not stomach such bald fact, launching instead into a long and passionate speech about the ancient civilization that inhered in my genes, about how steadily I should walk in such proud pigmentation. 'You are my wheaten daughter,' he declared, 'wheaten, and most beautiful!' Oh dear, I thought, looking down. How could I tell him that I was only trying to locate a difference, a fact that shaped my day much as weather did, the wet chill of an English spring? I had not the language to face up to his strong talk, and so looked down instead, almost as though he were right to assume that I had felt ashamed, inferior. 'Never call colour by its proper name,' I told myself, at seven. My mother did not say a word, but later that evening when I told her it was quite cold in the garden, 'How truthful you are, Sara,' she said with bright approval, 'What a truthful girl you are!'

For my mother loved to look at us in race. I have watched her pick up an infant's foot—Irfan's, perhaps, or Tillat's—with an expression of curiously sealed wonder, as though her hand had never felt so full as when she held her infants' feet. They were Asiatic, happiest when allowed to be barefoot or to walk throughout the world with a leather thong between their toes—a moving thought, to Mamma. Sometimes when we ran into a room she would look at the fascination of race in each of us, darting like red foxes round her room. 'And to this,' her wonder said, 'to these, I am the vixen?' When we made something, drew a picture that she liked, there was again a moment of glad surprise upon her face at the tangibility of what lay before her. I assume her mind was so preoccupied with all our tales, so abstracted with them, that the times when we became suddenly tangible were a form of recompense to her. Then she loved the way, what her mother called, our 'heathen names' became bodily events, calling attention to the accessibility of our difference. My father would look at his children with an equal delight, but somehow he seemed to notice only beauty, whereas my mother seemed subdued with awe at the commingling of colour that with our bodies we flung onto her, comminglings in which she had colluded to produce. And so there was a trace of sadness in her welcome, as though the aftermath of joy suggested fears that asked her, 'What will happen to these pieces of yourself— you, and yet not you—when you dispatch them into the world? Have you made sufficient provision for their extraordinary shadows?' The question made her retreat.

Where did she go when she retreated? Often away from us and into her own childhood, back to some Welsh moment that served to succour her when duty felt too great. She much admired her father, who used to sing: on some holiday mornings I would not wake to the sound of my mother calling up my name but instead to the sound of her privacy with some piece of music, her singing to it rather than to me. There was always some filial obligation that she paid in the pleasure she took to sit down at his piano, so when I stood at the top of the stairs and watched her play, I could see her spine swaying with loyalty. She was paying a compliment to some lost moment of her life, and I felt startled to observe such privacy. What great good fortune has flooded through this day, I would think, and then go slowly down the stairs, measuring my steps to the weaving movement of her body. When Tillat awoke I could see on her face too a sleepy gratitude, savouring the luxury of such a waking. For that span of time she was not my mother to me but a creature that had left itself and caught up with its voice, in voice's way of exceeding the limits of its body, so that the air we breathed was strung with secrets, luminous and sheathed.

Today, when I listen to that haunting Punjabi poet Baba Bulleh Shah being sung, he transports me to the days when I would wake to hear my mother sing. There could hardly be more different music, hers and his, but something in his cadence has to do with her: I feel perplexed at the incongruity of this connection, but when I listen to the old Punjabi poem *Hir Ranjha* being sung, I curiously enough think of my mother. The story is simple: Hir loves Ranjha and is separated from him, sent off to live in a strange tribe where, after much to-do, she dies, thus also killing Ranjha. At one point in the tale, however, Hir looks at the strangers that surround her and sings out: 'No one can call me Hir; I have named Ranjha so many times that I have become his name; I have become him by myself; you cannot call me Hir.' Now the passion in that voice is not my mother's—she was always wary of overpassionate tones—but in my mind she is linked to the gravity of Hir's posture: surely she would be familiar with that trick of mind with which Hir told the world that she had become someone else's name and now was Hir no longer? The romance of it has little to do with Mamma—where she rises gravely before my eyes is when Hir is living in a stranger's village, moving in the decorum of a repudiated name.

What an act of concentration it must have required, after all, the quick conversion through which Mair Jones became Surraya Suleri! She had to redistribute herself through several new syllables, realigning her sense of locality until—within the span of a year—she was ready to leave London and become a citizen of Pakistan. How literal-minded of her. Did she really think that she could assume the burden of empire, that if she let my father colonize her body and her name she would perform some slight reparation for the race from which she came? Could she not see that his desire for her was quickened with empire's ghosts, that his need to possess was a clear index of how he was still possessed? The globe was a bigger place in 1947, so her journey must have been arduous when she rose to put behind her every circuit of familiarity she had ever known. She left for what she imagined was a brand-new nation, a populace filled with the energy of independence, and arrived to discover an ancient landscape, feudal in its differentiation of tribes, and races, and tongues. For a woman who liked to speak precisely, she must have hated her sudden linguistic incompetence: languages surrounded her like a living space, insisting that she live in other people's homes. My mother was a guest, then, a guest in her own name, living in a resistant culture that would not tell her its rules: she knew there must be many rules and, in compensation, developed the slightly distracted manner of someone who did not wish to be breaking rules of which she was ignorant. For what choice had that world but to be resistant? The touching good faith of her Pakistani passport could hardly change the fact that even as my mother thought she was arriving, she actually had returned. There were centuries' worth of mistrust of Englishwomen in their eyes when they looked at her who chose to come after the English should have been gone: what did she mean by saying, 'I wish to be part of you'? Perhaps, they feared, she mocked.

Abnegating power is a powerful thing to do, as my mother must have learned to admit: in the eyes of Pakistan, her repudiation of race gave her a disembodied Englishness that was perhaps more threatening than if she had come with a desire to possess. In the necessary amnesia of that era, colonial history had to be immediately annulled, put firmly in the past; remembrance was now contraband in a world still learning to feel unenslaved. What could that world do with a woman who called herself a Pakistani but who looked suspiciously like the past it sought to forget? Then my mother learned the ironies of nationhood—of what can and cannot be willed—when she had to walk through her new context in the shape of a memory erased. Involved with his impetuous politics, my father probably did not notice the aura that now surrounded his wife, or perhaps he thought it was his need of her that gave Mair her new tread. She learned to live apart, then—apart even from herself— growing into that curiously powerful disinterest in owning, in belonging, which years later would make her so clearly tell her children, 'Child, I will not grip.' She let commitment and belonging become my father's domain, learning instead the way of walking with tact on other people's land.

No, it is not merely devotion that makes my mother into the land on which this tale must tread. I am curious to locate what she knew of the niceties that living in someone else's history must entail, of how she managed to dismantle that other history she was supposed to represent. Furthermore, I am interested to see how far any tale can sustain the name of 'mother,' or whether such a name will have to signify the severance of story. Her

plot therefore must waver: it must weave in her own manner of
sudden retreating, as though I could almost see her early surprise
when she found herself in Pakistan, on someone else's land. I,
who have watched her read a book, and teach it, should be able
to envisage the surrendering of black and white behind her
reading of the land. No wonder she felt nuanced, when her
progeny was brown.

For Mamma, in whom affection became so soon a figure for
obsolescence, must have learned years before I was conceivable
in thought what I have discovered only recently, that love
renders a body into history. Like litmus, apprehended love can
only turn historical, making of desire a social nicety,
companionable. 'I must say, Mamma,' I said to her as we went
walking in companionable conversation, 'It was most
incongruous, most perverse of you to take to Pip.' She looked
amused. 'You must not minimize my affection for him,' she
replied with slight reproof. 'But you're the one who says it
doesn't count!' 'Oh,' said Mamma vaguely, 'as conduct I
suppose it counts,' and then turned toward some nearby shrub,
but I pulled her back into our talk. 'If affection's conduct, then
what's history?' I asked her, curious. '...Bearing...' she
answered, vaguer than ever '...even posture, perhaps...' 'But
that's just like squirrel and marmalade!' 'Indeed it is,' she
laughed. And so I let her trail off away from conversation,
unable still to grasp why—despite her vaguenesses, retreats—
her finesse would always feel so sound.

How would I define her soundness? By the time I came to
consciousness, she had long since intuited the rules of
Pakistan—those hidden laws that people would not tell her—
and had come to terms with the ones she could and could not
keep. If she was attentive to my father, courteous with his
intensities, his ragings, then her attentiveness to Pakistan was
an even greater strain: her intimacy with place and way grew
habitual with the years but never changed her habit of seeming
to announce, 'It is good of you to let me live—in my own
way—among you.' She even had that habit with her children!
Why would not her manner of announcement register as

propitiatory, defensive? Because it was not acquisitive, perhaps? I cannot say, but Mamma moved through Pakistan with a curious relaxation that seemed unencumbered by any judgment—an odd claim to make about such a judicious woman, but she certainly appeared to suggest that the possibility of adding herself to anything was irrelevant to her. By the same token, she did not fear subtraction; her method of exchange functioned at the greatest possible remove from the structure of a bargain. Since the world she inhabited was so committedly fond of the language of bargaining, she became to that community a creature of unique and unclassifiable discourse. Her students, for instance, told their families, 'I think she is a saint.' But when such tales reached us, they caused my mother some annoyance and her children considerable glee. I immediately suggested that we set up some small trade, a stall in the Anarkali Bazaar, specializing in saintly portraits and other sundry charms: we could call the shop The Effects of Mrs Suleri (Personal and Otherwise). 'You can't treat people's feelings as though they were items in a marketplace,' she chided me, adding, in her habit of secret logic, 'I know how the human body is made.'

Her logic was indeed a secret. 'The only trouble with being female in Pakistan,' Ifat complained, years later, 'is that it allows for two possible modes of behaviour—either you can be sweet and simple, or you can be cold and proud.' 'No wonder they found Mamma difficult to decipher, then,' I agreed, 'whose coldness was so sweet...' 'As tactful as ice in water,' Ifat added passionately, 'and as sweet!' Tact, we knew, was far more difficult to define than a simple moral structure such as sanctity, and for us to place her meant we had to come to terms with what tact had to do with the idea of distraction. It was her element: sometimes when I watched her face, I would realize that she was not distracted from any one thing or in the direction of another—in her, distraction unalloyed was simply her habit of possible serenity. Out of that vagueness floated the precision of her judgment, and we were never able to determine which came first. Was precision the fodder for her vacant peace, or was it vacancy that allowed her to be lucid? She felt apologetic

that she could not explain her manner more exactly to her
children, who on occasion were exasperated with their need to
understand. I think she was too unconvinced by the stability of
logic to help us on this score, though she was sorry, she regretted
to me, to give us such denial. 'You don't deny us, Mamma,' I
told her—it was important that she know we did not feel denied.
'You must be just as you are, and we must discover why.'
'Why?' she asked me, gently, in the poignant structure of a
question that is really saying, 'Let things be.' 'Oh, you must
have had a child for each of your lost obsessions,' I muttered,
'so now it's just our business to work out which one we are.'
'Which one?' 'Which obsession?' When she looked at me, her
eyes were kind: I had to stop talking, then, uncertain whether
we were close to some forbidden boundary or had crossed it
long ago. For, with the years, our conversations would become
more dangerous, ready to say so much that they leapt back in
fear of distressing the illusion of lucidity.

Oddly, in her aftermath that single conversation haunts me.
Could we, I sometimes wonder just before I sleep—in the vagrant
clarity of thoughts that fight not to be dreams—work out which
one of us was which? Could it be an indelicacy in me, to so
catalogue what she kept quietly hidden? But still, the making of
such patterns has a magic to it, a pull I won't resist: Ifat was my
mother's lost obsession with being as passionate as my father;
Shahid, her hunger after gentleness; I could be her need to think
in sentences; and Tillat, an obsession with strange patience; Irfan,
her urge to be ignorant and pure. And Nuz would then become—
since Nuz was always in the room with us—her hankering for the
child she never had. For in the curious waiting of every pregnancy
I've witnessed crouches doubt: what child am I relinquishing,
maternity must ask, to give this growing thing my full attention?
What missing child will be the summation of my children? The
notion that she could have lacked a child is entrancing to me, and
so I must reconfigure my thoughts and then begin again. Ifat was
her lost obsession with beauty; Shahid, her nostalgia for the good;
Tillat...but now I am asleep...and then, Irfan.

Have I mentioned that I loved her face? I liked its posture of disinterest, the way she did not really fret over the wearing and tearing of her lovely things as they were shipped from town to town, getting lost and broken on the way. In a similar fashion, she took no notice of the beautiful wearing of her face, around which fatigue would register only as the burden of intelligence. 'One's aesthetic changes,' Mamma murmured to me, 'once one has a child.' I smiled at that: one, may be, but two? three? four? I wondered, and did not even need the rhetorical thrust of the fifth. But it made me reconsider the possible location of her inattention, of her lucidity: we were accustomed to assuming that my father's historical posture prevailed heavily on our home, but this could be our slight error. What if we questioned their joint apportioning of duty, looked again at what was literature, what history? I recall my father waking my mother up to say expressly, 'Mairi, look at the beauty—the balance—of this front page!' He made each front page fit into his control of the aesthetic of his history. My mother, however, let history seep, so that, miraculously, she had no language in which to locate its functioning but held it rather as a distracted manner sheathed about her face, a scar. 'Mamma was more political...' I essayed the idea to Tillat. 'She did not have to put it into print— it was the sheet in which she slept...' So of course she never noticed the imprint on her face as it wore, for she was that imprint: she was her own dust before her bones had dreamed that they could crumble.

We, her children, somehow must have sensed that she intended to become herself in every available manner, be one with her own history, her dust, in a way that made us just a moment in her successive transformation. And so we made ourselves complicit in her habit of hidden variety, glad to be brash foils to her neutrality of colour. 'I will be blistering daylight,' I decided, 'an exhausting thing to be, as long as such a posture gives to her the region of the afternoon.' 'I will be the flamboyance of the night,' declared Ifat, 'if only she would show me just one sentence of what her afternoon sleep must read!' And then we traded all the time, I taking from Tillat for a

day her dogged quietude, she from me the publicity of a
protection that knew it must fail, all of us never sure that what
we needed to buy today is what yesterday we sold. 'Well, she
makes her living by being a teacher,' our eyes said to each
other, and then smiled. We were the classroom in which she
had to walk and say with some reluctance, 'Take disappointment,
child, eat disappointment from me.' I saw us shift, uneasy to be
furniture to such a discourse. 'Since I must make you taste, let
me put gravel on your tongues, those rasping surfaces that years
ago I watered! If you cannot, will not, live—as I insist—outside
historical affection, then I must be for you the living lesson of
the costs of history.' She hated such a statement, which was
hard, quite hard on all of us, collaborating in the parameters of
where the giving of learning began, against the taking of
teaching.

Where are the lines that must be drawn between the teacher
and what can be taught? In my mother, distractedness erased
those lines, allowing instead for lucidity to take control of
context. And so we could not help but ask silently: Is it fair,
Mamma, is it fair that you have reached a point where you no
longer bother to differentiate between what the world imagines
you must be and what you are? Is that it, what you are saying?
For she would not discriminate, other than to enact for us her
vital promise that we would know disappointment. As students
it was hard for us to know so much about a teacher, about her
responsibility. Will she ever draw a line, I wondered, between
lesson and herself? Were we the ones to state the boundaries, to
make the limit, which is what her lesson said? I hated drawing a
limit. I hated my own youth, when I watched the ways my
mother sought to teach us of disappointment, and could not help
but grieve, 'Oh, look, she disappoints.'

Now fabrication fails me, and such fatigue signifies a possible
alternative to accomplishment. Against the quality of her
instruction, I must insist that I have said it all, said everything
that I must say. She smiles slightly at my pugilistic manner and
trails off before I have courage enough to ask her leave—
Mamma, marmalade, squirrel—to apprehend her name.

ANWER MOORAJ

The son of a German mother and Pakistani father, Anwer Mooraj was educated in India and England and is a graduate of the London School of Economics and Political Science. He started his journalistic career in *Dawn* in the 1960s as an assistant editor, was the founding editor of *The Herald* in 1970 and served as chief executive of *The Gulf News*, Dubai from 1983-85. He is the author of three books, including, *Wild Strawberries and People* (Royal Book Company, 1992) and *Harbour Lights* (Royal Book Company, 1992). He is currently executive director of the Pakistan American Cultural Centre, Karachi and contributes articles to newspapers and magazines.

KAMERADSCHAFT IN BERLIN

I was a kid when I had my tonsils removed in a clinic in Berlin, a city which we regarded as home ever since my mother's family moved to the capital from East Prussia around the turn of the century. It was a warm July night, two months before the outbreak of the Second World War, and I remember being grateful for the dish of ice cream a nurse in a crisp starched white uniform brought me.

Outside the first floor window, a street lamp gave out a pale leprous flush and lit the giant poster that extolled the virtues of the Third Reich. Somewhere in the distance I could hear the quick, measured tread of hard heels on a pavement slaked with the corrugated rust of a nation preparing for war.

'You have a visitor,' the nurse said the next morning, ushering in a boy of ten, who had a russet face like an apple and the clean-cut and well scrubbed looks of a prefect at an English boarding school. It was Hans Wasserman, who lived two streets away from my aunt's house in Wittenau. He was a sworn enemy of the Edelweiss Pirates and an active member of the Hitler Youth. He was also the oldest and tallest of the lads in the neighbourhood. I always admired his smart uniform and his total, unquestioned loyalty and commitment to the cause of the Fatherland.

I also marvelled at his sense of history, which began with the rise of the Iron Chancellor, Prince Otto von Bismarck—who united the great German nation and made it the most powerful military machine in the world—and ended with the dramatic rise of the National Socialist Party, which was determined to stamp out the crushing and humiliating thirty three billion dollar reparation imposed on a defeated nation by the Treaty of Versailles. Wasserman had brought some ice cream and the greetings of the lads who lived in my street... We called it *Kameradschaft* in those days. Pure, unsullied friendship.

Fourteen years later, I visited Berlin on an equally warm summer's day. The cafes in the western zone—etched against a backdrop of scaffolding which sprouted branches of leafed steel—served strawberries and whipped cream and Brazilian coffee, at a time when chocolates were rationed in London and were available against coupons. Entrepreneurs had already started to distil the urban landscape with markets that overflowed with merchandise, and happy shoppers went about their business without a care in the world. Germany had lost the war but was winning the peace.

The eastern zone, on the other hand, wore a melancholy look, compounded of threatened chaos and impending doom. Food was scarce and people were encouraged to avoid conversation with strangers. The portraits western artists painted of the place, showed a senile townscape, which had its heart cut out for a fresh disfigurement. The more sympathetic among them, projected a strange wistfulness and an air of poignant elegy. But the power and excitement of life was missing.

The East Berlin artists on the other hand, under state patronage, preferred what came to be known as socialist realism, as if somehow to express a longing for permanence, status and perpetuity. The Marxist order had been born and had to be preserved. The new communist czars had to discover *differences,* not similarities, between the two systems. The road to supremacy in the Olympics had been discovered.

I went back ten years later, again in the hot summer, when bathers at Tegel See were moored in the slow tides of flat, calm afternoons, and bright anatomies roasted in the sun. A warm dry breeze from the north blew the froth off tumblers and Lowenbrau, served by buxom girls in embroidered blouses. Boys with toy aeroplanes zoomed at their war games at the edge of the lake, while their sisters paraded skimpy swimsuits in a variety of colours, constantly threatened with photography.

Grandmothers in feathered felt hats and ankle-length skirts, bit into sausage and bread, and splashed themselves with 4711, while ice cream vendors offered them slabs of ice cream stuck between paper-thin wafers. I thought about Hans Wassermann and how his father had died in a merciless winter on the eastern front, fighting for the Fatherland.

The portrait in the eastern sector was darker in palette and mood. But I simply had to make another trip. The old Reichstag and Europe's most famous street, Unter den Linden, were housed in that part of the city, and I knew a walk down the avenue would trigger memories of a happy childhood. Besides, I had been told that the East Germans had developed a new collective sense of urban identity.

Haus Bucharst, a café in the eastern zone, where tourists were served delicious almond cake with icing and fresh lemonade, while a band played the tangos of Marek Weber, recaptured some of the charm of pre-war Berlin. Blondes, in white mackintoshes, flirted with swarthy southerners, while bored policemen sat in a corner sipping Schnapps or feeding pale red goldfish, ruffling the milky mucous on their skins.

The official family portrait on the streets was thirteen versions of one face, blown up at vantage points all over town. A kind face, that benignly watched over a populace that had accepted the principles of socialism, and glared at those that tried to flee the worker's paradise.

In the evenings, theatres competed for attention. For ten marks, you could get the Bolshoi Ballet, or take in a huge symphony orchestra that played Mozart or Mahler. I don't think I heard any Wagner, who was frowned upon for all the wrong reasons. Nor could I get a copy of any of Kafka's works. But the art galleries were simply brimming with wonderful expositions of modern art, asserting an artistic freedom from the entrenched conservatism of the past...

Though I've been to the Federal Republic many times after that, I just couldn't make it again to the Imperial City. It was always Frankfurt, where office towers appeared to be going up at every street corner amid the fretted structures of earlier generations. And so Sachsenhausen, a suburb of the metropolis, had to suffice.

In the winter evenings, when the Arctic wind chiselled the edge of the rivers and lakes, wayfarers flocked to the cloistered cosiness of the Apfelwein Kellers, where revellers linked arms and sang *Morgen muss ich fort von hier* and other bar room ballads. Good old-fashioned German hospitality.

On my last visit to Sachsenhausen, most of the people in the hall were American students or foreign tourists getting a taste of *Gemuetlichkeit*. They kept plying the accordion player with requests for *My Wooden Heart*, which was not a hot favourite in that part of the world, ever since Elvis Presley had sung it.

Suddenly, one of the students turned to me, by way of introduction and said, 'Wasserman'.

I was a little taken aback. 'You wouldn't be having any relatives who live in Wittenau, in what used to be the French zone in Berlin, would you?'

The American shook his head. 'Sorry, I can't help you there. I'm a second generation American. Anyway, what did this guy do? Pinch your girl? Owe you some money or something?'

'On the contrary, I owe him a bowl of ice cream. You see, it's a matter of *Kameradschaft*. But then, you wouldn't understand, would you?"

Nobody does, anymore.

ANITA DASS SCHWAIGHOFER

Anita Dass Schwaighofer (née Dass) was born in Simla and grew up in Karachi. She was educated at the Karachi Grammar School and College of Home Economics and won a scholarship to the Ecole des Beaux Arts, Paris. She has lived in France since, but continues to frequent Pakistan and has contributed a column in *Dawn,* 'Letter from Paris'.

A PARISIAN ODYSSEY

One summer morning thirty-four years ago, the phone rang announcing great tidings. It was the French Embassy. I had been awarded a scholarship to study art in Paris at the prestigious Ecole Nationale des Beaux Arts. Excitement, delirium, pandemonium followed in swift succession. Having never ventured beyond the borders of Pakistan, I could not wait to explore new worlds and taste the piquancy of adventure and freedom. Oh, yes! I was, as they say, in seventh heaven and full of dreams as I sped towards a land often conjured up through the rosy haze of Impressionist paintings.

Two years whirled by as I was sucked into the churning vortex of life in the Latin Quarter. I loved every minute of it. The student restaurants with their clatter of tin trays and hubbub of vociferous passionate discourse. The heady bliss of new found independence when the first packet of cigarettes was purchased. I sat for hours in cafés amongst my arty friends, desperately trying to be avant garde and bohemian. And oh, the confusion and blushes in drawing class when I had to sketch my first male nude model. The long afternoons spent wandering through the Louvre where room followed room, crammed with the most exquisite treasures amassed from the world over. I gaped at paintings hitherto poured over only in art books. These were indeed intoxicating elixirs for a young Pakistani girl with limited horizons.

The minutes, hours, months danced away. The term of my scholarship was ending and alas the time for departure approached. I was not ready to leave my lovely, lovely, Paris. But then happily destiny intervened. I fell madly and giddily in love with a young European.

It was springtime and the 'lark was on the wing'. Scores of young lovers strolled hand in hand along the flowering boulevards and there was I amongst them. My cup overflowed, truly God was in His heaven. We made plans for the future. Helmut was to finish University and I would return home and wait until such time as he would come to reclaim me as his bride.

The family was horrified at the very thought of my marrying a foreigner. They advised and admonished me to no avail. I neither believed nor reflected on their wisdom. After a year of languishing, I finally married and left home with dreams of living happily ever after.

We settled into a tiny Parisian flat and I took the first faltering steps down the long road of adjustment to the French mode of life. The carefree and ebullient student days were over. I now had to get down to humdrum daily life as a housewife. It was neither painless nor facile. How could I even think it could be easy to merge with a people of an entirely diverse culture to mine? After all it takes centuries of history and civilization to forge a people's ethos. To make matters worse, my own roots could not be so effortlessly discarded. But try I did to immerse myself and take on a French identity. From soup to nuts, I aped their ways. I was dying to be part and parcel of my husband's culture. I struggled and persevered and did manage to acquire a thin, shiny veneer of Frenchness. The desire for osmosis continued until four years later when my son was born. A most beautiful baby! He was the colour of wheat and honey, dark-eyed and with curling black hair. The other newborns in my maternity ward were like fragile peonies, pink and white. Whereas my first born was crafted from molten gold and touched by the sun which arises from the East.

Imperceptibly with this birth the first chinks in my French armour began to appear. I found myself cooing baby talk in my own vernacular and singing forgotten lullabies sung to me by my aged *ayah*. What stories was I to tell but those folk tales which had come down to me through centuries of old folklore— Laila and Majnun, Rustam and Sohrab and all those *lateefas* which had delighted me as a child?

The time came for him to start nursery school. We trotted off, his tiny hand clutching mine. His shoes had been polished and a brand new satchel swung from his back. He was agog with excitement and just a bit apprehensive. When he saw the classroom brightly painted and hung with posters, his eyes lit up. It was crammed with all sorts of wondrous toys, coloured chalks and noisy children for him to play with. How can I ever forget that autumn afternoon? When I picked him up after his first day at school the sunny smiling child had gone. Waiting for me was a little boy sobbing away. My son, a happy child secure within himself and his surroundings, who had been smothered in love, pampered, told how handsome and beautiful he was, had been cruelly taunted by the other children. Incomprehension and hurt poured out as he recounted the day. He was 'black, ugly, Arab...'

A mother's fury threw open the flood gates. An angry, rushing torrent swept away my unconditional love for France. From one extreme I swung to the other. In a complete turnabout the euphoria of living abroad was followed hotfoot by disillusionment and rejection of my adopted country. As the rejection became increasingly vigorous, I reverted to my Asian origins, unlocking those chambers where the pages of my history lay dormant. I yearned for my sun drenched land. I yearned for the dust and the blazing colours shimmering in an incandescent light, and the warm smells of the earth after a blessed monsoon. Above all, I yearned for the loud and effusive embrace of my own people. I started listening to *raags*, something I hadn't done before. The plaintive melodies conjured up our villages with the dew rising over fields of ripening wheat and the gentle lowing of buffaloes. I began to look for myself within the symbols and chimeras of a golden past.

I missed home, how I missed home. I'd pass my days dreaming about life in Pakistan. The airy homes I grew up in, the chatter of the servants; the Sindh Club where one met friends, swam, ate fat chips and fried fish. I retreated into a self-imposed exile and alienation from all that represented the West. Gone were the carefree student days when I viewed Paris through rose-coloured spectacles. Gone also were the happy laughing international set of friends. The hard winters, grey skies, and the rain and sleet were making me miserable. Inevitably this state of mind tainted my family life. There were splintering disputes with my husband on what I imagined to be schismatic and irreconcilable differences in basic ethics. We were young and stubbornly stuck to our pig-headed points of view. Our marriage went through turbulent years. I had lost all cohesion and balance. I noticed though that this was not the case with friends where both partners were Asian. They were at one and secure in their beliefs and values. They were not at war with the world and had carved out for themselves, in the midst of Paris, an island haven. Together, they shared and celebrated the rites of Ramzan, Eid, anniversaries and birthdays. They played rummy, gossiped in Urdu, and moved as a close knit clan. Their apartments were rich with carpets, the effluvium of spices and loud gay *desi* music. For them migration was, in great part, only geographical—a change of *situ* but not of mores. They had the moorings I lacked, for theirs was a world sheltered from the violence of cultural clashes and yet, they would say to me how fortunate I was to have in-laws in France. They had no family for solace and help in times of adversity.

Gradually, very gradually, I began to combine fragments of the jigsaw puzzle. The exotic and colourful Pakistani pieces were slipping slowly into the elegant, sophisticated French ones. The landscape was beginning to take shape and, with the birth of my daughter, the family portrait was now complete. After all, I argued to myself, the condition of exile does not exist anymore in today's world—in fact it probably never did. One just has to glance at India—the diversity and amalgam of culture and people, climate and language, not to mention the great 'melting pot', the USA.

The children too were growing up and settling down without problems into their bicultural world. They loved going off to see Nana and Nani. Once there, they would quite naturally slip into *shalwar kurta* and life in Karachi. Back in Paris, the flat was invaded with noisy school children who, whilst swallowing chocolate eclairs, listened round-eyed to my children's stories. Unbelievable tales of camel rides along the beach, dancing monkeys and snake charmers.

The wonder of waking up one morning to a glittering white Paris. The first snowfall of winter. Quickly, quickly the children pulled on boots, gloves, mufflers and ran out shrieking and laughing in the snow. Was it they who opened my eyes? Their sheer exuberance at being alive in both worlds made me realize the folly of battling against windmills. The children were definitely one of the factors which helped soothe the conflict within. Both were in French schools and now spoke French at home. This enabled me to improve my own language skills. I could now enjoy the theatre, literature and thus found it easier to make French friends, my gateway to integration. Today, dinners at home with Pakistani flavours accompanied by my husband's impeccable taste in French wines are much appreciated by our European friends, who enjoy this multicultural ambiance.

A second, not negligible factor, is that I come from a Christian family. My religious rites took on new dimensions. Christmas, for example, in Pakistan in no way resembled what I came to experience in France. The entire country gets galvanized for the event. I remember the children breathless with excitement when Paris was transformed into a magical fairyland of twinkling lights. At every corner stood towering fir trees strung with golden baubles and spangles. They watched in wonder at the enactment of Nativity plays—the anticipation of opening a tiny window every morning on their Advent Calendar. The climax of Christmas morning. Bells pealing from every single monastery, chapel, church and cathedral of the land announcing the birth of our Lord, Jesus Christ. Mass with the full throated organs accompanying Handel's Messiah, *'For unto us a Son is born. Hallelujah! Hallelujah! Hallelujah!'*.

Twenty-third March, Pakistan's National Day, would see us all gathered at the Embassy for the flag hoisting ceremony. There we were, a little Pakistani community dressed up in gaily embroidered clothes standing to attention as the national anthem played. How proud we felt. And what about the fourteenth of July, Bastille Day? What a grand and impressive march past down the Champs Elysees to the martial stirring 'Marseillaise'. Again we felt as proud as punch. And so it continued. The mingling of two cultures. From a tremulous start, with each passing day the welding process acquired strength and resilience.

As the years flow by, I get a deeper comprehension into French values. I realize it is only the modes of expression that are at variance in our different cultures. The icons are similar, only the colours, shades and nuances differ. The bedrock of basic tenets that govern our existence are constant.

Today I am older and perhaps wiser. I feel a new quietude and joy at being able to savour both worlds. How right Jung was when he said, 'racial history can never be eradicated from the unconscious mind'. He urged an active cooperation between the conscious and the unconscious self. Could it be that a western philosopher showed me the Tao? No matter how long I live abroad, the memories of childhood, the growing up years and my roots, will always be with me. Yes, I still miss and love to go back to my country. Yes, I also look forward to my return to Paris, my husband, my children and the Parisian life and friends. Have I developed a bi-faceted persona? Am I merely a chameleon who has learnt to deftly change colours? Or am I a cohesive whole of two worlds? Questions I am unable to answer.

HANIF KUREISHI

The son of an English mother and Pakistani father, Hanif Kureishi was born and brought up in Kent. He read Philosophy at King's College, London, where he started to write plays. In 1981 he won the George Devine Award for his play *Outskirts* and in 1982 he was appointed Writer in Residence at the Royal Court Theatre. Much of his work revolves around Asian Britons and in 1983, he made his first trip to Pakistan, which provided him with new insights. In 1984 he wrote *My Beautiful Launderette* (Faber, 1986), which received an Oscar nomination for Best Screenplay. His second film was *Sammy and Rosie Get Laid,* his third was *London Kills Me*, which he also directed. His first novel, *The Buddha of Suburbia* (Faber, 1990), won the Whitbread First Novel Award and was recently televised by BBC Television. He followed this up with two more novels, *The Black Album* (Faber, 1995) and *Intimacy* (Faber, 1998). He has written two collections of short stories, *Love in a Blue Time*, (Faber, 1997) and *Midnight All Day* (Faber, 1999). His story, *My Son the Fanatic*, has been made into a film and his stage play, *Sleep With Me,* opened at National Theatre in 1999. Hanif Kureishi lives in West London.

WE'RE NOT JEWS

Azhar's mother led him to the front of the lower deck, sat him down with his satchel, hurried back to retrieve her shopping, and took her place beside him. As the bus pulled away Azhar spotted Big Billy and his son Little Billy racing alongside, yelling and waving at the driver. Azhar closed his eyes and hoped it was moving too rapidly for them to get on. But they not only flung themselves onto the platform, they charged up the almost empty vehicle hooting and panting as if they were on a fairground ride. They settled directly across the aisle from where they could stare at Azhar and his mother.

At this his mother made to rise. So did Big Billy. Little Billy sprang up. They would follow her and Azhar. With a sigh she sank back down. The conductor came, holding the arm of his ticket machine. He knew the Billys, and had a laugh with them. He let them ride for nothing.

Mother's grey perfumed glove took some pennies from her purse. She handed them to Azhar who held them up as she had shown him.

'One and a half to the Three Kings,' he said.

'Please,' whispered Mother, making a sign of exasperation.

'Please,' he repeated.

The conductor passed over the tickets and went away.

'Hold onto them tightly,' said Mother. 'In case the inspector gets on.'

Big Billy said, 'Look, he's a big boy.'

'Big boy,' echoed Little Billy.

'So grown up he has to run to teacher,' said Big Billy.

'Cry baby!' trumpeted Little Billy.

Mother was looking straight ahead, through the window. Her voice was almost normal, but subdued. 'Pity we didn't have time to get to the library. Still, there's tomorrow. Are you still the best reader in the class?' She nudged him. 'Are you?'

'S'pose so,' he mumbled.

Every evening after school Mother took him to the tiny library nearby where he exchanged the previous day's books. Tonight, though, there hadn't been time. She didn't want Father asking why they were late. She wouldn't want him to know they had been in to complain.

Big Billy had been called to the headmistress's stuffy room and been sharply informed—so she told Mother—that she took a 'dim view'. Mother was glad. She had objected to Little Billy bullying her boy. Azhar had had Little Billy sitting behind him in class. For weeks Little Billy had called him names and clipped him round the head with his ruler. Now some of the other boys, mates of Little Billy, had also started to pick on Azhar.

'I eat nuts!'

Big Billy was hooting like an orang-utan, jumping up and down and scratching himself under the arms—one of the things Little Billy had been castigated for. But it didn't restrain his father. His face looked horrible.

Big Billy lived a few doors away from them. Mother had known him and his family since she was a child. They had shared the same air-raid shelter during the war. Big Billy had been a Ted and still wore a drape coat and his hair in a sculpted quaff. He had black bitten-down fingernails and a smear of grease across his forehead. He was known as Motorbike Bill because he repeatedly built and rebuilt his Triumph. 'Triumph of the Bill,' Father liked to murmur as they passed. Sometimes numerous lumps of metal stood on rags around the skeleton of the bike, and in the late evening Big Billy revved up the machine while his record player balanced on the windowsill repeatedly blared out a 45 called 'Rave On'. Then everyone knew Big Billy was preparing for the annual bank holiday run to the coast. Mother and the other neighbours were forced to shut their windows to exclude the noise and fumes.

Mother had begun to notice not only Azhar's dejection but also his exhausted and dishevelled appearance on his return from school. He looked as if he'd been flung into a hedge and rolled in a puddle—which he had. Unburdening with difficulty, he confessed the abuse the boys gave him, Little Billy in particular.

At first Mother appeared amused by such pranks. She was surprised that Azhar took it so hard. He should ignore the childish remarks: a lot of children were cruel. Yet he couldn't make out what it was with him that made people say such things, or why, after so many contented hours at home with his mother, such violence had entered his world.

Mother had taken Azhar's hand and instructed him to reply, 'Little Billy, you're common—common as muck!'

Azhar held onto the words and repeated them continuously to himself. Next day, in a corner with his enemy's taunts going at him, he closed his eyes and hollered them out. 'Muck, muck, muck—common as muck you!'

Little Billy was as perplexed as Azhar by the epithet. Like magic it shut his mouth. But the next day Little Billy came back with the renewed might of names new to Azhar: sambo, wog, little coon. Azhar returned to his mother for more words but they had run out.

Big Billy was saying across the bus, 'Common! Why don't you say it out loud to me face, eh? Won't say it, eh?'

'Nah,' said Little Billy. 'Won't!'

'But we ain't as common as a slut who marries a darkie.'

'Darkie, darkie,' Little Billy repeated. 'Monkey, monkey!'

Mother's look didn't deviate. But, perhaps anxious that her shaking would upset Azhar, she pulled her hand from his and pointed at a shop.

'Look.'

'What?' said Azhar, distracted by Little Billy murmuring his name.

The instant Azhar turned his head, Big Billy called, 'Hey! Why don't you look at us, little lady?'

She twisted round and waved at the conductor standing on his platform. But a passenger got on and the conductor followed him upstairs. The few other passengers, sitting like statues, were unaware or unconcerned.

Mother turned back. Azhar had never seen her like this, ashen, with wet eyes, her body stiff as a tree. Azhar sensed what an effort she was making to keep still. When she wept at home she threw herself on the bed, shook convulsively and thumped the pillow. Now all that moved was a bulb of snot shivering on the end of her nose. She sniffed determinedly, before opening her bag and extracting the scented handkerchief with which she usually wiped Azhar's face, or, screwing up a corner, dislodged any stray eyelashes around his eye. She blew her nose vigorously but he heard a sob.

Now she knew what went on and how it felt. How he wished he'd said nothing and protected her, for Big Billy was using her name: 'Yvonne, Yvonne, hey, Yvonne, didn't I give you a good time that time?'

'Evie, a good time, right?' sang Little Billy.

Big Billy smirked. 'Thing is,' he said, holding his nose 'there's a smell on this bus.'

'Pooh!'

'How many of them are there living in that flat, all squashed together like, and stinkin' the road out, eatin' curry and rice!'

There was no doubt that their flat was jammed. Grandpop, a
retired doctor, slept in one bedroom, Azhar, his sister and parents
in another, and two uncles in the living room. All day big pans
of Indian food simmered in the kitchen so people could eat
when they wanted. The kitchen wallpaper bubbled and cracked
and hung down like ancient scrolls. But Mother always denied
that they were 'like that'. She refused to allow the word
'immigrant' to be used about Father, since in her eyes it applied
only to illiterate tiny men with downcast eyes and mismatched
clothes.

Mother's lips were moving but her throat must have been
dry: no words came, until she managed to say, 'We're not Jews.'

There was a silence. This gave Big Billy an opportunity.
'What you say?' He cupped his ear and his long dark sideburns.
With his other hand he cuffed Little Billy, who had begun
hissing. 'Speak up. Hey, tart, we can't hear you!'

Mother repeated the remark but could make her voice no
louder.

Azhar wasn't sure what she meant. In his confusion he
recalled a recent conversation about South Africa, where his
best friend's family had just emigrated. Azhar had asked why,
if they were to go somewhere—and there had been such talk—
they too couldn't choose Cape Town. Painfully she replied that
there the people with white skins were cruel to the black and
brown people who were considered inferior and were forbidden
to go where the whites went. The coloureds had separate
entrances and were prohibited from sitting with the whites.

This peculiar fact of living history, vertiginously irrational
and not taught in his school, struck his head like a hammer and
echoed through his dreams night after night. How could such a
thing be possible? What did it mean? How then should he act?

'Nah,' said Big Billy. 'You no Yid, Yvonne. You us. But
worse. Goin' with the Paki.'

All the while Little Billy was hissing and twisting his head in
imitation of a spastic.

Azhar had heard his father say that there had been 'gassing'
not long ago. Neighbour had slaughtered neighbour, and such

evil hadn't died. Father would poke his finger at his wife, son and baby daughter, and state, 'We're in the front line!'

These conversations were often a prelude to his announcing that they were going 'home' to Pakistan. There they wouldn't have these problems. At this point Azhar's mother would become uneasy. How could she go 'home' when she was at home already? Hot weather made her swelter; spicy food upset her stomach; being surrounded by people who didn't speak English made her feel lonely. As it was, Azhar's grandfather and uncle chattered away in Urdu, and when Uncle Asif's wife had been in the country, she had, without prompting, walked several paces behind them in the street. Not wanting to side with either camp, Mother had had to position herself, with Azhar, somewhere in the middle of this curious procession as it made its way to the shops.

Not that the idea of 'home' didn't trouble Father. He himself had never been there. His family had lived in China and India; but since he'd left, the remainder of his family had moved, along with hundreds of thousands of others, to Pakistan. How could he know if the new country would suit him, or if he could succeed there? While Mother wailed, he would smack his hand against his forehead and cry, 'Oh God, I am trying to think in all directions at the same time!'

He had taken to parading about the flat in Wellington boots with a net curtain over his head, swinging his portable typewriter and saying he expected to be called to Vietnam as a war correspondent, and was preparing for jungle combat.

It made them laugh. For two years Father had been working as a packer in a factory that manufactured shoe polish. It was hard physical labour, which drained and infuriated him. He loved books and wanted to write them. He got up at five every morning; at night he wrote for as long as he could keep his eyes open. Even as they ate he scribbled over the backs of envelopes, rejection slips and factory stationery, trying to sell articles to magazines and newspapers. At the same time he was studying for a correspondence course on 'How To Be A Published Author'. The sound of his frenetic typing drummed into their heads like gunfire. They were forbidden to complain. Father was determined to make money from the articles on sport, politics and literature which he posted off most days, each accompanied by a letter that began, 'Dear Sir, Please find enclosed...'

But Father didn't have a sure grasp of the English language which was his, but not entirely, being 'Bombay variety, mish and mash'. Their neighbour, a retired schoolteacher, was kind enough to correct Father's spelling and grammar, suggesting that he sometimes used 'the right words in the wrong place, and vice versa'. His pieces were regularly returned in the self-addressed stamped envelope that the *Writers' and Artists' Yearbook* advised. Lately, when they plopped through the letter box, Father didn't open them, but tore them up, stamped on the pieces and swore in Urdu, cursing the English who, he was convinced, were barring him. Or were they? Mother once suggested he was doing something wrong and should study something more profitable. But this didn't get a good response.

In the morning now, Mother sent Azhar out to intercept the postman and collect the returned manuscripts. The envelopes and parcels were concealed around the garden like an alcoholic's bottles, behind the dustbins, in the bike shed, even under buckets, where, mouldering in secret, they sustained hope and kept away disaster.

At every stop Azhar hoped someone might get on who would discourage or arrest the Billys. But no one did, and as they moved forward the bus emptied. Little Billy took to jumping up and twanging the bell, at which the conductor only laughed.

Then Azhar saw that Little Billy had taken a marble from his pocket, and, standing with his arm back, was preparing to fling it. When Big Billy noticed this even his eyes widened. He reached for Billy's wrist. But the marble was released: it cracked into the window between Azhar and his mother's head, chipping the glass.

She was screaming. 'Stop it, stop it! Won't anyone help! We'll be murdered!'

The noise she made came from hell or eternity. Little Billy blanched and shifted closer to his father; they went quiet.

Azhar got out of his seat to fight them but the conductor blocked his way.

Their familiar stop was ahead. Before the bus braked Mother was up, clutching her bags; she gave Azhar two carriers to hold, and nudged him towards the platform. As he went past he wasn't going to look at the Billys, but he did give them the eye, straight on, stare to stare, so he could see them and not be so afraid. They could hate him but he would know them. But if he couldn't fight them, what could he do with his anger?

They stumbled off and didn't need to check if the crêpe-soled Billys were behind, for they were already calling out, though not as loud as before.

As they approached the top of their street the retired teacher who assisted Father came out of his house, wearing a three-piece suit and trilby hat and leading his Scottie. He looked over his garden, picked up a scrap of paper, which had blown over the fence, and sniffed the evening air. Azhar wanted to laugh: he resembled a phantom; in a deranged world the normal appeared the most bizarre. Mother immediately pulled Azhar towards his gate.

Their neighbour raised his hat and said in a friendly way, 'How's it all going?'

At first Azhar didn't understand what his mother was talking about. But it was Father she was referring to. 'They send them back, his writings, every day, and he gets so angry...so angry...can't you help him?'

'I do help him, where I can,' he replied.

'Make him stop, then!'

She choked into her handkerchief and shook her head when he asked what the matter was.

The Billys hesitated a moment and then passed on silently. Azhar watched them go. It was all right, for now. But tomorrow Azhar would be in for it, and the next day, and the next. No mother could prevent it.

'He's a good little chap,' the teacher was saying, of Father.

'But will he get anywhere?'

'Perhaps,' he said. 'Perhaps. But he may be a touch—' Azhar stood on tiptoe to listen. 'Over hopeful. Over hopeful.'

'Yes,' she said, biting her lip.

'Tell him to read more Gibbon and Macaulay,' he said. 'That should set him straight.'

'Right.'

'Are you feeling better?'

'Yes, yes,' Mother insisted.

He said, concerned, 'Let me walk you back.'

'That's all right, thank you.'

Instead of going home, mother and son went in the opposite direction. They passed a bombsite and left the road for a narrow path. When they could no longer feel anything firm beneath their feet, they crossed a nearby rutted muddy playing field in the dark. The strong wind, buffeting them sideways, nearly had them tangled in the slimy nets of a soccer goal. He had no idea she knew this place.

At last they halted outside a dismal shed, the public toilet, rife with spiders and insects, where he and his friends often played. He looked up but couldn't see her face. She pushed the door and stepped across the wet floor. When he hesitated she tugged him into the stall with her. She wasn't going to let him go now. He dug into the wall with his penknife and practiced holding his breath until she finished, and wiped herself on the scratchy paper. Then she sat there with her eyes closed, as if she were saying a prayer. His teeth were clicking; ghosts whispered in his ears; outside there were footsteps; dead fingers seemed to be clutching at him.

For a long time she examined herself in the mirror, powdering her face, replacing her lipstick and combing her hair. There were no human voices, only rain on the metal roof, which dripped through onto their heads.

'Mum,' he cried.

'Don't you whine!'

He wanted his tea. He couldn't wait to get away. Her eyes were scorching his face in the yellow light. He knew she wanted to tell him not to mention any of this. Recognizing at last that it wasn't necessary, she suddenly dragged him by his arm, as if it had been his fault they were held up, and hurried him home without another word.

The flat was lighted and warm. Father, having worked the early shift, was home. Mother went into the kitchen and Azhar helped her unpack the shopping. She was trying to be normal, but the very effort betrayed her, and she didn't kiss Father as she usually did.

Now, beside Grandpop and Uncle Asif, Father was listening to the cricket commentary on the big radio, which had an illuminated panel printed with the names of cities they could never pick up, Brussels, Stockholm, Hilversum, Berlin, Budapest. Father's typewriter, with its curled paper tongue, sat on the table surrounded by empty beer bottles.

'Come, boy.'

Azhar ran to his father who poured some beer into a glass for him, mixing it with lemonade.

The men were smoking pipes, peering into the ashy bowls, tapping them on the table, poking them with pipe cleaners, and relighting them. They were talking loudly in Urdu or Punjabi, using some English words but gesticulating and slapping one another in a way English people never did. Then one of them would suddenly leap up, clapping his hands and shouting, 'Yes—out—out!'

Azhar was accustomed to being with his family while grasping only fragments of what they said. He endeavoured to decipher the gist of it, laughing, as he always did, when the men laughed, and silently moving his lips without knowing what the words meant, whirling, all the while, in incomprehension.

RUKHSANA AHMAD

Rukhsana Minhas Ahmad graduated from Government College, Lahore, did her Masters from Karachi University and moved to Britain after marriage. A feminist consciousness permeates all her work and she was a founder member of the Asian Women Writers Collective in London. Her short stories have appeared in several anthologies including *Right of Way* (Women's Press, 1988), and *Flaming Spirit* (Virago, 1994), which she co-edited. She has written a novel, *The Hope Chest* (Virago, 1996) and is now working on another. Her extensive work as a playwright, includes *Song for a Sanctuary* (1990), which was a runner-up for the Susan Blackburn Smith Award and was published in *Six Plays by Black and Asian Women Writers* ed., Kadija George (Aurora Metro Press, 1993). The radio version was runner-up for the 1993 CRE Race in the Media Award. Her radio work includes *An Urnful of Ashes* (1995), and her 1994 adaptation of *Wide Sargasso Sea* by Jean Rhys, which was runner-up for the 1994 Writers Guild Award and the CRE Media Award. She has written three film scripts, translated Urdu poetry into English, *We Sinful Women* (Women's Press, 1991) and an Urdu novel, *The One Who Did Not Ask* by Altaf Fatima (Heinemann, 1993).

THE TREATMENT

'You know what I've been thinking...I think...may be we should tell her,' Abbas ventured. He had decided to broach the subject after a long debate with himself—hoping his wife might have mellowed and changed her position in the intervening years.

But Zaitoon swung round quicker and more sharply than ever before, 'You promised me, you won't interfere, Abbas, you promised.'

He looked at her green eyes ablaze, blood coursing up her fair throat and neck in an angry flush. It always surprised him that she could turn red like that...like white people do. He sighed, surrendering in the face of such visible and mighty rage.

But a fraction resentful of her easy victory, he could not help muttering, 'It was different then. I couldn't have known how things would turn out... How I feel now... I wasn't to know. I feel like a fraud somehow, and I never did before.'

She retaliated, double-quick, 'You better get used to it then. Now, more than ever, I don't want her to know.'

'But, Zaitoon, what if she finds out?'

'She can't. There's absolutely no way she can. And, if she does, I'll know who to blame.'

He looked at her warily. 'I had this idea back then it would be good to tell Mona... just before her twenty-first birthday or...thereabouts. But... if you feel like this...,' he broke off in the face of her snarling rage. 'I suppose I can live with it. I don't care. Not really.'

He knew her too well to argue when she was in the mood for pitched battle. So, he changed into his nightclothes. His white muslin *kurta* and *lungi* flapped sulkily, swishing round him in a hushed protest—a lifelong habit refusing to cave in to the London winter.

'Where is she, anyway?' he asked, exercising his paternal right to know her whereabouts with unusual vehemence.

'In bed. She has a...a migraine.'

'Again? Maybe she should see someone about it.'

'Hum.' Zaitoon was afraid to say more, lest her voice should give her away.

Abbas appeared to have forgotten that Mona was taking this... 'treatment'. He had been told about it. They had discussed it with him; he had only laughed, dismissing the idea. She wished she had made more of his opinion then. He may have helped her dissuade Mona. It was a mad idea, and... now... it seemed... more than a little dangerous.

The treatment had turned into a kind of Pandora's Box letting out new phantoms and fears daily to hound her. Spectres billowed out of it, growing larger. Mona's behaviour that afternoon had shaken her more than she dared admit even to herself. The girl had returned home in a strange trance-like state, her eyes seeing without seeing, brow heavy with a darkling frown. She had pushed her mother, goaded her, begged and wheedled, altogether unaware of herself.

Such complete and utter faith in the healing abilities of this man, this so-called hypnotherapist! She was like a woman possessed—driven by her faith in his theory that the migraines would vanish if he could regress her far enough into the past to discover what painful memory was producing them. 'They are a protest of your innermost psyche,' he had told her, 'an assertion of a deep psychic truth which you've been denying unwittingly. A truth at odds with your real self—struggling to be recognized!'

Mona's healthily dark brown skin had greyed under the stress of these forced journeys into the past. Zaitoon looked at her daughter anxiously, 'Are you sure this thing is working for you Mona? You seem exhausted!'

'It was...a bit draining...but only today. All those years of growing up, in Jeddah, in Birmingham, and then here in London were all right. Happy days! He's explored them all. He sends me into them, I enter, look around, and there's no pain, no problems. A good life...ordinary and comfortable, so...trouble-free! But, today, when he regressed me...to...the time of my birth...it was just awful...*I was writhing in pain, screaming with it*. I came out feeling shattered. He thinks, if I could only confront that memory, deal with it, I'd be cured. Forever! Imagine that! Never another one of these, stupid blinding headaches. All the painkillers. Dark room, balm, nausea and pain...! Gone forever ! Wouldn't that be brilliant? Imagine how wonderful it would be for me, Maa.'

Mona followed her mother round the house as she went through the rooms collecting vases with dead flowers to re-arrange them with fresh ones. She had a real way with flowers. They gave the house a rather special caring and cared-for look.

'So, come on, Maa, tell me then. I need you to remember every detail... to help *me* remember. I'm sorry for being such an awful baby, hurting you like that. How long were you in labour?'

'Mona, you don't want to go into all that!' Zaitoon protested feebly, 'I... I... really don't remember much...!'

'Surely you must remember some things...? Maybe the doctors said something about foetal distress, or the baby's heart beat...? Did I nearly die? Is that the pain I've been trying to forget?'

Zaitoon did not know how to face this inquisition. A slow flush was creeping up her throat. When she spoke again her voice had tensed in her effort to strangle some forgotten bitter emotion rising into her throat.

'*You've* been trying to forget?' she asked. 'I'd say *I've* spent my life trying to forget...to...blank it all out of my memory. And I'd rather not remember. Look! I'm sure it has nothing at all to do with your migraine...it can't have!'

The bitterness threatening to choke her raised her voice by several decibels, gave it a hysterical edge. She banged the irises on the table with an uncharacteristic roughness and turned her back on Mona.

'That's impossible, Maa. No one ever forgets. Ever! It's the most important time in a woman's life,' Mona persisted, challenging her mother in a manner she had never done before.

Zaitoon looked at her in anger: a strange shivery coldness pitched her into a visible tremor this time. The unfamiliar look alarmed Mona: she drew back a little, almost subconsciously. Silenced. Retreated into her every day docile self again. Almost afraid of the icy glimpse.

Mortified by that small involuntary movement, Zaitoon retracted immediately, 'Let's see... hum...? It was... twenty four hours of labour... may be more...! Not that it means anything, I'm sure.'

'Is it that no one talks about these things back home?' Mona sounded wistful.

'Yes, that too. And the, I... I... had such a painful and humiliating time...! I couldn't bear to remember...' Zaitoon stuttered, her voice gentler, appeasing. 'Mona, your father was right. It's all quite nonsensical, you know.'

Steadily, Zaitoon continued her assault on the efficacy of the treatment. 'The man's some kind of a quack. After all, hypnotherapy isn't really a science! Only yesterday there was this psychiatrist on television saying how people elaborate the memory themselves, building it up you know, once they're given the go-ahead from the hypnotist. They kind of plant things in your head, these therapists, don't they?'

Mona said nothing. She had left the lounge.

'She's been a good child, hardly any trouble at all!' Zaitoon reminded herself. True, her lack of ambition was disappointing. The world could have been hers and she chose to be a teacher! An anti-climax at the time! But then, it had its little bonus...she found a job round the corner and at least, she didn't move out! She was happy enough, and, had just got on with her life.

Except for the vicious attacks of migraine, sudden and quite debilitating. The episodes became longer, gradually, a little more frequent. Someone at work who had been cured by a hypnotherapist suggested she try him. Mona, suggestible as ever, decided to give it a try.

'If only I had talked her out of it then,' Zaitoon kicked herself mentally. It started with yoga and mediation, health foods and holistic treatments, all harmless stuff, seemingly. In retrospect, you could see how all that had altered her too, slowly but steadily, if not so dramatically...but this latest experiment threatened to change their lives forever.

Hours later Zaitoon found her cocooned in a quilt and a haze of balm, suffering from another migraine. She refused dinner. In the dim light her mother looked around the room with distaste at the piles of photo albums and ribboned bundles of old letters on the floor which she must have ploughed through!

Zaitoon returned to the dining room feeling defeated. After a long period reasonably free of attacks, this was worrying. She tried to restore her faith in the future with food and drink, only to have her calm shattered again by the shrill telephone bell. She jumped. Quite unduly threatening, that loud bell! Or, perhaps not unduly? It was her brother-in-law... a disembodied voice... at such a distance, calling almost from another world!

She tried to concentrate, sound welcoming, note the details....
'This weekend?'... 'Yes, both of us. Razia's coming with me too.'... 'Looking forward to it.'... 'Nothing you want from here,

sure?'... 'Nothing, thank you.' 'Nothing, nothing at all,' she sighed to herself. 'No one can bring me what I need! Peace of mind.'

The news of their visit added to her worries; she went to bed feeling fraught. Mona would surely raise the unmentionable subject with them... like a blood hound digging up an old grave. Zaitoon saw her migraine exactly for what it had been that day... a weapon, an obvious protest at her mother's refusal to remember.

'Forget, forget, let the world forget!' For years Zaitoon had hoped and prayed, and then believed that it would happen. That they would all forget. How could she now remember?

Yet the memory assailed her, clear and precise in every detail. Slowly, the hot and humid day of Mona's birth replayed itself in her imagination still suffused with the odour of blood and pain, damp with tears, filled with cries of anguish... and... and... a burning sense of shame! How she had struggled through every moment as it had slipped by: turning the wheel of fortune for her.

'Yes, for me, only for me because I alone had the courage. *I had to have it for both of us*. Abbas had wanted a child too, but there was not the despair in him or the longing. When it came to the crunch, he surrendered responsibility for the decision to me. And I shall keep hold of it now.' Again, she firmed the choice she had already made that afternoon. There was no way she could risk the future. It was not a gamble she could afford!

I could do some *badaami halva* for dessert, she tried to divert her attention to the practical problems the weekend presented. Just as she settled down to sleep, an image flashed through her head, unbidden. It was Tara's face—covered in beads of sweat, chalky lips parted in the suffocating mid-June heat of the kitchen, as she rolled out the dough for *chappatis* which she insisted on cooking at home. 'But what's that got to do with anything?' She wondered, longing for sleep, and turned over once again, banishing the memory.

Zaitoon was still in bed when Mona stepped out of the house and pulled the front door shut. The sound woke her with a start.

An early morning nightmare, rife with misleading clauses and
crisp images, splintered, giving way to a wild fearful
throb...she's gone, run away, left us forever.

Terrified, Zaitoon went through Mona's room, tidying,
touching things, smelling them, holding them close to reassure
herself. She knew, she must not panic. That would be fatal.

The whole week was filled with anguished nights. Saturday
morning came far to soon. She crinkled her eyes tiredly against
the sunlight weaving through the chinks in the curtains, fearful
of what the day might bring. But it was soon apparent that
Mona was not going to pursue her uncle and aunt with questions
about the past. What could they know of her birth? She
calculated... if her own mother had chosen to forget that moment
of infinite intimacy between mother and baby, who else could
bring it alive for her? Zaitoon was tense but hospitable. 'Try
some dessert, Razia. Everyone says my *badaami halva* is
excellent.'

'I remember that! Tara used to make it... so well. Same recipe,
haan?'

'Who's Tara? I've never heard that name before!' Mona
asked.

'Haven't you?' Her aunt seemed surprised. 'Your mother was
very fond of her. But then...she was only a maid in the house,
and she probably died long before you were born! Wasn't it in
1971, Zaitoon, just before you had to leave for Jeddah quite
suddenly?'

'That's *not* long before I was born. I'm June 1971...!' Mona
smiled pleasantly, intrigued by her mother's discomfiture.

'But you wouldn't remember that time...!' Her aunt explained.
'Anyway, she died, poor woman, in childbirth.'

'Childbirth? How sad!' Mona's heart missed a beat for some
reason.

'Your mother looked after her!' Razia continued her story.
'But her relations caused poor Zaitoon such grief. Imagine,
blaming her for bringing Tara bad luck during her labour. The
shadow of a childless woman is always a curse, they said
afterwards...! Ignorant, ungrateful wretches, if you ask me! Cruel

things they said, nasty things. Even the husband made a fuss, kept saying he wasn't shown the baby's face.'

'Tara died in 1970, not '71,' Zaitoon replied. Her voice trembled, dying in her throat. Abbas directed a warning glance at her, but she ignored it.

'No, no! It was the year our Jawaid was born, just before the war,' Razia was looking at Zaitoon suspiciously now.

'Why wasn't her husband shown the baby's face, Maa?' Mona rounded upon Zaitoon.

Silence shrouded the room.

'Did the baby die too?... Maa?' she persisted, even more desperate for the truth.

'God forbid!' Zaitoon replied, her voice a mere whisper.

Mona looked round the hushed table. Perhaps a spirit had walked through the room. Spellbound, they were all watching her. She looked at each face as if her bewildered eyes had opened to the world for the first time. She gasped for breath, struggling with the atmosphere like a newborn baby, expelled from the womb, and rose to leave the table.

TALAT ABBASI

Born in Lucknow, Talat Abbasi grew up in Karachi, was educated at St Joseph's College there, Kinnaird College, Lahore, and the London School of Economics. She moved to the New York in 1978 and has worked in the UN since. Her short stories, which deal extensively with class and gender, have been broadcast on the BBC, appeared in many literary journals, anthologies and included in college text books in the United States. Her collection *Bitter Gourd and Other Stories,* is to be published by OUP soon.

A BEAR AND ITS TRAINER

3 pm in New York, midnight in Karachi, thought Mrs Mirza, as she said thank you ever so much to the saleswoman for the empty cartons, half a dozen of them, three sizes, small, medium and large and started to wheel her shopping cart out of A and P. Such a funny thought, even she had to laugh and then she tried hurriedly to turn it into a cough at the look which the saleswoman gave her. But really—3 pm in New York, midnight in Karachi—coming so unexpectedly like snow in Karachi... snow...now really! And she couldn't help the laugh which escaped her at that. And she couldn't blame the saleswoman, not at all, for telling her so rudely to get out of the way, move on. She started to say sorry but looking at the woman she laughed again—after all snow in Karachi—as if they were sharing a private joke. Only they weren't of course and the poor woman probably thought she was laughing at her because she had these funny long hairs sprouting from her chin like an old Chinese man. Only she wasn't Chinese though her hair was dead straight and she probably wasn't even a man. God knows what she was, where she'd come from, grown up. On a health farm of course, where else, grown organically with a face as

purple as an eggplant. And Mrs Mirza, laughed her way down
the aisle towards the front door.

There she hesitated because it was raining now but the door
had opened automatically even before she'd reached it as if it
were conspiring with the saleswoman to throw her out, as if she
were right there behind her, her purple hands pushing her out.
And so with the purple hands on her shoulders she dove into the
rain.

Crazy, he'd say, isn't that just like you, still calculating the
time difference after twenty-five years of living here! As if
she'd landed here yesterday or was going home tomorrow, as if
there was a home for her there now, with Papa just waiting to
make things right for his Dolly! And crazier still she'd have to
admit—pointless—this sudden discovery, this resentment almost
as if that she hadn't so much as come to America as been
brought here. Oh not as a slave or anything so melodramatic.
As his wife of course. Followed him willingly—actually without
a thought—leaving home, leaving everyone thousands of miles
away. And she'd have followed him to Mongolia, made no
difference, family was country. So anywhere, everywhere, all
the same as long as *he* was there for her to follow. But now—

In any case, wasn't everything else also crazy? As for
instance, walking out in the rain, hunched over the cart, holding
the umbrella over the cartons, getting soaked. Yes, that too was
all wrong—shielding empty cartons, letting the rain drown her.
What a funny sight! Almost tipping over the cart, holding the
umbrella over it as if some celebrity, royalty no less, were in it
and she a slave in attendance! Not that she herself could pass
for an attendant to royalty.

Under the circumstances! He'd be the first to point that out,
not with those hips! One of the first things he'd pointed out to
her, described what a shock it had been to him to see her, really
see her for the first time. He'd seen her only once before they'd
got married and then Mother had instructed her to keep sitting,
not to get up no matter what, to drape the shawl this way, let it
fall down, never mind the shoulders, let it spread round you,
thank heavens it's winter, imagine this in the hot season! And

then after their marriage, he'd described his surprise at really seeing her hips for the first time, how suggestive they were of...of...

She didn't think it proper that they should discuss her hips, that wasn't the way she was brought up, but he was her husband now, what could she say?

Cranes! He'd said it snapping his fingers suddenly, construction sites, bricks, mortar, not sex, not fun, not even motherhood, and he'd gone on to explain, just plain, solid weight...

She wasn't stupid then. She wasn't stupid now. She'd known what she'd looked like then. She knew what a funny sight she must make now, this minute, the legs of her *shalwar* rolled up high above her ankles, above her rubber bathroom slippers, ready to wade through ditches flooded with monsoon rain, not just walk five blocks to the supermarket and back on a perfectly good road in Elmhurst.

But she'd been in the bathroom when he'd called, folding dirty clothes in the laundry hamper, rearranging them in a neat pile, the heavy bath towels at the bottom, bedsheets next, then her clothes and right on top of everything, the smallest items, her scarf, her socks. She was smiling, she couldn't help the thrill which shot through her every time she stood before the hamper and admired the neat pile of dirty laundry, so neat, fit to be displayed in a shop window! She laughed—perhaps a bit overdone—a display of dirty laundry. But honestly if there were a competition for neat piles of dirty laundry—and after all they had all kinds of competitions in this country, the weirdest competitions—watermelon seed spitting contests—she'd win hands down. Oh she would, thanks to Mr Mirza of course. Entirely, Mr Mirza couldn't stand sloppiness of any kind whether it showed or not, that didn't matter. It was the principle of the thing. That's why he couldn't stand the idea of rumpled clothing stuffed anyhow in the hamper as she used to do in the beginning. Right in the beginning when he brought her to America. The hamper had a lid and it always closed, she made sure of that, she had that much sense. So she herself couldn't understand what difference it made, especially when he never touched it, left his clothes on the floor for her to pick up, neat piles of course. But then understanding had never been important to her.

Until now, she thought, pushing down hard, almost squashing the top carton, which was threatening to roll out of the cart. Maybe it was simply the cold rain, simply being drenched while the cartons remained bone dry. Maybe it was—yes crazy or not—maybe it was because it was midnight in Karachi then. And how Papa had cried, saying good-bye to Dolly—like a woman, Mother had said—when Mr Mirza had married her and brought her all the way to America. You'll see her again, Mother had chided him. But he hadn't, he'd known how ill he was, that's why they'd rushed her marriage to Mr Mirza, because Dolly was holding up the younger two sisters. That's why her brother Ahmad had been persuaded to marry Mr Mirza's sister in exchange, because there was no money on either side, Dolly was no catch, everyone knew that. But Mr Mirza had sacrificed his own chances for a better match, just like Ahmad, because his own sister was equally difficult to dispose of. That's why understanding had never been important to her.

But now, all of a sudden, she wanted to know why she was doing what she was doing, why she'd dashed out like that at the very sound of his voice. He'd called to say he was coming round for the last of his things this afternoon. Just odds and ends left. He'd moved to Memsahib Nipples' over a year ago. Not what he called her of course! That was Dolly's own pet name for them all, for all his blonde floozies. She didn't have to see even one of them to know what they'd look like. She recognized them on buses, on subways, in the streets, everywhere in short, such plentiful supply—the time difference wasn't the only difference—recognized them by the sale sign they wore instead of bras: Sex is on sale year round!

So now that he and Memsahib Nipples had signed the lease for some store and they'd begun to renovate it, he needed some things, tools, some box he'd marked with skulls and crossbones, exterminator's stuff. Best leave that lot to him, lethal stuff, enough to burn holes in the floor. Everything else she could...

Within the hour, she'd said, straightaway, she'd said and dashed out of the apartment immediately with the cart, forgetting to change her shoes, forgetting to turn off the alarm clocks which would be ringing soon, first in the bathroom, then in the kitchen reminding her that it was Monday, her day for the cleaners, forgetting above all that Mr Mirza was not her husband anymore!

That was the strangest thing of all to forget, she thought, glancing fearfully up at the sky which was darkening as if it were night. She pushed the cart harder but no use. It was still royalty moving in slow procession while everyone round her walked briskly in rainboots and raincoats and umbrellas held over their heads. Then she remembered the wheel, which was loose. She'd meant to have it repaired but she hadn't needed the cart since Mr Mirza had left with just her own grocery to do. She hadn't got round to it and of course when she'd heard his voice she'd dragged it out forgetting that too! She nudged it slowly along now, afraid the wheel would come off, afraid at the same time that if she didn't get home soon, the cartons would get wet after all. She was trying her best with the umbrella, leaning over the cart till her back began to ache quite dreadfully but the rain was coming down at a slant and the sides would get splashed soon.

Forgetting her broken glasses too, forgetting the band aid she'd stuck on the frame which was coming off now in the rain so that she had to keep switching her nose, tipping her head back. Hilarious! Like a clown she'd seen years ago, balancing a tumbler on the tip of his nose, his head tipped back just like this, tense as a tight rope walker but his hands free while she must shield royalty with one arm stretched out, the other steadying the cart.

So nose high up in the air, looking snooty as royalty herself, she sedately pushed the cart across the road. Ages to get just half-way across. The two old ladies supporting each other seemed to shoot across by comparison. Ages not only because the loose wheel and her glasses slowed her down. Her *shalwar*, which she'd also forgotten to change had turned a simple walk into an obstacle race. Of thin flimsy georgette, light as a circle of air round her legs, it had changed at the first drop of rain. The balloon had been pricked, the air had gone out and now it clung to her here and there unpleasantly, stickily, like reptiles slithering up and down her legs. She paused, stamped her feet to shake off the reptiles and heard a string of obscenities yelled at her. A motorist then and the lights must have turned again. She twitched her nose, held her head even higher because the glasses were slipping down now so fast as if she'd greased her nose. Motorist after motorist honking. So what? Royalty after all holding up traffic. And so, like royalty she continued her slow sedate march until she reached the shelter of the gold and red fringed canopy of Taj Mahal Restaurant, 'famous world over for Indo-Pak-Bangla Quisine' just as the alarm on her watch went off.

More like a cow, she thought, turning off the alarm. Far more, he'd agree and point out that they also hold up traffic—in India for instance. She set the alarm for five minutes later for yes, she'd allow herself a little rest, stand up straight, both hands free. Five minutes, no more. She couldn't afford to waste more time.

Time. One of the first things he'd changed about her, for her own good of course, was to teach her about time. Not to tell it, she wasn't that stupid, but to give her what he called a 'concept' of time, a 'respect' for it. She was totally lacking in that, he could tell that within a week of marrying her, knowing her, bringing her to America. Some people were like that, starting something, not finishing it and then starting something else, easily distracted. Some might call them easygoing, they themselves might consider themselves easygoing. But this snacking when you felt hungry, picking up the phone when you felt chatty, dashing out of the house simply because it was such a beautiful day, watching a late night movie because you didn't feel sleepy—all this was sheer self-indulgence. Fortunately it could be corrected by inculcating in her the notion of time. And so that she might have some concept of time, alarm clocks were placed in every room, all three bought at a sale, each with extra large numerals. She's burst into tears. But he said impatiently, matter-of-factly, that the shop was overstocked with items for the visually impaired, there was no need to be so touchy. She cried some more but as usual once she'd got used to the idea she outdid herself. Went out and bought a watch with an alarm. And today no one had a better concept of time than she herself. So much so that now her hand moved to turn off the alarm practically before it started to ring and she began to walk towards the apartment building.

No not a cow, it struck her immediately she entered the apartment, stopped a moment before the foyer mirror. A bear. A real bear, that great, big, dark mountain bear brought down from the hills to the plains, hundreds, maybe thousands of miles to Karachi where she'd seen him years ago when she was just a child. He was standing right in front of her and the other little boys and girls, face to face with her, just like this close, as this mirror. Standing on his hind legs, poor thing, dancing to the tune of his trainer. Bells on his neck, bells on his feet, garlands of marigolds, tinsel. A monkey in a brocade jacket and cap embroidered with mirrors might look sweet. But not this huge furry creature. Yet how she had enjoyed it, how everyone had enjoyed it. But how wrong it all seemed now as she stared at the mirror, how painful, unbearably painful, that large dumb creature, dragged down to the desert and made to dance on the hot sands. And he still in his fur coat! And how well he was dancing, performing in front of the clapping laughing children. But of course he wasn't born dancing, you had to hand it to the trainer, he'd trained him so well. That bear would never stop dancing…

So, still laughing somewhat sheepishly at his own clumsy way of putting things and hardly blaming Patty Jo for going off into one of her gales of laughter the moment the words were out of his mouth—in America he had discovered girls, he'd said in all seriousness, earnestness—Mr Mirza stepped out of 'Spiceistan Two' and unfurled his umbrella. He did this with such perfect timing that not a drop fell on his raincoat though the rain was coming down hard. The forecast was heavy rain with thunder. Not quite the day to go and collect the last of his things from Dolly's, that is from his old apartment where Dolly still lived.

And no hurry either because as Patty Jo pointed out they'd signed the lease for the store yesterday. There was so much work to be done to the place it would take them the rest of the week at least just to clean it up. Look at the cobwebs, look at the dust, at your hand—just turn the doorknob—see, as if coated with flour! Open the windows—half the panes missing. Had he thought of that? What was the point of spraying the place, putting out traps and poison until the windows and cracks were fixed? Really he was letting the exterminator in him run away. True, he laughed, true, but he couldn't help it, seeing those cockroaches and mice just made him itch to get rid of the lot of them.

And so here he was, on his way to Dolly's. Poor dotty Dolly, playing the role of the good wife to the bitter end, even after the bitter end! How she'd jumped to it! Straight away, she'd said, within the hour, she'd said, everything would be packed and ready for him. And then she'd hung up, cutting him off as he'd started to say, Don't bother with sorting and packing, he was going to throw most of it out, he needed only a carton or two, he knew which ones, his tools, the exterminator's box. He'd do it himself, preferred to in fact, lethal stuff, she wasn't to touch— but she'd shot out of the apartment immediately, buying boxes and tapes and whatever was needed to pack up the last of his belongings and by the time he arrived, she'd have everything packed, waiting for him. He imagined them, the boxes, all the same shade of brown, neat as coffins, all with the same shiny tape running over the tops and down the sides, disappearing underneath, stretched so tightly there wasn't a single wrinkle anywhere. They might as well have been ironed on. All with the labels stuck in front, the same place, exactly in the middle. And

Dolly herself going round and round sizing them up, giving them marks, medals, like a judge in a beauty contest.

Dolly all right, Dolly the good wife. Brewing his herbal cold medicine, straining it through a piece of spotless white muslin and bringing it to the table. Himself at the table, astonished, making a face at the thick muddy looking mixture with its strong unique smell—the umbrella shook hard at the memory—and only then he became aware that his throat was ticklish, on the way to becoming sore. How had she known before him? Perhaps he'd cleared his throat a few times that morning. Perhaps he'd sneezed. Perhaps he'd thrown the ice out of his water without thinking why he was doing it. Perhaps his voice had sounded just a little hoarse. Perhaps but what was the use? He'd never known what it was that had told her before he himself knew it, that he was getting a sore throat. Something had told her and there she was, a steaming cup of the herbal remedy in hand. And after he'd finished watching the football game on TV and went to the bathroom before retiring, there, on the sink a big mug of hot water and salt for him to gargle with. And so it would continue for three days and without even thinking he would drink the mixture, gargle with the hot water and salt. And on the fourth day, would wake up just fine, not a trace of the sore throat. And she knowing that, would put away the mixture, remove the mug from the bathroom, all without a word passing between them, either of thanks on his part or of concern on hers. Uncanny, the way she seemed to understand, anticipate his physical needs. All except one of course. Dolly on night duty, Dolly jumping off the bed immediately afterwards, going to wash up, have a bath, cleanse herself head to toe!

Too much for the umbrella, which had been shaking non-stop but now rolled upwards, then down again, up again, ready to collapse. And the rain—really pelting down—came straight at him, not from up there, but as if someone were standing right in front of him turning a hose on him. His raincoat was splashed but he didn't mind, not at all, not a bit. Even if his feet had got wet—impossible of course because he'd remembered his rain boots on a day like this, who wouldn't—he wouldn't have minded. Still laughing he made it to the bus shelter, stood right in the middle of it but the hose was still turned on. He straightened the collapsed umbrella rib by rib, held it in front of him like a shield and again he laughed. A game, boys playing with sprinklers. How easily he laughed.

How easily. And how marvellous to feel this warmth, this closeness, this empathy, oneness, with the whole world, even total strangers like this bus driver. Ugly, surly fellow—who could possibly love him, his own mother had abandoned him in a garbage can the day he was born. Who but himself, Mr Mirza himself, so that he greeted the fellow' with a huge smile and Good Morning. And how marvellous not to mind, not a bit, when the oaf barked back in return, To the back with you, to the back. And not to mind either the old lady behind him who was prodding him to move with the sharp end of her umbrella, not a word, driving cattle. He felt the hard end of the umbrella in the small of his back but even that made him laugh as if she were tickling him. And he didn't mind his laugh being misunderstood by the tall elegant black woman in the red raincoat and emerald green turban. So shiny the raincoat she looked like a giant red pepper glistening in the rain as she poked him with her umbrella in the stomach, no lower, thank goodness. And then when the bus screeched to a sudden halt, everyone yelling at him as if it were all his fault, his stop after all. And to all this saying only, So sorry, excuse me please, smiling pleasantly, easily as at a dinner party, all the way down the aisle, getting off, walking towards the apartment, turning round suddenly, walking in the opposite direction, to the shops instead to buy Patty Jo a present because it *wasn't* her birthday!

It was Thursday, a good enough excuse, because it happened to be a Thursday when they met for the first time at the restaurant where Patty Jo was a short order cook and where he'd gone in connection with his exterminating business. And while some things were being exterminated, others were flowering, as Petty Jo had said later. She had such a marvellous way with words—'Spiceistan' was her idea, all he could come up with was Indo-Pak Spices—which he didn't have, that's why he came up, quite unintentionally of course with hilarious things like in America he had discovered girls! Unforgettable things, because he'd never live it down now, he knew it from the way she'd kissed him goodbye and warned him to be careful, America was a continent mined with girls!

And now the Sikh shopkeeper came up to him and agreed they were funny, weren't they, see tail moves, battery extra, how old child is? The monkey's tail, long as a whip and curled at the edge suddenly began to move to and fro as if flicking off flies. And Mr Mirza laughed, threw his head back and laughed, because he'd said it so solemnly, so earnestly too, holding Patty Jo close. And being a bit of a fool and imagining that she hadn't understood had even gone on to try and explain what he'd meant. Nice girls, he'd meant. There too, obviously, but he never knew any, not really, not the way you could here, not the nice ones, not before marriage...

Eight, he said to the shopkeeper who'd asked for the third time, how old the child was. Eight because that's how old he must have been when he'd sat in the cinema hall in Karachi, with those funny glasses on his nose, watching for the first time a 3D movie. He didn't remember the movie, not a thing about it, but the excitement came back to him, the thrill, the disbelief almost, of people, of things, coming towards you, reaching out to you. Not just endless wide open spaces stretching ahead of you. More than that, far more. Life reaching out to you with both hands. And it was that boy in the darkened cinema hall who'd propelled him into the toyshop in the first place, who made him buy on an impulse the funny teddy bear chosen precisely for that reason, you couldn't help laughing the moment you set eyes on him. Not cute, not cuddly, perfectly ugly, shapeless, a strange shade of brown-black, large and clumsy and a pouch in its belly, of all things, like a kangaroo, for holding goodness knows what. Pillow teddy, the salesman had called it.

And it was that same boy who filled him with false energy, who made him bound up the stairs when the elevator didn't come immediately. He stood on the top of the first landing, hand on rail, huffing puffing too much to laugh at himself. He tried the elevator, this time waited till it came, got off on the fifth floor. Yes the fifth! He was going to run up five flights of stairs! At his age, he thought, walking down the corridor to the apartment. And yet what did age matter here in America! New beginnings at any age—Patty Jo, a whole new life in middle age, Spiceistan Two, their second grocery store in less than a year, one day a chain. Yes a chain, why not, had he never in his wildest dreams imagined that life held anything for him but roaches, mice, Dolly, ants, spiders? And the best part was that he didn't know what he'd done to deserve it, any of it, he'd just been present at the right place, at the right time like that boy.

He heard the alarm clocks going off inside the apartment before he rang the doorbell. All dozen of them, Dolly and her alarm clocks. Always one going off somewhere or the other reminding her to do this or that in such and such a length of time. At the end of which the next alarm went off. To please him. Oh of course. He knew that. Some remark of his no doubt about time years ago soon after Haris was born within ten months of their marriage—that was the whole trouble—when he'd tried to get her to organize her work, her pregnancy over after all now, told her she had to be her own servant here in America. And alarm bells had been assaulting his ears ever since. He hadn't even bothered to explain, moved out of the bedroom, leaving her with the baby, stayed out as much and as late as he pleased. Pleased her too, he knew, because Dolly being Dolly could hear only one kind of alarm bell until it was too late. No going back for him though, so that when Haris was four or five and they were in the car one night and Dolly finally forced herself to laugh and say Haris was demanding a brother, he turned on the car radio to save her further embarrassment.

He rang the bell but no one came. He rang again, still no answer. He knocked loudly, called out Dolly but still nothing. Well obviously, because she wasn't in, that's why the alarms were going off. Stupid of him. He shifted the bear, propping it under his left arm and with his right fished out his key chain. Lucky thing the key still being there so he could let himself in, turn off the damn things after tossing the bear in the direction of the fire engine red sofa. Three of them going off, he could tell. Crazy himself too, putting up with her for so long. In America of all places where there was no family, no interference, where everybody minded their own business, where he was utterly free. And he dashed round the apartment, flew from room to room as if putting out fires. He returned to the living room, calm again. Just as well she was out, he'd take what he needed and clear out before she came. He turned on the light.

But—and this was crazier still—she wasn't out. She was sitting on the sofa, a wet mess just fished out of a sewer. He half smiled as he drew closer, taking in the cartons in the shopping cart, then drew his breath in exasperation at the box with the skull and crossbones at her feet, with some of its bottles and tins spread on the carpet, ready to be repacked neatly. Really! Stupid even for Dolly. Lethal, hadn't he warned her, burns holes in the floor. Well lucky for her he was here. Poor predictable Dolly. Exceeding herself. To please him. And the sofa was wet too. Must've been sitting there sometime then, must've heard the doorbell, must've seen him come in, seen him throw the bear—

Heavens! Straight in her lap it had landed1 No wonder her state of shock. Frozen, staring disbelievingly at the bear in her lap, falling backwards as far as she could go on the sofa, feet just off the floor, recoiling as if it were a real live one so that she was powerless to touch it, throw it off. And holding the position for his benefit! Crazy even for Dolly! Poor dotty Dolly, who could possibly love her? And yet towards her too, strangely enough perhaps most of all towards her, he felt—no he was overcome by—this warmth, this sympathy so that he resisted the urge to laugh and sitting down on the wet sofa next to her reached out to touch her, yes actually touch—

The bear went whizzing past his head and at the same instant Dolly swooped down to the box at her feet, grabbed the bottle. His mouth was still hanging open when she threw it on his face.

He screamed, jumped to his feet and danced.

ADAM ZAMEENZAD

*B*orn in Pakistan, Adam Zameenzad lived in Nairobi until he was eight and grew up in interior Sindh and Lahore. He graduated from Government College, did his Masters from Karachi University, became a teacher and moved to Britain in 1974. All his novels deal with the disadvantaged, the dispossessed, and the outcasts of this world. His first novel, *The Thirteenth House* (Fourth Estate, 1987), set in Karachi, won the 1987 David Higham Award. Famine-stricken Africa and a South American shanty town form the backdrop to *My Friend Matt and Henna the Whore* (Fourth Estate, 1988) and *Love Bones and Water* (Fourth Estate, 1989) respectively. His bawdy, gargantuan fourth novel, *Cyrus, Cyrus* (Fourth Estate, 1990), spans several continents and he has written a fifth, *Gorgeous White Female: The Comic Adventures of a Demented Nonager* (Penguin, 1995). In 1996, he was a VSO volunteer in Namibia and says his many travels which include Europe and North America have been essential to his intellectual, political and spiritual growth as a writer.

JUST LIKE HOME

'Back home, home was home. Here...it is just a house. Brick and wood and windows. With blinds. Horrible word, blinds. Horrible to look at, blinds. Horrible to look out of. Can't see anything. Or anyone. Just a blur. A grey blur. Doesn't feel like home at all.'

'Ohhh you're just new here, Razia. That's why you feel like this. Just a few months more, and this will be like home too. You wait and see. This will be just like home!'

That was six months ago, when Razia, heavily pregnant, had arrived in England with daughters: Nima, seven, and Naila, five; to be with her husband and their father, Jamil.

Nima remembered that dialogue between her parents as she sheltered behind her mother against the harsh winds of October. 'Can't we go home Ammi? I am cold.' She wasn't sure which home she wanted to go back to. In many ways she liked it here, in England. She liked her school, she liked her...

'You should have worn that thick sweater I told you to!' Razia interrupted her thoughts. 'You never listen, do you? Then you complain. Look at Naila. She has her woolly jumper on, and her parka. She is not cold.'

'I've got my parka on,' droned Nima, 'Naila's not cold because she's fat! And ugly.'

'Hush, you bad girl. Naila is pretty, the prettiest girl in the whole village, town...in the whole world. Same as you. And it is good to have some meat on your bones. You are just a skeleton. Hardly eat anything. Whatever I make, you don't like. Can't have granny's mince and *saag parathas* here every morning, like we used to back home, can we?' She looked accusingly at Nima as if it was her fault that they could not have granny's mince and *saag parathas* here every morning, then added, 'No wonder you are cold.'

Nima stuck her tongue out at Naila, but said nothing.

'Let's go to the park, Ammi. I want to feed the ducks,' Naila tugged at her mother's *dupatta* while at the same time trying to push Nima away from her mother.

'Don't push Nima away like that,' Razia waved a finger at Naila. 'She is hugging me because she is cold.'

'I don't want to go the park,' whined Nima. Actually she loved going to the park, to feed the ducks, to run around; but not if Naila suggested it first. Then she owed it to herself to oppose the idea.

At this, both the girls started to hit out at each other. Little finger jabs at first, then a slap on Naila's face by Nima resulting in a violent tug of her pigtail by Naila even as she let out earth-shattering squalls. Not to be outdone, Nima joined in with her own louder howls of pretended pain and genuine affront.

Razia had a hard time trying to play fair between the two girls. They were always pushing to gain her attention at the expense of each other. If only Jamil helped a little, she thought. Spent some more time with the girls, then perhaps they would not fight so hard for her time, all the time. And what with the little baby...it was all getting too much. She let the girls fight it out. She was too exhausted to bother. *They* will soon get exhausted, she thought. Hoped!

Back home her mother would have helped. And her sisters. Not to speak of the neighbours. And she had Badi Bee coming round to do the dishes and sweeping out the rooms every afternoon.

Razia heaved a heavy sigh as she pushed the pram with baby Seema lying in it, mercifully still asleep. Next to two Tesco shopping bags bursting at the seams. Another bag swung this way and that way hanging loosely from the pram handle. Two others, Razia was carrying herself; one in her left hand, the other slung across her right shoulder. Back home she had only to walk across to the local cabin-shop for whatever little was needed at any given time. Or better still, send Salloo next door to run down and fetch it for her.

'I want to go the park. To feed the ducks,' screamed Naila, this time coming to a standstill and stamping her feet on the pavement.

'I *don't* want to go the park. I want to go home,' Nima screamed at the top of her voice, pulling at Razia's *kameez* tail and pointing homeward.

Seema chose just that moment to wake up and began simpering.

'Look what you have gone and done, now. Both of you. Woken your baby sister up. Don't know what I am going to do with the lot of you! Allah *toba*. You girls will drive me to my grave before I am dead. Then you can cry all you like and I'll see who comes to fill your needs, much less pander to your whims.'

'All right then,' Nima sobbed, rubbing her eyes with her fists, 'Let's go to the park then. She always gets her way, Naila does!'

The park was further up the High Street, on a turning to the right. A longish walk, but in the general direction of home, just a slight diversion along the way. *It will keep the girls happy*, thought Razia, *and I could do with a sit down*.

In the park at last. The girls were running around; Nima chuckling to herself at the sight of the ducks waddling about, chasing them round the edge of the pond, and generally enjoying herself more vigorously than Naila.

Razia put her bags down by her feet and relaxed back on a sunny bench. The trees were still green, and chequered shadows of branches heavy with leaves played hide and seek with the shadows of the girls, now hand in hand, and in harmony with each other, and nature. The mating cry of a lonesome wood pigeon could be heard to their right, while above them skylarks sang and house martins chirped in an incessant chorus of delight. Somehow the singing and fluttering of birds seemed to intensify, even create, a feeling of silence, of stillness, rather than drown it or wash it away.

Closing her eyes Razia stretched her legs out as far as they could reach, and lost herself in the rhapsodic tranquility of the moment.

Life wasn't too bad here, after all. Jamil was right. It was beginning to feel like home. There were difficulties, of course; but there were advantages too. There were so many things to choose from. So many types of food. Even Pakistani and Indian foods. And it was clean, pure. Not like back home: chilli powder mixed with brick-dust and milk with water and *ghee* with *banaspati*...not to mention cowpat with...she stretched her arms above her head and decided not to think of all the impurities she used to complain about in the foods back home. Or any of the...other...problems back home. Problems she had blacked out. Rather concentrate on all the good things here. Some too good to be true, too good to last...but no. She wouldn't go into that. Even though that was the best part of being here...the shopkeepers were nice and polite, generally; the white ones often better than our own kind. The people were friendly too, most of them, in spite of...but no. She was going to steer clear of all negativities today. Time had come to be positive. This was going to be her home now, and she had to make the best of it. See the best in it. Enjoy what was on offer.

She loved going to the big shopping mall out of town. And the jewellers in London had the most fabulous jewellery she had ever seen, even if the gold here wasn't as good as the gold back home. Not 24 carats, like her father spent his life savings on to buy for her wedding. But the diamonds here… yes, the diamonds were absolutely fabulous. And some of the clothes, too…though she could never wear them. Wouldn't dare. And you could get all the best and latest Indian films on video. The summer had been nice too. Despite what the British say about it. She never liked it too hot back home. Dried her skin, making it go black. Lovely skin creams here, even if she couldn't afford to buy the best of them. But maybe, one day…she would like to go to Scotland. It was beautiful there, among the mountains. Better than Simla, one of her neighbours said. A Sikh girl, but quite nice, nonetheless…though Jamil didn't like her seeing much of her. She was studying to be a lawyer. So many facilities, here, even for girls to study. That was good. She would have liked to have finished her BA, but had to give up when her marriage was arranged. Jamil was only a matriculate, and it would not have been right…nice, to be more educated than him. But he was good in business, smart…brought in enough money, and that was what counted. She would see that Nima got a good degree, became a lawyer, like Kuldeep, or a doctor. Though Naila would be better as a doctor. She knew how to look after her health. Nima argued so much, she would be a good lawyer. And Seema, well, she'll have to wait and see. She was so pretty. Like a model. But Jamil would never have that…

She was woken from her reverie by a scream. It sounded like Nima. It was Nima. She jumped to her feet and looked to see where she was. She had only fallen over. Nothing to worry about.

'Naila tripped me, deliberately,' she yelled.

'No I did not, did not, did not,' Naila yelled back.

'Let's go home now,' said Razia. 'I have no time to sort your problems out here. Baby has to be fed again, and I must get back to warm her milk. Come on, hurry up, both of you, before I lose my patience. And then I'll give you something to really cry about, both of you. Come. Come, come, come.'

Almost close to home and 'Shi…' Razia nearly said the word, and blushed. Jamil was right. She had to watch herself very carefully here. *The West can corrupt you before you realize it*!

'I forgot to buy some shaving cream and razors for your Abbu,' she said half to herself, half to the girls. 'We'll have to walk all the way back to Boots. He told me to get it from Boots, even though there is a shop closer...anyway. If we have to walk back, might as well walk a little more. Won't kill us, will it now?' The question was not so much directed at the girls as to quell her own doubts.

By the time she had got the shaving cream and razors for her husband, from Boots, and returned home, the sun was almost on its way out. And she was so tired she could lay herself down on the settee and go to sleep for a few days. She was thinking about that impossible prospect while fumbling in her bags to find her keys when the door opened.

Jamil was already home. He stood aside to let her in as she staggered with her bags and the pram.

'You're home early,' she began, as she made her way to the kitchen, 'I was thinking of making some meat *korma* and some...'

'And where have you been all this while?' Jamil advanced upon her. 'I've been here for a hundred hours wondering about you, you cheap slut.' He brought the back of his right hand fast and furious upon her right cheek. And as she struggled to keep her balance, he hit out with his left, 'You will make sluts out of these girls as well. That is why you only have girls. So you can have more sluts to keep you company. I don't even know whose they are. My family always has sons. I was hoping this last one...but no. No. Not from you.' And another back hander, 'I tried to control myself a lot. I honestly did. Up until today. I had promised myself. Not here. Not in England, where the busy social worker bitches get on your case for nothing, for being a man. But there is only so much a man can take.' And with that another blow, which finally sent Razia, sprawling on the kitchen floor, hitting her head against the steel edge of the cooker.

Nima cowered back against the opposite wall, her arms protectively round Naila.

Her Abbu was right. It was like home, now, here too. After only a few months. Just like he had said. He is always right, he is. Just like he always says.

PART III
VOTING WITH THEIR FEET

IRFAN HUSAIN

IRFAN HUSAIN was born in Amritsar and educated at St Patrick's School, Karachi and at L'Ecole Active Bilingue, Paris. He is a well-known freelance columnist for several newspapers and journals, both in Pakistan and abroad. He is the editor of an encyclopaedic work, *Pakistan* (Stacey International UK, reprinted OUP Pakistan, 1997) and author of several demographic and educational reports. He was in government service for thirty years and now heads a private university, The Textile Institute of Pakistan

VOTING WITH THEIR FEET

Recently Shakir, my 23-year old son, moved to Abu Dhabi to begin a career in portfolio management. He had graduated last year from a liberal arts college in the States, and was clear that he wanted to live and work in Pakistan. After applying at various places, he got a job with a magazine in Karachi. He enjoyed the job, but felt this society was too stifling for him. So when he got the offer from the Gulf, he was off like a shot. I know several of his friends and contemporaries who did not even attempt to return to Pakistan after completing their studies abroad, choosing instead to brave the red tape and legal hassles involved in staying on in the West, usually in the States.

While I miss Shakir, I can understand why he left. As he said, it was not just the money or the job, but the quality of life that made him decide to leave. Actually, he was more comfortably off than most young men his age: he had free room and board at the family house, a car, and access to my beach hut. On top of that he had a salary of Rs 15,000 plus what he made freelancing for various publications. So what drove him to leave family, friends and a familiar setting to try and make a life in a foreign country?

It is difficult to quantify one's 'quality of life'. This concept is a composite of many ingredients that are of different weightage for different people. I may bemoan the absence of good cheese and wine, but these may be of no concern to someone else. Similarly, others may relish the atmosphere of religiosity that permeates society, while you and I yearn for a more liberal society. Though such intangibles play a major role in helping make up a person's mind, the biggest single factor pushing Pakistanis to emigrate is the lack of job opportunities: with over a million entering the job market every year, unemployment has become an enormous problem for the young and their parents. A moribund economy is unable to create jobs at anywhere close to the required rate, and merit is largely ignored as the few jobs that are available go to the children of the well-connected.

Frustration and desperation combine to produce a fierce desire to migrate to countries that offer a degree of hope, despite the many hurdles. Pakistanis drive taxis in New York, sell newspapers in London, polish shoes in Rome, chop wood in Brazil and farm in Saudi Arabia in order to ensure a better life for their children. These same Pakistanis would have sneered at the same jobs in their motherland, but think nothing of doing them in foreign countries. Thousands of our citizens have bartered their life-savings and future earnings for a chance to escape. Unscrupulous agents have prospered as a result of this lemming-like rush to emigrate.

Apart from purely economic compulsions, increasing expectations are also driving thousands of Pakistanis abroad. While their fathers may have accepted their lot with stoic fatalism, the younger generation, raised on a diet of films and TV, has decided that what was good enough for their elders is not good enough for them. Many of them get admissions in unknown educational institutions in the West, obtain student visas, and then go underground only to surface when they have completed residency requirements. Driven by desperation and attracted by the liberal lifestyle, our best and brightest are leaving in hordes to make a life for themselves in countries that offer opportunities and a bright future.

The fact of the matter is that Pakistan does not offer many attractions for the young. A stifling hypocrisy, an overpowering religiosity and a rigid hierarchy, discourage creativity and initiative. Indifferent students suddenly blossom when they are placed in the challenging environment of Western universities. Aimless young Pakistanis are transformed into go-getting entrepreneurs abroad.

Our best academics and scientists are enriching societies from Bonn to Boston. In music, literature, the sciences and the arts, there has been no outstanding contribution from any of the post-Partition generation living in Pakistan. This is a sobering thought. India, by way of contrast, has produced a galaxy of young stars in every field.

If we are to understand why Pakistanis are voting against their country and their society with their feet, we must analyze the reasons underlying the frustration and cynicism that are gnawing at the foundations of the state. Most Third World countries have economic problems similar to ours: a high rate of population growth, low incomes, low literacy levels and abysmal average incomes define our underdeveloped status. These countries supply the bulk of the migrant population the world over. From Tunisia to Turkey and from Indonesia to India, the poor are leaving at the first opportunity to escape the vicious cycle of poverty in which they are trapped. Despite draconian laws that most developed countries have enacted to keep these hungry hordes outside their boundaries, desperation gives them the ingenuity and the fortitude to make it to the promised land.

What is different about Pakistan is that apart from the poor, even the privileged professional class wants to leave. Many of them despair of the violence endemic in our cities; others see no future for their children; still others crave the freedom Western societies offer. Whatever the reason, I am convinced that if the West were to suddenly and miraculously open its gates to all comers, the only people left in Pakistan would be crooked politicians, racketeers and mullahs. We are rapidly reaching a stage where only the losers will be left behind, while those with initiative, drive and ambition will jump this rapidly sinking ship.

The problem is that these are the very people required to make Pakistan a viable state. Unfortunately, they are alienated to the point where they feel there is no longer any place for them in this country.

The sad fact is that they are right. The war between a liberal, secular world-view and a harsh, reactionary monopoly of religion has been comprehensively lost by the former, and anybody holding such views now lives here on sufferance. The minorities and the Ahmadis learned that long ago, and their continuing persecution provides a strong impetus for them to leave. But now it is people from the ruling classes who have begun to feel marginalized. One factor is the weakness of successive elected governments: they have given in again and again to extreme demands to such an extent that Pakistan has drifted very far from Jinnah's vision of a secular state for the Muslims of the subcontinent. We are now a theocratic state, and those who feel distinctly uncomfortable (and even endangered) in this dispensation are now seriously examining their options.

Many parents like me feel that for better or worse, we have spent the bulk of our working lives in Pakistan and no longer have the option of getting jobs abroad. But where our children are concerned, we think they are far better off elsewhere. We therefore spend large amounts on their education in Western universities in the hope and expectation that they will make their lives in foreign lands. Indeed, people like me go into debt to finance a good education for our kids because due to the virtual collapse of higher learning in Pakistan, most of our degrees are no longer recognized abroad.

As a result of all these factors, thousands of bright, energetic young Pakistanis are voting against their motherland with their feet. Their departure is creating a vacuum that is being steadily filled by all that is retrograde and backward in this society.

HUMAIR YUSUF

*H*umair Yusuf was born in 1973 and educated at the Karachi Grammar School. He did a triple major at the Massachusetts Institute of Technology in Engineering, Philosophy and Film Theory, and did his masters in Creative Writing from Boston University. He has been writing fiction since 1995. His stories have appeared in the *Agni Review* and received the Transatlantic Award from the Henfield Foundation in 1997. He spent a year writing for *The News* and local publications in Pakistan. He now lives in Karachi where he manages a marketing company and writes fiction.

MM HASHMI, SUPERINTENDENT OF THE PASSPORT OFFICE

Now that he was Superintendent of the Passport Office, MM Hashmi didn't do anything but authenticate passports. He loved the way his signature and official rubber stamp, which said *Given this __ day of ___, 19__, by the Superintendent, Immigration and Passport Control, on behalf of the President of Pakistan* was enough to make up for page numbers that weren't in sequence or pictures that had quite obviously been changed—he didn't even need to fill in the date. And although not selfish by temperament he had made sure that nobody else had the authority to authenticate passports because the going rate for one with a Canadian immigrant visa was eighteen thousand rupees, twenty-five if accompanied by a work permit, which was more than enough to tempt everyone from the typists to telephone operators to start issuing passports on their own.

He had been busier than usual since the Prime Minister's Self Employment Scheme—collateral free loans for qualified youth to start their own businesses—because all the young men who managed to secure loans went straight to travel agents and bought one-way tickets to Toronto or Montreal, and then to money changers to buy Canadian dollars with whatever they had left. As expected the embassy rejected all such visa applications, at which point their travel agents offered, for what they insisted was a very reasonable fee, to arrange everything. They bought stolen passports with Canadian visas from the black market, changed names, photographs, expiry dates and sometimes genders, ripped out pages and added new ones, and then made their way to Hashmi with brand new notes of five-hundred or a thousand rupees in sealed envelopes that said 'Entertainment Expenses.'

Hashmi invariably ran out of passports as soon as he was beginning to enjoy himself, so to prolong the activity he spent a long time staring at the passports—impotent without his signature—before he began. And then, while working his way through them, he took frequent breaks during which he just looked around, examining the typical government office with its ineffective ceiling fan, distempered walls, and metal desk of indeterminate colour as if he was seeing it for the first time. He was in the middle of one such break when Kamran, the office peon whom he had appropriated for himself, came into the room. Hashmi was surprised because Kamran was usually quite perceptive and somehow knew exactly when he wanted mango squash or cigarettes or laxatives, and entered only to place whatever was required on Hashmi's desk. But at that moment there was nothing that he wanted, and in any case Kamran was empty-handed. 'There's a woman outside to see you,' he said. 'Shall I bring her in?'

She had to be married to somebody important because nobody else would have dared to turn up unannounced. Like all bureaucrats Hashmi made it a point to be shamelessly servile to wives of politicians in power, who were flattered to engender more servility than their husbands and often recommended promotions. 'I'll receive her myself,' he said.

Hashmi rushed downstairs, planning an elaborate welcome as he negotiated the staircase two and sometimes three steps at a time. But as soon as he reached the reception it became obvious that she wasn't a politician's wife because she lacked the defiant corpulence and over-embroidered clothes typical of women with political affiliations. She had a tired looking face, and instead of the arrogance that Hashmi had expected, the type that could fill a room, she seemed intimidated by Moazzam, the senile receptionist. Hashmi was both relieved and disappointed.

She introduced herself. 'My name is Mrs Zulfikar—'

Still, one could never be sure so Hashmi greeted her with all the effusiveness of which he was capable. 'So kind of you to come,' he said. 'So *very* kind of you.' He inquired about her health, told her that her husband was a fine man, a thorough gentleman, her father and brother as well, and sent Kamran to get tea and biscuits. He was in the middle of offering to put off the air-conditioner if she was feeling cold, or turn it up if she was feeling hot, when she interrupted him.

'You can relax because I'm not anybody important,' she said.

'Did somebody send you?' Hashmi asked. Promising careers had been destroyed because second cousins or neighbours of important personages hadn't been treated with sufficient respect.

'I came myself.'

'So what do you want? If it's about a passport you're not supposed to come directly to me. I can tell you where to go.'

'Look,' said Mrs Zulfikar. 'I'm not interested in going anywhere. I'm here because my son Farooq is trying to go to Canada. I made sure the embassy rejected him and now I want you to reject him as well. You can keep whatever money he paid you—I don't care about that—just don't issue his passport. That's all I want.'

'That's it?' he said, only because he couldn't think of anything else.

'That's it,' she replied with a smile that seemed to mock him.

Hashmi was about to ask her to leave when Kamran walked in with tea and two kinds of imported biscuits. Still under the impression that she was somebody important he served her with exaggerated deference. Since neither Hashmi nor Mrs Zulfikar knew what to do she ended up accepting a cup of tea but declining the biscuits.

First Hashmi simply watched her, and when that got too awkward he asked her why she didn't want her son to leave. 'He could make lots of money in Canada,' he said. 'Probably even send you some.'

'I already have two sons in America, one's in Houston, the other's in Chicago. I don't need money. I need a son to stay with me.' She finished her tea, drinking noisily like the security guards at official dinners. 'So are you going to give him the passport or not? It won't cost you anything.'

'I'll see what I can do,' he said.

Hashmi's first instinct was to ignore Mrs Zulfikar, but her request was so peculiar that he ended up locking Farooq's passport in the top left-hand drawer of his desk, where he put all the things that he didn't know what to do with. He then tried to find out who had let her in but everybody—Kamran, the police guards outside, Moazzam at the reception—denied it and blamed each other. All Hashmi could say was 'It shouldn't happen again.'

But it did, the next day and the day after that. Both times she made her way straight to his office, asked if he had done what she wanted, and then left when he said, 'I still have to take a final decision.' And again, nobody knew how she got in.

When she turned up for the fourth day in succession Hashmi resigned himself to Mrs Zulfikar coming and going as she pleased. She made herself comfortable, sent Kamran to bring a cup of tea with no sugar and very little milk, and emptied a manila envelope of family photographs on Hashmi's desk. 'Kazim, my eldest, on his fifth birthday...look at him all pompous in his bow-tie...the tricycle was a present from his grandfather...Jamal when he won second prize in the elocution contest...all three of them playing cricket, destroying my garden...must be more than twenty years ago...me with the boys when we went to Lahore...I can't remember the last time we were all together...'

'Let me warn you that people have tried everything and nothing has worked,' said Hashmi. That was only partly true; he

was shown family photographs all the time, but never to refuse
a passport.

'All right,' said Mrs Zulfikar. 'If that's what you want.' She
put the pictures back in the manila envelope. Hashmi was
surprised at how easily she had given up. But while drinking
her tea, Mrs Zulfikar told him how much she missed her sons.
'When I look at my watch I automatically subtract eleven hours
for the time in Houston and Chicago. Then I wonder what they
are doing, if they are asleep, at work, with friends, watching
television—it kills me not to know. Sometimes I lie in their
beds or open their cupboards so I can remember what they used
to smell like, their deodorant, their after-shave, and then I feel
their empty rooms pitying me.'

Hashmi was moved. He didn't tell Mrs Zulfikar but he had
decided to reject her son's application. When she had left and
Kamran was clearing up, he said, 'Tomorrow this whole thing
will be over.'

But the next morning when he reached his office there was a
young man waiting for him. Hashmi knew exactly who he was
because he had the same tired face as his mother.

'It's been more than a week and you haven't issued my
passport,' said Farooq. 'Why?' He was smoking, something
nobody ever dared to do in the Superintendent's office, and
flicking ash all over the floor. 'I've given you everything you
asked for, signed affidavit, notarized copies of my birth
certificate, three passport size photographs with light blue
backgrounds—and the money.'

'How did you get inside?' Hashmi asked.

'Is it because of my mother? Don't listen to her. She's mad.
Both my brothers are in America, why should I stay here?'

'But you're going to Canada.'

'Once I'm in Canada I can go to America, no problem. All
that matters is that I get out of here.'

'What about your mother?'

'What about her? She's old. And I told you she's mad, she doesn't know what she's talking about.'

It was Farooq who ended the conversation. He handed Hashmi a plastic shopping bag. 'Here's eight thousand three hundred rupees. I had saved this to buy dollars to spend in Canada until I found a job. Now release my passport.' For the first time in his career Hashmi was reluctant to accept money. But when he tried to return it, Farooq refused. 'I'm leaving the bag right here. If you don't take it somebody else will.' All Hashmi could do was lock it in the top left-hand drawer with Farooq's passport.

A vague and unfamiliar feeling that things weren't right began to bother him—it was obviously Mrs Zulfikar and her son. Previously emigration had been simple: Hashmi just had to multiply the number of passports issued by the going rate and then calculate everybody's share. But this was nothing like that. He tried talking to the Additional Director, his immediate superior who got a percentage of whatever Hashmi received in the envelopes marked 'Entertainment Expenses.' The Additional Director was first thoroughly amused, and then said, 'Now ask the mother how much she's willing to pay. It'll be open bidding, a completely transparent process—what could be better than that?' Hashmi would have liked to do that, but for some reason that he couldn't explain, even to himself, it wasn't that easy.

Then everything got worse: Farooq began to stalk him. Like his mother he had the ability to elude the police guards and the others, to come and go as he pleased; he was there in the morning when Hashmi got to office, and after lunch when he returned from the canteen. He rarely said anything, he just smoked and dropped ash all over the floor. Soon he became a regular feature of the Passport Office and Kamran arranged for an ashtray and began to serve him tea—made the way he liked it, with two tea bags and powdered milk. And whenever Hashmi tried to avoid him, either by coming in late or taking an early lunch, Farooq changed his timings accordingly.

'Look,' said Hashmi when he had had enough. 'Why don't you just stay here? Some people are making lots of money. And if you have money here you know what it's like: you live like a *badshah*, do whatever you want, and have as many servants as you like. In Canada you'll always have to cook your own food and clean your toilets yourself, and if you hit your wife or don't pay the phone bill, you get in trouble with the police. And the police there are nothing like the police here.'

'People that rich have connections.'

'So do you. I can get you a job anywhere you want.'

'What's the point? I'll get eight thousand now, and after ten years if I work hard I'll get twenty. But by then twenty will be worth nothing.'

'What about a government job? By next week you could be an inspector in the Labour Department.'

'You want me to go from to office to office demanding bribes of two or three hundred rupees?'

'What about a multinational? Philips, Proctor and Gamble, IBM if you like computers.'

'You need a proper education.'

'Name any university and I'll get you a degree—MBA, doctor, engineer, accountant, whatever you want. First Division, position holder, even gold medallist if you like.'

'Local degrees are worthless.'

Hashmi knew he wasn't being very convincing. The problem was that he agreed with Farooq: the sensible thing for a young man was to get out of the country as soon as he could. He decided to make one last attempt.

'Your mother loves you very much,' he said. 'She'll be devastated if you leave.'

'If she really loved me she'd want what's best for me. And what's best for me is to go to Canada.'

Hashmi told him to come and pick up his passport tomorrow.

The next morning, instead of Farooq, Mrs Zulfikar was waiting for Hashmi. 'I knew you'd do this,' she said. 'But I want you to know what you've done.' Then she emptied her handbag over his desk. It was full of medicines, pills and tablets and capsules, most were in blister packs, others were loose. Hashmi's desk, which had been an indeterminate grey-brown as long as he could remember, was suddenly overcome by the colour of prescription medication: pink, green, blue, orange, white, silver, red, purple and possibly others that he had missed.

One by one Mrs Zulfikar held up each pill and told him what it was. 'Trazodone,' she said. 'It's an antidepressant.' 'Melleril, also an antidepressant.' 'Doxepin, another antidepressant.' All the pills were antidepressants. Then she listed the side-effects: water retention, drowsiness, dry skin, flatulence. 'You know what my psychiatrist told me. "Surround yourself with grandchildren and you won't need any of these." And where am I supposed to get grandchildren from? Tell me Superintendent Sahib, where can I get some grandchildren for myself?'

'Your son hates you,' said Hashmi. 'Why don't you let him go?'

'My sons who are thousands of miles away love me. Let Farooq hate me if he wants. As long as he's here it doesn't matter. And how many years can he hate me for. One? Two? Not more than that—hate requires stamina which he doesn't have.'

Hashmi tried to say something but Mrs Zulfikar didn't let him.

'You people care about just one thing: money. Well I don't have any money. All I have are these.' She threw a sheaf of papers at Hashmi, aiming them at his face as if she really meant to hurt him. The papers scattered all over the room. 'Defence Saving Certificates. My husband bought them with his pension just before he died. You can encash them whenever you want, but if you wait three years you get eighteen percent extra.' He gathered the certificates and locked them in his drawer. The feeling of things not being right was no longer vague or unfamiliar; in fact Hashmi would have been quite miserable if he wasn't so used to it that he didn't notice it anymore.

❈

Mrs Zulfikar resumed her regular visits. Initially they were mercifully short because she suffered from spondylitis and couldn't sit for very long. But then Kamran arranged for cushions from the Additional Director's office and somehow got his hands on a tube of analgesic cream, the same one that her doctor had prescribed. Mrs Zulfikar started coming in every morning at eleven to drink two cups of tea, three if she was feeling particularly talkative.

'Have you gone totally mad?' Hashmi asked Kamran once the routine had been established.

Kamran blamed him for not making it clear who was to receive royal treatment and who wasn't. 'It's not my fault,' he said. 'How am I supposed to know?'

❈

Since there was nothing else he could do, Hashmi tried to convince Mrs Zulfikar to let her son go. It was easier than convincing Farooq to stay because like all Immigration officials he had a vast repertoire of stories about corruption, incompetence and general depravity. He told her about a religious leader who sodomized his students as part of their training and about a senator who had his hooligans trash the television studios because his speech wasn't shown on the news. Neither story had the desired effect so he told her about a wholesaler who stripped two women naked and then paraded them around the market because they had caught him overcharging them. If he couldn't think of a suitable story he simply made one up: 'Have you heard about the gang of policemen who randomly arrest young men, shove iron rods dipped in red chillies up their arses until they confess to murder, and then charge thirty-thousand to let them go?' Every account, true or false, ended with, 'We refuse to act like civilized people, and the problem is we're never going to change.'

'That's unfortunate,' Mrs Zulfikar would reply, 'but what does it have to do with me?'

Hashmi tried to be more specific. He told her about the Prime Minister's sugar mills in Kenya and properties in London, and when she remained unimpressed he told her that not one of the last four Pakistani ambassadors to Canada had returned because they had used their diplomatic connections to become Canadian citizens. 'The post is auctioned off every year,' he said. 'Retired generals, bureaucrats, the really big industrialists, all of them try and the Foreign Minister himself receives the bids. That's his way of making money.'

'So?'

'So if they're leaving why should anybody stay? Why should your son stay?'

'You're not going.'

'I'm different. I'm in the immigration business.'

Hashmi gave up after that.

Farooq placed an excessively taped and stapled orange booklet on Hashmi's desk. 'Registration papers for my motorcycle,' he said. 'It's a Honda, four years old. I should get at least twenty thousand for it.'

Kamran came in to vouch for the motorcycle. 'I've seen it,' he said. 'It's in excellent condition. Superintendent Sahib, he'll definitely get more than twenty.'

'Now you know what it's worth,' Farooq said to Hashmi. 'It'll take me two or three days to get you the money.'

Hashmi tried to return the booklet. 'I don't want anything,' he said. 'Please don't make this more difficult than it already is.'

'I'll have the money for you in three days,' Farooq said, and then left.

The vague feeling that something was wrong had now progressed to full-fledged depression. Hashmi no longer enjoyed authenticating passports and had stopped meeting his friends to discuss postings and transfers and scandals in the bureaucracy— he spent all his time thinking about Mrs Zulfikar and Farooq, wondering what to do about them. And when Farooq gave him the registration papers of his motorcycle Hashmi decided to authorize fifteen days of medical leave for himself.

For the first few days he sat at home doing absolutely nothing, just getting irritated with his wife and servants. Every afternoon he called Kamran to find out if Mrs Zulfikar and her son were still stalking him, and every afternoon Kamran told him that there was no sign of them. 'Superintendent Sahib,' he would say, 'please come back. The office doesn't function unless you're here.' Hashmi appreciated the flattery but wasn't ready to return until he was certain that they were gone for good. But he couldn't last very long at home and soon began to dismiss his servants one by one. Nobody minded when he fired the chauffeur, but after the cook—who his wife had spent years teaching how to make roasts and cutlets and puddings—was thrown out, he was asked to return to work. However he still didn't dare go back to the Passport Office—so he decided to go to the airport.

Just the idea of going to the airport lifted Hashmi's spirits. It was there, twenty-six years ago, that he'd begun his career in the Immigration Cell and even then people had been leaving the country. First it was the Kashmiris, entire villages of them, the men wearing cardigans under their mismatched suits, the women over their shiny saris, who had moved to Bradford and Birmingham. Hashmi had been at Passport Control then, and had personally stamped 'Exit' on many of their passports. Now it seemed absurd that everyone had resented the Kashmiris and considered their emigration a betrayal. He remembered calling the men bastards in front of their families, pinching the women and then feeling thoroughly proud because he was defending his country's honour. Many years later when turbaned and bearded tribals who stank up the Departure Lounge with body odour left to work in Saudi Arabia as labourers, he had learned

how to be bribed without demeaning himself. Occasionally he
had walked over to International Arrivals to watch the same
people, still filthy and malodorous, but now carrying huge
cassette players and woollen blankets. Their prosperity pleased
him; he was indirectly responsible for it, which made him feel
good about himself. But the best years had been the recent ones,
when the Departure Lounge was constantly full of doctors and
engineers and accountants leaving for the United States. They
were polite and respectful, they stood in line and Hashmi loved
to watch as they waited for their flights, dressed in their best
clothes and so excited about beginning a new life that they
already spoke in exaggerated American accents taken from
television programmes. By then it was an accepted fact that the
country was decaying and he was sincerely happy that they
were getting out, so happy that he sometimes got carried away
and wanted to congratulate them, to shake their hands and wish
them well. He never actually did that, but he did circulate a
memo that they were not to be unduly harassed.

All Hashmi needed was to be there while a flight to New York
or Toronto was boarding, and he knew he'd be fine.

But he had been spending too much time with Mrs Zulfikar—he
didn't even make it to the Departure Lounge. He spent the day
outside in the waiting area watching the more emotional groups,
the ones in which the women cried in unison and the men looked
grim. For the most part he kept a safe distance, but couldn't
help overhear a seemingly composed mother get hysterical as
she told her son over and over again to wear two pairs of socks
on cold days. Embarrassed, Hashmi hurried away, only to find a
second mother suddenly realize that her son hadn't eaten *biryani*
in the two weeks that he had been home. She started sobbing
and refused to be pacified by promises that he didn't mind and

that he'd eat it when he came back next year. He decided to stay away from mothers after that, but sisters were as bad, particularly the two who were trying to convince their brother—who insisted on communicating by fax—to call home every other Tuesday so that they could at least hear his voice. The one grandmother that he came across was amusing, she warned all the young men in the vicinity against American women because they carried vaginal lice, while the fathers were generally depressing because they tried to disguise their sadness as pride and then failed quite badly.

Hashmi had always thought of migration in terms of people going away; he had never thought about those left behind. Now he noticed that they always stayed until the flight actually departed, even if that meant waiting for another two hours after saying goodbye, more if there was a delay. He tried to talk to the Airport Manager about it. 'Who knows when they'll meet again?' he said. 'One year, two years, six years? Let the families spend at least two more hours together.' But the Airport Manager wasn't interested.

He went back to work the next day. His office, which Kamran had assured him would be deserted, was suddenly like a train station. When he arrived Farooq was waiting for him, with brand new notes of five-hundred and a thousand rupees neatly arranged on his desk.

'I sold the motorcycle,' he said. 'Here's twenty-eight thousand.'

'You were expecting twenty.'

'It's a popular model. The resale value is very high. Ask your peon, he'll tell you that there's great demand for this model.'

Hashmi didn't argue; it was all going into his desk anyway.

'Look,' Farooq continued. 'Now there's no way that my mother can pay you more. Just give me my passport.'

'We'll see,' said Hashmi. He gathered the money and then locked it in his drawer.

A short while later Mrs Zulfikar turned up. 'How much did my
son give you?' she asked.

'He sold his motorcycle. It has nothing to do with you.'

'He doesn't own a motorcycle. He doesn't even know how to
ride one. He stole my jewellery—jewellery I was saving for my
daughters-in-law.'

'I saw the registration papers.'

'Those were for his cousin's bike. Farooq borrowed them.'
She handed Hashmi two gold bangles. 'Somehow he missed these.
You keep them, you might as well because you've got everything
else. But whatever money he gave you, it goes into my account.
You have to treat it as coming from me.' She waited for a moment
and then asked again. 'So how much did he give you?'

'Twenty-eight thousand.'

'It was worth much more. Whoever he sold it to cheated
him—keep that in mind.' Mrs Zulfikar got up to leave. 'Now
you'll have to decide because I have nothing left to give you.
And neither does Farooq.'

Hashmi had decided. He was going to empty his drawer, return
everything, and tell both mother and son to go to hell. But
before he could do that another lady, whom he had never seen
before, walked into his office. Like Mrs Zulfikar she had a tired
face, but also had an air of defeat about her. Her clothes were
shiny and cheap, and for some reason Hashmi felt that they
were her best, which made everything worse.

'Superintendent Sahib,' she said. 'Forgive me for disturbing
you. I know that you're an important man, you must be very
busy, but there's nobody else who can help me. You see I'm a
widow, I have no family except for one son and now he wants
to go to Canada—'

Hashmi couldn't believe this was happening.

'Superintendent Sahib,' she continued. 'You have to understand. I'll be all alone if my son leaves. All you have to do is—'

Suddenly Hashmi knew: Kamran. He was the only one smart enough to do something like this. And nobody could get into his office unless Kamran let them in. 'It was my peon, wasn't it?' he said.

All the Mrs Zulfikar look-alike could do was stare at Hashmi, horrified. 'Oh no, oh no, oh no,' she said. 'Kamran Sahib was very helpful. He didn't take any money, not even one rupee. He told me that you were a decent man, not like all the other officers. He said that you'd listen, that you were—'

Her discretion didn't matter because Kamran admitted to everything. For a while now he had been seeking out widows who would be all alone once their sons left. Initially his scheme hadn't worked because most of them had aunts or cousins or nieces who lived with them and others had simply resigned themselves to their loneliness. Mrs Zulfikar had been the first to agree to his proposal: a hundred rupees a visit, fifty for him, fifty to be shared between the police guards outside and Moazzam the receptionist. Convincing Hashmi wasn't his responsibility, all he did was let her into the Superintendent's office. And then Farooq had turned up, but Kamran only charged him for every other visit because he felt sorry for him.

'Aren't you ashamed of yourself?' Hashmi asked Kamran.

He wasn't. 'Three years I've been in the Immigration Cell,' he said, 'and not once have I got one paisa more than my salary. Superintendent Sahib, every day you get your envelope—but I get nothing. Do you know that at the airport the porters eat chicken for dinner every night? Or that the typist has his own car and the clerks come and go on motorcycles? And that last month the manager's peon shifted to a new house with an air-conditioner in his bedroom.? I'm ashamed to show my face before him because I still live in a house without electricity. Before his house was just like mine, but since he got transferred to the Immigration Cell he's bought a colour television and a Korean refrigerator. And next month, his wife tells everybody, he's going to buy a VCR. I've been in the Immigration Cell longer than him and I don't even have a black and white television. Thousands of people have gone to Canada in front of me and I got nothing! Aren't I in the Immigration Cell? Isn't it my right also?'

Hashmi didn't disagree. But at the moment he was more concerned about Mrs Zulfikar. Taking money from people because they wanted to get out of Pakistan was one thing, but taking advantage of widows because they were terrified of being alone was quite another. Hashmi felt that he had been involved in something shameful, and wanted to make up for it.

He sent everybody away and locked himself inside his office. He tried to think but ended up staring at the distemper which was flaking badly. The more he tried to concentrate the more closely he examined it. But by the afternoon he knew exactly what to do. He'd come up with the perfect solution—everybody would be happy. He didn't move from his desk, he just sat there thinking how brilliant, how absolutely brilliant, his idea was. And for the first time in his life Hashmi felt genuinely good about himself. He had pretended to many times before, but then it had just been to justify the bribes he had accepted. This time it was real. Hashmi was so moved that he was on the verge of tears. He tried to be patient, perhaps even cry a bit for proper melodramatic effect, but he was too excited to wait any longer.

He called Mrs Zulfikar. Then he called Farooq. When they were both in his office, glaring at each other and drinking the tea that he had made because Kamran had disappeared, Hashmi announced his plan. 'H-1 visa,' he said. 'For the United States. I'll arrange it. These days it's impossible but I have contacts in the embassy. And it costs at least eighty-thousand but I won't take anything. Farooq you'll be able to work anywhere in America. And for you Mrs Zulfikar, a J-2 residence permit. That's also difficult but I'll get it done. Then you can live there for as long as you want.'

Neither Mrs Zulfikar nor Farooq said anything.

'It's perfect,' said Hashmi, disturbed by their silence. 'Now the whole family will be together. Both of you get what you want. Farooq you'll be living in America and Mrs Zulfikar you'll have all your sons near you, not just one but all three of them.'

He couldn't understand why they weren't as pleased as he was. 'It's perfect,' he repeated.

Finally Mrs Zulfikar spoke. She was calm and composed, there was no sign of her previous histrionics. 'Go,' she said to Farooq. 'Go to America. You have an opportunity, so take it. See if I care. Do whatever you want.' Then she turned to Hashmi. 'You people think you know everything. But you don't, you know, you don't. My sons, their entire lives are unnatural—frozen foods, Hindu friends, even the way that they themselves speak—and most of the time nothing makes sense. But one thing always makes sense: home. They know that they have a home because it's here in Karachi, and because I'm here. If I leave, the house that they were born in will still be here, but it won't be home anymore. Do you expect me to take their home away from them? Do you expect any mother to do that to her children? You can keep your J or H or whatever it's called visa because I'm not going anywhere.'

Farooq laughed, a loud and sarcastic laugh. 'I told you she was mad,' he said.

Hashmi, who had unlocked his desk drawer to take everything out, locked it again.

MAHIR ALI

Mahir Ali was born in Lahore in 1959, educated at Cathedral School, Aitchison College and Oxford University. He has worked as a journalist in Pakistan for *Dawn* and *The Frontier Post* and in Dubai for *The Khaleej Times*. He has written extensively on politics and culture and contributed to periodicals such as *Viewpoint* and *Herald* as well. He now lives in Sydney and works for *The Australian*.

A LETTER FROM A FATHER TO HIS DAUGHTER

Dear Tanya,

The primary purpose of this letter is to explain why your mother and I deemed it prudent to nurture you in Australia, a continent so far removed from Pakistan, the homeland you have never really known. By the time you are old enough to wonder about such matters, and perhaps to query our motives, we may no longer be around, or our perspectives skewed and our powers of recollection dimmed.

Hence this epistle. A pre-emptive self-defense exercise, if you like, though I would be more inclined to view it as a contribution, however meagre, to the constant tussle between memory and forgetfulness. It's hard to tell where you are going if you can't remember where you are coming from. Or why.

I wouldn't like that observation to be misinterpreted, though. I have never been too enthusiastic about the 'roots theory' dividing humanity. In fact, I would probably have been rather well-disposed towards that be-all and end-all catchphrase of the Nineties—globalization—had it implied a world without borders. But that privilege is reserved strictly for capital, for multinational corporations, for profits *sans frontieres*.

Excuse the digression although the issue isn't unrelated to Pakistan. For at least two decades successive governments have wished to convert the country into a sweatshop at the service of foreign capital. Their lack of success is attributable chiefly to an environment hostile to foreign investment: not, unfortunately, in the shape of resistance from organized labour, but the threat of veritable anarchy.

I don't suppose the foregoing would mean much, minus the socio-historical context, but you'll have to seek that elsewhere. Nor is objectivity my objective. However there is room for broad agreement on the contention that follows: namely at the time we left Pakistan in 1987, not long after your brother Rahul had been born, the sense of oppressiveness was palpable. In terms of political suppression, the worst was perhaps over by that time, although the military General Zia-ul-Haq still had a few tricks up his khaki sleeves. But there was something that went well beyond the ordinary repressive apparatus of the state: an atmosphere inconducive to unrestrained application of the intellect, a culture of limitations. The so-called 'ideological frontiers' of the state, defined in appallingly narrow terms, exercised a choking influence in a multitude of ways, of which censorship was but the most blatant manifestation.

The Zia regime cannot be lumped with sole responsibility for this feat; although it extended the phenomenon far beyond earlier high water marks, it was essentially building on foundations that had been laid in the nation state's infancy. Notwithstanding the military dictatorship's excessive zeal in blocking conceptual avenues, it is well worth remembering that the Zia years were, paradoxically, also a period of high hopes. Resistance to the trauma, which manifested itself in a variety of ways, held out the prospect of a liberated nation, redefining itself in the aftermath. It turned out to be a fond hope. But it nonetheless helps to understand why our self-exile, an act of desperation though it may have been, did not initially bear the stamp of permanence.

The combination of a superficially benevolent despotism and ostensibly laissez-faire economics offered by a nearby Gulf sheikhdom was a temporary, and mildly embarrassing, refuge. Let it also be said that the scarcity of high priests choking you with moral concoctions based on dubious ingredients was refreshing; it was a pleasant surprise to find the same religion, that in Pakistan was employed as a tyrannical mantle, playing the role of a relatively innocuous backdrop. You may also find it interesting that when your grandparents visited us in Dubai, they found the cultural mix vaguely reminiscent of pre-Partition India. But the high sheen veneer of vibrant commerce conceals a darker reality: the conditions under which the labourers, recruited largely from the subcontinent, live and toil, are not substantially different from the economic bondage in India or Pakistan that they seek to escape. Yet they are in most cases willing to put up with the exploitation in exchange for wages that enable them, if they spend next to nothing on themselves, to purchase education for a son or dowry for a daughter. Their plight serves as a searing indictment not just of capitalism in the Gulf, but of those who sustain the circumstances that compel them to leave home.

As you probably know, the Zia era ended suddenly, with a thud, on an August day in 1988. At the time of writing, the circumstances of the General's fortuitous flight into oblivion are still shrouded in mystery. The truth may emerge at some point, although I wouldn't count on it. We still don't know, and nobody is trying to find out, whether the assassination of Pakistan's first Prime Minister was part of a broader conspiracy. In the case of the country's first popularly elected Prime Minister, the identities of those who conspired to secure his elimination through blatantly unjust judicial means are well known. Yet his final moments and the manner of his quietus reside in the realm of rumours despite his daughter Benazir's two stints in power.

And it is the same daughter with whom one must pick a quarrel over the unrelieved mediocrity of the post-Zia period. It's harder to argue with her chief rival, Nawaz Sharif and his priorities, because of considerably lower expectations. After all, he still pays obeisance at the shrine of Zia-ul-Haq, the mentor who plucked him from industrial obscurity and nurtured his political career. His authoritarian predilections therefore come as no surprise, nor have his limitations ever seriously been doubted. Benazir Bhutto's is a somewhat different case, not because of her genetic heritage but as a consequence of what she succeeded in symbolizing, courageously, during the darkest days of martial law. And because of the widespread assumption that her education, not her academic career at Radcliffe or Oxford, but her political initiation as a victim of oppression, and her gender would propel her towards a liberating role.

There were, admittedly, warning signs. Such as the way in which she looked to Washington's blessings, rather than the accumulated goodwill and sympathy of the masses, as the surest route to power. And her apparent lack of qualms about entering into complex and self-defeating compromises with the military-bureaucratic elite. Yet I was frankly appalled by the extent of her negligence while presiding over two spectacularly flawed administrations. Its social-democratic reputation compromised beyond redemption, the Pakistan People's Party decimated at the last election has chosen her as its Chairperson-for-life. It is quite literally a diminished responsibility. Ms Bhutto's do-nothingness included a refusal to tamper with the fundamentals of an agenda set by the Zia administration. This echoes, perhaps, a wider trend: for example, Bill Clinton and Tony Blair have exhibited a wanton willingness to play the game according to the rules established during the Reagan-Thatcher years. But that doesn't really mitigate Ms Bhutto's refusal to even attempt a substantial reordering of priorities. She has thereby facilitated the continued degeneration of Pakistan's polity as well as its economic imbalance.

Lest the foregoing be construed as casting any sort of doubt on Mian Nawaz Sharif's contribution to the process, I must hasten to add that his role in the reduction of politics to competitive corruption has been second to none. One could claim that Pakistan has come full circle, with the political process returning to what had become the norm before Ayub Khan introduced the jackboot into the equation. Except that now the level of chicanery and deception goes well beyond the wildest imagination of the average 1950's politician. Besides, one can ill-afford not to take cognizance of an element whose significance has grown manifold since those days: obscurantism, harnessed secular purposes by the scheming mind of General Zia, and epitomized by the creeping Talibanisation of Pakistan. It may not have come to this, had Ms Bhutto and Mr Sharif had the good sense and the courage to dissociate their governments from sponsorship of the unending strife in Afghanistan, which had served a crucial strategic purpose for their military predecessor, encouraging him to ignore the destruction it wrought on both sides of the border.

By the time you read this, you will have the advantage of knowing how matters have turned out. But at this point I dread to think what lies ahead, given the multifaceted and uniformly ugly legacy of the Zia years, the trends that have evolved since then, and now the nuclear factor. It is pleasanter to look back, although perhaps largely because past realities are hard to disentangle from generally warm personal memories. I find it difficult, for example, to contemplate the Ayub era in an entirely negative light as images of a happy childhood interfere with the process. Even an instance of victimization, such as the fact that your grandfather was prevented from working as a journalist for the duration of that particular dictatorship, carries with it a corollary. Having him at home meant that I was at the receiving end of all the paternal attention I could possibly have hoped for. It was only much later that I was able to appreciate how agonizingly frustrating those years of enforced inactivity must have been for him.

On a broader plane, if Ayub Khan's so-called Decade of Development had a redeeming feature, it was the means of its demise: a popular revolt that reflected the international mood of the times. It's a different matter that Ayub was followed by another repulsive dictator, during whose reign I, for the first time, felt truly ashamed of being a Pakistani, especially a Punjabi. I vividly recall the excitement generated by the nation's first general election in 1970. A December night. Mattresses on the floor in the TV lounge. Coffee and sandwiches to sustain your grandparents and me through the night as we witnessed the ovel spectacle of a popular verdict being recorded. And then, ust a few months down the line, the unspeakable horror of the electoral aftermath. Mass slaughter, rape and pillage on a scale hat has earned Pakistan a place in twentieth century history alongside Nazi Germany, Cambodia and Rwanda. A steady orrent of ever more fantastic falsehoods issuing forth from the government's mouthpieces. And, perhaps worst of all, barely a whisper of domestic protest at the enormity. Nary an expression of sympathy for the victims of gratuitous bloodletting. When outrage eventually flowed out into streets still plastered with ading and frayed Crush India posters, it was directed at the lecision by Pakistani forces in Bangladesh, the butchers ttendant at the birth of a nation, to surrender.

Whatever his role in these traumatic events, the inauguration of Zulfikar Ali Bhutto's era was enveloped in an aura of reshness. I would not wish to idealize the early Seventies, or to gloss over the fact that the flower of democracy wilted within a ouple of years. The country's first popularly elected Prime Minister surrounded himself with opportunists, sycophants and ools setting in motion a process that led meanderingly to July 977. One can only lament that his undoubted ability to make a lecisive break with the past and to transform the relations of roduction remained underutilized. But those were interesting mes (not least because of Mr Bhutto's unpredictability) and he possibility of change for the better continued to hover verhead almost till the end. Among his various other flaws, Mr Bhutto's arrogance did not serve him well. But, unlike his aughter, he at least had something to be arrogant about.

His successors have succeeded in creating a climate of nduring inhospitability for the imagination, for fresh ideas, for e truth. For hope.

I retain a particularly delightful childhood memory of runching underfoot on winter mornings the frost that could be ound on patches of grass in Lahore. There has been no sign of for at least a couple of decades, although the winters are still old. The last time you and I visited that city, we were stranded t the airport in Karachi for ten hours or so, because all flights

northwards were delayed. Reduced visibility, they said, because
of smog. The flight controllers were waiting for a window of
opportunity... I'm not sure whether it makes sense to perceive
the rising level of pollution as a metaphor for the loss of
innocence, but I do fear that the pall is semi-permanent. It may
not, just yet, be all encompassing. Perhaps it is still possible, on
a clear day in Nathiagali up in the Murree Hills, to gaze across
the mountain ranges and catch a glimpse of Nanga Parbat
standing tall in the distance. It's an elevating experience. Yet all
around you there is grinding poverty amid conditions that have
barely changed across generations, the summer cottages of the
bourgeoisie serving only to underline the contrast.

In cities, towns and villages across the country, the
deprivation of the many is combined with change-resistant levels
of superstition, ignorance, fatalism. And despair.

I share the despair. At the same time, I harbour boundless
respect for the men and women, especially the women, who
continue, in a hostile environment, to rage against the dying of
the light. I wish them success. I envy their ability to find silver
linings amid the deepening gloom. Yet, given the choice, I would
not wish my children to grow up amid the stultifying,
asphyxiating atmosphere of the land of lengthening shadows.
Should you, in your adolescence or later, wonder out of
curiosity, resentment, or whatever, why your parents exercised
that choice on your behalf, I hope these observations will serve
as an explanation of sorts.

Yours lovingly,
Bab
Sydney, 16 March 199

HUMERA AFRIDI

*H*umera Afridi spent her early years in Karachi, grew up in Abu Dhabi and graduated from Mount Holyoke College in the United States in 1993 with a major in English and a minor in Asian Studies. There she also started to write short stories. She went on to do a teaching certificate in San Francisco, and an MA in Literary and Cultural Theory at Carnegie Mellon University. She lived in Jeddah, and Dubai where she was a full-time feature writer for the *Gulf News*, before she became a lecturer in the English Department of a Dubai college and started to write freelance for various publications. She now lives in Dallas, Texas and continues to write.

(TRANS)MIGRATIONS OF THE HEART

Sifting through picture albums dusted with history in search of photographs of my weddings—plural not in terms of partners, but rather in terms of ceremonies and states of mind—I discovered after thumbing through an inordinate heap of pictures, that over the course of our many travels, my husband and I had managed to lose most of our wedding photographs. We were thus obliged to call on parents, siblings and friends to replenish our memories of the ceremonies that spanned continents and then cities.

I have been married seven years and three months or six years and nine, depending on which wedding I take as my frame of reference. Having either option has actually proved more confusing than convenient, and consequently my husband and I, at a loss as to when we really got married, have the dubious distinction of not having celebrated a single anniversary on any of the sanctified dates.

The haphazardness began when I was a sophomore at Mount Holyoke. At the time, if someone had suggested we were a nation obsessed with marriage, I would have had no qualms in giving the bigot a dressing down, and pointing out that he was obviously blind to the radical changes taking place in our society. He had only to look at my generation of independent, career minded women, to realize how mistaken he was. It was only months later that foregoing my original plan to take New York by storm with a bunch of dorm-mates during Thanksgiving break, I braced myself, on my family's prodding, to visit a set of long lost cousins who had migrated to the United States decades ago.

I returned after five days, engaged—of my own volition—to be married to someone I didn't know, much to the puzzlement of my parents, then based in Abu Dhabi, who had only met my fiancé once when he was a scowling ten year old, and to the subliminal horror of my feminist friends who thought I had 'absolutely lost it.'

So why did I opt for the semi-medieval ritual of getting acquainted with my fiancé after betrothal? Thoughts of marriage had, after all, been as far from my mind on my trip to Waterloo as they should be for any healthy undergraduate! But for my husband and I, it became quietly lucid during an engaged conversation three days in to my visit that ours was a meeting of minds, a match destined to take place, and thus when he proposed the following day, I thought, 'Ha! A post-modern rendition of the arranged marriage!'

Our decision to get married was not about submission but rather about subversion, at varying levels—it defied the codes of modern dating and thus brimmed with novelty; it negated the claim that women either marry men or their careers (I went right back to college, on to do an MA followed by a full time career). The novelty of getting engaged in a snow-ridden hinterland in somebody's drawing room over a hot cup of tea and cake and my husband's grandmother's engagement *dupatta* draped over my sweater and trousers for the sake of tradition, (and the camera) was deliciously unceremonious.

For many Pakistanis the obvious next step would have been to make preparations for the wedding 'back home'. However, we were faced with a dilemma: how does one orchestrate a

Pakistani wedding when the bridegroom, essentially Iowan, upholds Midwestern values antipathetic to the hullabaloo of aeons-old tradition, while the bride, a rootless expatriate, who left Karachi at the age of eleven, secretly craves the pomp and ceremony of a traditional wedding? Tussles over location were rapidly diffused by the ugly realization that for our union to be *halal* in the United States—Ahad's country of allegiance and my soil of residence—we had to first have an American wedding. 'A civil ceremony!' I exclaimed, the cold sibilance of the words replete with images of musty courtrooms manned with hoary judges in gowns.

The 'courtroom' of our American wedding turned out to be an old church that had been converted into a mosque, a hub for the growing Muslim population of Waterloo. Within the hallowed walls of the mosque, Ahad and I were pioneers: for although circumscribed by American civil law, our wedding ceremony, the first of its kind in this establishment, was at least taking place at a site that ostensibly represented our religious heritage. But as I looked around at the newly painted walls decorated with streamers and balloons, and the wide-eyed audience of well-wishers anxiously awaiting the next act in the drama, I cringed inwardly. Bereft of parents and grandparents, cousins and childhood friends, bereft of the wedding anthems that consecrate all marriages, I balked at the horror of the unfolding spectacle. This is not how I had imagined my wedding.

The irony of this hybrid ritual was rendered all the more pungent when Judge Walt Rothschilde, (who, I recently discovered, is Jewish), directed us to stand side by side and instead of reading out our American rights and making us sign the dotted line as we had anticipated, ordered me and then Ahad to repeat after him as he broke into the sedate but sing-song litany of Christian wedding vows, 'In sickness and in health', 'For better or for worse'. Tripping after him, reluctant to keep up with the script I'd heard so often in movies, I barely managed to suppress reams of hysterical laughter as the ritual spiralled to a close with, 'You may now kiss the bride!' There was a collective gasp in the hall and then community members murmured and tut-tutted their disapproval of the sacrilegious injunction.

My first wedding demonstrated the raging cauldron of America's converging traditions, and left me more than anything else, cold with longing for my own. Needless to say, the choice of venue for our real wedding had now been made infinitely easier. Both Ahad and I looked forward to the festivities, less than three months away, in our ancestral village, Babri Banda, in the North West Frontier Province, followed by a ceremony in Karachi, my old home town. Making wedding arrangements from afar is almost as complicated as directing a big-budget movie, I discovered helplessly, as my parents in Abu Dhabi and my in-laws in Iowa endeavoured to co-ordinate the logistics of clothes, trousseau, guest lists and menus with relatives scattered all over Pakistan.

My expectations of a traditional wedding hadn't prepared me in the least for the hyperborean gusto of a Pathan wedding. Nostalgic in my rootless identity as an expatriate for the signifiers that bind one to a culture, I was utterly unprepared for the reverse—for tradition to claim me. This was no superficial rehearsal of a time-worn ritual for sentimental or novelty value. As Kalashnikovs fulminated my arrival into the village, and residents thronged the route to my grandmother's house, I realized I was no longer the navigator of my wedding. The next couple of days in *mayun* made me cranky, oversensitive, and withdrawn, the way Pathan brides are perhaps meant to be, acutely aware in these last days of the change in hands from father to husband, of his family's gain and the loss of mine. Out of respect for the stringent moral codes of the village, I remained in seclusion. Ritual gradually colonized mind and spirit, and my only succour in those pre-*nikah* days of virtual isolation were hours spent chatting with Saman, a childhood friend who had travelled from Karachi for the wedding.

The day of the *nikah* arrived after what seemed an unctuous eternity in *mayun*. Flanked by the women of my family, I waited for the 'messengers' to arrive from the village mosque where

he actual ceremony, consecrated by the *maulvi* and attended
only by males, would be consolidated by my Nana whom I had
chosen as my witness. The two messengers finally arrived.
According to tradition they were there to ask me whom I wanted
as a male representative and witness in the mosque, and to
thrice confirm my acceptance of the *rishta* from Ahad and his
family. However, having fulfilled the first half of their mission,
the messengers abruptly got up and with a flourish of their
voluminous shawls strode back to the mosque. Minutes later, a
volley of gunshots decimated the late morning calm with a festal
violence: I had been married, once again, but this time it was a
condition bestowed upon me. I was neither agent nor participant.

The *rukhsati* followed a day later, and embellished in a gold
and *ferozi gharara*, amid much rejoicing and clamour of drums
and trumpets I was bundled into a garlanded palanquin that
toured the route from my house to Ahad's, flanked by the village
youth. The occasion of my 'delivery' was baptized once again
by a deafening volley of Kalashnikovs that refused to let up
until we stormed through the gates. Ahad, who had been an
integral participant in the festivities, told me later that his
moment of fame had involved having to sit on a chair, turban
and all, surrounded by hundreds of people as the military band
serenaded him. My 'moment'—and I have yet to find words
that will reflect the diction of emotions that washed over me—
was to come when fumbling out of the palanquin I was led to a
stage about three feet high. 'Keep your head bent and look
modest,' Aunty Abida commanded in my ear. 'And don't forget
to turn slowly so the women can see your finery!' Before I
knew it, I was being hauled up to face the masses.

The ingredients that made up the final stage of our wedding
at the Boat Club in Karachi—faces familiar to me from childhood, the quiet sophistication of a city ceremony devoid of
drama, the fact that Ahad and I were considered equal partners
in a union—made me feel as if I had finally arrived. And yet in
a few days we would all go our separate ways again—Ahad
back to his job in Minneapolis and I back to Mount Holyoke.

In our contemporary diasporas, our expatriate and exilic communities, and our multinational dispersions, is the maelstrom of tradition worth the hassle? As an expatriate, I felt compelled to garner the rituals and rites of my marriage in the battle of memory. And yet as hard as I tried, I was often struck by the hollowness of traditions that no longer corresponded with my world-view. How then does an expatriate appease her fear of not belonging when the fact is she will never wholly belong again?

IA RAHMAN

*I*A Rahman is one of Pakistan's most distinguished journalists, columnists and human rights activists. He has been writing professionally since 1949. He worked with *The Pakistan Times* for many years and rose from sub-editor, to film critic, leader writer to chief editor. He went on to become the editor of *Cinema* briefly, was managing director of an Urdu publication, *Azad,* and served as the executive editor of the weekly *Viewpoint*, during the harsh oppression from 1978-88. He has written a book, *Arts and Crafts of Pakistan*, co-edited *Jinnah as a Parliamentarian* and put together a collection of his own columns, *Pakistan Under Siege*. Since 1990, he has been working as Director, Human Rights Commission of Pakistan and writes freelance for various publications, including *Newsline.*

IN THE NAME OF HONOUR

Lahore. April 6, 1999. Time: 5.54 pm. Samia Sarwar is sitting in advocate Hina Jilani's room. For the first time in years she feels a sense of relief. Her parents have sent word that they have agreed to her getting a divorce from an abusive husband. In fact, her mother is bringing the settlement papers. It is only to meet her and receive the documents that Samia has been brought here from Dastak, a shelter for women in distress. Well-known intermediaries have persuaded her lawyer to arrange this meeting and they have offered complete assurances of good faith. Samia will soon be free to make a new life, there is a tangible feeling of optimism all around. The mother arrives. But she is not alone. She is accompanied by a tough-looking man. Samia rises in her chair out of respect for her mother. At the same time Hina Jilani asks the mother to send the man accompanying her out as his presence in the room is not permitted. The latter answers in English, 'He is supporting me as I have difficulty in walking.' She has barely finished her sentence when the male intruder whips out a pistol and takes a shot at Samia's head. In a split second her dreams are shattered as she slumps on the floor, her young blood forming a pool around her lifeless head.

The assassin and Samia's mother run out of the room—the latter apparently has no difficulty in racing through the corridor, towards the exit door where another man, Samia's uncle, is standing guard with a pistol in his hand. Their getaway plan however, goes awry somehow. Perhaps the vehicle needed for the great escape has not arrived. Perhaps the appointed driver has changed his mind and not shown up. The man at the door notices Shahtaj Qizilbash, a key figure at AGHS Law Associates, grabs her, puts his pistol to her head, forces her to accompany him, and warns everyone against following him. Meanwhile, the assassin notices the police guard crouching behind the reception desk and takes aim at him, but the policeman is quicker. He, who had a few moments earlier taken a life, thus loses his own. Amid this chaos, Samia's mother and uncle with their captive, Shahtaj, in tow manage to scramble down the stairs.

They are spotted by the security guards of a private organization, but when the latter see Shahtaj being taken hostage at gunpoint, they desist from intervening. Her captor then pushes her and the other woman into a rickshaw, squeezes in and off they go. Lahore has just witnessed one of the most foul murders of its kind in recent years.

The premeditated and cold-blooded killing of Samia Imran Saleh in the law office of widely reputed campaigners for human rights, especially of women's rights, Asma Jahangir and Hina Jilani, was a crime of extraordinary daring. The culprits knew that they could not gain access to their prey at Dastak as no man is allowed entry there. The only place they could hope to reach her were the advocate's chamber and that too was proving difficult since Samia had refused to meet anyone—even her father. Thus, they had to assign a key role to Samia's mother.

A mother being used to help assassinate her offspring is not an ordinary matter, even in Pakistan's violence-ridden society.

Men have been guilty of such cruel behaviour, but instances of a mother's heart being hardened to such a degree, of being an accomplice to her child's murder, are rare.

It was an even more extraordinary crime because the culprits were aware of the nature of the venue chosen for the dastardly act. They knew that any violence committed at such a place would immediately attract the attention of the media, the lawyers' community, the NGO fraternity and the public at large. They were also fully aware of the high profile contacts they had to use to persuade the advocates to allow Samia's mother to see her, and that too for delivering a settlement deed that would rule out recourse to a court of law. Yet they were not deterred from committing a capital offence at these premises.

It was also an extraordinary crime because the characters involved were no ordinary persons. True, Samia Imran came from Peshawar, but she was not one of those Pathan women who have never tasted freedom. Her husband's parents had accepted the fact of her incompatibility with her husband, the son of her mother's sister. They had been maintaining her in their home for about four years and providing her two children with a comfortable upbringing and education. They had not only allowed Samia's younger sister to study medicine and become a doctor but had also permitted Samia herself to study law after her separation from her husband. And the parents themselves were not ordinary persons—her father enjoyed eminence in the business community of Peshawar and her mother was a doctor. They had just returned home after performing Haj, a rite that symbolizes in its essence the best and most pure in life, that conjures up images of peace and sanctity. How did the seeds of a murder plot strike root in such a household?

And then it was an extraordinary crime because it was not warranted nor understood in any way—not even as a crime of passion. Samia was seeking a divorce four years after her separation from her husband that had been accepted by both sides. It was not a sudden development. Nobody had enticed her to Lahore. Neither Dastak nor the AGHS had suggested to her that she should seek refuge with them. She had, in fact, gone to a law college in Lahore about which she might have heard after deciding to take up the LLB course, and it was the principal of that institution who had advised her to take refuge at Dastak and engage Hina Jilani for the divorce proceedings. There was no immediate provocation, and divorce is not unknown even in tribal society.

Ironically, it was this extraordinary crime that exposed the Prime Minister and the Punjab Chief Minister's hollow rhetoric about instant retribution for all killers for what it really is. They apparently believe an innocent woman's brutal murder is not a heinous crime.

'A brutal killing', 'senseless', 'cold-blooded murder', shouted women activists, human rights defenders, media personnel, *et al.* Certainly not for the first time. Were they crying out in vain?

They had cried out when Kanwar Ahsan was shot and critically wounded on the premises of a court in Karachi—targeted because he and an adult woman had decided to live together in marriage.

They had cried out when the country's most outstanding painter, Zahoorul Akhlaq, and his talented daughter, Jahanara, were mercilessly gunned down in Lahore.

And they cried out each time a woman fell victim to the evil custom of *karo kari*. Samia's murder demonstrates only too graphically how each time their cries were in vain.

Is there a link between Samia's murder, the killing of Zahoorul Akhlaq and Jahanara, the murderous attack on Ahsan and the increasing incidence of *karo kari* killings?

These orgies of wanton killing cannot be wholly explained by the theory of the progressive brutalization of Pakistani society over the past few decades. True, society has been brutalized each time the state has used arms to deal with political dissidents among the Pakhtuns, the Bengalis, the Baloch, the Sindhis and the new Sindhis who call themselves *muhajirs*. It was brutalized when capital punishment was made a trivial matter by prescribing it as the minimum punishment for a variety of breaches of martial law regulations, and when several new offences were added to the list of capital crimes. It was brutalized when Ziaul Haq gathered crowds to witness a hanging in public, or to listen to the shrieks of victims who were flogged in public squares, or when individuals in authority harangued their audiences with the resolve to hang people by lamp-posts. And so on. These are surely some of the more commonly identified factors that have contributed to the culture of violence in Pakistan. But it is time to take a critical look at some other factors that have encouraged the perpetrators of mayhem.

To begin with, murder is not treated as a crime against society since the promulgation of the *Qisas* and *Diyat* law in 1990.[1] This law has made it possible for murderers to go scot-free if they are rich enough to buy a pardon from the victim's heirs or notorious enough to scare the latter off law courts. Nothing is proved by the argument that murderers continue to be sentenced to death, that indeed their number has been growing year after year. What is important is the creation of hope in the criminal's mind that he can escape retribution even if his legal defence is untenable.

This hope is greatly reinforced if a killer has the *wali* of the victim on his side. A man can kill anyone so long as he is sure of being pardoned by the *wali*. A man killed his daughter and told his son to take the rap. Later, he pardoned the 'killer' and both were home free.

The gravity traditionally attached to the crime of murder and the respect for law have both been undermined by the rise of the belief that laws do not apply to offences committed in the name of religion. We have seen treason and lawlessness justified on the grounds of belief. Thus, the *ulema* of Peshawar can instigate their followers to kill Asma Jahangir without any authority taking notice of their offence and newspapers can publish their call to crime without realizing that they too are committing an offence. The freedom allowed to clerics to preach

---

1. Law promulgated during the regime of Zia-ul-Haq, which legalized the ancient Muslim custom of giving blood money as atonement for a murder, instead of the death penalty, subject to agreement for the next of kin: the sum liable to a woman victim's family is half that due to a man's.

violence and practice it at will has dealt a fatal blow to the supremacy of law.

The authorities have to realize that once exemption from the law is allowed on the ground of religious belief, the concession will inevitably be claimed on other grounds—such as tribal codes. It is not a coincidence that increased recourse to tribal codes has followed the process of the so-called Islamization of laws. Nobody should therefore be surprised to find a business group of Peshawar justifying Samia's murder as an act protected under tribal customs.

While the factors mentioned above have made all citizens more vulnerable than before, women suffer additional disadvantages. Whenever a woman is killed, the police, the media and the public invariably try to find fault with the victim. When a woman wants to marry of her free will she is described as a rebel. Samia is killed, Asma and Hina are assailed for encouraging her to defy her family. Zahoorul Akhlaq is killed, he is described as the father of a *raqqasa*, and Jahanara cannot even be granted the status of an artist. Finally, the judiciary has made no small contribution to raise killing of women to a virtue. It has decreed by assorted judgements that those who kill women for the sake of family honour merit only light punishment. At a recent seminar presided over by the Chief Justice of Pakistan, Supreme Court Justice Nasir Aslam Zahid candidly conceded gender bias on the part of the judiciary. He admitted that the moment a doubt was created about the character of a woman victim, the court became prejudiced against her.

A whole series of cases show how the judiciary's gender biases affect the course of justice. When two brothers killed their sister to uphold their *ghairat*, they were let off with an 18-month prison term, which they had already undergone. A killer's sentence of death was reduced to a few years imprisonment because the court held that capital punishment could not be awarded in a case of honour killing.

The question is, what is family honour? The breaking off of an engagement is considered legitimate provocation for murder. A man killed his wife and the court sympathized with the killer because he might have felt frustrated at the woman's failure to bear a child. And there was a case in which an honourable court observed that if a Pakistani Muslim saw a woman of the family in a compromising position with an outsider he had not only the right, but in fact it was his duty to kill her. Can we still pretend ignorance of where the rot lies?

A Punjabi girl leaves her home and takes refuge in Karachi's Edhi Centre and the police of Punjab and Sindh collaborate with one another in conducting a raid on the Centre, in utter violation of the law, and drag the poor girl out. An innocent woman is killed in Lahore and the same mighty police force of the Punjab is denied the right to arrest the culprits by the Frontier authorities. There is one law for the murderous patriarchs and another for their women victims.

The message is clear. No woman of independent mind can be given quarter in the present state of Pakistan.

AKBAR S AHMED

$\mathcal{D}$r Akbar S Ahmed is a distinguished civil servant, anthropologist, writer and a media commentator on Islamic Affairs. His book, *Discovering Islam: Making Sense of Muslim History and Society* (Routledge, 1988), was translated into many languages and inspired the BBC television series, *Living Islam,* for which he wrote a tie-in book, (BBC-Penguin, 1993). He later published a revised and expanded version, *Islam Today: A Short Introduction to the Muslim World* (IB Tauris, 1999). His many other books include *Postmodernism and Islam: Predicament and Promise* (Routledge, 1992), which was nominated for the Amalfi Award. He has been a Fellow of Selwyn College, Cambridge for the past decade. He was also Visiting Professor at Princeton and Harvard and the Allama Iqbal Fellow at Cambridge (1988-1993). He was the first Pakistani to have been elected a member of the Council of the Royal Anthropological Society. He has been awarded the Sir Percy Sykes Memorial Medal by the Royal Society of Asian Affairs and the *Sitara-e-Imtiaz*. His 'Jinnah Quartet,' consists of four projects: a television documentary, *Mr Jinnah and the Making of Pakistan;* a feature film, *Jinnah;* an academic book, *Jinnah, Pakistan and the Islamic Identity: The Search for Saladin* (Routledge, 1997); and a graphic novel, *The Quaid: Jinnah and the Story of Pakistan* (OUP, 1998), which won the President's Award. He has also been Pakistan's High Commissioner to the UK.

MIGRATION, DEATH AND MARTYRDOM IN RURAL PAKISTAN

This chapter* focuses on migration, its impact both on the individual and his or her society, and the social processes which may be triggered by a migrant's return home. Although several economic studies have been conducted on Pakistani migratory labour, a social anthropological or cultural perspective of this migration is, on the whole, notably missing. How do Pakistanis abroad adapt to new ideas? What do they do with them on

---

* Author's note: This is a slightly revised version of a paper which first appeared in *Man* (21 (1) 1986) under the title 'Death in Islam: The Hawkes Bay Case'. I am very grateful to the editor and to the Royal Anthropological Institute for permission to use the material again.

*return? Do they shift away from so-called 'traditional' culture
once home again? Do they accept or challenge—the traditional
leadership, class and social structure from which they escaped?
Do kinship loyalties survive or fade?*

*These questions raise a number of other related issues.
Notions about women, status in society, sacrifice and social
order may all be affected by migration. So too is the way in
which people relate their daily lives to their concepts of the
afterworld. The case study presented here thus also raises
important issues about concepts of death, sacrifice and
martyrdom among Shi'a and Sunni Muslims, a subject scarcely
discussed in anthropological literature.[1] Migration, the case
shows, is only one phase which needs to be analyzed as part of
a migrant's total life-cycle.*

In late February 1983, thirty-eight people—all Shi'a from
Chakwal Tehsil in Punjab—entered the Arabian Sea at Hawkes
Bay. The women and children in the group, about half the
number, had been placed in six large trunks. The leader of the
group, Sayyid Willayat Hussain Shah, pointing his religious
banner at the waves, led the procession. Willayat Shah believed
that a path would open in the sea, which would lead him to
Basra, from where the party would proceed to Karbala, the holy
city in Iraq. A few hours later almost half the party had lost
their lives and the survivors emerged in varying stages of
exhaustion and consciousness.

Pakistan was astonished at the incident. Religious leaders,
intellectuals and newspapers discussed the event extensively.[2]
The discussions revealed almost as much about those
participating in them as they did about the incident. Some
intellectuals saw the episode as evidence of 'insanity'

---

1. See for example, Banton, 1966; Bloch and Parry, 1982; Douglas, 1970;
   Evans-Pritchard, 1937, 1965; Geertz, 1966; Keyes, 1981, 1985; Lewis,
   1971; Werbner, 1977; Winter, 1966.
2. A committee was set up by Dr M Afzal, the Minister of Education, to
   examine the problem. It was chaired by Dr ZA Ansari and included some
   of Pakistan's most eminent psychiatrists and psychologists. I represented
   the social scientists (Pervez, 1983).

(Salahuddin, 1983) and the leaders of the group were described as 'mentally unbalanced individuals with twisted and deviant personalities, the source of death and destruction' (Irfani, 1983). Sunnis dismissed the matter as yet another Shi'a deviation from orthodox Islam. The Shi'as, on the other hand, pointed to the event as a confirmation of their faith (Jaffery, 1983; Yusufzai, 1983). Only Shi'as, they argued, were capable of such extreme devotion, of such a sacrifice. It was, undoubtedly, a case rooted in Shi'a mythology, which preconditioned the community to respond to, and enact, the drama.

I. Chakwal Tehsil

Willayat Shah's family lived in a small village, Rehna Sayyadan, about ten miles from Chakwal Tehsil in Jhelum District. The town of Jhelum, on the Grand Trunk Road, is about seventy miles from Chakwal Tehsil. A population of about 250,000 live in the Tehsil. Chakwal and Jhelum are areas of rain-fed agriculture, unlike the canal colonies of Lyallpur (now Faisalabad) and Sahiwal, with their rich irrigated lands. The population of the village itself is about 2000 mainly consisting of Sayyids, the upper social group, and Arain, the lower.[3] The latter are challenging the authority of the former, through new channels of employment, hard work and frugality (Ahmed, 1984b). The village is somewhat isolated from the rest of Pakistan. Electricity has only recently arrived and the road to Chakwal is not yet metalled. This is one of the hottest areas in the country. Winters are short and the rainfall (about 20 inches) is unreliable. Poor harvests have pushed people off the land to look for employment outside the Tehsil. Many have joined the armed services (Jhelum District is a rich recruiting ground for the Pakistan Army) and from the 1960s the Arab states offered

---

3. The organization of Punjab society into agricultural peasant groups, defined by ethnicity and occupation, is well-documented (Ahmad, 1973, 1977; Ahmed, 1984c; Alavi, 1972, 1973; Balneaves, 1955; Darling, 1925, 1930, 1934; Eglar, 1960; Ibbeston, 1883; Pettigrew, 1975).

opportunities for employment. Willayat Shah, after his service as a junior officer in the Pakistan Air Force, left to work in Saudi Arabia. He returned to Pakistan in 1981 after a stay of four years.

Rehna Sayyadan is self-consciously religious. Its very name announces a holy lineage, that of the Sayyids, the descendants of the Holy Prophet, and means 'the abode of the Sayyids'. Many of the Shi'a actors in the drama bear names derived from members of the Holy Prophet's family: Abbass and Hussain for men, and Fatima for women. But there is tension in the area between Shi'a and Sunni, a tension made more acute by the fact that their numbers are equally balanced. The economic subordination of the Sunni by the Shi'a, reinforces the tension. Conflict between Shi'a and Sunni easily converts into conflict between landlord and tenant. This opposition also runs through the local administration. The local government councillor, for example, is Sunni, but the village *lambardar* (headman) is Shi'a. Even families are divided along Shi'a–Sunni lines and where individuals have changed affiliation, relationships have been severely strained. (There are at least four known cases of Sunni affiliations closely related to the main actor in the drama, Naseem Fatima.) The tension is exacerbated by the current emphasis on Sunni forms of religion by the government of Pakistan. The Shi'as, about 20 per cent of Pakistan's 100 million people, resent this emphasis. The Jamaat-e-Islami, the major orthodox Sunni political party of Pakistan, is active in the area. In the background is the larger ideological tension between the Shi'as and Sunnis in Pakistan. From 1980 onwards this tension became severe and led to clashes between the two, especially in Karachi. Beyond the south-western borders of Pakistan, a vigorous Shi'a revivalism in Iran has unsettled neighbouring Sunni states allied to Pakistan, such as Saudi Arabia.

Willayat Shah was living in Saudi Arabia when Imam Khomeini returned to Iran at the head of his revolution in 1979. Being a devout Shi'a he would have been inspired by the message and success of the Imam, but Saudi Arabia was no place to express his rekindled Shi'a enthusiasm. He would, however, have been dreaming dreams around the themes of the revolution: sacrifice, death, change, and martyrdom. His first act on returning home was to begin the construction of a mosque.

II. The Hawkes Bay Case

On 18 February 1981, Willayat Shah had been engrossed in supervising the construction of the mosque. Late that evening Naseem Fatima, his eldest child, entered his bedroom and announced she had been visited by a revelation—*basharat*. She had heard the voice of a lady speaking to her through the walls of the house. The apprehensive father suggested she identify the voice. For the first few days the voice was identified as that of Bibi Roqayya, the stepsister of Imam Hussain, the grandson of the Holy Prophet (PBUH) buried in Karbala.

Some handprints next appeared on the wall of Willayat Shah's bedroom. They were made with henna mixed with clay. A handprint has highly emotive significance among the Shi'a. It is symbolic of the five holiest people in Islam: the Holy Prophet (PBUH), his daughter, Hazrat Fatima, his son-in-law, Hazrat Ali, and his grandsons, Hazrat Hassan and Hazrat Imam Hussain. The news of the handprints spread rapidly in the area. The impact on the village was electric. One informant described it as follows:

> [F]or the next fifteen days or so the usual business of life came to a halt. People gave up their work, women stopped even cooking meals. Everyone gathered in the house of Willayat Hussain to see the print, to touch it, to pray and to participate in the mourning (*azadari*) which was constantly going on (Pervez, 1983).

The *azadari,* a recitation of devotional hymns and poems in honour of, in particular, Hazrat Hussain, was a direct consequence of the handprints. It created a highly charged and contagious atmosphere among the participants.

Sunnis, however, were cynical about the whole affair. They would remain adamant opponents of Naseem's miracles (*maujza*). Opinion was divided among the Shi'a. Established families such as the Sayyids scoffed at Naseem and her miracles and, at first, both Willayat Shah and his daughter had their doubts. As if to dispel these doubts Imam Mahdi, or Imam-e-Ghaib, the twelfth Imam, himself appeared in the dreams of Naseem. Earlier, Bibi Roqayya had announced that the Imam rather than she would communicate with Naseem. The Imam wore white clothes and was of pleasing appearance (Ansari, 1983). All doubts in her mind were now dispelled and he addressed her as *Bibi Pak*—pure lady.

The Imam, with whom she now communicated directly, began to deliver explicit orders (*amar*). One commanded the expulsion of the carpenter who was working for Willayat in his house (ibid.) and who had overcharged him by Rs 1,000, in connivance with the contractor. He was ordered never to work at a Sayyid's house again, or both would be losers in the transaction. To compensate Willayat, the Imam placed Rs 500 in a copy of the Holy Qur'an, and ordered the carpenter to pay the remaining 500. The orders increased in frequency and soon included matters of property and marriage. The family, at least, no longer doubted the miracles and obeyed divine orders without question. During the revelations Naseem would demand complete privacy in her room. Her condition would change. She would quiver and tremble. Noises would sound in her head beforehand and the trauma of the revelations often caused her to faint afterwards. The orders would come to her on the days the Imams died or were made martyrs. 'The Imam,' according to her father, 'had captured her mind and heart.' (ibid.).

Local Shi'a religious leaders and lecturers (*zakirs*) acknowledged Naseem and visited her regularly. Of the three most regular visitors one, Sakhawat Hussain Jaffrey, was particularly favoured. Naseem claimed that she had been especially ordered by the Imam to single him out. They were often alone for long periods. Naseem began to organize *azadari* regularly. These meetings were charged with emotion and created devout ecstasy in the participants. They were held next to the local primary school; so many people attended, with such noisy devotion, that the school had to close down. Naseem now completely dominated the life of the village. Before moving to the next phase of the case, let us pause to examine the effect of the revelations on some of the main actors in the drama.

Naseem was a shy, pleasant-looking girl, with an innocent expression on her face, who had a history of fits. There was talk of getting her married. Although she had only studied up to class five, her teachers recall her passionate interest in religion, especially in the lives of the Imams. She had a pleasing voice when reciting *nauhas* (poems about Karbala), many of which she composed herself. After her revelations there was a perceptible change in Naseem. She began to gain weight, wear costly dresses and use perfumes. She became noticeably gregarious and confident. In a remarkable gesture of independence, especially so for a Sayyid girl in the area, she abandoned the *purdah* or veil. According to Shi'a belief, any believer may become the vehicle for divine communications. Naseem turned to the dominant person in her life, her father, upon receiving communications and he interpreted them in his own light.

Willayat Shah now reasserted himself in village affairs after an absence of years. His daughter's religious experience had begun soon after his retirement from Saudi Arabia. He had an older brother to whom, because of the traditional structure of rural society, he was subordinate. His period in Saudi Arabia had enhanced his economic, but not his social position. Because of the miracles and revelations of his daughter, however, he gained a dominant position in the social life of the area. Sardar Bibi, Naseem's mother, was influenced by her husband and daughter and identified wholly with the latter. She was said to have been a Sunni before her marriage and this created an underlying tension in the family. In an expression of loyalty to her husband, she severed relations with her parents and brothers because they disapproved of her conversion. She unhestitatingly obeyed her daughter's revelations.

Another actor in the drama was Sakhawat Jaffrey, a *zakir* of Chakwal. He was not a Sayyid and his father was said to be a butcher. He had thus risen in the social order. Willayat Shah rewarded him for his loyalty with gifts—refrigerators, televisions and fans. When he needed money for a new business he was presented with about Rs 20,000, and with this sum he opened a small shop selling general goods. He was given such gifts on the specific orders of the Imam to Naseem. In turn, he was the only one of the three *zakirs* who personally testified to the authenticity of the miracles of Naseem. Naseem was regularly visited by Sakhawat Jaffrey and she visited his house. In a gesture of affection, contravening social custom, Naseem named Sakhawat's male child—a few months old—Rizwan Abbass. Such names, deriving from the Holy Prophet's family, were traditionally reserved for Sayyids.

Most people were cynical about the relationship between Naseem and the *zakir*. Sakhawat's own wife, who had complete faith in Naseem, said people had spread 'dirty talk' (*gandi batey*) about Naseem and her husband (ibid.). In spite of his belief in the revelations, Sakhawat Jaffrey did not join the pilgrimage to Hawkes Bay. He had recently opened his shop and explained that abrupt departure would ensure its failure. Naseem was understanding: 'This is not a trip for *zakirs*. We want to see you prosper.'

After the visions, Naseem's followers bestowed on her the title already used by the Imam, *Pak Bibi*, or pure lady. The transformation in her appearance and character was now complete. She radiated confidence. Her following spread outside the village. In particular, she developed an attachment to the people of a neighbouring village, Mureed, who were recently converted Muslims (*sheikhs*) and who wholeheartedly believed in her. Most of them were *kammis*, belonging to such occupational groups as barbers and cobblers. Naseem, as a Sayyid, represented for them the house of the Prophet while her father, being relatively well off, was a potential source of financial support. Seventeen of the villagers of Mureed would follow her to Hawkes Bay.

The normal life of the village was disrupted by the affair. The Shi'a, in particular, 'wholeheartedly accepted the phenomenon' but, not unnaturally, 'the regular routine life of the village was paralyzed.' In particular, 'women stopped doing their household jobs' (Jaffery, 1983). Some placed obstacles in Naseem's path, teasing her family members (especially children on their way to school), and dumping rubbish in front of her house. Sayyids who did not believe in her ill-treated her followers from Mureed.

Meanwhile, a series of miracles was taking place which riveted society. Blood was found on the floor of Willayat Shah's bedroom. Naseem declared this to be the blood of Hazrat Ali Asghar, the male child of Hazrat Hussain, martyred at Karbala. On another occasion visitors were locked in a room and told that angels would bear down a flag from heaven. When the door was opened, indeed, there was a flag. On one occasion four children disappeared, to appear again later. But the greatest miracle of all remained Naseem's constant communication with the Imam. Supplicants would pray in front of Naseem's room, expressing their demands in a loud voice. The Imam would be consulted not only on profound matters but also in trivial ones, such as whether a guest should be given tea or food. Naseem, who received many of her orders during fainting fits, would then convey a reply on behalf of the Imam.

There came a time, however, when Naseem's authority was disputed. Doubts arose first from the failure of certain of her predictions and, second, from a public refusal of her kin to redistribute their property according to her orders. Naseem had been making extravagant predictions regarding illness, birth and death. Some of these came true, others did not. In one particular case she predicted the death of a certain person within a specified period. He did not die. In another case, the elder brother of Willayat was asked to surrender his house for religious purposes, which he refused to do. A cousin also refused, when asked, to hand over his property to Willayat. In yet another case, Naseem, perhaps compensating for a Sunni mother in a Shi'a household ordered the engagement of her cousin to a non-Shi'a to be broken: it was not. Naseem and Willayat responded to such rebellion with fierce denunciation. The rebels were branded as *murtid*, those who have renounced Islam and are, therefore, beyond the pale. Their relatives were forbidden to have any contact with them. In some cases, parents were asked not to see their children and vice versa. While taking firm measures against those who did not believe, the followers were charged with renewed activity, calculated to reinforce group cohesiveness. The frequency of religious meetings increased as did visits to shrines. Participation was limited to believers.

Naseem's physical condition now began to correspond with the revelations: she lost weight and her colour became dark when she was not receiving them; she glowed with health when she was. People freely equated her physical appearance with her spiritual condition. She lost *noor*—divine luminosity—in her periods of despondency and regained it when receiving revelations. For those who believed in her it was literally a question of light and darkness. But the crisis in Naseem was reaching its peak; so was the tension in the community.

Exactly to the day, two years after the first communication began, Naseem asked her father a question on behalf of the Imam: would the believers plunge into the sea as an expression of their faith? The question was not figurative. The Imam meant it literally. The believers were expected to walk into the sea from where they would be miraculously transported to Karbala in Iraq without wordly means. Naseem promised that even the 124,000 prophets recognized by Muslims would be amazed at the sacrifice (Ansari, 1983).

Those who believed in the miracles immediately agreed to the proposition. Willayat was the first to agree: he would lead the party (ibid.). There was no debate, no vacillation. They would walk into the sea at Karachi and their faith would take them to the holy city of Karbala. Since the revelations began, Willayat had spent about half a million rupees and had disposed of almost all his property. He now quickly disposed of what remained to pay for the pilgrimage. The party consisted of forty-two people, whose ages ranged from 80 years to 4 months.

Seventeen of them were from Mureed and most of the remaining
were related. Willayat, his brother and cousin, distributed all
their belongings, retaining one pair of black clothes (symbolic
of mourning) only. They hired trucks to take them to Karachi.
With them were six large wooden and tin trunks. They also took
with them the Shi'a symbols of martyrdom at Karbala; *alam*
(flag), *taboot* (coffin), *jhoola* (swing) and *shabi* (picture of the
holy images).

Stopping over at shrines for prayers in Lahore and Multan,
they arrived in Karachi on the third day. Karachi was in the
throes of anti-government demonstrations and the police had
imposed a curfew. The tension in the city directly reflected the
rivalry between Shi'as and Sunnis in Pakistan. In spite of this,
the members of the party were not stopped as they made their
way to Hawkes Bay. For them this was another miracle (Ansari,
1983). At Hawkes Bay, the party offered two prayers (*nafil*) and
read ten surahs from the Holy Qur'an including Al-Qadr, an
early Meccan surah, which states 'the Night of Destiny is better
than a thousand months' (Surah 112, verse 3; M. Asad, 1980).
The verse was well chosen: for the party, it was indeed the
night of destiny.

The Imam then issued final instructions to Naseem: the
women and children were to be locked in the six trunks and the
virgin girls were to sit with her in one of them. Willayat was
asked to hold the *taboot* along with three other men. Willayat's
cousin, Mushtaq, was appointed chief (*salar*) of the party. He
was ordered to lock the trunks, push them into the sea and
throw away the keys. He would then walk into the water with
an *alam*. At this stage four young people from Mureed, two
men and two girls, became frightened. This fear, too, 'was put
in their hearts by the Imam' (Ansari, 1983). Naseem therefore,
willingly exempted them from the journey. The remaining thirty-
eight entered the sea. Mothers saw children and children saw
old parents descending into the dark waters. But there 'were no
ah (cries) or *ansoo* (tears), (ibid.). Those in five out of the six
trunks died. One of the trunks was shattered by the waves and
its passengers survived. Those on foot also survived; they were

thrown back on to the beach by the waves. The operation, which had begun in the late hours of the night, was over by the early morning when police and the press reached Hawkes Bay. The survivors were in high spirits; there was neither regret nor remorse among them. Only a divine calm, a deep ecstasy.

The Karachi police, in a display of bureaucratic zeal, arrested the survivors. They were charged with attempting to leave the country without visas. The official version read: 'The incharge, FIA Passport Cell, in an application filed in the court said, it was reliably learnt that one Willayat Hussain Shah, resident of Chakwal, along with his family had attempted to proceed to a foreign country, Iraq, without valid documents through an illegal route i.e. Hawkes Bay beach', (*Dawn*, March 1983). The act came within the offence punishable under section 3/4 of the Passport Act 1974. The accused were however, soon released.

Rich Shi'as, impressed by the devotion of the survivors, paid for their journey by air for a week to and from Karbala. In Iraq, influential Shi'as equally impressed, presented them with gifts, including rare copies of the Holy Qur'an (ibid.). Naseem's promise that they would visit Karbala without wordly means was fulfilled.

III. Social Change, Leadership and Kinship in Chakwal Society

In an attempt to find a sociological explanation of the Hawkes Bay Case I shall begin by putting forward a thesis based on the so-called *Dubai chalo* (let us go to Dubai) theme in Pakistan society (Ahmed, 1984a). Briefly, the thesis suggests that Pakistani workers, returning from the Gulf with their pockets full of money, are no longer prepared to accept the status quo of the social order from which they had escaped. Those who return demand more social status and authority in society. In their own eyes they have earned the right to be respected by their long and usually hard periods abroad. But they may have little idea how exactly to go about changing society, or even whether they wish to move it 'forward' or back to older, more traditional, ways. Their new social confidence, backed by economic wealth and combined with frustration at the slow pace of change, may result in tensions and dramatic developments of which the Hawkes Bay Case is an example.

Consider Willayat Shah. Belonging to the junior lineage of a Shi'a family and with a Sunni wife, he escaped to Saudi Arabia determined, it may be assumed, to make good on his return. After four hard years there, he returned with considerable wealth, but society had remained the same and there was no perceptible change in his social position. Willayat's immediate family was acutely aware of his predicament. His closest child and eldest daughter, fully grown and intelligent, and herself under pressure to get married, responded to the crisis in their lives with a series of dramatic, divine pronouncements. In her case, the social crisis had triggered psychological reactions. The revelations were calculated to disturb the social equations of the village forever. Naseem dominated not only the social but also, and more importantly for the family, the religious life of the area. Willayat Shah had finally arrived. Both he and Naseem now reached out towards the better, truer world that, for Muslims, lies beyond death. Through their deaths they would gain an ascendancy which would be final and unassailable. They would triumph through the Shi'a theme of death, martyrdom and sacrifice.

For the actors in our case, society provided the stress but failed to suggest cures. We know that at least four individuals closely related to the key actor, Naseem, suffered from tension due to mixed loyalties in the Shi'a-Sunni line up; her grandmother, her mother, her uncle and her aunt's husband were rumoured to have been Sunni in the past. It was known that her grandmother's family were Sunni. By assuming the role of a Shi'a medium, Naseem was socially compensating for the Sunni connections in her family. Under such complex pressures, religion is the most convenient straw to clutch. The stress thus assumes a form of illness, but the illness is both mental and physical and 'in its expression culturally patterned' (Fox, 1973). One must look for cultural acts and symbolic forms which have local significance, including sacrifice and martyrdom. This case is certainly patterned by the religious sociology of Chakwal Tehsil.

Willayat Shah compared the sacrifice of his family to that of Karbala because 'he and his group had been assigned a duty to save the religion and the faith,' (Pervez, 1983). In an interview given to Tariq Aziz on Pakistan Television, he explained why Karachi was selected. He could have died in a pond in the village, he said. But the world would not have known of their faith. The prediction of his daughter had indeed come true. The world was amazed at the miracle of Hawkes Bay and people would talk of them as martyrs forever. Throughout the interviews he remained proud and unrepentant. His perception of those hours at Hawkes Bay is revealing. 'He insisted that he had been walking on the sea all the while like a truck driving on flat road' (Irfani, 1983). He felt no fear, no regret. Most significantly, he remained convinced that the revelations would continue, even after the death of Naseem, through a male member of the family (Ansari, 1983). Willayat's wife, Sardar Bibi, reacted with a fervour equal to that of her husband. 'If the Imam tells us to sacrifice this baby too,' she said, pointing to an infant she was feeding during an interview, 'I'll do it' (Jaffery, 1983, p. 27).

Willayat's eldest sister, Taleh Bibi, divorced and living with her brother, lost one daughter in the incident. She herself survived because she was in the trunk that did not sink. She, too, believes the miracle will continue through a male member of their family. In relation to the Islamic concept of death, it is significant that she had mixed feelings about her own survival. Although relieved to be alive and although she gives this as another proof of the miracle, she is none the less envious of those who died and thereby gained paradise.

Was the psychological condition of Naseem cause or effect of her religious experience? We know that her peculiarities of temperament became acceptable after the revelations. Her fits, her rapture, her ecstasy now made sense. She was touched by the divine. Even her acts defying tradition in Chakwal—such as abandoning the veil or being alone with a man—expressed her transcendent independence. Examples of trance, spirit possession and ecstatic behaviour have been recorded among Muslim groups from the Turkmen (Basilov, 1984) to the Baluch (Bray, 1977). It is commonplace that highly gifted but disturbed individuals adapt religious idioms to consolidate their social position or to dominate their social environment. Women have heard voices before, all over the world. Joan of Arc's voices advised her to lead her nation into fighting the English. Naseem's urged her to lead her followers into the sea. In order to understand the motives of those involved in this case, we need to combine an appreciation of religious mythology with an examination of certain sociological factors. There was more than just *jazba* (emotion, ecstasy, passion) at work in Chakwal. What did the followers think was awaiting them at Karachi?

Both local leadership and kinship helped to determine who would be on the beaches that night. The importance of a leader in an Islamic community, Shi'a or Sunni, is critical. The group is judged by its leadership (The Holy Qur'an, Surah 5: 109; and Surah 7: 6-7). In different ways Willayat, Naseem and Sakhawat Jaffery played leading parts in the drama, but we look in vain for a Savonarola figure in either Willayat or Sakhawat. Leadership was by consensus. They were all agreed upon Naseem's special role in the drama. She led, as much as she was led by, her father and the *zakir*. The followers were responding not to one leader in their immediate community but to the concept of leadership in Shi'a society. They were responding to symbols centuries old and emotions perennially kept alive in Shi'a society. What is significant is the lack of ambivalence in the majority of the followers. Even the call for the ultimate sacrifice evoked an unequivocal response among most of them. Asad's interesting question, 'how does power create religion?' (T Asad, 1983) may therefore be turned around. The Hawkes Bay Case provides an interesting example of how religion may create power.

Willayat Shah was a forceful person who mobilized public opinion behind his daughter. The *zakirs*, especially Sakhawat

Jaffery, supported him and he in turn assisted Sakhawat Jaffery financially. Apart from assisting the *zakirs*, Willayat also paid sums to a variety of other people. Among the beneficiaries were members of the traditionally lower social class—mostly artisans, barbers, and blacksmiths. The seventeen people from Mureed who were prepared to walk into the sea were from this class. In fact, four of this group backed out at the last minute and although thirteen entered the sea, only three of them died. The people of Mureed were recent converts to Islam and, like most converts, they were eager to exhibit their religious fervour. They looked to Willayat Shah for religious and financial support. For them he was both a Sayyid and a man of means and they were enraptured by his daughter. Through him and his daughter they found access to a higher social level.

Whatever the levelling effect of religion and the loyalties it created, the Sayyids rarely allowed their genealogy to be forgotten: the rural Punjab class structure was recognizable despite the experience at Hawkes Bay. Even in death, class distinctions remained: three of the four men who held the *taboot* as they stepped into the waters were Sayyid, and the non-Sayyid was swept into the sea. Later, with a strange twist of logic, Willayat explained this by suggesting that his faith was weak (Pervez, 1983). His faith was weak because he was not a Sayyid, while the three Sayyids who survived, did so because their intentions were pure. And yet he also argued that those Sayyids who died, did so because of their purity. Sayyids obviously won either way. The Sayyids, of course, provided Willayat's main support and many of them were his relatives. Of those who walked into the sea, twenty-five were related. For these, Willayat was the elder of the family: father to one, brother to another and uncle to yet others. Of the eighteen who died, fifteen were his near relatives, while ten of his kin survived. Religious loyalty was here clearly buttressed by ties of kinship.

There was, however, structural resistance to Naseem and her revelations. The Sunnis dismissed them out of hand and even the Shi'a were not unanimous in supporting her. The Sayyids, senior in the Shi'a hierarchy, ill-treated Naseem's followers, especially the poorer ones, and teased her family. The older, more established, Shi'a lineages felt threatened by the emergence of Naseem since she challenged their authority. Willayat's own brother, Ghulam Haider, suspected to having Sunni affiliation, kept away from the entire affair. The *zakir*, himself a close confidant and beneficiary of Naseem, but wordly-wise, chose not to accompany the party on some pretext. And at the last moment, by the sea, four followers backed out. But, although there was opposition and resistance at every stage, thirty-eight people were prepared to sacrifice their lives on the basis of Naseem's commands and revelations. The explanation for their behaviour partly lies, I have argued, in the forces of social change, leadership and kinship in Chakwal society. But there are also other, more ideological and mythological dimensions to consider.

IV. Death, Sects and Women in Muslim Society

There is no substantial difference between the core theological beliefs of Shi'a and Sunni. Both believe in the central and omnipotent position of Allah; both accept the supremacy of the Holy Prophet as the messenger of Allah. The Holy Qur'an is revered by both as the divine message of Allah and its arguments relating to notions of death and the afterworld are accepted by both. Discussion of death is indeed central to the Holy Qur'an, which has many verses on the theme that 'every soul must taste of death'.

Death in Muslim society is seen as part of a natural preordained, immutable order, directly linked to the actions of the living and part of a continuing process in the destiny of the individual. It becomes, therefore, a means to an end, 'the beginning of a journey' (Abd al-Qadir, 1977). Humans 'transfer' from this to the next world (the word for death in Urdu and Arabic *inteqal* derives from the Arabic *muntaqil* 'to transfer'). The Holy Qur'an warns 'unto Him you shall be made to return' (Surah Al-Ankabut, verse 21). On hearing of someone's death, a Muslim utters the words 'from God we come, to God we shall go'. For Muslims there is no escaping the consequences of death (Muslim, 1981).

In Islam—both Shi'a and Sunni—life and death are conceptualized as binary opposites. *Al-akhira*, the end, is the moment of truth, determining the future of a person. The individual is alone in that hour; all ties including those with parents and family are repudiated (Surah 82: 19). At that time all veils between man and 'the objective moral reality will be rent' (Rahman, 1980). *Al-akhira* is opposed to *al-dunya*, the here and now, which may mean base pursuits. Indeed, *Alam-e-Uqba*, a popular book in Urdu on death in Islam, has sections called 'Your death is better than your living' (Sialkoti).[4] Given the awesome facts of *al-akhira*, human beings must prepare for it in this life. Together, *al-akhira* and *al-dunya* are a unitary whole, the latter determining the nature of the former. Life after death is explicit in Islam and central to its theology. In a general sense, this partly explains the attitudes to death shown both in the traditional religious war, *jihad* and in contemporary events in the Muslim world. Those who killed President Sadat in Cairo and, like Lieutenant Islambuli, awaited death calmly, during the trials, and those who died following Imam Khomeini's call in Iran, first against the Shah and later against the Iraqis, believed they were dying for a just, Islamic, cause. Matters are complicated when *jihad* is freely translated as a struggle against any enemy, including Muslims (Ahmed, 1983). But the problems between Shi'a and Sunni lie in this world and are rooted in the history, not the theology, of Islam.

---

4. See also Saeed, 1982. In another popular book the author promises the reader, in the subtitle, 'Glimpses of Life Beyond the Grave'. One section in the book is entitled 'The Depth of Hell: if a Stone is Thrown into Hell it will Take Seventy Years to Reach its Bottom' (Islam, 1976, p. 284). For discussion of *djhannam*, the Muslim hell, see Gibb and Kramers, 1981, pp. 81-2. Maulana Maududi discusses the importance of death, the afterlife and its relationship to man's life on earth, in dispassionate analysis of Islamic society (Maududi, 1968). See also chapter 6, 'Eschatology', in Rahman, 1980.

Islamic history, Shi'as maintain, began to go wrong when Hazrat Ali, married to Hazrat Fatima, daughter of the Prophet(PBUH), was not made the first Caliph after the death of his father-in-law. To make matters worse Hazrat Ali was assassinated. Hazrat Ali's two sons, Hazrat Hassan and Hazrat Hussain, following in their father's footsteps, opposed tyranny and upheld the puritan principles of Islam. Both were also martyred. Hazrat Hussain was martyred, facing impossible odds on a battlefield, with his family and followers, at Karbala. Among those killed at Karbala was Hazrat Hussain's 6-month-old son, Hazrat Ali Asghar (who appeared to Naseem in Chakwal). The Prophet(PBUH), Hazrat Fatima, Ali, Hassan and Hussain are the five key figures for Shi'a theology and history. These are the *panj tan pak*, 'the pure five', of Shi'as in Pakistan, including those in Chakwal. Since five of them were martyred in the cause of Islam, death, martyrdom, tears and sacrifice form a central part of Shi'a mythology (Algar, 1969: Fischer, 1980; Khomeini, 1981; Schimmel, 1981; Shariati, 1979). Members of the Shi'a community are expected to respond with fervour (*jazba*) to a call for sacrifice by the leadership. A sense of sectarian uniqueness, of group loyalty, faith in the leadership, readiness for sacrifice, devout ecstasy during divine ritual, characterizes the community. It has been called 'the Karbala paradigm' (Fischer, 1980) and would have been exhibited in Chakwal.

In Pakistan today, where about 20 per cent of the population of 100 million are Shi'as, Shi'a-Sunni differences can degenerate into conflict. This is especially so during Muharram, the ten days of Shi'a mourning for the events at Karbala. During this period Shi'as mourn, flagellate themselves, organize processions symbolic of Karbala, and recite moving poems of the tragedy at Karbala which reduce those present to tears and quivering rapture. Conflict with Sunnis is often sparked as a result of overzealous Shi'as abusing figures respected by Sunnis, such as Hazrat Umar. It was one such riot which had paralyzed Karachi when the party from Chakwal arrived there on its way to the Arabian Sea. Chakwal society itself is riven with Shi'a and Sunni opposition, which has a long and bitter history. Local politics, marriages and economics are based on this opposition. Sectarian tension and loyalties also divide families. Some of Willayat's own nearest kin were either secret Sunnis or suspected of being sympathizers. These divided loyalties must have led to severe tension both for him and his daughter.

An appreciation of the five central figures of the Shi'as also helps us to understand the role of women in that community. The position of Hazrat Fatima is central. Her popularity among the Shi'a in Chakwal may be judged by the fact that seven women in Willayat Shah's family carry her name. Two of these are called Ghulam Fatima, or slave of Fatima. Always a great favourite of her father, Hazrat Fatima provides the link between her father and husband and between her sons and their grandfather. The Sayyids, those claiming descent from the Prophet(PBUH), do so through Hazrat Fatima. So do the twelve Imams, revered by the Shi'a. In addition, Fatima's mother and the Prophet's(PBUH) first wife, Hazrat Khadijah, is also an object of reverence. Two other women feature in Shi'a mythology, but neither is a popular figure. They are Hazrat Ayesha and Hazrat Hafsa, both wives of the Prophet(PBUH). The reason for their unpopularity is linked to the question of Hazrat Ali's succession. Ayesha was the daughter of Abu Bakar and Hafsa of Umar, the two who preceded Ali as Caliph. Ayesha is singled out as she opposed Ali actively after her husband's death.

Thus, one of the five revered figures of the Shi'a is a woman. Among the Sunnis a similar listing—of the Prophet(PBUH) and the first four Righteous Caliphs—consists entirely of males. In other matters too, Shi'a women are better off than Sunnis. Shi'a women, for example, often inherit shares equal to that inherited by male kin, whereas among educated Sunni, women receive, at best, one half of what a male inherits. In the rural areas they seldom inherit at all. Shi'a women also play a leading role in ritual. The organization of *marsyas* and *azadari,* the enactment of the death dramas of Karbala, all involve the active participation of women.

Of the eighteen people who died at Hawkes Bay, ten were women, a notably large number in view of the fact that only sixteen of the forty-two who set out on the pilgrimage were women. Willayat Shah lost both his mother and daughter. It may be argued that the women were unequivocally committed to sacrifice. By locking themselves in trunks they had sealed their own fates. For them there was no coming back from the waves. Their sense of sacrifice and passion for the cause were supreme.

The attitudes of the two communities to the Hawkes Bay incident reveal their ideological positions. Sunnis, as we saw above, condemned the entire episode as 'bizarre' and dismissed it as 'insanity'. This, they argued, was mumbo-jumbo and quackery and not in keeping with the logic and rationality which is Islam. For Shi'as all the ingredients of high devotion were amply displayed. Through it they felt they had once again established their superior love for Islam. Here there was sacrifice, persecution, death, and martyrdom, the Shi'a paradigm. Educated Shi'as, who found it awkward to explain the Hawkes Bay Case, nonetheless applauded the *jazba* of the group. As one journalist concluded his report: 'There are millions who don't have the slightest doubt that they have demonstrated the highest degree of sacrifice by answering the call and order of the Hidden Imam' (Yusufzai, 1983). The idea of sacrificing life and property for Allah exists both in Shi'a and Sunni Islam and is supported in the Holy Qur'an. Sacrifice and its symbolism are part of Islamic religious culture. Abraham's willingness to sacrifice his son Ismail, for example, is celebrated annually throughout the Muslim world at Eid-ul-Azha. But for the Shi'as, sacrifice holds a central place in social behaviour and sectarian mythology. Here it is necessary to distinguish between suicide—throwing away life given by God—and sacrifice, or dedication of that life to God. Suicide is a punishable offence in Islam (Islam, 1976). Sunnis, therefore, seeing the deaths at Hawkes Bay as suicide, disapproved. They saw the episode as a throwing away of valuable lives, whereas Shi'as saw it as a sacrifice which would confirm their devotion. Willayat Shah was convinced his mission was divine and that he had proved this through a dramatic act of sacrifice. Reward, he was certain, would be paradise in the afterworld (Pervez, 1983).

In interviews after the event he expressed his wish to be martyred (*shaheed*). There was no remorse; there was only *jazba*. To a remarkable degree Shi'a tradition, and the practice of death and sacrifice, coincided in this case. For the Shi'as in Chakwal, text and practice were one.

Suffering thus became as much an expression of faith as of social solidarity. 'As a religious problem, the problem of suffering is, paradoxically, not how to avoid suffering but how to suffer, how to make of physical pain, personal loss, worldly defeat, or the helpless contemplation of others' agony as something bearable, supportable—something, as we say, sufferable' (Geertz, 1966). Suffering, martyrdom and death, the Karbala paradigm, create an emotionally receptive social environment for sacrifice. Death in our case, therefore, became a cementing, a defining, a status-bestowing act for the community. It consolidated the living as it hallowed the memory of the dead.

Through the Hawkes Bay Case, we have attempted to examine complex and largely unstudied issues in Pakistan society resulting from migration. We have noted the impact of the years abroad on the migrant and his actions on his return, and how they affect those around him. We have pointed out answers to the questions raised at the beginning of the chapter. We have also discussed notions about the status of women, sacrifice, death and the afterworld.

We are thus able to note some unexpected answers to our questions. Clearly, the role of women is a much more important and central one than we are led to believe on the basis of conventional wisdom about rural Pakistan society. The Hawkes Bay Case revolves around a woman.

Another interesting and perhaps unexpected observation arising from the case is that the returned villager does not necessarily shed his 'traditional' world-view for a new one. On the contrary, this traditional view becomes even more extreme, as migrants are exposed to politicized religious movements, calling for a return to a purer Islam. A returning migrant may thus call for a renewed emphasis on his society's particular culture or religion and thereby provide a lead to others in his family. In challenging the existing class and leadership structure, he invokes 'traditional' ideas. In a world of change such a migrant wishes to recreate a pure and absolute world-view. He appeals to his kinsmen and to kinship loyalties, just as he appeals to a revitalized and purified religion.

Clearly, then, an act with a pragmatic motive such as migration can generate—indirectly—an opposite move, one towards martyrdom and wealth may end, as in the case we discussed here, with the ultimate act of sacrifice. Migrants are inevitably caught up in the course of their migratory careers in broader cultural movements. They bring this heightened consciousness back to their home villages. The mundane act of migration thus needs to be analyzed in its cultural context, as it comes indirectly to impact on broader philosophic ideas about personhood and the hereafter. Inevitably, then, as Pakistani labour migration increases, so too does the polychromic complexity of Pakistani society.

NADEEM ASLAM

*B*orn in Pakistan, Nadeem Aslam grew up in England. At 25, he published his first novel, *Season of the Rainbirds,* (Deutsch, 1993), which employs the narrator's magical childhood as a foil to the politics and violence in a small Punjab town. The book won the Author's Club Best First Novel Award, a Betty Trask Award and was shortlisted for the Whitbread First Novel Award and the *Mail on Sunday*/John Llewelyn Rhys prize. He lives in Huddersfield and is now working on a second novel, *Maps for Lost Lovers.*

RAINBOW DUST[1]

Mother promises she'll buy me a whole rupee's worth of *falsé* if the postman calls today. She is expecting a letter. I sit on the doorstep. The postmark is five wavy, river-like lines across the top of the envelope, overlapping the stamp. Father has gone away to find work in Saudi Arabia. Mother had to sell her bangles and her necklace and the five-fingered *punjangala.* If the postman likes a stamp he tears it off, and the letter arrives in an envelope which has one corner missing

The flowers of *ishq-é-péchan* grow in clusters. Each flower has five petals at the end of a long hollow stalk. The thick stalk can be bent into a circle and inserted into the hole at the centre of the five petals. A wedding ring. Rings can be looped into each other to make a chain—a necklace for the bride or a garland for the bridegroom.

Nothing used to grow in the courtyard. Then Sujata told Mother to pour sheep's blood on to the soil. The blood came in an aluminium bucket. In the bucket, and on the soil, the blood looked dark, almost black; but during its journey from the tilted bucket to the barren soil it was bright red—ruby coloured. A

---

1. From the novel, *Season of the Rainbirds.*

bucketful was added every month. And now we have jasmine and seven-winged *gul-é-lala* in the courtyard. Birds come to eat the nectar. A young bird pecks at a dry seed concealed in the webbing of a mat.

Sujata and Mother grew up together. After Father left, Mother told her her dreams. She seemed to fall through a hole, and continued to fall for such a long time that, above her head, the rim of the hole disappeared.... Nothing but darkness, and yet she still kept falling.

She stops by on her way back from the bazaar and tells Mother who she saw at the shops. She buys satin ribbons and dragonfly hair-clips for my hair. She makes two plaits—four stranded!—and arranges one before the shoulder and the other behind. She paints my lips red and inserts a sprig of lilac into my hair, just above the nape of the neck. And then she plants a kiss on my forehead. A tiny silver snake holds her index finger in a fivefold embrace. Her fingernails look like rose petals.

Sujata's bangles chime inside the room. Mother is laughing.

Mimosa encircles the window frame, the leaflets sparkling in the sunlight. The thin branches are held up by strings, tied to drawing pins pushed into the wall. Some strings have lost their colour—bleached away by the sun; others were recently put up, attached to the younger branches. Purple flowers peer into the room. Mimosa leaves react if you touch them; the leaves snap shut like a Japanese fan. I look through the glass into the room. The mimosa leaves contract at the touch of my skin, and a light enters the room—a small blue clearing in the darkened room. Sujata's *mukaished* stole is on the floor. Her arms are wrapped around Mother's body; their lips touch each other. Behind them, on the shelf, the yellow rose swivels through an arc in its vase, almost as if it's stretching and yawning. Father's picture looks down into the room, one shoulder higher than the other.

The postman knocks on the door. Birds fly above the courtyard in curved paths like sagging marquee roofs. Singing, they cut the air into strips with their scissor beaks. I take the letter into the room. When you step out of the sun into the shade, your forearms notice the cold before the rest of you.

Sujata's face is covered in flaky pink powder as though she had opened a large box and a thousand butterflies had rushed out, leaving rainbow dust on her skin. Mother reads the letter. Father says he'll be home for Eid this year. He will bring a television. He tells Mother she is not to hit me, ever 'not even with a flower on a stem'. The night before he left, Mother says, he stayed awake and stroked my face and hair. Sujata is eating a hill-station apple, her fingers curved around the fruit like the little prongs that hold a ruby in a ring. Her brother-in-law also went away to work and has sent them a television and a camera. In the evening me, Lubna, Uzma, Aamar, Mitho, Sabahat and Farzana go to Sujata's house to watch cartoons.

TARIQ RAHMAN

*E*ducated at Burn Hall in Abbottabad and at Peshawer University, Tariq Rahman did his doctorate in English Literature from the University of Sheffield and an MLitt in Linguistics from the University of Strathclyde. As professor and chairman to the University of Azad Kashmir, he introduced Linguistics and English Language Teaching at the masters level. He has also taught at the University of Peshawer, the University of Sana'a, Yemen, and was a Fullbright Scholar at the University of Texas at Austin. He is now associate professor at the National Institute of Pakistan Studies at Quaid-e-Azam University, Islamabad, and the honorary chief editor and research advisor at the Sustainable Development Policy Institute. He has written *A History of Pakistani Literature in English* (Vanguard, 1991) and three collections of short stories: *The Legacy* (Commonwealth Publishers, 1989), *Work* (Sang-e-Meel, 1991), and *The Third Leg* (Sang-e-Meel, 1999). He has also published several scholarly works including *Language, Education, and Culture* (OUP, 1999) and *Language and Politics in Pakistan* (OUP, 1996), which won the Patras Bokhari Award, and the National Book Foundation Award.

THE ZOO

'We cannot do without more funds for the Zoo,' said Ikram Arif with conviction.

'But Ikram Sahib,' said the Secretary wearily, 'you constructed that lovely place for the birds we imported for you, when the money should have gone for the bears.'

'Sir, that was inevitable. Every animal has to be given its place—its ecological niche—I mean the kind of place it is naturally used to.'

'I know,' said the Secretary, raising his hand. 'But there has to be a limit.'

'Look at it this way, Sir,' put in another official from the Finance Ministry. 'The Zoo is seen by so many foreigners. What kind of impression will we give them, if the animals are not lodged properly?'

Ikram Arif nodded in enthusiastic agreement. The Secretary looked doubtful and then smiled, as if conceding defeat.

'Lodge in style. Money for the bears, the big cats and the giraffe. OK.'

'Thank you, Sir,' said Ikram Arif graciously.

The next few months were very busy at the Zoo. An Austrian firm created the appropriate landscape for different types of animals. By the end of the summer there were verdant grasslands for the antelopes, the deer, the wild bison and the zebras. There were tall trees in the giraffe's enclosure, which had been enclosed into another island with a canal around it, as well as concealed fences.

The dens for the lions were in terraced plateaus with groves of trees. They too had a moat around them with drawbridges leading to an inner fence. The lions strode majestically around and stared into the eyes of the curious. While lions often lay sleepily around, the tigers paced in their part of the enclosure almost all the time. But they too retired to their dens or sat away from the spectators whenever they wanted to. The elephants lived in a swampy area with a thick growth of trees and fields of sugarcane, which they munched lustily most of the time.

The Zoo was a success. Ikram Arif, its manager was commended by the Governor of the Punjab himself. Now the Governor had another place—besides the Badshahi Mosque and his own palace—to take foreign dignitaries to. The cost of the upkeep made financial jugglers almost give up in despair, but they found the money somehow, as they always did, when the Governor really wanted something.

Hashmat Ali was new in Lahore. He had come from Sargodha, where he was an agricultural labourer. But the Malik Sahib who employed him had turned his land into a large orchard. He now required less people and the family had to seek a living in the city. The day he left for Lahore, his wife, Fatima, had cooked him *parathas*. His children, Azmat Ali and Zainab Bibi, had clung to him till the end of the village. When the green fields ended and he stood on the pot-holed road, he felt elated: he was going out to fabulous Lahore, the wide world. And yet, stuffed in the heat between brown bodies, he could not help looking at the intensely green fields flying past at incredible speed.

Lahore was fabulous indeed, Chacha Barkat Ali told him, but not for village men like him.

'Work is not easy to find, son,' he said, solicitously.

Indeed, for about a month Hashmat did hardly anything more than carry people's luggage to waiting taxis and rickshaws at the railway station. The huge gate of the station overwhelmed him and the roof was the highest he had ever seen. Huge caterpillars of dark titanic trains rushed into the dome of the station. And not even weeks of seeing this, day in, day out, made him accustomed to it; it was awesome and impressive. The milling crowd, the fight for cramped places in the compartments and being knocked about by people in a great hurry, was somehow a routine. He did not complain. Then he left Chacha Barkat's little room where ten people slept and rented one for himself. Hashmat had found a job—as a gardener in a small school.

The room was not far from the school. It was up four flights of stairs, in a blind alley. It faced another dark wall and the only window was covered with newspapers because all the window-panes were broken. It was so dark that he stumbled and almost fell when he entered it.

'Electricity is expensive,' said the property agent, who had brought him to see it. 'So the bulb will have to be a small one.'

'But the children will study in a school,' he answered in desperation.

He wanted to blurt out that his children would go to school. They would not be labourers. Of course, Zainab would get married to an educated boy. For that too, she had to go to school.

'They can read in the daylight,' mumbled the property agent shrugging his shoulders. Then he smiled slyly and said, 'Of course for a different rent—only a bit more—you can have a meter. You can even have a heater for the winter.'

Hashmat dismissed the heater with a laugh but after some haggling they agreed to a new figure for a separate electric meter.

He went to fetch Fatima and the children. They emerged looking harassed, after having been cooped up in the bus for five hours. The city with its noises enthralled them; it was with suppressed excitement that Fatima climbed up the stairs to her room.

'It is a bit dangerous,' she commented when Azmat tripped on a steep, worn out, step. 'The landlord should get it repaired.'

'The landlord,' he laughed. 'The man looks like a reptile. He should have been in a Zoo!'

They were in front of a termite-eaten door. Hashmat was struggling with a rusty lock.

'Zoo?' echoed his wife, blankly.

Hashmat cursed the lock. Fatima pressed her daughter close. The little girl was afraid of foul language. Somebody had cuffed her on the ears with some such words. The lock opened and the door creaked ajar. The fetid stench of dirty quilts assailed their nostrils. It was dark and cavernous inside.

'Yes, Zoo. In the city they have animals in it. Enter. This is our home.'

'*Bismillah, Bismillah*,' murmured Fatima, reverently. 'Don't look down, Zainab. Come on, Azmat. Lions too?'

'Enter. *Bismillah*. Yes, and elephants, bears and what not.'

'Lions, Father?' Little Azmat shouted. He stood holding a piece of stale bread. 'Father, you ate this?'

'Father could not have. It is old bread,' said Zainab. 'Yes, we should see the animals. But will they not bite?'

'No. No,' Hashmat laughed.

Fatima sat down on the cot and put her things down. The conversation about the Zoo, so mixed up with the homecoming, petered out. The woman busied herself with cooking. The man allowed himself the pleasure of lying back on the cot and closing his eyes. The children started quarreling.

More than two months later, the Zoo came up for discussion again. 'This house is so dark. In our village the fields were so green and open,' said Fatima.

'You should thank God we have a roof at least,' he said, angrily. 'Women never do thank God. I work overtime to get you decent food and send the children to school.'

'I scrub and scrub the floors and the utensils, and still everything is dirty. This hovel. The sun never peeps in here nor does the wind blow and...and we are suspended somewhere. It is not like being on the earth.'

Hashmat kept quiet. Suddenly his heart ached for the earth, the feel of the wind on his hair. He did at least work in the garden but she and the children stayed in this suspended hole, this dark, fetid cave where neither stars, the moon, nor even the sun ever peeped through.

'Let us go to the Zoo,' he said.

Fatima extended her hand and clutched his with emotion. He knew she was crying.

'Tomorrow,' he said.

The next day, Fatima was almost ecstatic with joy as she walked with Hashmat and the skipping children in the Zoo. She had forgotten that it was spring. The wind was balmy and the trees were laden with blossoms.

'Why did they not plant crops in these large fields?' she waved her hand vaguely at the grassland in which zebras grazed quietly.

'Oh, are you mad?' Hashmat laughed, looking at Azmat who was also grinning. 'They are not like us poor farmers who would not leave even bits of land unused.'

'Wasteful,' she expostulated.

'It is for the animals,' he said.

'See Mother, they are grazing there,' the children pointed this out to her.

'They are only animals,' she commented.

They were now looking at the bears being fed. Combs of honey lay before them. The lethargic big beasts waddled up to them and their snouts dug into the soft swept thickness of the honey.

'Pure honey,' she said incredulously.

'I bet the bears would not touch the impure one the shopkeeper palmed off on us when Zainab was ill,' Hashmat said jokingly.

'Why should they?' Fatima replied.

A bear came and stood lazily near the gate. Children threw him food and he obliged them by nuzzling at it. Azmat and Zainab too threw their pastries in.

'God curse you both!' cried their mother, in genuine indignation. 'He is so fat he can't walk and here these two imps go wasting our hard-earned money.'

'They are only children,' said Hashmat indulgently.

The children ran away towards the baboons who were making faces at them from the other cage. This was not a small cage but a huge area with trees, swings and ropes. Large monkeys swung from them and nibbled at apples, guavas and radishes. Here again the children threw in biscuits—their last biscuits—and a large impudent chimpanzee gobbled them up.

'This cursed brute thinks it buys these biscuits,' said Fatima bitterly. The chimpanzee turned around impudently, presented his hindquarters to Fatima, and swung himself up a tree. The other apes chattered and looked down at the human beings.

The sinking sun peeped out of a cloud and the monkeys were bathed in gold. A cool wind started blowing and the children started clapping their hands in sheer exuberance of spirits.

'Time to close,' said Hashmat regretfully. He knew they could not afford such an outing—the tickets cost quite a bit—for quite some time.

'Will they sleep in these lovely wooden huts?' asked Azmat, pointing at the apes.

'Those, or out in the open under the stars,' he replied.

'They have many houses,' said Zainab.

'A big, lovely, green house,' said Azmat.

Fatima turned to go. She was thinking of her room where the sun would never shine, nor would the stars ever be visible. The sun set in a splendour of fiery gold and dark red, but by the time they got into the bus, it was dark. She sat between two fat women thinking about the stars which would be twinkling at the monkeys.

TAHIRA NAQVI

Tahira Naqvi grew up in Lahore and did her masters in psychology from Government College. She moved to the United States with her husband in 1972, joined an MEd programme, and started to write fiction. She has published two collections of short stories, *Attar of Roses* (Lynne Reiner, 1997) and *Amreeka, Amreeka* (Lynne Reiner, 1999). She has translated Urdu fiction in *The Life and Works of Saadat Hassan Manto* (Vanguard, 1985), *The Quilt and Other Stories* (Kali, 1991) by Ismat Chughtai, which she co-translated, *The Heart Breaks Free, The Wild One* by Ismat Chughtai (Kali, 1993), *The Crooked Line* by Ismat Chughtai (Kali\Heinemann\OUP, 1995), *Cool Sweet Water* by Khadija Mastur (OUP, 1999), *My Friend, My Enemy: A Prose Anthology* by Ismat Chughtai (Kali, 2000), and *Remembrance of Days Past* by Jahanara Habibullah (OUP, 2001). She now teaches Urdu and Hindi at New York University.

HIATUS

An uneasy awakening guarantees that whatever little coolness had insinuated itself into the night as darkness prevailed, has now vanished. The heat in the room weighs me down like a heavy blanket, forcing me to leave the bed quickly. Any desire to linger further is dispelled by the appearance of white-hot strips of sunlight along the margins of the curtains where they have strayed from the window casings. Standing next to the window I resist a momentary impulse to lift a corner of the weighty cotton drape and look out; encountered head-on, the livid rays of morning light can make one cringe and fall back, and I know there are no clouds as yet. Which means we can't go to see our lot today. That must wait another day, perhaps two, depending on when the rains come.

Tea, I think, splashing water on my face from the bathroom tap. Already the water is lukewarm, the flow weak and irregular. As the day progresses and the sun rotates around the water tank on the roof of my parents' new house, finally beating upon it with full force around noon, one can be assured of a hot bath, an oddity, one might say, in hundred-degree weather. But one doesn't worry about such oddities when there are streams of sweat to contend with and the stale overpowering odour of perspiration that not even soap and talcum powder have the power to quell.

The weather in Lahore has changed. Surely it was never as hot as this, when we were children, when we lived in Garhi Shahu in the old four-storey house, which rose only a short distance away from the road like an aging fortress. We never talked about the weather then, nor did the adults, I think. But these days, seemingly endless summer afternoons are filled with lengthy, lethargic discussions of how the rains have abandoned us, how nothing is as it used to be.

I arrive in the kitchen, which is as large as my oldest son's bedroom in Connecticut, and find Ayesha nursing her ten-month old daughter, her shirt-front lifted discreetly. Only two years older than me, she is my cousin from my mother's side and has my mother's deep-set eyes and wide forehead.

'Where's Amma?' I ask, surprised to see Ramzan silently turning omelets in the soot-black frying pan with bent edges, a souvenir from our childhood days, favoured more than the five or six Teflon-coated pans I have brought over the years from the US for Amma. I've never known Amma to trust anyone with the omelets at breakfast, but then Ramzan has been with her since he was a boy.

'She's outside, with the *mali*,' Ayesha says, pulling out a stool for me. Her daughter squirms at her breast, the tiny wet mouth groping for the nipple that has been momentarily lost.

I look out the kitchen window. Amma's back is to me. She's talking to the gardener who is crouched low, retrieving for her what's ready to be pulled off the branches. There'll be *bhindi*, called okra where I live, to bring in, also small tight tomatoes tinged with green, so different from the full, pulpous orange-red tomatoes in the fresh-vegetable section at Stop and Shop, so slight in comparison.

'Zenab, did you ever see such beautiful *bhindi*?' Amma will ask me, cradling the vegetables in one pale, squat palm while she strokes them with the fingers of the other hand, separating one grooved pod from the other as if she has, spread out on her palm, not just olive-green *bhindi*, but emeralds.

Ramzan hands me tea and going to the sink busies himself with clanking pots. His long white cotton *kurta* is diagrammed in the back with elongated perspiration stains. He is nearly as tall now as my brother MH with whom he used to fly kites on the roof in the old house when they were both children. Dressed in nothing but loose, knee-length khaki shorts that flapped against their spindly legs, the two boys ran from one end of the verandah to the other with the cord clutched tightly in their hands, the wind in their hair, their faces ruddy from the exertion of the game. This year Ramzan became a father.

'Drink your tea Zenab, it's getting cold,' Ayesha says. She's here to see me. With her husband and three children, she lives in a village on the outskirts of Lahore. The village has an unusual name I can never remember, and is one of innumerable others that are strewn about in a haphazard way on the boundaries of larger towns and cities. Her husband, Rafique, a tall, thin man who walks with a stoop and has tired eyes, teaches at a boys' school in that village, earning about one thousand rupees a month. It's easy to calculate that's only forty dollars; the dollar is twenty-five rupees this year.

'Allah! It's so hot!' I pull back the hair from my forehead and neck so I can keep it from touching my face. It flops right back. How foolish that I had cut it so short, that I had forgotten how I would curse myself for not being able to tie it up. Ayesha's baby is staring at me. I lean over to pinch her cheek. The girl pouts, narrows her small, round, coal-black eyes, then hastily burrows her face in her mother's breast.

'Don't you think she's too old to be still nursed?' I ask Ayesha.

'I don't know what to do, she's so spoilt,' Ayesha replies, smiling sheepishly. 'Now tell me Zenab, when are you going to build the boundary wall on your plot?' She pulls her shirt down over her breast and covers the child's face with her cotton *dupatta* to keep off the flies.

I tussle with semantics. 'Lot' in the US, 'plot' in Pakistan.

'I don't know Ayesha,' I say, feeling uncomfortable that I have to lie. We had bought some land not far from my parents' new house when we thought that soon, very soon, we were to come back from the US and settle in Lahore. In those days making elaborate plans to return was not only a prerequisite of our condition, it was also fashionable, a coffee-table subject that we debated hotly and animatedly at get-togethers. Now my husband and I, like others before us, will only return for visits. Phupi Anjum called me a traitor when we brought our decision to the family, and Amma was so angry she couldn't bring herself to speak to me, and Ayesha said, in a pitying tone, 'You'll regret this.'

But the land remains. An investment we're told. And we should build a boundary wall like all others who have empty lots, and if we fail to do so the authorities, who know nothing of, and care little about, our dilemma, will confiscate the land. These were the conditions of the sale. I should go and see our lot, re-examine its possibilities. Yes, as soon as the clouds come.

'Building a wall isn't cheap, you know,' I begin seriously. 'At this time we don't have the money for it. It is a big expense after all.' Stretching out my legs, I rest my head against the door of the reddish-brown cabinet behind me that still exudes a mildly lingering odour of varnish. 'And not one we can't put off for a while.'

Ayesha chuckles. 'If you don't have the money then we should be out on the streets begging.' Her eyes crinkle at the corners as she smiles again and shakes her head. She thinks I'm trying to be funny.

'I mean it, Ayesha,' I tell her in a serious tone. 'Maybe next year.'

But what good is a boundary wall when in the dead of summer afternoons young boys from the colony, impervious to the unyielding heat, will carry bricks off one by one to use as wickets when they play cricket on the main roads of the colony?

Gradually, imperceptibly, like other solitary walls housing empty lots, ours too will become irregular, misshapen, and will slowly diminish in size. Then we will be expected to repair and rebuild.

I bend over and kiss the child's cheek, which smells of sweat, milk, and the mustard oil Ayesha uses in her hair. 'But what about you?' I ask my cousin. 'When are you going to stop having children?' Ayesha is pregnant, although, being stocky, she doesn't show as yet.

Again the timid smile. 'Ahh, what can I do? It's God's will.' Ayesha's hair is thickly patched with grey, a sight completely at odds with her chubby, unlined face. She raises long black brows, tilts her head to one side and sighs. Her mouth, which is tiny, stretches in a childish grin. Her face doesn't seem to belong to the body below it, nor does the smile, waif-like and naive, appear to have anything to do with bearing unwanted children.

'But you can help me, Zenab.' Her tone changes. 'Only you can help me,' she says tremulously.

'How?' I ask in amazement. 'Do you need pills?'

She shakes her head vigorously. 'No, no, that's not what I meant. I mean if only my husband could go to *Amreeka*,' she breaks off helplessly.

'What?' I start laughing, then realize she's on the verge of tears.

'Well,' she continues with a sniffle, 'if he isn't here, there won't be any more children and perhaps he'll also find better work in *Amreeka*.'

'But what about birth control?'

'Rafique says we shouldn't interfere with God's will, you know what he's like.' The child in Ayesha's lap has fallen asleep. She rocks back and forth as she talks in a whisper. 'How are we going to raise four children, buy the girls' dowries, pay for their education?'

'Someone has to drill some sense into his head, Ayesha, *Amreeka* isn't the answer to anyone's problems.' And I embark on a lecture about keeping husbands in line.

'Zenab I've tried, ' Ayesha says earnestly, 'I've tried so hard, but he has such stubborn ideas about everything.'

Amma walks into the kitchen with my three boys in tow.

'Come on everybody, it's time for breakfast...children, go to the dining room...Ramzan, here take these vegetables and put some water on for tea and hand me the frying pan...Zenab, finish your tea...it's cold, why do you let it get cold? Such nice *bhindi* today, just look at it...Zenab get your children up here at once...everyone should have breakfast at the same time. The cleaning will start soon. Zenab, go in with your sons, see that they eat properly.'

I marvel at the energy my mother exhibits. Mine is drained already, although it's only nine in the morning and the only activity I've engaged in since waking up has been the trip to the bathroom and later the walk to the kitchen.

The three boys, still groggy and upset—they have been awakened so early—stagger toward the dining room like zombies, their hair awry, their faces puffed up and sullen. I follow them, wondering again if there will be any rain today. July is coming to a close and the monsoons should bring the city a reprieve soon, unless something has really changed, unless something as predictable as the monsoon downpour is no longer the same. I peer at the sky through the dining room window, timorously, hopefully, like a young woman sneaking a look at her prospective bridegroom. The sky, stretched taut and unrelenting, is white and clear, a disappointment. The glare rankles in my eyes like sand and I pull back. I yearn for rain, I have the monsoon blues.

'Mom can we fly kites today?' Haider, bleary-eyed, asks.

'Yes Mom, can we please?' Asghar and Kasim reiterate energetically with one voice. In some things at least they're united.

'But it's too hot on the roof at this time of day.' I'm troubled that I have to say no.

'Please Mom, Ammi, we can't do anything else, there's nothing else to do. We can't go out because it's too hot, we can't play in the lawn because it's too hot, why did we come?' Asghar, twelve now and always questioning, grumbles, noisily bangs a spoon on the checkered plastic tablecloth and scowls.

'You know why. Anyway, eat your breakfast and then we'll see.'

'We'll see, we'll see, that means no.' Kasim sticks out his lower lip and his whole face falls like a collapsed souffle and in the very next moment his eyes fill with tears. His older brothers exchange cynical glances.

'Don't start Kasim, eat your *paratha*, Nanima took so much trouble to make these for you, and when it's cooler, you can go up with Ramzan. He'll get some kites and help you fly them.'

Ramzan, standing nearby with a plate heaped with perfectly round, sticky-brown *parathas*, nods.

'Could we walk to our lot then?' Kasim asks, a spoon raised in the air.

'Yes, later.'

Where are the monsoons? I ask myself angrily as if I had a secret rendezvous with them, as if they had made a promise and retracted. I'll have to let the boys go. Around five in the evening they finally make the trek to the roof in the company of Ramzan and three large, multi-coloured tissue-paper kites that look so fragile it's a wonder they can go up at all without ripping into shreds. Ramzan gingerly holds them aloft, and like the Pied Piper, he leads the boys to the roof.

Amma and I stand at the foot of the dark, winding cement staircase and anxiously watch the children disappear, hearing only snatches of their excited chatter, as they talk to Ramzan in broken Urdu.

'Amma, let's go and sit down for a while,' I tug at my mother's sleeve.

She follows me into the family room, her thin, sparse brows curled with concern.

'They're so wild, your boys,' she says.

The sofa on which I sit has been upholstered for the third time in fifteen years, in blue woven tapestry now. The long, heavy drapes on the French windows, also new, have been drawn to let in some air. But the air is as distressing as everything else around us—the seat of the sofa which seems to emit heat, the abrasive touch of my cotton shirt against my skin, the hair on the nape of my neck which feels like fur, the steaming third cup of tea in my hand.

Perspiration gathers on my face like a thin film of oil. My thoughts wander to the unwalled parcel of land with which my connection is becoming more and more tenuous, to the yellowed lifelessness in my mother's eyes.

'Did you see the house across the street from us?' she asks, averting my glance, her gaze pinned to some point above my person.

'Yes, who are the owners, do you know them?'

Amma shifts in her seat. In spite of a meagre breeze from the ceiling fan, which whirs so fast the blades are just arcs of light, tiny beads of sweat have gathered on her forehead.

'A retired railway officer and his wife. Sometimes she comes over to see me.'

'And the children?'

'They're not here. Two sons are in America, and the daughter, she's married and lives in Karachi. Only last month the mother was sick and the daughter flew in from Karachi in a few hours.'

A heavy silence, as rough as a cloak of coarse wool, falls over us.

Amma rubs an imaginary stain on the arm of the sofa. 'You should build your boundary wall now, Zenab,' she says quietly.

It's my turn to seek an imaginary spot on the arm of the sofa. 'Hmn, yes,' I murmur.

'The council is threatening to reclaim the land if people don't build. The idea was to populate a new colony, not have people buy lots and disappear. Your investment will go down the drain.' Her hands, small-fingered with blue veins on the back that remind me of old scars, rise and fall as she speaks.

'I know, but we can't rush into this,' I say, my voice rising in exasperation. 'Suppose we change our mind and decide not to build at all.'

Amma's eyes move restlessly and I notice for the first time that her left eyelid is drooping, giving the face a melancholy look.

'But what is this laziness, Zenab? You should go and see the plot at least, it's yours isn't it? Why did you buy it?' She emits a tight, shallow cough. She's angry.

'It was a mistake, we shouldn't have been so impetuous. But we would be making another mistake if we rush into this construction.'

She coughs again, then wipes her brow with a corner of her white chiffon *dupatta* and points to the window. 'Look, do you see those clouds in that corner? That means we'll have rain soon.'

All I can see is a minute cluster of fluff, which, in the enormity of the whitewashed, pale sky is like a forgotten speck of dirt on a mirror.

'That's nothing!' I exclaim.

'Don't be silly,' Amma scolds. 'You're too impatient.'

Around seven, Phupi Anjum and Uncle Shah come to visit. The sun hasn't relinquished its place on the horizon, but is spent, dulling the sharpness of the heat somewhat. We sit in the family room where the air from the ceiling fan isn't as humid now as it was in the afternoon.

Phupi Anjum is my father's youngest sister. When I was five, she taught me the names of colours in English from *The Radiant Reader Book One* in which two children, Jack and Jane, forever hopped and skipped on cobbled walks winding through English gardens adorned with vividly yellow daffodils, white-speckled daisies, clusters of violet hyacinths, purple and yellow round-petalled pansies, bold red poppies, and multi-coloured primroses. Phupi Anjum was eighteen that year and in love with a cousin who was studying to be an engineer, and I was her first student.

Now, each year during my visits to her house, we spend long afternoons in the guest room, chatting tirelessly over cups of tea and *samosas,* forgetting she's nearing fifty and I'm thirty-something. Today I notice that the creases on her brow have thickened, and around the corners of her mouth are cobweb-thin lines I don't remember seeing before. I've been waiting for her.

'Zenab, you haven't changed,' she says, as we hug.

I point to the grey strands in my hair no one can see because I've dyed them and shake my head. 'But I have,' I protest, laughing. Sometimes I think I wait for her with childlike eagerness so she can see me and say, 'Zenab, you haven't changed.'

'Well, if you have, I can't see it.' She holds my hand and looks at me closely, then pats my cheek. 'No, you're the same.'

'Nobody is the same any more Phupi ji, and nothing is the same. Take Lahore. Was it ever so dusty and so dry?'

'Well, this is progress, my dear. The government is digging up roads to lay down fibre optic wires so people can have telephones without the long waits.' A bitter expression accompanies the smile on her face.

'Well, why not, we're not to be left behind in the race for progress, are we?' Uncle Shah remarks with a snicker.

'I agree,' I say. 'So, what will it be? Tea? Squash?' I know it will be tea for Phupi Anjum and mango squash for Uncle Shah. I run out to tell Ramzan who's in the kitchen again, preparing *bhindi* for dinner. A bittersweet, mellow vegetable smell pervades the kitchen. Amma, I discover, is taking a bath. The children are on the front lawn, playing cricket, Ramzan informs me, and only one kite went up. 'We'll try again tomorrow,' he adds with a smile of reassurance, knife poised in one hand, a small green okra pod held securely in the other.

On my return to the family room I find Phupi Anjum and Uncle Shah contemplative. The heat is enervating so that even conversation is an effort and slipping into uneasy silences is easy.

'And how is Navid? He has written he will be moving to another house in a month. Have you seen his new house?' Uncle Shah idly fingers the corners of his crisp, white *malmal kurta* and raises eyebrows in query.

Navid is Phupi Anjum's oldest son. There aren't that many of us left here. She is bitter. She hasn't let me forget I was

among the first to go to America and the first to cancel plans to
return. 'You and your husband have set a bad example for all
the young people in the family,' she said accusingly once.
'Telling them it's all right to condemn parents to lives of
loneliness in big empty houses.' Her voice frightened me. I felt
I was a little girl again, stuttering and stammering with answers
in response to her questions, confusing blue with purple, red
with orange.

'Navid is fine, and so is Saima, they're so excited about the
new house. And Phupi ji, they'll finally have an extra room so
now you have absolutely no excuse not to come to the States.'
Phupi Anjum has been stubbornly avoiding the trip for three
years.

Ramzan brings in tea, squash in a jug, and a plate of white
burfi speckled with pistachio bits. Phupi Anjum waits for me to
pour tea in her cup. 'We'll see,' she says with a sigh. 'So, when
are you building your wall?' The question comes as a surprise. I
had forgotten about the wall, about the lot.

'Perhaps next year,' I say hesitatingly, extending the cup
toward her.

'What? Next year?' She retorts sharply. 'If you don't start
building the land will be taken away from you, child.'

Like the refrain of a song, the words follow me. She gives
me a wounded look, as if I had violated a promise yet again.
Setting the cup down on the table before her, she wipes her face
with a corner of her green *dupatta* and shakes her head. I know
she's upset. Like Amma and Ayesha, she'd like me to build
quickly. Why wait, they're all saying? 'Yes, I've been told about
that.' I stir the ice cubes in the tall glass of mango squash
before handing it to Uncle Shah.

Phupi Anjum becomes agitated and fidgets in her seat. 'No,
no, my child, you can't wait, there's no more time. Do you
know, we've already constructed ours?'

'But you're not putting a house on the lot, are you?'

'No, the land is for Navid, he can do what he wants with it
when he comes back. At least no one will take it away.' She's

drinking her tea slowly, a chunk of *burfi* in one hand, the cup in the other.

'But is he coming back to live here?' The question falls from my mouth as if it were a morsel that had to be spat out. I hadn't meant for it to sound the way it did, cruel. Helplessly I look at Uncle Shah who has finished his mango drink and is now busily wiping his face with a sparkling white handkerchief.

The smile on Phupi Anjum's face freezes. 'If he doesn't, then his mother is dead for him.' Tears gather in her eyes, her lips quiver. 'You can tell him that.' She wipes her eyes with her *dupatta*.

'Phupi ji, now don't cry, please.' My eyes smart with unshed tears. We can easily have a weeping session, and Amma will join us, gladly.

'So Zenab, when are you coming to have dinner with us?' Uncle Shah asks me, ignoring my remark, ignoring his wife's tears.

'Friday. Is that all right Phupi ji?' I turn with relief to my aunt who is biting into the *burfi* intently.

She smiles. 'Of course it's okay, any day is all right, my dear. I'll make *kulfi*, you like *kulfi*, I know.'

The last of the sun has dipped into the horizon when Phupi Anjum and Uncle Shah leave. The verandah is darkly grey. As the three of us come out on the porch, I notice there are still no signs of clouds in the sky. Only inky darkness sprayed with the glitter of stars. And a sliver of a bright, yellow moon.

Moths flutter and dash agitatedly against the naked light bulb attached to a long wire dangling from the ceiling in the porch. The chattering of frogs, grasshoppers and other night creatures has gained momentum. The air, still and burdened with lingering evening heat, is thick with the incense of *raat ki rani,* July roses and *chambeli* from Amma's summer garden.

'Well Zenab, my dear, we'll see you then.' Uncle Shah slips behind the wheel of his immaculately kept white Toyota. I notice that the flesh on his lean cheeks hangs in loose folds, and his deep-set eyes have sunk further back into their sockets. I remember his taut smile, his aloofness and his severe manner when we were children and Phupi Anjum had just been married. But that was many years ago, and he was a civil servant then.

'*Khuda hafiz*,' I clutch my aunt's hand before she gets into the car. Her hand is warm, the skin roughened, corrugated to the touch. In the dark, her eyes shine the way they did when she was eighteen, when she was my first teacher. '*Khuda hafiz*,' I keep waving although I know they can no longer see me.

Ayesha has come out on the porch, her daughter straddled on her hip.

'Let's walk to your plot, Zenab,' she says.

'Walk all the way with her in your arms?' I ask, wondering how with a ten-month-old baby in her arms and another inside her, she can contemplate a long walk at this time of night.

The children have gone indoors to watch TV and gulp down bottles of Coca-Cola Amma has kept chilled for them in her refrigerator.

'I work around the house all day long with her straddled on my hip,' Ayesha remarks with a laugh. 'Let's go to your plot.'

'It's still too hot,' I mumble. The words are like blinking an eyelash or breathing, always with you, always meaningful, necessary. If only it would rain.

'We'll go tomorrow,' I hedge. 'Maybe we'll have rain tomorrow.'

'All right, come and sit here for a while. Inside, the house is like an oven.' Ayesha points to a rope cot in the far corner of the porch.

Darkness falls here in its truest sense, like an unwieldy blanket, cumbersome with the weight of stillness, its oppressive touch tangible upon one's skin, upon the grass which is already seared by the July sun, upon the grey cement walls of my parents' new home, upon Amma's rose bushes which will flower wildly in March when I'll be in Connecticut wondering if there's going to be more snow. Upon Ayesha and her baby.

In the encroaching darkness I can't see the grey in Ayesha's hair, or the look in her eyes, and the child's honey-brown face is also turned away from me. I hear Amma calling Ramzan, the voice I hear thinned and weakened by distance. Soon Abba will be home from his clinic. Each time the city is deluged during the monsoons, Abba's clinic is flooded with water overflowing from the low-lying streets, and he has to stay home. That's when he takes my children out for rides in the car, a trip to the Zoo, the Fortress, Shalimar Gardens, the Lahore Museum, and Kasim gets a new toy. The memory is deeply etched in my mind, yet I'm impatient.

Closing my eyes, I rest my back against Ayesha's as she croons absently to her daughter, rocking to the languid rhythm of her lullaby. I want to rise from the *charpai* and walk to the gate, and out, towards the lot which will have soaked the day's fever, and will now be drenched with torrid vapours. There won't be much to see, I know, but I must go.

Getting up, saying nothing to Ayesha who won't move for fear of waking her sleeping child, I lumber toward the wrought iron gate only to find it shut, padlocked. But, within seconds, the lock hangs open of its own accord, like a mouth gaping in surprise. I free the latch from the latch's hook, and force it to yield, the bolt squeaking as if each movement were a jab in the heart. Over a clump of mulberry bushes in Amma's garden, I see the moon suspended in the sky like a pale gold half-disk cleverly stitched to an indigo blue *dupatta*.

The gate is ajar. I leave the porch to come out on the unlighted road, which will take me to my lot in ten minutes. Feeling as if I've travelled this route a hundred times, I quickly turn left and start walking. On my face the darkness is suddenly cool, wet with moisture I hadn't known about. In the absence of street lights, a rarity in the new colony, the moon's half-disk offers some illumination. But soon, beneath my feet, the dirt road, gnarled with uneven gravel, stones and sodden brick ends, becomes darker than the sky overhead. The moon fails to light my path.

At a pile of new bricks and earth, which is only a misshapen mound in the darkness, I make another turn and continue walking. The houses strung on both sides of the road and shrouded in fogged shadows are silent. I wonder about the silence and then tell myself, as if I was torn in half to become two people, that everyone is asleep at this hour.

Finally, my destination appears before me, all one-tenths of it, an acre of it. On crossing the road I find myself at the point where the road, which will one day qualify as a boulevard, merges carelessly with the western boundary of the lot. I notice a tree. Why didn't someone tell me a tree had been planted here? I come closer. It's a large tree, a *peepal* perhaps, or maybe an overgrown, dense poplar. With little notice the moon takes off somewhere and it's dark again.

As if it had sat there all this while and I had merely failed to notice it the first time because of the darkness, is the verandah of the old house. In a corner at the farthest end of the small lot, it is directly across from me and distanced from the tree under which I stand. I see it clearly now. It seems to have been sliced out of the house in Garhi Shahu and transplanted in its entirety on my lot. And on a *charpai*, sharply visible in the light from a naked ceiling bulb swinging from a fly-infested wire is Dadima, my grandmother, Phupi Anjum's mother. She's alive, I tell myself happily, without surprise.

'Come here, Zenab,' she's saying, her voice ringing in my ears like the echoes of a distant bell.

'Is it *Yusuf Zuleikha*, Dadima?' I run to sit beside her on the bed. A cool breeze moves across my face and ripples through my hair. Henna, golden-yellow like the skin of winter tangerines, covers all of Dadima's hair; her narrow shoulders are hunched forward, a black shawl draped over them loosely. A book sits in her lap. A book with amber pages and olive green covers edged with a gold lining. I can even see the script, the couplets jumping at me with blinding clarity.

'I'm going to read now, so be still child.' She wets her forefinger and pauses before lifting the corner of the page.

I edge forward. 'Are you going to read the part about Yusuf's brothers?' On Dadima's woollen shawl the familiar paisley forms, inverted in pairs, look like birds in embrace.

'No, I'm reading the part where Yusuf's father, the Prophet Yaqub, has become blind from crying for his lost son. Remember? And he's been told the King of Egypt wants his next favourite son in exchange for grain? Remember?' Dadima's eyes, glazed over with age, peer closely at my face.

'Yes, I remember, I remember, read, read some more,' I beseech like a child, tugging at a corner of her black shawl.

'All right, all right, don't talk now,' she admonishes. 'Here, get under the covers and listen quietly.'

And Yaqub thrashed his breast
As tears flowed from his visionless eyes.
He lamented, crying like a child,
I will not give away my beloved son.

My eyes fill for Yaqub. For his loss, for his loneliness. I cover my face and cry with a girl's abandon, tears trickling thickly through the gaps between my fingers like rain seeping through the slackened joints of an old window frame.

The words of the poem become tangled with each other, jumbled; Dadima's voice grows faint and soon all I can hear is a whisper. Anxiously I move closer to her and still I cannot hear. My chest constricts with a stabbing pain, then with some emotion that pushes aside my breath.

Her hand is on my arm. 'Did you build your wall yet, child?' she's asking, her head lifted toward me, her old woman's voice suddenly loud in my ears.

I look closely at my grandmother's face through the film of moisture in my eyes. 'No, no I didn't,' I answer between sobs, wiping my cheeks with my palms, dragging my hand across my face fiercely. 'But I will, I will.'

Dadima lifts the book from her lap and holds it out to me. 'Take this Zenab,' she instructs simply, 'and turn off the light when you leave.'

On my grandmother's face are lines I contemplate with surprise. Tiny, yet deep, forming a web, they remind me of the skeleton of a leaf gnawed through by a persistent gypsy moth, its veins drained of chlorophyll, white.

'Can I stay?' I lean toward her, my hand closing tightly on the edge of her shawl, my eyes heavy again with unshed tears.

Pulling the shawl from her shoulders, Dadima raises it with one hand while with the other she pats the bed sheet, her long thin fingers, knotted at the joints, so much like my own, aflutter with the movement of her hand. 'Come,' she says.

Unable to move, I sit on the *charpai* that squeaks noisily as Ayesha rocks back and forth with the child in her lap, and wonder if the monsoons will gather in the muted silence of the night. Will I suddenly wake up and hear the rain thrashing upon the walls of my room like urgent hands on a door? And, as I hurriedly leave my bed to shut the window casements and a sprinkle of rain alights on my face, will the room be filled with the heady aroma of wet, rained-on earth? And will I finally, in the aftermath of the deluge, get to see my lot? And what will I find there?

Ayesha's baby stirs in her lap. 'Hmn...hmn... ' she croons, her eyes half-shut.

In my ears my grandmother's recitation resounds faintly, like a faraway, failing sound. And the blind prophet's face, resembling the face of an old man from a Biblical film, perhaps that of Charlton Heston's Moses, fills my vision. I look at the sky for the clouds that don't come. I see nothing, not even a cluster of fluff.

KAMILA SHAMSIE

Kamila Shamsie was born in Karachi, in 1973 and educated at the Karachi Grammar School. She went on to the United States and received degrees in Creative Writing from Hamilton College and the University of Massachusetts at Amherst. Her first novel, *In the City by the Sea* (Granta, 1998) was short-listed for the 1999 *Mail on Sunday*/John Llewellyn Rhys Award in Britain and received The Pakistan Academy of Letter's 1999 Prime Minister's Award. Her second novel, *Salt and Saffron* (Bloomsbury, 2000) about a family divided by class and by Partition, has been translated into Italian. She has now written a third novel, *Kartography*. She lives between London and Karachi.

MULBERRY ABSENCES

When you grow up among mangoes it's hard to have any regard for the mulberry.

I speak from experience, of course. For the first twenty years of my life I don't think I ever stopped to consider a mulberry for any longer than the time needed to transport it from plate to palate, and in its absence I certainly never missed it the way I miss mangoes when summer is over. Ah, mangoes! whose magical ability it is to blend the culinary devotee's Holy Trinity of taste, texture and smell into an experience that can only be heightened by the messiness incurred in the devouring

Seriously now—if we are ever to be friends you must know: no ardent mango-lover *eats* mangoes. We guzzle, gormandize and gorge on mangoes. We wolf down, stuff our faces on, gobble up mangoes. We linger over, relish every bite of, just about wallow in mangoes. We learn new languages in the—dare I say it—fruitless search for words to adequately describe what exactly it is we do to mangoes, and they to us.

But you see what I mean. Mangoes overtake mulberries completely, even in the writing of a mulberry story. Hardly surprising that for twenty years the mango consumed the fruit-conscious part of my brain, with occasional allowances for pomegranates. Even now, I can't remember what made year twenty-one of my life so different; I only know that one day in 1994, while home in Karachi for the summer holidays, I looked across the dining table at my sister and said, 'What's happened to the mulberry crops? We haven't seen, let alone eaten, mulberries in years.' She regarded me in silence for a moment, the way she does when I say something particularly stupid, and said, 'Nothing's happened to the mulberry crops. I ate mulberries this year. You're just not around during the mulberry season.'

Oh, the treachery of mulberries. That a fruit so seemingly innocuous should be the instrument by which the illusion of four years is shattered! Prior to this moment, I'd had no trouble convincing myself that though I was at college in America, the fact that I returned home for four months of the year meant I was not really missing out on life back home. After all, I was home for at least parts of: the crabbing season, the beach season, the monsoon season, the wedding season; home for pomegranates, pears, oranges, apples, *chikoos*, lychees, watermelons, melons and, yes, mangoes. Home for everything, I had thought, except the Cricket World Cup, and while this was a big exception I took it as The Symbolic Exception which rolled around once every few years, and to which I would be able to point in later years to remind myself, 'Yes, I was in America for a time.'

Everything was so simple before the mulberries, but after...what could I do but become obsessed? I stayed awake all night trying to remember what else I had forgotten. I raced through cookbooks, family albums, old diaries, in search of the once familiar, made unfamiliar, by absence. I spent a whole week interrogating people about October at home—and got nothing more than the shrugged-off description, 'It's like September becoming November.'

At some point it occurred to me that reacquainting myself with the mulberry would be the only sane way of reclaiming those eight lost months of the year. I started with food magazines; but while there was plenty of space given to berries of the straw- and black- variety, I couldn't find a single mul- in two years of back issues. I did find an entire issue devoted to avocado, and this incensed me immeasurably. What has the avocado ever done to deserve such attention except flaunt its own blandness?

Encyclopedias were my next stop, but I only paused there long enough to see that there were no pictorial accompaniments to the entry 'Mulberry', though in the course of flipping to 'M' I had seen pictorial accompaniments to: Brazil Nut, fan tracery, Ivory-Billed Woodpecker and Jesus Christ. You see why I moved quickly on.

I came at last to the dictionary, and lo and behold! In the parenthetical etymology for *mulberry* I read: Middle English *merberie, mulberie*, fr. Middle French *moure*, from Latin *morum*—and finally—from Greek, *moron.*'

Moron indeed, I chided myself. A mulberry was never a mulberry to you when you ate it. It was always its Urdu self: always *shaitoot.*

Shaitoot, I say out loud.

The word drips—ripe and purple—from my tongue.

AAMER HUSSEIN

*B*orn in Karachi, Aamer Hussein is connected to Sindh and Central India through his father and mother, respectively. He was thirteen when his family left Pakistan for Britain. He joined the Blue Mountain School, in Ootacamund, India and arrived in England, two years later. He graduated from the School of African and Oriental Studies and in 1984, he started writing English fiction. He has published two collections of short stories, *Mirror to the Sun* (Mantra, 1993) and *This Other Salt* (Saqi, 1999)—reprinted in India as *The Blue Direction* (Penguin, 1999)—and an English translation of Urdu writing, *Hoops of Fire: Fifty Years of Fiction by Pakistani Women* (Saqi, 1999). He teaches Urdu at the Language Centre, SOAS, is a lecturer in South Asian Studies at the London branch of Pepperdine University, and has taught at Queen Mary and Westfield College too. He is also a literary critic, contributes to *The New Statesman*, *The Independent* and *The Times Literary Supplement*, and is on the editorial board of *Wasifiri*.

SUMMER, LAKE AND SAD GARDEN[1]

Why should I stop, why?
The birds have gone in search
of the blue direction.

– Forugh Farrokhzad

I think that we are those people on whom misfortune has fallen and I am he who is most at fault.

– Intizar Husain

---

1. Written for *Leaving Home* and developed into 'Skies: Four Texts for an Autobiography', published in *This Other Salt*.

August 1996
This is the dream:
There's the man, on a playground—not a painter's impression,
just a dusty patch. He's with his lover, or at least he thinks it's
her. And there's a child, with wild grey eyes and straw coloured
hair, leading a band of other children. He knows the child, but
he can't remember who he is. Hal Mera, his lover says. That's
his name. Come here, Hal. The child looks back at them with a
cold fire. Shouts something vicious, crude, at the man's lover.
Then he runs. Angry, the man chases Hal. The child runs down
to where a ladder's propped up against a rocky slope, leading
to a barren field. The sky above is a forbidding grey. Then he's
halfway up the ladder. The man has the child's foot in his hand.
Hal's holding on to a rock. Struggling to get away. I'll kill you,
you little bastard, the man says. But he doesn't know where the
anger is coming from, the hot violence. He's only a child, Hal,
though his grey eyes are a mercenary's.

Forget turquoise and the hissing of summer green. And the
sea's out of style this summer. The sky and the city and you are
draped in grey dust from dawn till nightfall. But there in the
desert landscape you suddenly see a bright patch of red blooming
in the dust. And just as suddenly the grey refracts a touch of
hidden sun. It turns to gold. Even the dust. Then the darkness
falls, like a winding sheet. On such a night they drove out,
down wide new avenues lined by tall towers of glass and
chrome, through squares enclosing asymmetrical marble
monuments to modernity, past the Boating Basin with its throngs
of people eating grilled meats at small tables in the cooling
night breeze, to a lane bathed in purple. The smell of salt and
the sea wind hung over their heads. Against a purple-black
horizon that seemed quite close there were long, long bands of
icy white. He turned to Zoya and asked: Are those bands of
salt? Come on Sameer, she said. It's surf. Can't you see the
waves coming at us? So that's my sea, he thought. I thought
they'd chased it away from here.

Karachi, star of the sands, jewel of the green Arabian Sea...

They'd built an amusement arcade on reclaimed land not far away in Clifton, near the ancient shrine. Carloads of young men in tight jeans and flower-laden girls dressed in their mothers' old saris in imitation of Indian film stars cavorted here late into the night. He sat on a wall from which you would once have seen the sea at high tide and the sand at low. Now there were Ferris wheels. Ribboned in blue, yellow and red. There he talked about Hal Mera and his violent, unexpected fury. And about that other recurring dream: he's standing on a stage, prepared. It's a grand performance, a special occasion. And suddenly his lines are all gone. His lover—or at least he thinks it's her—is prompting him from the wings. But it's no good. He can't go on; he's stammering. He walks off the stage in shame. I can't, he stutters. I just can't.

—That's when I started stammering, Sameer said. I just couldn't speak English any more. Who was the child? And why did he take my tongue away? And why isn't there any blue left here after the miles I've travelled to find it? And why am I still stammering?

—All I know is that those dreams brought you here, Zoya said in response. Hal mera? *Haal mera.* The state you're in. In an English accent. Stop looking for the past. It's gone from here.

That was the only time he saw the sea that summer.

But then there was also the walk to the old house. They were on a faintly lit street lined with low trees. He felt he knew some of the houses there, but when he wanted to turn down the familiar lane that would lead him home, the street seemed to have come to an end, and there were no more lights beyond that corner.

—There were two little lakes here. One on either side of the road. One was blue and one was green. They used to call the green one the man-eater. We used to wade in the blue one. They built a park around it later.

—Let's turn back, Zoya said. You've made a mistake. The lake's been dead for years. It's a garbage-dump. We're in the wrong place.

He didn't speak; just grabbed her hand and turned left into the darkness.

—We're here, he said. I told you I'd find it.

And there it is, the lane he remembers, flooded in white light: the old house barely changed, the low walls around the sunken garden barely changed, the tall proud coconut palm he'd looked at from his window now leaning to one side and strapped to a wall, the jasmine bushes stripped away. Changed but recognizable. Still there. Like our relationship with remembrance: light suddenly floods forgotten corners, darkness envelops places once so bright. And sometimes we're fortunate enough for time to bring us back to stare our dreamscapes in the face.

At his lecture the next day he said:

—We probably all live in three rooms at once: the room of memories, the room of dreams and the room of our chore-burdened present. And that's the attic, crowded with the debris and the phantom toys of the other rooms. Being a migrant is something like that, too: only more complex, because we inhabit about as many houses as well; but our continuities are shattered and even words play games with each other as memories suffer the distortions of other languages. We become, to quote an Indonesian writer, cultural stammerers. (Take me, for example: I read the world from right to left, though I find it hard, sometimes, to decipher the right-to-left passages of my mother tongue. But a web of Arabic letters, in invisible ink, underlines my sentences, forms a palimpsest, crosses and recrosses and mutilates the words I write. Sometimes I feel I write English from right to left.) Perhaps the only difference between those of us who write and the rest of you is the amount of time we spend locked up in our little attic, reckoning with the decor and the embellishment of the other rooms.

—Chic expatriate nonsense, thundered a veteran Hindu communist from Sindh. Here we're struggling with our children turning to one or another sectarian party. Or various separatisms.

—But I think I was meant to talk about language, exile and the imagination, Sameer said. I teach literature, not ideologies.

—Go home to your smart university then, the communist said, before the dumbstruck chairman silenced him.

Sameer hadn't returned just to search for the house or decipher his dreams. Or then perhaps he had. The story he'd written about his childhood city had come out here to some recognition. But the other project, the book he'd come to launch, was the official reason for his visit. Two years in the planning, six months in the writing. And no end to the problem of working on a social history of fiction that some—including his editor—felt was arcane, conservative and politically irrelevant. Others saw it as a work of impeccable scholarship, a tribute to language and heritage. After all, it was his doctoral thesis from one those western universities people here respected so much. The recently-established Allama Iqbal Academy Press, funded by the World Council of Muslim Intellectuals, had offered for it while it was still in its thesis stage. The word Muslim was enough to set the ears of certain local *litterateurs* and self-appointed secular arbiters of the nation's conscience on fire, but others, including Zoya, gave him some grudging support.

—Don't you feel we've advanced at all since the turn of the century? he was asked by editors and journalists alike at an informal press conference in the post-modern coffee bar of a hotel which was the haunt of radical and impecunious writers who debated the day's issues over very expensive cups of tea.

He was watching on a video monitor the antics of a singer who looked like a smart clerk in a mirror-encrusted Sindhi jacket. To the robust accompaniment of a brass band with a particularly raunchy tenor saxophonist playing a local folk song, the boy was raising thin fingers like a dozen little earthworms above his head and writhing his jean-clad hips.

His answer, distracted and lame, was that the occurrence of one *fin de siecle* demanded an examination of another.

—But what about the riots, the terrors, the ethnic conflicts we've known lately, here in this very city to which you once belonged? they asked.

—The swans have flown, and the crows and the caravans of camels have left the deserts, and now only loves' name remains in the burning sand, sing *allahallahallah*, sang the clerk on the video monitor in a voice piercing and sweet as a teenage girl's.

—The city I belonged to has become invisible now, Sameer said. Only its ghosts and its shadows remain.

He was reminded of an incident in his childhood. His mother and their neighbour would take turns to drive the children of both households to school. One day their neighbour, hit by the driver of the car in front of him, had got out of his own car on the crowded bridge that connected Victoria Road to Clifton, dragged the perpetrator of the accident by the collar to the street, and created a traffic jam while he punched the little swarthy proletarian's ears and nose until he bled. When Sameer got to school, late, he was ostracized by his entire class. Even his friendly Parsi desk-mate Spenta moved away to sit alone in the dark corners of the back of the classroom. Later, during recess, his Goan teacher, Mrs Menezes told him the cause: he'd been part of an incident in which a white man had beaten up a native and a poor man at that. Somehow, he'd let down the side; as if he'd touted for an alien cricketer, say Gary Sobers, at a match. (But Gary was a dark man from the Queen's Commonwealth, which muddled matters slightly.) Colonial times were over, Mrs Menezes remarked, but these white wretches still stalked around like rulers. Sameer, who'd never yet spared a thought (his ten years spent in a polyglot city) for skin colour or nationality, now realized that—of course—kind, gruff Schneider was American. White, or rather red, and identical in appearance to the rough Englishmen still remembered by older locals. And today—there are small groups of gun-bedizened youths lolling against walls, cigarettes hanging from pursed lips. Self-styled vigilantes, nostrils twitching for trouble like dogs for bitches on heat. The rich ride in armoured cars. *Since the Afghan War, we've become an arms dump, a drug dump, a city besieged. Blame Uncle Sam. We sold our souls and when the Cold War was over the rednecks flushed us down the drain.* That's what his friends say. And he retorts, when are we finally going to learn? Stand up to them. Take your own responsibility. Find yourselves a half-honest leader.

Don't speak in the first person, he tells himself each moment. Your pronouns get mixed up halfway through your phrases.

—Times have changed since my days here, he told a journalist ruefully. (They were seated on the roof terrace of a house not far from the neighbourhood he'd grown up in. Smells of night-blooming flowers mingled with smoke and the indefinable odour of lanes. Illicit gin was flowing over ice and slices of tart green lime. There was a power failure, but the light of a misty half moon lit up their discussions.) There's a city of dust and squatter's shacks I don't recognize, by the side of our city of illusions and bright lights. Once we were all Pakistani. United against the power of the intruder. I didn't even know that I belonged to the Sunni majority till I was eight. Or, indeed, that Sunnis were a majority. Now we're at each other's throats, using sects and dialects to create spurious causes. I don't know what to say because I condemn violence and I fail to understand the reason why there should be carnage instead of peaceful debate. I can't say whose side I'm on because I'm only on the side of the peacemakers.

On a wall beyond, a poster freshly painted in red proclaimed:

OUR FATHERS SHED RIVERS OF THEIR OWN BLOOD TO COME TO THIS LAND. THIS IS OUR ONLY COUNTRY NOW. OUR GOLDEN LAND. WE, TOO, ARE CHILDREN OF THE INDUS RIVER.

The second book for which he's just signed a contract AIAP—
the one his university will probably give him a sabbatical to
research, and a very decent grant—is concerned, once again,
with the past. Though a personal past, this time. His mother's
uncle Aman had been a very fine writer; he'd found out about
this just by chance, when his mother—on a cold, cold afternoon
in a Greenford semi-detached to which he'd taken her by tube
and minicab—was talking to an old friend of hers, Annie Q, a
renowned novelist who'd lived and written for many years in
Karachi after Partition, and then returned to India. She was
narrating a traditional ballad. A tribal chieftain's wife begs him
to bring her a string of legendary pearls that belong to a powerful
prince's wife. She threatens to leave him for the King's harem
if he doesn't fulfil her desire for the jewels. The chieftain holds
up the lady's caravan and, bandit-like, makes off with the
precious loot. Intrepid as a robber, the chieftain, also a fool like
many of the courageous, doesn't have the guile to cover his
tracks; he's hunted down, he confesses his crime. My lady asked
for the pearls and I did what I did for love, he says. The prince
responds: God and the King love the man who tells the truth.
They let him go.

—I know the story, Annie Q said. It has a tragic end in the
version I know, though. The Queen's brother has him arrested
and imprisoned again. He sends his wife the jewels and says:
May these replace the youth you'll now surrender to a widow's
life. It was written as a long story in a beautiful collection of
tales called *The Teardrop*.

—So you know my uncle Aman's work? His mother asked.
He died so young, I thought he'd been forgotten. Virtually at
the start of his career. And I don't even have a copy of his
book...

—It's been out of print for years, Annie said. But you have
to realize he was one of his time's leading literary lights. And
wasn't there some terrible scandal around his death? He and the
writer Afkar were both in love with the same woman and they

made a suicide pact. Afkar lived—became a ghastly bureaucrat. Aman died. Betrayed. I think there was a touch of skullduggery.

Sameer's mother went white and said nothing.

...Flash back to another August. Last year.

He's waiting outside a little guest house in Islamabad for someone he doesn't know: Zoya Zamaan, who's translating parts of his dissertation to include in a volume she's editing, *The Forgotten Women Writers of Pakistan.* Over the blue-green silhouette of hills in the distance hangs an orange-red globe that could be either sun or moon; with a good sense of direction, he might have been able to tell. But then it's difficult to make out anything in this new town.

The August breezes felt almost cool. It had drizzled all day, but now the sky had opened a huge golden eye. An ambulance drew up. A tiny woman in white *shalwar qameez*, with a waterfall of silky hair cascading over her crushed white *dupatta,* tumbled out. She extended a hand to take his firmly and introduced herself. It emerged, in conversation, that she divided her time between running a division of the local Health Authority, and writing in various genres.

Zoya had started her career as a celebrated romantic poet, taught by her male mentor—himself famous for his espousal of progressive causes—to observe the Boundaries of the Heart. But at the age of twenty she strayed into the territory of savage social satire in her verses, then she wrote an elegy after the national disgrace of the Bangladesh War. She earned the censure of erstwhile flatterers. She soon made a public statement to the effect that all poetry today—even the supposedly political— was dust and ashes, written by geriatrics and aspiring bureaucrats. Women poets merely fulfilled drooling senile male fantasies. She took up radical reportage instead. But as more than half her targeted audience—the country's disenfranchised women—was illiterate, she reached them through the medium of entertainment most popular with the proletariat, the teledrama, fulfilling the irrepressible urge that only the shadowplay of word with image could satisfy in her. She was prolific in her production of scripts for prime-time soaps with women's issues at the core of their rather scandalous narrative complexities, combining the expected escapist romance with reformist messages. Rather in the manner of those irrelevant early novelists you're so fond of and insist on writing about, she'd later delight in telling Sameer. She had left Karachi in a rage about the deteriorating relationship between communities and massive evidence of resulting police brutality. The journal she had run single-handedly there had been targeted by several oppositional groups, with bomb threats, menaces and hate mail directed at its drive towards communal harmony. Religious conservatives had also condemned—for its disregard of moral values—a short play she'd written about a woman choosing to terminate a pregnancy that, under the law, could jeopardize her pending divorce from a violent and domineering second husband. It was a portrait of Zoya's own first marriage.

...Present tense. Again.

Zoya's come back to Sameer's native city: she left Islamabad a few months after their first meeting. She's set up a new publishing company, an NGO that foregrounds feminist concerns but also highlights obscure and valuable aspects of national culture. She decided she'd taken a coward's way out by running away from Karachi; she could only deal with her problem by confronting it. She's a confrontational woman.

Her frequent pronouncements about the ambiguous position of migrant intellectuals seem to imply that Sameer, the archetypal expatriate scholar, is in flight from his past here; but he, too, she realizes, is unable to stay away. One of her first publishing projects is to be the Urdu translation of his dissertation. It is at her behest, and with her encouragement that he came here to launch the book she'd encouraged him to complete and is still busy translating. His obsession with cultural history though (she suggests) is also an escape; a quest for a lost moment of innocence and optimism in a patriotic Neverland.

He finds it hard to explain that his is a fascination with the dying throes of dreams. What are we, he reflects in his journal one night, but a single tear, frozen into a bell of glass that chimes the music of its own destruction? And isn't a poem, a painting, a prayer or a piece of writing nothing but a vain attempt to gather fragments of glass when the bell of our bodies is shattered by the sound of its own weeping?

But Zoya and he, from the start, have got on surprisingly well. Her political correctness, compounded of socialism, feminism and a dedication to the plight of ethnic minorities, is undercut by a mad, subversive sense of humour and the sound and detached aesthetic that makes her so fine a polemicist, poet and editor. She believes greatly, too, in the translator's craft, which she sees, to Sameer's surprise, as an art—but then she's a woman who sees little difference between artists and artisans. If, in conversation, her attitudes err towards the ardent and judgemental, her writings and her critical finesse overturn her zeal, balance her fervour. Her comments on his research were, at first, occasionally patronizing, though he soon became aware that it was the time and period he was chronicling, and its reformist zeal, of which she was dismissive, not his methodology or approach.

She also loves fancy food, and many of their debates took place over the cosmopolitan delicacies—Japanese, Afghan, Italian—that the seaside city provided. They were eating in one of those restaurants that seemed to be everywhere in the chic new neighbourhood called Zamzama, glass menageries with exotic menus perused by luminous young matrons lunching with teenaged sons or liaising with them on vodaphones propped on elegant shoulders, when she'd proposed—over a heaped bowl of green ribbon pasta succulent with chicken, cream and mushrooms bearing little resemblance to any dish he'd savoured in Italy—that he write another book.

—The elegance of your style, she said, your passion for language and its vagaries, raises your writing above the level of academic research. It carries its own significance and conviction, transforming critical discourse and historical anecdote into subjective art.

The conversation veered, as it always did, to the legacy and the state of the nation. Suddenly the image of Annie Q and his mother in that Greenford salon came to him. But it wasn't the delicacy of Aman's visions, known to him only in his mother's lyrical versions, that he cited; it was the moment in which Aman—a moment duly recorded in his one essay that survived the short blaze of his life—had left for Pakistan after Partition.

—He didn't belong to the Muslim League, or to any other party. He was in Delhi, a lecturer at a university, when a friend of his warned him that sectarian zealots had marked his door with a great white swastika. The friend spirited him out of a window, draped in a woman's black veil, and put him on the next chartered Dakota to Pakistan. You didn't need a ticket or a passport in those days. So he found himself in Lahore, a city completely alien to him, against his will. Shortly after that, he moved to Karachi. He remained an isolated romantic. He didn't join the Progressive Writers Association...

—But he adopted this country as his own with a passion...he wrote so many stories about the incomers and the tragicomedy of Partition...

—Do you have his book?

—No, but I know someone who might. Have you come across Nadeem Zahidi?

—I know his work.

—Talk to him. He'll point you in the right direction so you can retrieve all sorts of archival papers. What I really like about his work is the identification with his new land. And when you think of what they do to us now—do you remember when Ayub told us Mohajirs—so-called refugees—that if we didn't like what was happening to us at that time—I was about thirteen—we could just walk into the deep blue sea? Well, it seems neither sea nor sky wants us any more. Oh, this state we're in.

Zoya's family had come to Karachi from Dhaka in 1951, the year before she was born. They'd left their home in Patna at

Partition. Her real surname was Siddiqui and Siddiquis were once, she said when in cynical mood, low-caste Hindu weavers.

—Hooch-makers, I've heard, which is worse, Sameer retorted late one evening in Clifton, waiting to be served at a fast-food bar that served several varieties of *biryani*. At least you're not a tanner. Nor a horse-trader like my lot.

—Pale-skinned horse-traders, she said, who rode across the borders from foreign lands. Makes all the difference to our lot. We still think in terms of caste. Look at our Christians, poor souls. The Untouchables have the finest church which the Catholics won't attend because they converted from higher Hindu castes.

—But my people...my grandfather's grandfather was brought up by a dyer and had to work at his trade for a while, so they say...

—Haven't you ever thought of writing about your Sindhi family instead of Aman? Now there's an idea for your third book...

—It's already been done. In Sindhi. All you need is to get a translation. Which I can't do.

Though Sameer had a working knowledge of Siraiki and Punjabi, his Sindhi was not even functional. But Zoya chattered away in several local languages; she'd married and divorced a doctor who'd worked in the interior Sindh, and her children's Sindhi was as fluent as their Urdu and as their Sky TV-inspired Ameringlish. For people like Zoya, India held no loved or loving memories, no sensations of loss or yearning. It was a foreign country, to be enjoyed, on a holiday, simply as that. For years she—and people like her—had ignored the growing sense of nation as alienation that was being imposed, quite artificially, upon them. Then taunts, factions and politics of the blood, soil and native son variety, had forced them to search for a third solution, which often made them espouse positions that occasionally appeared mutually contradictory. Sameer, who was born and brought up here and had long, deep roots in Sindh and the northern region, had always despised ethnic separatism. And yet the pain he felt from people like her—coming at him like the smell of fenugreek or fried onions—made him feel sorry, not to say guilty, about the sturdiness of his claims to this soil. On the other hand, his mother's people were still in India, and he travelled freely to that country. Some of his most passionate memories still breathed beneath Indian skies. Often, on this trip, he would find himself voicing stances as contrary, as confused as those that echoed around him.

The seed of his new project, sown over a meal of green pasta with Zoya, germinated under her green thumb. But he began to discover that what he was planning, far from being a critical study or even the biography expected by the AIAP, was a new selection of his uncle's stories, prefaced and placed in context by a long piece he'd write. AIAP could publish the English version with a biographical introduction; Zoya would produce the Urdu version of the book for him. He envisaged it as a sequence of song-like fragments, a caravan of images of travellers in grief and joy, multiple migrations, cross-pollination and seed dispersal. Crossings from Iran and Iraq and Afghanistan and Uzbekistan. Some members of his mother's Indian family had mixed their blood with craggy Pathans and mild-mannered Sindhis here. He's a product of such a union. His uncle's story will be one of such crossings, ending, perhaps, in his mother's story and his own: an epilogue in which the stories of the past live on, in rented flats in Greenford.

He travelled around Pakistan on that trip, but he didn't go back to Karachi. The sky and the sea were calling out to him: We are not for you. This state we're in. You've left us to our troubles. Now go back to your own. And he did. To the lengthy hours of his new lectureship and the disaster of separations. To the city where slimy drops running down drainpipes remind you that happiness is a dirty word.

But look at him now. Here he is, again. Surrounded by scattered dreams of lost turquoise and summer green. Back, once more, to dreams of the city at the sea's edge. The story of Uncle Aman is relegated, unfinished, to a drawer.

Late one night, on the tube, after an evening class and a reception, he thinks: at least I should write a story of homecomings and leave takings. About love and partings and a poet, perhaps.

He made a list on the back of an envelope.

HIBISCUS DAYS:

1. The futility of writing.
2. A few drops of absence on a page.
3. Colours lost in summer, lake and sad garden.
4. White sea, unshed, behind your eyes.
5. On your lips this other salt.
6. So many skies to choose from. Calling you away, alone, towards your own stretch of blue.

ROSHNI RUSTOMJI

Roshni Rustomji Kerns was educated in Karachi, at the Mama Parsi Girls' High School and attended the College of Home Economics for two years. She graduated in English Literature, from the American University of Beirut, did her masters in American and English Literature from Duke University, North Carolina and a PhD in Comparative Literature from the University of California at Berkeley. In between she taught in Beirut and Karachi and worked as a scriptwriter and programme producer for the Transcription Service at Radio Pakistan. From 1973-93, she taught at Sonoma State University, where she is now Professor Emerita. She has been appointed a Visiting Scholar at the Center for Latin American Studies at Stanford University, where she conducts a reading and research course on the subject of Asians in Latin America. She has edited the anthologies, *Encounters: People of Asian Descent in the Americas* (Roman & Littlefield Publishers, 1999) and *Living in America: Poetry and Fiction by South Asian American Writers* (Westview Press, 1995). She is the co-editor of *Blood and Ink: South Asian and Middle Eastern Writers Write War* (Westview Press, 1994). Her short stories have appeared in various magazines, journals, and anthologies such as *Her Mother's Ashes and Other Stories by Women from South Asia in Canada and the United States I* and *II* (TSAR Publications, 1994 and 1997) and *Growing up Ethnic in America: Contemporary Fiction about Learning to be American*, edited by Maria Maziotti Gillan and Jennifer Gillan (Penguin, 1999).

ELEPHANTS AND JAGUARS

It was past midnight and the place was the city of Oaxaca in Mexico. I was sitting with friends around a dining table, listening to a very old gentleman, Senor Juan, as he recounted a long story about his youthful encounter with a jaguar. The story began when Senor Juan turned to me and said, '*Usted es de la India? Que bueno! Hay muchos tigres y leones y serpientes y elefantes in su pais. Si?*' Before I could tell him that I was from both India and Pakistan, and that it was camels that I grew up with and dragonflies that I remembered the best and fireflies that I missed the most in California, he assured me that although there weren't any elephants in Mexico, there were many jaguars. And he launched into his jaguar story. Everyone around the table made appropriate noises of fear, terror, horror and awe at the strength of the jaguar and the courage of the storyteller. I had just begun to learn Spanish and soon got lost as far as Senor Juan's words were concerned. But I could not retreat from his voice, the gestures of his hands, the intensity of his eyes as he looked at each of us in turn to make his point when the story became truly dramatic. As I followed his voice, his eyes, his gestures, I remembered my Mamaiji's home in the city she always called Mumbai and her voice as she told me stories about warriors and lovers, heroines and heroes from the *Shahnamah*, from the *Arabian Nights*, from the *Mahabharata* and the *Ramayana*... my favourite stories were the ones about Mamaiji's life in Japan and her memories of her daughter, my mother, when she was a young girl.

Sitting in that dining room in the valley of Oaxaca, mesmerized by Senor Juan's performance, looking out from the window at the dark, lush enclosed garden where the raucous birds had at last gone to sleep, I remembered sitting on the old wooden bench in our garden in Karachi, listening to my paternal grandmother, my parents, my aunts and my uncles telling us, the daughters of the house, stories. Family history, ancestral memories, books and newspapers gave rise to these stories. *Gupshup*, gossip, rumours and films were not denied their rightful place in these stories. 'Garden' maybe a misnomer for the storytelling place in my paternal home in Karachi. It was nearly impossible to grow any flowers in our garden but my grandmother always hoped that flowers would appear in profusion one day. The first time I lamented my mother's death was the morning after her funeral as I looked out at our front yard and realized that I would never again see her at dawn carefully, lovingly pouring water at the roots and over the leaves of the five short bushes that grew against the far wall. But in the days of my childhood, the kites had soared high above the scattered tall trees in our front yard, screaming their shrill cries deep into the late evening sky as the stories grew longer, more complicated, spiraling outwards and then inwards, as different voices remembered different stories, different variations of the same story. The words would begin to blur and I would doze off. Because I was a little girl then. But I refused to go to bed. I knew that the storytellers' voices and gestures had to be learned, memorized. Because I might be called upon to recreate those stories, create new stories. Sometime. Somewhere.

And many years later, I, a grown woman from India and Pakistan, with ancestral roots in Iran and China, with memories of Lebanon, living in the United States of America, sat listening to an old Mixtec man recounting his jaguar story in Oaxaca, Mexico. That night in Oaxaca, I imagined a place from where my stories would start. I called the place Devinàgar and situated the town of Devinagar between Bombay and Karachi. The main characters in my stories would have connections to both Karachi and Bombay and would either live in Devinagar, come from Devinagar, visit Devinagar or hear about Devinagar. Many of them would end up living out their lives, dying in peace or otherwise, in Oaxaca.

The first story I thought of in this series of Devinagar-Oaxaca stories was of an old woman, who comes from Devinagar to Dallas, Texas, to stay with her son-in-law. Bored by Texas, searching for one last adventure before she dies, she eludes border patrols and immigration-customs officers and finds herself in the mountains of Oaxaca. A pair of knitting needles and a ball of yarn is all she carries. She creates her world through her knitting. But since she has only that one ball of yarn, she is forced to unravel her work before she can continue to knit. The unravelling part interested me the most.

While I was creating my story, Senor Juan was continuing his story. It obviously ended well for him because there he was, sitting with us, wonderfully alive, telling us about his long-ago encounter with the jaguar. I had no idea as to how it ended up for the jaguar.

A few years later, and once again in Oaxaca, I told my friend Laura, who had been with me the night of the jaguar story, that

I hadn't been able to follow Senor Juan's story well enough to find out how he had escaped and what had happened to the jaguar.

Senor Juan, Laura informed me, had seen that particular jaguar not as a common, ordinary jaguar but the restless, sad soul of his friend who had drowned in a river one night when he was accosted by the ghost of the legendary wailing, weeping woman, La Llorana. Senor Juan had recognized his friend even though he had been transformed, reborn as a jaguar. Senor Juan had sung to his friend and talked to him and the jaguar had made jaguar noises and gone off into the forest. Never to be seen again.

That led me to tell Laura the legends about the great king Vikramaditya who had some rather strange encounters with a shape-changing ghoul. I also told her a story about a Buddhist elephant caught in a series of different lives. That story had been told to me in Karachi by a very old Muslim lady when I was about eleven years old. It had taken the lady seven consecutive evenings to tell the story. It was during Ramadan and she would continue her story evening after evening, right after she had broken her daily fast. I summarized the shape-changing ghoul as well as the elephant stories for Laura in a few hours, between a late afternoon lunch and late evening supper on a Tuesday during Holy Week in Oaxaca.

After my stories, Laura and I discussed reincarnation, Hinduism, Buddhism, Sufism and Zoroastrianism, the complexity of saints and the frustrating history of angels and such beings. And then she said, 'It is surprising. All these people. All these different ideas and stories. And we all live in Estados Unidos and in Mexico!' 'Yes,' said I. 'But I don't think that the Buddhist elephant was ever reincarnated in either Mexico or the United States of America.'

Last year when I walked into the same room, in which Senor Juan had told us about his encounter with the jaguar, I heard Laura telling a story to her niece. It was about an elephant who had lived all over the world. In Laura's version, the Virgin of Guadalupe played a very important role when the elephant had found himself in the San Diego Zoo. If I remember correctly, Mary helped the elephant escape from the Zoo.

While I listened to Laura's story, I thought about how, in the stories I write in Oaxaca, or in Half Moon Bay, I hear the voices of my ancestors, my grandmothers, my parents, my aunts and uncles, who had tried to prepare me for life by telling me about the world of histories, legends and mythologies. I also thought of the last time I had been in Mumbai with my aunt, Dossi Bhujwala. She was eighty-seven years old and I had asked her to tell me about her memories of Karachi. She began with the familiar story about how my father, always so independent, always so stubborn, always so careless (she always used that phrase in that story!) had lost a precious watch in the sands of Old Clifton when he was five or six years old. All of a sudden, before the end of her story, she turned to me and said, 'Now Roshni, tell me about Mexico. I want to hear your stories. They are a part of my life too.'

She sat on the verandah of her house on Babulnath Road, listening to me as she looked out at the traffic, which has created a new circle of hell—an eternal rush hour. As I told her about the mountains and the coffee-growing fincas of Oaxaca and about the Zapotec and Mixtec women in the markets speaking to one another and their children in languages that predated the presence of Europeans in the Americas, I watched my aunt's elegant, beloved face and realized that it is people like her and Senor Juan, two people, from two different continents, who have trained my ears to listen to stories about jaguars, elephants—grandfathers who loved children and impossibly expensive pastries, grandmothers who travelled to China, Japan, Africa and Europe, parents who sang lovely songs when they were children—and La Llorana, whose ghost appears in Mexico, California, Texas weeping for the murdered children of the world.

These storytellers haunt me. I am always searching for their voices in the world of critically acclaimed, canonized books, award winning films and closely monitored literary conferences. As I live on the constantly dissolving, constantly reconstructed borders between countries and cultures, as I try to smuggle stories and ideas, facts and fiction across politically fantasized borders, the voices of my grandmothers, my parents, my aunts, my uncles, of Laura, of Senor Juan, of the Zapotec and Mixtec women selling their weavings and their embroidery in the streets of Oaxaca, their husbands and sons singing songs to earn money from the tourists, the insistent call of the woman who went through our neighbourhood in Karachi every afternoon selling *papads*, '*Pa-a-pad, sa-a-ria*! *Baiji pa-a-pad sa-a-ria*!' echoed by the desperate call of the woman in Oaxaca selling *tamales* late into the night, '*Tama-a-a-l-es*! *Tama-a-a-les!*' bring Asia to the Americas. The Americas to Asia.

GLOSSARY

Aao	come
Abba	Father
Ada'ab	elegant salutation, offering respects
Ahl-ai-zaban	one who speaks a language as a mother tongue
Alam	the banner of Imam Hassan and Imam Hussain, grandsons of the Prophet (PBUH)
Alap	musical term
Aligarh pyjama	a straight cotton pyjama worn in Aligarh
Allah toba	God forbid
Amar	order, command
Amma	Mother
Andaz	a stylish grace
Angrez	English
Ankhein	eyes
Ansoo	tears
Ajrak	block printed Sindhi shawl
Arra pyjama	tight-fitting pyjama, creased around the ankles, also known as *churidar*
As salaam aleikum	Peace be on you

Azadari	mourning during Moharrum
Baba	Father
Baboo	clerk
Badaam	almond
Badshah	king
Banaspati ghee	*ghee* made of vegetable fat, instead of the more expensive, genuine article from butter
Bande matram	Indian national anthem
Baniya	merchant
Bara gosht	beef
Basharat	divine revelation
Batchi	child (girl)
Batey	talk, gossip
Begum	Lady
Bhai	brother
Bhangra	Punjabi folk dance
Bharat	India
Bismillah	In the Name of Allah
Biryani	luxurious meat and rice dish
Bhaenchod	sister fucker
Bhindi	okra
Bibi	Lady
Bong	simpleton
Bubber Sher(a)	lion